PUBLIC EXPENDITURE

ALDINE TREATISES IN MODERN ECONOMICS

edited by Harry G. Johnson
University of Chicago and
London School of Economics

PUBLIC EXPENDITURE

Jesse Burkhead | *Jerry Miner*

Syracuse University

ALDINE PUBLISHING COMPANY / *Chicago*

ABOUT THE AUTHORS

JESSE BURKHEAD is Maxwell Professor of Economics at Syracuse University. Educated at the University of Wisconsin and Harvard University, he has taught at Lehigh University as well as at Syracuse. Professor Burkhead has served on numerous professional and advisory boards. His books include *Government Budgeting, State and Local Taxes for Public Education,* and *Public School Finance — Economics and Politics.* He is coauthor of *River Basin Administration and the Delaware, Decisions in Syracuse,* and *Inputs and Outputs in Large City Education.*

JERRY MINER, Professor of Economics at Syracuse University, received his Ph.D. in Economics from the University of Michigan. He has been Senior Research Economist for UNESCO in Paris, and an Assistant Study Director of the Survey Research Center at the University of Michigan. The author of *Social and Economic Factors in Spending for Public Education,* Professor Miner has contributed widely to the literature of economics.

First published 1971 by Aldine · Atherton, Inc.
Address all inquiries to
Aldine Publishing Company
529 South Wabash Avenue
Chicago, Illinois 60605

Library of Congress Catalog Number 76-91725
ISBN 202-06042-X

Printed in the United States of America

Second printing, 1973
Third printing, 1974

Foreword

The purpose of the Aldine Treatises in Modern Economics is to enable authorities in a particular field of economics, and experts on a particular problem, to make their knowledge available to others in the form they find easiest and most convenient. Our intention is to free them from an insistence on complete coverage of a conventionally defined subject, which deters many leading economists from writing a book instead of a series of articles or induces them to suppress originality for the sake of orthodoxy, and from an obligation to produce a standard number of pages, which encourages the submergence of judgment of relevance in a pudding of irrelevant detail. The Aldine Treatises seek to encourage good economists to say what they want to say to their fellow economists, in as little or as much space as they consider necessary to the purpose.

The present volume treats of the economics of public expenditure. This is a relatively new and rapidly growing field of economic analysis and policy. Economics in the past has tended to concentrate on the economics of taxation, on the assumption that the scope of the objects of public expenditure is given by nature or society and the main problem is to allocate the tax burden equitably and with minimum loss of economic efficiency. It is only recently that economists have come to enquire into the reasons why certain kinds of expenditure are assigned to the public sector (the theory of public goods), the logic of the assignment and of the processes by which the total amount of public expenditure and its allocation among alternatives are determined, the criteria for efficiency in the spending of public money, the implications of the division of responsibility for expenditures among different levels of government, and the actual behavior of governmental units viewed simply as economic units attempting to maximize their objectives subject to a budget constraint.

The analysis of the public sector, more so probably than other economic units such as the firm or household, lends itself to many different approaches, from that of the pure economic theorist interested in public goods, externalities, and market failures to that of the cost-benefit analyst interested in assessing alternative public investment opportunities and in relating expenditure programs to social objectives, and from that of the theorist interested in the philosophical problems of social choice to that of the coldly applied economist seeking to find empirical regularities in the behavior of governmental units. One can concentrate on the purely theoretical issues, or on the operational problems of decision-making with respect to public expenditure, or on empirical observation of governmental behavior.

One unfortunate consequence of this variety of possible approaches, for the student of the subject, is that the relevant literature is widely scattered as regards place of publication, and that the techniques employed for different aspects of the problem are extremely heterogeneous. To keep up with the field, the student and his teacher must read omnivorously, and be extremely versatile in their capacity to use the various tools of economic analysis. For the economist actually engaged in the formulation of public policy, the task might well seem hopeless.

The authors of the present Treatise realized the need for a monograph that would bring together, survey, and synthesize the main developments in the analysis and treatment of the public sector, and decided to pool their talents in order to make the survey as authoritative as possible over the extremely wide range of topics that rightfully demanded inclusion. Each has made independent contributions to the development of the field, and can write authoritatively about it. The result of their collaboration is a happy blend of individual expertise raised to a higher power, in which the reader is furnished with a carefully evaluated summary of the major contributions of a great variety of authors, set within a broader context of concern about the major issues revealed by past scholarship, and illuminated by a conscientious awareness of those issues that remain unresolved. Readers at all levels should find this Treatise a useful guide to the nature and merits of the work done so far in this rapidly-developing field, as well as to the problems and issues that remain open.

HARRY G. JOHNSON

Preface

In the years since World War II economists generally and public finance economists in particular have become increasingly involved in both the theory and policy analysis of public expenditures. No doubt the growth of the public sector, in both developed and underdeveloped nations, has contributed to this involvement. And no doubt the increased importance of military expenditures in the budgets of many nations, with a resultant pressure on public resources for nonmilitary purposes, has also contributed to a heightened concern over the composition and level of public outlay.

The traditional analytic framework of economics has not been wholly adequate for the tasks that have been confronted. Theory and policy analysis in economic stabilization are reasonably well developed; we have not attempted here either to synthesize or to add to this body of knowledge. But other areas are less secure. The nature of preferences and their relationship to individual and group welfare is not yet satisfactorily resolved.

The concern for attaining efficiency has continued to be significant, but in recent years has been joined by a concern with the distributional aspects of public expenditures. A successful conceptualization of the ideal merger of efficiency and distributional objectives in the public sector has not yet been attained. The "new" welfare economics has been no more successful in specifying an optimum for the public sector, and its integration with the private sector, than in specifying an optimum for purely market-type conditions. As a result, the field of public expenditure is in a somewhat unsettled state in both theory and practice, and the authors of this volume find themselves writing into and about a number of areas where neither doctrine nor practice has yet been resolved.

In consequence, we feel that we owe to our readers a statement of the presuppositions on which this volume rests. These are first, that fiscal theory has significance only in an operational context — in the analysis of policy alternatives, in the choice among fiscal instruments to achieve societal goals, and in particular in the context of budget procedures and budget systems. Thus we move from an examination of the pure theory of public goods to an examination of the political context of budget making and to the development of program budgeting and its principal analytic tool, benefit-cost analysis. We also stress that the theory and practice of multilevel finance is relevant to the analysis of public expenditures, both to their objectives and to their outcomes.

A second presupposition on which this volume rests is that every effort must be made, in the analysis of expenditure policy, to embrace distributional objectives. We are convinced that the failure to combine distributional considerations with efficiency considerations is a major continuing deficiency in fiscal theory, and we are also convinced that distributional considerations are, at minimum, capable of being handled systematically, even if not definitively, within the theory and practice of public expenditures.

In addition, this volume is characterized by a continued concern for the nature of preferences, their aggregation, and their expression in a political context. The study of public expenditure is, of course, a study in the politics of economics. This must be approached both through an examination of the "purely" economic considerations that are relevant and with recognition that noneconomic considerations also are significant.

Our acknowledgments of indebtedness are substantial. Many graduate students in economics have been subjected to these materials, in one form or another, and we have profited greatly from their critical comments. Our colleagues in the Department of Economics, Syracuse University, have been most generous in their efforts to improve these chapters. In particular, we are indebted to Melvin A. Eggers, John Henning, Katharine Lyall, Seymour Sacks, Edward J. Stevens, Sidney Sufrin, and A. Dale Tussing. Our colleagues in Political Science, Alan K. Campbell, Julian Friedman, and Dwight Waldo, have also been most helpful, as has Harry P. Hatry of the Urban Institute. One of the authors (Burkhead) is indebted to the Brookings Institution for its hospitality and intellectual stimulus in the fall of 1966 when these chapters were in their first stage. Harry G. Johnson, the editor of this series, has been unsparingly critical of earlier drafts of these chapters; his comments have been of great value.

Finally, we would acknowledge the patience and skill of Virginia Halsey who typed the numerous revisions of these chapters, and the assistance of Steven and Philip Miner in the preparation of the index. Also, we express our appreciation to Christine Valentine of Aldine · Atherton, who contributed so much to the transition from manuscript to book.

Contents

ix

ONE

The Nature of the Public Sector

Perhaps the most general observation that can be made about government activities is that they have grown, both relatively and absolutely, in all countries of the world. This commonplace observation must necessarily serve as the starting point for any systematic treatment of the political economy of public expenditure, for the growth of government lies at the heart of continued controversy over the role of the public sector. This controversy is particularly acute in a mixed economy where the public sector is growing more rapidly than the private and where it often appears that this growth is at the expense of, or contributes to a diminution in, private economic activity. In any economic system, regardless of the relative growth of public and private activities, there will be continuously difficult and controversial choices in selecting the appropriate composition of government expenditure and in choosing among alternative government programs that are intended to accomplish social goals.

It is, therefore, useful at the outset to describe the major factors that have contributed to the growth and changing character of governmental outlay.

The Growth of Government

Wagner's law, that there is an expanding scale of state activity, is empirically verifiable, but somewhat deficient analytically (Musgrave, 1969, pp. 73 – 75). The question is, What are the political and economic causes of the growth? Relevant empirical evidence is examined below (see Chapter 9).

There is no doubt that wars among nations have been a major factor contributing to the increase of government activities. National governments expand the scope and range of their activities greatly in the conduct of war. New programs of regulation and direction of the private economy are undertaken.

1

To secure increases in output, governmental outlay is expanded for productive facilities, as well as for transportation and other social overhead capital. Not all of these facilities are dismantled after the war. Peacock and Wiseman argue that a "displacement effect" occurs (Peacock and Wiseman, 1961, pp. 25 – 31). Public revenue grows during the war, both from higher rates of taxation and from the imposition of new levies. This leaves the public sector in a relatively affluent state at war's end. With new and unmet social wants, public expenditure will increase in response to the availability of tax revenue. The displacement effect appears to have operated briefly in Great Britain and West Germany after World Wars I and II, but less strongly in the United States (Musgrave, 1969, pp. 91 – 109).

The growth of government in developed and underdeveloped countries in the years since World War II is also attributable to a high level of international tension and the accompanying importance of the military and its technology. Indeed, modern military technology appears to have a dynamic quality of its own, absorbing increased public resources almost without regard for the existing state of international tensions.

Economic growth is a factor that has both facilitated and made necessary the expansion of the public sector, at least in absolute terms. In most countries, in most circumstances, government expenditures are limited by the availability of tax revenues. Since tax revenues have a positive elasticity with respect to national income, economic growth brings an increase in the volume of revenue from the existing tax structure. This increase is typically accompanied by an increase in government expenditure. The classic Gladstonian phrase is that "expenditure depends on policy." Expenditure also depends on revenue.

An additional factor that has contributed to the growth of the public sector is urbanization. A common pattern appears in all economies that have moved to higher stages of development. The processes of economic growth are initiated in manufacturing. The growth of manufacturing involves an increase in urbanization and a decline in the relative importance of agriculture. The growth of an urbanized area provides the necessary complement of service activity to accompany manufacturing and the concentration of population. Economic activity becomes more specialized and interdependent; new increases in the level of output require additional facilities for communication and transportation. Occupations and firms within the developed and urbanized economy are thus more highly specialized. A larger volume of social overhead capital is necessary to sustain the increased complexity of patterns of transportation and communication, and to further encourage specialization and interdependence. Additional services for police and fire protection and sanitation are required to meet the needs of a concentrated population.

In this setting, increases in economic activity, and the accompanying specialization and interdependence, tend to generate a large volume of externalities.[1] These may be in the nature of private external economies made available to producers, as where a new steel fabricating plant can sell to firms in an area at lower transportation cost. Externalities may also impose costs on other producers, as where the congestion of city streets by delivery trucks reduces the volume of retail trade.

Externalities may also affect households. Consumers may enjoy an external benefit from the location of specialized warehousing facilities within an urban area. But households may suffer losses from a new factory, as in the common example of smoke pollution.

The privately induced external costs of an urbanized existence, whether they affect producers or consumers, are often the occasion for governmental intervention. Frequently this takes the form of regulatory activity, as with efforts to control air pollution or water pollution, or to control patterns of land utilization through zoning and subdivision regulations. In some cases the externalities from the private sector require additional governmental programs with major expenditures. Traffic congestion in the urbanized area is met by new facilities for urban transportation. Water pollution will require additional public facilities for water treatment.

In other cases public programs in the urbanized area emerge from externalities that contribute to the failure of private markets. In a declining residential neighborhood no one property owner may have adequate incentive to rehabilitate his property. The rationale for a public urban renewal program is that government intervention is required to internalize the externalities of neighborhood decay, by substituting public control over land use for private control. A different type of externality, with distributional consequences, occurs in housing. In this country the private market is apparently unable to provide housing at a satisfactory price and of a quality to meet the needs of low-income urban residents. In the absence of direct income subsidies a partial income redistribution is made available by means of public housing, with a consequent growth in the public sector.

The growth of the public sector in response to these externalities and other sources of market failure, including inequities in income distribution, assumes many and varied forms. In some cases, as with regulations for air and water pollution abatement, it is intended that private costs should more nearly reflect social costs; there should be a resulting improvement in aggregate resource allocation. In other cases public programs will express a range of preferences that are not reflected in market forces, as where governments consciously redistribute income to the less affluent. The public sector will alter the private market choices that are available to households, as it taxes away a part of their income.

---

1. Externalities are defined and discussed at length in Chapter 4.

An additional factor that has contributed to the growth of government is generally described as economies of scale. There are certain kinds of economic activities that may be provided at lower cost per unit of output when the scale of the enterprise is enlarged. Individual householders cannot economically provide their own police and fire protection, water supply, waste disposal, and the maintenance of streets in front of their homes. The traditional range of municipal services has come to be provided publicly because economies of scale exist and because there are substantial external benefits from the provision of such services to all households. And again, most of these services and their growth are associated with urbanization. The increased urbanization generates the needs. The higher levels of income that are associated with urban employment are accompanied by a willingness to pay for an expanded level of public activities, at least in developed countries. Activities that were formerly private consumer goods now become collectively provided public goods.

The growth of government attributable to economies of scale implies that this kind of public sector expansion yields a larger real output in relation to a given cost of inputs. But there is an additional characteristic of government output in mature economies that works in the other direction and is attributable to the predominance of services in the composition of government expenditures.

Productivity increases occur in industries that are capital intensive; very little government output is of this nature. Moreover, prices paid by public agencies for inputs must stay roughly in line with private sector input prices. In consequence, as Baumol points out, if there are relatively inelastic demands for public services, resources must be continuously shifted from the high productivity sectors of the economy to the "unprogressive" service sectors (Baumol, 1967, pp. 415 – 26). Since a wide range of government activities, particularly in urban areas, consists of the provision of services, and hence suffers from low rates of productivity increase, there is an inexorable increase in government expenditure, and average productivity for the economy as a whole will tend to fall (see Chapter 9).

The relationship between economic growth and the growth of the public sector is by no means a simple phenomenon, in either developed or developing countries. In a developed country with a mixed economy, such as the United States, much of the growth of governmental activity arises, as noted above, from the social overhead requirements and external costs generated by the private sector. The public sector is not the prime mover, although often public sector activities induce a favorable growth response in the private sector. For a developing economy the growth stimulus is more likely to reside directly in the public sector. The developing country will assume responsibilities for economic planning and hence for the provision of infrastructure development that impose a heavy burden of government expenditures.

The relationship between urbanization and the growth of the public sector in developed and developing countries is strikingly similar in one respect. As the agricultural sector declines in importance, the agricultural population moves to the urbanized area more rapidly than it can be absorbed. Public authority is required to provide minimum levels of subsistence for the unabsorbed population, a requirement that often entails an expanded public expenditure for a broad range of social services. The developed countries of western Europe and the United States and the developing nations of Africa and South America have shared this pattern of experience.

To a greater degree than developed countries, most of the developing countries with mixed economies encounter a continuing need to strengthen and supplement private market structures. Where there are impediments to the organization and financing of private activities, national governments often assume additional responsibilities for the inadequacies in both product and financial markets.

Apart from the generalized forces that appear to operate in almost all economies to produce an increase in the public sector, there are influences that may be operative and important in special circumstances. The age composition of the population may shift as birth rates rise; this will cause increased demands for expenditures on public education. The proportion of the aged may increase, with additional expenditures for pensions, medical care, and other social insurance measures. The agricultural population, whatever its size, seems to occupy a favored position vis-à-vis the public purse in a great many countries, as shown by farm price supports in the United States.

Given both the generalized and specialized forces at work, and their different impact from country to country, it is not surprising that patterns of statistical regularity are somewhat elusive (Musgrave, 1969, pp. 91 – 124). The ratio of either total government expenditures or civilian expenditures to gross national product shows only approximate regularity over time, and a cross-section analysis of these ratios at a point in time produces a much less satisfactory fit.

Public Sector Goals

The economic objectives of the public sector are conventionally described under four headings: the efficient allocation of resources, the stabilization of economic activity, an equitable distribution of income, and the promotion of economic growth.

The public sector may also pursue entirely noneconomic objectives or objectives that are only loosely related to economic objectives. Participation in international organizations might fall into this category, or a concern with highway beautification. The pursuit of noneconomic objectives may or may not require additional public resources. Where resources are required, traditional efficiency considerations enter; that is, there will be choices among the means for accomplishing noneconomic objectives, and it may be possible, in some but not all circumstances, to establish trade-offs among economic and noneconomic objectives.

The four economic objectives or responsibilities of the public sector can be elaborated briefly.

The public sector, in all modern governments, should adopt policies that assure full employment and confine fluctuations in the price level to limits that do not interfere with the effective operation of the economy.

The public sector has a responsibility for the efficient allocation of resources, both in private markets and within the public sector itself. Regulatory public policy should be directed toward offsetting or countering imperfections in private markets so that such markets may serve more effectively as guides to private decisions. Regulatory activity is not important as resource-using for the government itself; rather it affects the private use of resources, as with zoning regulations and building codes. Such activity is usually set apart from the economic objectives that require budgetary outlays for their implementation.

Within the resource-using activities of the public sector there should be attention to technological efficiency in order to maximize outputs from a given volume of inputs, and there should also be attention to efficiency in the sense of satisfying the wants of the citizenry for public goods.

Governments have responsibility for influencing the distribution of income among the regions of an economy and among producer groups, and may implement this responsibility by controlling or offsetting market imperfections. In addition, governments assume responsibility for the distribution of income among the rich and the poor. If private markets do not yield a distribution of income that is socially acceptable, modifications by way of taxes or transfer payments may be necessary for correctional purposes. Redistributional measures need not be limited, however, to tax and transfer payments but may also embrace government expenditures for goods and services that are directed to specific regions or specific groups in the population (see Chapter 9). Moreover, the redistributional measures themselves, that is, the devices employed and not just the outcomes, are a matter of policy concern. As Marglin has pointed out, the size of the economic pie and its division may not be the only factors of concern to the community — the method of slicing the pie may also be relevant.[2]

The fourth general goal is economic growth, defined as an increase in per

2. Stephen A. Marglin, "Objectives of Water-Resource Development: A General Statement," in Arthur Maass et al., *Design of Water-Resource Systems* (Cambridge: Harvard University Press, 1962), pp. 17–18.

capita real income over time. Real economic growth is necessary if the conditions of material existence are to improve. Improvement, measured in these terms, has come to be very widely demanded as evidence of progress.

These four broad goals or responsibilities of the public sector are widely accepted and generally understood. What is less understood is that the interrelations among the goals are most complex. In some cases the goals are reinforcing and in other cases they are in conflict one with another.

The pursuit of the goal of economic growth, for example, may contribute to the achievement of a more equitable distribution of income. Every nation has its submerged one-tenth, one-third, or perhaps a submerged 90 percent of its population, with incomes below those necessary for minimum standards of health and decency. Where a good part of the increment of economic growth can be channeled toward lower-income groups, distributional problems can be alleviated. It is easier to redistribute shares of a growing national income than shares of a static level of national income. Decisions with respect to allocation will also have an important effect on distributional considerations. An expansion of collective consumption for education and health, for example, should contribute to an improvement in human resources and may, if widely distributed among the population over time, alleviate a part of the need for more direct redistributional measures. In addition, an improvement in human resources augments the capital stock of the nation, and this contributes to economic growth.

In other cases there are conflicts among the goals. A rapidly rising domestic price level may call forth public policies in the interests of economic stabilization. To halt the increase in the price level may require a temporary cessation in the rate of growth, as with the deflationary policies pursued by Great Britain in 1966 – 67 and by the United States in 1969 – 70. Moreover, policies pursued in the interests of inflation control may redistribute income upward, as when heavy reliance is placed on monetary policy and an increase in interest rates. Deflationary policies often lead to unemployment, and efforts to control the price level will burden those in the working force who lose their jobs. The conflict among the several aspects of economic stabilization is most often observed in the choice between price stability and employment stability. At some point, in the absence of wage and price controls, a further reduction in unemployment can be purchased only at the expense of an increase in the price level. A continued policy directed to a low level of unemployment may lead to continued inflation.

The goals of the public sector, whether harmonious or in conflict, are pursued in an organizational context. This context is, or should be, coordinated by means of administrative and legislative instrumentalities, among which budget policy and procedure are the most important. Before examining the general characteristics of public sector behavior, it will be useful to describe the major organizational patterns.

Organizational Characteristics

Government activities are conducted in three reasonably distinct organizational forms — general government, public enterprise, and trust funds. Although the specifics of these forms necessarily vary among countries, each has certain common characteristics that may be described.

General government typically embraces those activities that are organized as departments or agencies and headed by appropriate ministers or secretaries of cabinet rank. General administrative services, the military, the conduct of foreign relations, and a large number of other domestic economic activities in the fields of education, health, transportation, and housing will be embraced under the term "general government." General government programs will influence the distribution of income, and economic growth and stabilization. But most of general government is allocational — the provision of collective goods and services.

It is characteristic of these activities that they are financed from general revenue. There is little, if any, earmarking of funds to establish a linkage between specific taxpayer contributions and specific outlays. There is no quid pro quo relationship between the taxpayer and the beneficiary of expenditures. There are no price tags attached to general services, and it is the absence of price tags that crucially differentiates general government activity from market activity. It is therefore necessary to conceptualize and analyze the economic activities of general government very differently than in the case of activities in the market sector.

For example, it is customary in first-year textbooks in economics to depict a market economy in terms of a flow chart showing the interrelationships between households and business firms. The chart traces the way in which the business firm purchases factors at their market prices and sells goods back to households with price tags attached.

A flow chart showing the interrelationships among households, business firms, and governments must depict a different pattern. Factors are purchased at their market prices, but general government goods and services are not sold to households or business firms. Consequently, individual valuations of public goods are not manifested in exchange prices and there must indeed be a process of social valuation. This social valuation is conceptually more difficult than the valuation process for private markets. In the latter it is conventional for economists not to look behind the demand curve. That is, there is no effort to measure utility itself — the satisfactions that individuals can appropriate from the consumption of goods and services purchased in the market. Neither do economists attempt to explain the sources of preferences or determine whether consumer behavior is optimal (see Chapter 9). But in the absence of market prices for public goods, valuation requires measured estimates of benefits; much of the effort of students of public finance, in recent years, has been directed toward the measurement of government output in terms of explicit or implicit utilities.

A second consequence of the absence of price tags on divisible units of government activity is described in fiscal theory as the nonapplicability of the exclusion principle. In its provision of goods and services, general government does not and often cannot exclude possible beneficiaries. The national defense establishment that protects one household protects other households regardless of their tax contributions. This is a fundamental difference between the public sector and the private market sector; in the latter the exclusion principle prevails and benefits are individually appropriable. The major consequence of this difference is that consumers of public goods are unwilling to reveal their preferences or willingness to pay.[3]

The second organizational form for the conduct of the economic activities of government is typically designated as public enterprise or public undertakings. The patterns that prevail among governments are immensely varied, but the basic characteristic of enterprise activity is that it operates more or less along commercial lines, providing goods and services with specific price tags attached. In the United States familiar examples are the post office department, the Tennessee Valley Authority, and municipally owned electric utilities. Frequently, although not invariably, such activities are organized formally as government corporations with a general manager and board of directors. For some government corporations, both here and abroad, financing is provided by issues of stocks and bonds. Accounts are maintained to show annual profit or loss and the status of assets.

Public enterprise does not fit neatly into any of the conventional categories of public sector objectives. In this country government enterprise often pursues allocational objectives — the public provision of goods and services, even though on a fee or price basis. But distributional considerations also enter, when a part but not all of the output of the enterprise may be priced at marginal cost, to favor specific classes of users. Postal services are a case in point. Public enterprise is often utilized to achieve objectives that are not satisfied by private market institutions, as in the provision of insurance and financing for farmers, homeowners, and small businessmen. Again, there is a mixture of allocational and distributional objectives. In countries undergoing development public enterprise often has responsibility for the pursuit of growth objectives or for supplementing inadequacies in private markets.

3. The implications of this distinction will be explored in Chapter 2.

The degree of central administrative control to which public enterprise is subject varies greatly among governments. In the United States federal government corporations conform to a pattern of central control that is almost as rigorous as that applied to general government departments and agencies. In Great Britain, on the other hand, the nationalized industries operate more independently with respect to pricing policy, and are required only to follow general guidelines. Investment policy, however, when additional funds are required, depends on the central government.

The third form for the conduct of government activity is the trust fund. In most governments, trust funds have found their widest applications in the field of social insurance; they thus implement distributional objectives. The trust fund distinguishes a class of contributors who provide earmarked revenues and a class of beneficiaries who are entitled to draw from the fund under specified conditions. Accumulations in trust funds are typically loaned to general government, thus reducing borrowing or taxing requirements from the public. The distinguishing characteristic is the earmarking of revenue and expenditures and the segregation, at least on a bookkeeping basis, of a set of accounts. Although trust funds are most often used for transfer payments, as in social insurance, they are also utilized for goods and service transactions, as in the highway trust fund of the U.S. government.

In the Anglo-Saxon governmental tradition there have always been reasonably sharp lines drawn between the public sector and the private sector, as well as among the forms of government organization. The mixed undertakings that characterize the activities of many South American governments and those of the Scandinavian countries have been largely absent from the traditions of Great Britain, Canada, Australia, and the United States. In the former countries public enterprises are often conducted by boards of directors which represent a mixture of public and private interests. Capital may be provided in part publicly, in part privately. Operating policies with respect to prices and wages may be subject to a measure of public control. The possible mix of public and private interest is almost infinitely varied (Hanson, 1955).

After World War II, governments in the Anglo-Saxon tradition initiated experiments with more complex patterns for public undertakings. In Britain the nationalized industries developed much more independence from the central government than the older British corporations had.[4] In the United States, government corporations, such as local housing authorities, were financed by the sale of debt obligations to the public. Post office department construction during the 1950s was partially financed from private capital sources, as was the TVA. These developments were undoubtedly encouraged by the abun-

4. For interesting comments on these developments see John Kenneth Galbraith, *The New Industrial State* (Boston: Houghton Mifflin, 1967), pp. 99–101.

dance of liquid capital accumulation in the private sector in these years and the resulting generalized pressure for additional investment outlets.

In recent years, particularly in the United States, the traditional sharp lines between public and private economic activity have been even further blurred, and not alone by way of changes in the characteristics of public enterprises. The new mixtures now emerge from changes in the traditional operating patterns of general government departments and agencies.

A large part of the research and development activities of the U.S. government has been contracted to private corporations and universities. A large part of the research and operations of the space programs is under the management of private firms, only generally supervised by the National Aeronautics and Space Agency. The antipoverty programs of the Office of Economic Opportunity have further blurred the lines between the public and the private sector. Many activities that would once have been conducted as a part of general government administration are, again, contracted to universities and business firms. And the financing and operation of the communications satellite (COMSAT) illustrate an extreme case of the complex mixture of public and private economic activity.

In the last instance a corporation was chartered by act of Congress in 1962 to be governed by a board of fifteen — three appointed by the president, six elected by the stockholders, and six elected by the telecommunications industry. Capital is private; technology is the product of public research and development. Both the Federal Communications Commission and the National Aeronautics and Space Agency are involved; the organization is conducted for private profit. The complexity of this organizational pattern greatly exceeds that of the traditional forms of state capitalism in western Europe.

The organizational multiplicity and complexity of modern governments poses a great many difficulties, in conceptual, operational, and measurement terms, for designating that which is public and that which is private. Unfortunately, for most purposes, it is necessary to lay the complexities aside and to approach questions of public expenditure as if the lines were reasonably sharp. In this way it is at least possible to describe and analyze the important operational differences between public and private activity.

The Government Budget

The principal instrumentality that attempts to impose a sense of order on this multiplicity of organizational forms is the government's budget. The preparation of the annual budget for a government is the occasion for a review of existing programs and of executive recommendation as to their expansion or contraction. It is the occasion for introducing new programs and interrelating them with existing operations. It is the occasion for the review of considerations affecting operating efficiency.

A government budget is a plan of revenue and expenditure for the forthcoming fiscal year, and should be related to plans and projects for a longer period. The preparation of the budget becomes the occasion for decisions about the composition and level of government output and about the relative importance of the goals of stabilization, distribution, and growth. In their legislative aspects, budget review and authorization are the occasion for assuring administrative accountability. Legislative action on the budget is also the occasion for enforcing the requirements of constitutional democracy by assuring that revenue and expenditure programs are responsive to the wishes of the representatives of the electorate.

Budget procedure in any government will vary widely in its applications to the three organizational forms described above. As a formal document, the budget may comprehend only the activities of general government, omitting the activities of enterprises and trust funds. The decision processes inherent in budget review may similarly be restricted. But as an information document, the budget, even when procedurally restricted in its review, may comprehend government activity in all of its forms. That is, a budget may be informationally comprehensive.

The budget process is in some ways similar to private market processes. Like market processes, the budget reflects decisions concerning the allocation of resources. The optimum allocation of scarce resources is the common objective of both. The procedures for budgetary examination and review impose a kind of discipline which is ordinarily associated with the discipline of expenditure decisions by households or business firms in a reasonably competitive market. But in other ways the analogy is faulty (McKean, 1965, pp. 496–506).

A market is usually described as an impersonal mechanism generating and responding to price signals for factors and for products. The prices, in turn, interact with preferences and technology to constitute the basis for decisions by households and business firms. The budget, however, does not generate comparable price signals for budget-makers to respond to. Rather, the budget reflects the representations of the executive and of the citizenry with respect to the appropriate level and composition of government output and the revenues that should be associated therewith. The representations of the citizenry are often made to both administrators and legislators. Or, administrators and legislators may react to indirect evidences of the demands and preferences of the citizenry for public goods and services. Or, administrators and legislators may acquire a kind of independence of the citizenry and shape and influence the demand for and acceptability of their programs. But in any case there are no quantitative signals to be interpreted in the way that an increase in copper prices, for example, suggests to copper producers that output should be expanded, or when an increase in unsold inventory is the signal to cut back production.

The budget process in government thus differs from the market process in ways that are significant for economic analysis. The market is a social, man-made institution that serves up information on which consumers and producers make decisions about the purchase and sale of factors and products. The market does not "make" the decision; the market does not allocate resources. The market provides information.[5] Even as producers and consumers make decisions, so do those government officials who propose and adopt budgets. The budget document reflects these decisions; as it details the transactions of the prior fiscal year, it is a record of immediate past actions with respect to the composition and level of expenditure for the public sector. It is also a plan for the immediate future of revenue and expenditure, reflecting the administration's proposals as presented to the legislature. As a record of past decisions the budget document has its counterpart in the books of account of households and business firms. As a plan for the immediate future, the possible private market counterpart of the government budget is the business firm's investment or sales plan for the forthcoming period.

Behavioral Characteristics

The organizational multiplicity of government and the conflicts and the complex interactions among the goals of public policy make the subject of public economics inherently intricate. No single rule for decisions can be followed with simplicity.

The contrast with the private market is sharp and clear on this point. There the profit yardstick is continuously available. Profits are measurable as a guide to the decisions of business firms. Decisions related to price policy, to current levels of output, and to investment can be structured in accordance with profit possibilities. This does not mean that the decision is uncomplicated. There may be difficult choices between short- and long-run profit possibilities, and choices between current profit and the preservation of asset values. Decisions to accept or oppose costly public regulations in the interests of maintaining cordial relations with community opinion may be difficult. But there is at least a single rule — profit maximization — that can serve as a guide. Both operating and capital programs can be projected in relation to this guide. Results can be measured in these terms.[6]

5. Even the most careful of economists sometimes lapse on this point. For example, "In a free enterprise system markets allocate scarce resources among firms. . . ." (Anthony Downs, *Inside Bureaucracy* [Boston: Little, Brown, 1967], p. 29).

6. There is no intention here to enter into the controversy over whether profit maximization

Governmental program objectives are never this clear-cut. For example, technologically inferior methods may be perpetuated by a government agency in the interests of protecting its employees from unemployment; that is, the social service aspects of the government program may be as important as its output of goods and services. Thus, government programs may be hampered in their pursuit of technological efficiency. It would be more appropriate, however, to describe these situations as ones in which government programs are intended to accomplish multiple goals; and economic efficiency judgments, as such, are only partial judgments.

The pervasive presence of multiple goals in the public sector is underscored when government program decisions are shaped and structured not only by the wants of the consumers of government goods and services but also by the wants of producers of public sector goods. Private producer groups — the suppliers of intermediate goods to government programs — may have a great influence on the volume and composition of such goods. The suppliers of cement and steel and road-building equipment have been important in increasing the "demand" for highway facilities in somewhat the same fashion as producers have shifted the demand curve for their products through advertising. The level and composition of highway programs will necessarily be conditioned by the interests of such producer groups as well as by the consumers of highway services. And, in terms of the theory of consumer demand, it is most difficult to conceptualize a demand function for final product that embraces both the demands by factor suppliers based on anticipated profits and the demands of final consumers based on the utilities generated by the consumption of these products.[7] Any attempt to conceptualize the demand for highways as this demand impinges on public decisions must embrace both the demands of the consumers of highway services and the demands of those who supply products to the governments that pay for the highways.

There are other differences in the behavioral characteristics of the public and private sectors. Viewed solely as an institution for the attainment of economic efficiency in resource allocation, and in relation to the availability of information, the political process is probably inferior to private decisions guided by competitive markets. But this does not make the private sector a superior

---

or profit maintenance is the significant rule that guides the behavior of business firms. For some aspects of this controversy see Galbraith, op. cit., pp. 109 – 127 and James S. Earley, "The Impact of Some New Developments in Economic Theory," *American Economic Review,* May 1957, pp. 330 – 35.

7. This case is to be distinguished from that of producers who demand government services as intermediate product for their own output, as with the manufacturing firm that uses the highway. The aggregation of this kind of derived demand with consumer demand poses fewer problems.

institution. The public sector is simply a different institution, with goals that involve considerations other than those of economic efficiency.

The same kinds of considerations affect the evaluation of the relative efficiency of management in the two sectors. As has often been pointed out, the public sector manager typically has little incentive to reduce costs or to return appropriations unspent. Neither is he likely to be accountable, in the same fashion, for mismanagement as in the private sector (Alchian, 1967, pp. 77–79). As public sector programs become increasingly complex, the task of devising an adequate incentive system becomes a matter of crucial importance (Schultze, 1970, pp. 145–72). This includes such formidable tasks as assuring that private incentives produce a behavior pattern consistent with public objectives, and that within the public sector performance-measures be developed as guides to administrators (see Chapter 6).

The differences in goals and management incentives require different definitions of efficiency. Peacock and Wiseman say: "we do not have any simple unambiguous measures to offer by which the efficiency of government spending might be assessed. Indeed, we would assert that there are no such measures" (1968, p. 37).

Economic and political objectives cannot always be distinguished or traded off as if they were independent efficiency criteria. The criteria of effective government operation may appropriately extend to the satisfaction of specific and narrow clientele interests, the contentment of government employees, the furtherance of the political careers of elected officials, the tenure of bureaucrats. All of these and numberless other objectives are a part of the "function" that is maximized by government agencies and departments (Gross, 1964, pp. 467–537).[8]

There are other differences. In the market, intensity of demand is revealed by the willingness of purchasers to offer more than the prevailing price. In the political process voting at the polls does not reveal the intensity of demand, but there are other mechanisms that do. The vociferous minority is often in a position to trade support on a series of issues over time in order to make its demands effective. Interest group representation, with crucial shortcomings and omissions, contributes to the expression of the intensity of citizen demands for public goods and identifies emergent demands (see Chapter 5). Also, government programs differ greatly in character. Some groups benefit more than others — as consumers, as producers or as residents of one area rather than another. This is true even in the case of pure public goods where one person's consumption of the public good does not limit another person's (see Chapter

---

8. For an interesting general discussion of these issues see P. D. Henderson, "Political and Budgetary Constraints: Some Characteristics and Implications," in J. Margolis and H. Guitton, *Public Economics* (New York: St. Martin's Press, 1969), pp. 310–25.

2). In fact, some will consume and benefit more than others, even when no one is excluded.

Finally, government programs are marked by an element of coercion which is absent in the private sector. In the market no one is required to buy any specified quantity of goods and services. But, at some point, after a government program has been proposed, reviewed, and adopted, taxes are levied for its support. These taxes are levied coercively, that is, persons are required to pay. Some persons will necessarily be required to pay for specific kinds of government goods and services from which they themselves will not benefit and which they themselves would oppose. It is in this sense that government programs, however democratically arrived at, will restrict, to a greater or lesser degree, private economic freedom. The quantity of coercive restriction on private persons through compulsory taxation, however, may be offset by what happens on the expenditure side. It may be, for example, that the offsets are very great for programs of human resource development, such as education, that expand the limits of personal choice; on balance, there may be no net freedom restriction for such tax-expenditure programs. In short, a "general equilibrium analysis" of this complex situation would require a balance sheet that estimated the economic freedom losses to taxpayers against the economic freedom gains of program beneficiaries, and some in each group may be the same individuals. The absence of a monetary calculus for such gains and losses, however, precludes comprehensive analysis of this kind.

Economic Analysis

An economic theory of government activity is typically a product of two sets of influences. The first is the set of real world conditions that surround the observer and that structure the kinds of problems to which he addresses himself as well as his view of economic and political society. The second set of influences consists of the contemporary body of economic and political theory itself. In a general way, any theory of the public sector that attempts either to describe consequences of public sector decisions or to prescribe how those decisions ought to be made, must depend heavily on the general state of economic theory as it prevails. A theory of the public sector cannot be divorced from the general body of economic theory.

Sometimes it is relatively easy to discern the real world conditions that give rise to particular approaches and to discern the problems to which theorists address themselves. It is frequently more difficult to perceive why a given body of theory or a particular approach, in this case to the public sector, persists over time, often lasting beyond the conditions that gave rise to its existence. A given pattern of thinking may perhaps have an internal dynamic of its own to encourage elaboration and extension beyond the original conditions of relevance. Or it may continue its existence as prescription, not as theory that explains reality. The development of classical and neoclassical theory about the economics of government illustrates the kind of degeneration that can occur.

Classical theory starts, of course, with Adam Smith's writings about the role of government. Smith's major policy preoccupation was a desire to contribute to the decline of mercantilist practices. He wished to change the responsibility of government from one of interference in the market sector to one of noninterference. Competitive markets required no regulation. The "invisible hand," that is, man's rational desire to improve his own economic position, would be able to achieve efficient results for society as a whole. The market does not allocate resources, nor does man's propensity to "truck, barter and exchange." The regulatory mechanism is the rationality of economic, individualistic man.

Smith wished to restrict the role of government activity generally, to strengthen competitive market forces, and to restrict in particular those governmental practices that encouraged private monopoly. This would free the economic system to facilitate growth and, in particular, the growth of manufactures.

To serve this policy purpose it was not necessary for Smith to theorize about the role of government. Rather, he could prescribe, as he did in the famous passages which proposed to limit the sovereign to specified duties and expenses. These were to be restricted to defense, justice, and public works and public institutions, with the latter to include institutions for facilitating the commerce of society, institutions for the education of youth, and institutions for the instruction of people of all ages; and finally, Smith allowed the expense of supporting the dignity of the sovereign (Smith, 1937, pp. 653 – 768).

Although Smith's approach to the economics of the public sector was highly restrictive — indeed, that was its intent — he was nevertheless sufficiently perceptive to give the restrictions flexibility. His noninterventionist approach was by no means a rigid one. For example, he was not preoccupied with the dangers of unproductive public expenditure, at least as compared with his successors.

At the hands of his followers in the British classical tradition, Smith's prescriptive approach became narrower, the flexibility he imparted tending to be lost, particularly in the writings of McCullock, Nassau Senior, and James Mill. Even Ricardo made little advance in terms of a general theory of the economics of government, although he made notable contributions to such particular problems as the analysis of public debt.

As classical political economy yielded to neoclassical economics at the end of the nineteenth century, there was a continual decline in attention to the theory and problems of the public sector. The first edition of Alfred Marshall's *Principles,* published in 1890, contained no chapters on public finance, unlike the treatises by Smith, Ricardo, and Mill. Marshall made frequent reference to the use of taxes and subsidies to control externalities in private markets, but he was not concerned with the role of government expenditure in achieving economic goals.

It may be that British economists' concern with the public sector could be dropped in the last part of the nineteenth century simply because decisions about the size and composition of government outlay were safely left to the political process. The British system of central budgeting was well established with the Gladstone reforms of 1866. The budget procedures of that time have continued with a high degree of effectiveness and with surprisingly little alteration to the present day. Moreover, the relative size of the domestic public sector was not growing in Britain during the last half of the nineteenth century. The public sector did not appear to be encroaching on the private. The expenditure side of the budget was under control.

With expenditures safely left to administrative and political processes, economists in the British classical tradition concentrated their attention on the distribution of tax burdens (Musgrave and Peacock, 1958, pp. ix – x). This was economics, not politics. James Mill, McCulloch, and particularly John Stuart Mill, devoted considerable care to a generally fruitless effort to refine various concepts of sacrifice and ability to pay.[9] But the British economists were not concerned with what would be called today a general equilibrium analysis of the public sector. There was no effort to look at revenue and expenditure together or at the composition and size of the public sector in relation to the total of economic activity. Public expenditures were to be determined in accordance with traditional and restrictive rules. Public revenue policy was to be judged in accordance with concepts of sacrifice, benefit, or ability to pay. By the first quarter of the twentieth century the flexibility of the early classical approach had degenerated into a series of meaningless prescriptions, most of which were directed toward the distribution of tax burdens.

The continental tradition in public finance during the nineteenth century was very different. Again, the real world conditions were different, and this is nowhere more evident than in Italy, which produced a remarkable body of fiscal theory in the last quarter of the nineteenth century.[10] In Italy, unlike Britain, there was no well-established central government budget system; the political processes of decision-making were hardly to be trusted. In this period, Italy was emerging as a national state from the previously autonomous provinces. Standards of public administration were lax; public revenues were uncertain. It was perhaps easier in those circumstances for the Italian economist to

---

9. For a critical examination of these efforts see Gunnar Myrdal, *The Political Element in the Development of Economic Theory,* trans. Paul Streeten (Cambridge: Harvard University Press, 1954), esp. pp. 156 – 76.

10. For an excellent review of the theory, although unrelated to its historical setting, see James M. Buchanan, *Fiscal Theory and Political Economy* (Chapel Hill: University of North Carolina Press, 1960), pp. 24 – 74.

look at both revenue and expenditure; certainly it was necessary to do this in order to devise some rules for the guidance of governmental authorities.

Italian fiscal theory, beginning with the writings of Ferrara in the 1850s and continuing with the later work of Pantaleoni and Mazzola insisted that social choice must be based on individual choice (Buchanan, 1960, pp. 17–30; Musgrave and Peacock, 1958, pp. xiii–xiv). This emphasis required that the public budget be viewed as a part of a general equilibrium system; expenditures could not be neglected, as in the Anglo-Saxon tradition.[11] Both the public sector and the private sector are to be guided by the wants of individual, sovereign consumers. The collective decisions of the public sector must reflect individual preferences. But how are these collective decisions to be made and how are individual preferences for public goods to be aggregated?

Through attempts to answer these questions, two distinct strands of Italian fiscal theory emerged. In one, represented by the writing of de Viti de Marco, emphasis was placed on treating the public sector as if it were a market, that is, on the establishment of proper prices for public goods and the maximum utilization of fees and charges.[12] For the remainder of the collective services the task of political authority is to interpret the preferences of individuals as if they were purchasing public goods in a market.

The other strand, represented by such economists as Mazzola, Montemartini, and Barone emphasized that it was the responsibility of political authority, not to price out the public services, or to attempt to make decisions on the budget as if it were a market, but to impose a policy of general welfare based on a careful conception of the public weal as it affects both taxpayers and the beneficiaries of government expenditures (Musgrave and Peacock, 1958, pp. 37–47, 137–51, 165–67). This model attempted to explain fiscal decisions in terms of the behavior of the ruling group, and was undoubtedly influenced by the authoritarian conceptions of the state advanced by Pareto and Mosca (Buchanan, 1960, p. 32).

This latter approach, which in contemporary literature has come to be called the "organic theory," is thus to be distinguished from approaches that may be termed "individualistic." The term "organic" is unfortunate because it carries so many of the authoritarian connotations that marked its initial use by the Italians. This authoritarian association should not be the case. One of the

11. Buchanan suggests that in the Anglo-Saxon tradition it was implicitly assumed that there was democratic participation in political processes, or that, at worst, the public sector was managed by a benevolent despotism that could interpret the wants of individuals. Thus there was no need for theorizing about the nature of the state or the relationship of individual choice to social choice (ibid., pp. 33). See also Buchanan, *The Demand and Supply of Public Goods* (Chicago: Rand McNally, 1968), pp. 191–93.

12. De Viti's major work is one of the few treatises of the Italians that is translated in its entirety. See Antonio de Viti de Marco, *First Principles of Public Finance* (New York: Harcourt Brace, 1936).

important contemporary approaches to fiscal theory is "organic" in the sense that it looks at social decision as political processes that are not essentially guided by individual, sovereign consumers. This approach is in no sense authoritarian or undemocratic (see Chapter 5).

The developments in marginal utility economics in the last quarter of the nineteenth century contributed to both strands of Italian fiscal theory. Shortly after the elaboration of the principles of marginal utility by Menger and Wieser, they were applied to the public sector in 1883 by Emil Sax (Musgrave and Peacock, 1958, pp. 175 – 89). This approach was formulated in terms of the marginal sacrifices through tax payments that must be imposed on each individual in order to yield for him the maximum satisfaction of personal needs. From this individualistic approach there was a leap to a comparable rule for the collectivity: the sum of individual sacrifices must be balanced against the sum of satisfactions from collective activity to attain an equilibrium welfare position. This formulation is frequently stated in terms of a prescription: the public sector is to be ordered so that the aggregate private sacrifice occasioned by the last dollar of taxation equals the aggregate private benefit occasioned by the last dollar of public expenditure. The operational content of this prescription was then, and remains today, rather empty.

Marginal utility economics can be used to justify a pricing approach to the public sector in which goods and services are to be provided, if possible, on a fee or charge basis so that individuals can equate costs and gains. It can also be used to justify an organic approach in which the sovereign or the political process reaches a decision such that costs and benefits are equated at the margin. In any event, marginal utility economics did serve to emphasize the duality of revenue and expenditure and to underscore the need for both sides of the budget to be examined together.

This kind of general equilibrium approach to the public sector reached an even higher stage of development at the hands of Wicksell at the turn of the century (Musgrave and Peacock, 1958, pp. 72 – 118). Wicksell proposed to utilize market-type solutions for much of public activity. For the remainder of general government the size and composition of public outlay were to be determined by establishing linkages between specific taxes and specific expenditures. In Parliament, the tax expenditure packages would be voted successively. The members of Parliament could thus balance costs and gains. Moreover, a specific tax expenditure package would require more than a majority vote for passage. Wicksell favored a unanimity rule, but recognizing that a small minority could then exercise considerable power, he proposed a rule of "approximate unanimity," ranging from two-thirds to 90 percent. A somewhat smaller majority would be required to reduce existing tax expenditure levels.

There are a great many difficulties, both conceptual and operational, in the

Wicksell proposal, as critics have pointed out (Black, 1955, pp. 7 – 23). In a general-fund budget the pairing of specific expenditures with specific taxes would impart independent decision authority to those charged with responsibility for the pairing. Moreover, the ordering of the tax-expenditure pairs will influence the outcome. Voting results will differ if Proposition A is considered before Proposition B, since the success or failure of A may influence votes on B.

On the conceptual side, Wicksell's unanimity rule would satisfy the welfare requirement that gains exceed losses for all members of the community (as interpreted by the Parliament) for any specific addition to the budget. Approximate unanimity would obviously satisfy the welfare criterion approximately. Thus the unanimity rule is the public sector counterpart of Pareto optimality in competitive private markets (Buchanan, 1968, pp. 155 – 58; see Chapter 4 below).

The political aspects of the Wicksell proposal are not without interest. Wicksell was a social reformer and favored confiscatory taxation for some types of property income, such as rents and inheritances (Uhr, 1953, pp. 366 – 68). With a preestablished "just" distribution of income, public expenditures and revenue determination could proceed in terms of voluntarism (Buchanan, 1952, pp. 599 – 602). Wicksell did not feel that an equitable distribution of income had yet been attained in Sweden. In the 1890s the Swedish tax system was heavily regressive and the Swedish parliament contained few representatives of the working class. The rule of unanimity would operate usefully to block the passage of indirect taxes that would burden the poor. Wicksell anticipated, however, that, as working class representation increased, the rule of unanimity would prevent the undue expropriation of the rich by the poor.

The Wicksell proposal is an important contribution to fiscal theory, not because of its practicability, but because it centers attention on the rigorous requirements for an optimal welfare solution in budget determination. This development in fiscal theory, however, had very little impact on the mainstream of British neoclassical thinking about public finances.[13] As late as the 1920s, the principal British fiscal economists, Pigou and Dalton, in discussing general budget principles, elaborated guidelines that equated marginal social benefit with marginal social cost; the two made no attempt to fill in this formulation, either conceptually or operationally. It was not until the Keynesian revolution that new approaches were attempted.

The impact on fiscal theory of Keynes' *General Theory* in 1936 was a mixed one. The great contribution of the *General Theory* in this field was to restore

---

13. Baumol has been successful in finding some neglected references to a welfare approach to public finance in the writings of John Stuart Mill and Henry Sidgwick (Baumol, 1965, pp. 189 – 96).

the economics of public finance to the mainstream of economics. This restoration was accomplished, not by calling attention to the problems of resource allocation and the general equilibrium aspects of the public sector, but by attention to the role of the public sector in economic stabilization. Keynes, of course, was not much concerned with the efficient allocation of resources, in either the public or the private sector. His concern was with the employment of resources, and with the role of public economy in the control of aggregate demand. This great contribution, both to theory and practice, had the effect of relegating the concern with questions of the size and composition of government outlay to a subsidiary position.

Not until the 1950s did economists return to the resource allocation aspects of public economics. Again, real world conditions had something to do with this renewed interest. Government budgets were large and growing. The most serious of public policy problems in both developed and underdeveloped countries were with the size and composition of government outlay. At the same time, for more obscure reasons, economists turned their attention to market solutions for assistance in resolving allocational problems in the public sector. In terms of fiscal theory this meant a revival of interest in a general theory of allocation common to both the public and the private sector. For specific policy problems economists increasingly proposed the utilization of pricing mechanisms for public activities, and the application of benefit-cost analysis — a modification of market economics — in the analysis of public investment decisions. Public policies, it was urged, should be judged in terms of private opportunity cost.

The contemporary concern for resource allocation in the public sector has received undoubted stimulus from the new welfare economics, although it is often difficult to trace the direct linkages. The concern with externalities has been carried over into fiscal theory (Baumol, 1965, pp. 24 – 36). Applications such as benefit-cost have also profited from the infusion of concepts from welfare economics. But it would surely be a mistake to regard any of the contemporary approaches to fiscal theory as a primary outgrowth of welfare economics.

The historical antecedents are closer to those developed by the Italians in the nineteenth century and modified by Wicksell. Although no taxonomy is fully adequate to classify the present diffuse state of contemporary fiscal theory, there are a number of major categories that can be distinguished. The individualistic approaches, associated with the work of Samuelson and Musgrave, seek to build a theory of the public sector on the assumption of consumer sovereignty. Government decisions with respect to the public fisc are viewed as a reflection of individual preferences and the institutions of government are accorded no independent role. This type of fiscal theory is examined in detail in Chapters 2, 3, and 4.

A second group of theorists starts not with the individual and his preferences, but with the institutions for collective decision-making, and hence is intellectually descended from the "organic" theorists among the Italians of the nineteenth century. The work of Colm and Lindblom is representative of this approach.

A third group of theorists is primarily individualistic in outlook — consumer sovereignty is again the starting point — but explores the interactions between fiscal institutions and individual maximizing behavior. Buchanan is the principal exponent of this approach. These "public interest" and "self-interest" approaches, as they will be termed here, are examined in Chapter 5.

Chapters 6 and 7 explore the operational characteristics of public expenditures as expressed in program budgeting and benefit-cost analysis. Chapter 8 introduces the complexities that are ever-present in a system of fiscal federalism, and Chapter 9 examines both the methodology and the major empirical findings of "positive theory," that is, the determination of public expenditure outcomes and the measurement of input-output relationships. Although there are a number of references throughout this volume to stabilization objectives in the theory and practice of public expenditure, no specific chapters are devoted to this topic. The literature would not be enriched by anything that could be added here on this subject.

In contrast with the older traditions of public finance, all contemporary fiscal theory has two characteristics in common. First, it seeks to reconcile the divergent and often conflicting goals of economic stabilization, growth, efficient allocation of resources, and equitable distribution of income. Second, fiscal theory is concerned with general equilibrium solutions in the sense that (1) for the public sector revenues and expenditures must be viewed together, and (2) public policies must be formulated with a view to their impact on the private sector; there must be a conscious effort to "balance" costs and gains, both public and private.

References

Alchian, Armen A. "Cost Effectiveness of Cost Effectiveness," in Stephen Enke, ed., *Defense Management.* Englewood Cliffs: Prentice-Hall, 1967, pp. 74 – 86.

Baumol, William J. *Welfare Economics and the Theory of the State.* Cambridge: Harvard University Press, 1965.

———. "Macroeconomics of Unbalanced Growth: The Anatomy of the Urban Crisis." *American Economic Review,* June 1967, pp. 415 – 26.

Black, Duncan. "Wicksell's Principle in the Distribution of Income," in J. K. Eastham, ed., *Economic Essays in Commemoration of the Dundee School of Economics.* London: Economists' Bookshop, 1955, pp. 7 – 23.

Buchanan, James M. "Wicksell on Fiscal Reform." *American Economic Review,* September 1952, pp. 599 – 602.

————. *Fiscal Theory and Political Economy.* Chapel Hill: University of North Carolina Press, 1960.

————. *The Demand and Supply of Public Goods.* Chicago: Rand McNally, 1968.

Gross, Bertram M. *The Managing of Organizations,* 2 vols. New York: The Free Press, 1964.

Hanson, A. H. *Public Enterprise.* Brussels: International Institute of Administrative Sciences, 1955.

McKean, Roland N. "The Unseen Hand in Government." *American Economic Review,* June 1965, pp. 496 – 506.

Musgrave, Richard A., and Alan T. Peacock. *Classics in the Theory of Public Finance.* London: Macmillan, 1958.

Musgrave, Richard A. *Fiscal Systems.* New Haven: Yale University Press, 1969.

Peacock, Alan T., and Jack Wiseman. *The Growth of Public Expenditure in the United Kingdom.* Princeton: Princeton University Press, 1961.

————. "Measuring the Efficiency of Government Expenditure," in A. R. Prest, ed., *Public Sector Economics.* New York: Augustus M. Kelley, 1968, pp. 37 – 67.

Schultze, Charles L. "The Role of Incentives, Penalties, and Rewards in Attaining Effective Policy," in Robert H. Haveman and Julius Margolis, eds., *Public Expenditures and Policy Analysis.* Chicago: Markham, 1970, pp. 145 – 72.

Smith, Adam. *The Wealth of Nations.* New York: Modern Library, 1937.

Uhr, Carl G. "Wicksell on Fiscal Reform: Further Comment." *American Economic Review,* June 1953, pp. 366 – 68.

TWO

The Pure Theory of Public Expenditure: Partial Equilibrium

Although the underlying ideas have had a long history (Musgrave and Peacock, 1958, and Musgrave, 1938) the term "the pure theory of public expenditure" came into being as the title of an article by Paul A. Samuelson (1954).[1] In a subsequent treatment of the subject, Samuelson (1955) was led by comments on the earlier article to modify the title from "the pure theory" to "a theory" on the ground that "public expenditures and regulation [also] proceed from considerations other than those emphasized in my models."

It is, nevertheless, extremely useful to attempt to develop a pure theory of the public sector which, insofar as possible, mirrors the theory of the private sector. Such an endeavor serves to illuminate the conceptual framework and behavioral assumptions which must be made to permit analogous analysis of resource allocation through private and public arrangements. At the same time, development of a pure theory helps distinguish those characteristics of the analysis of the public sector which arise as a consequence of imperfections from those attributable to the fundamental character of public goods or of public decision-making mechanisms.

While there may be several alternative conceptions of a pure theory of public expenditures, there appears to be one set of assumptions that has proved to be highly fruitful and, as a consequence, has served as the basis for most economic analysis and discussion. In general, what marks this conception of the pure theory of public expenditures is that it is a narrowly economic approach which

1. References to works cited in Chapters 2, 3, and 4 appear at the end of Chapter 4.

omits institutional details and takes conformance with individual preferences as the basis for the evaluation of alternative economic states. Within this framework it attempts to specify the conditions for the determination of that level and composition of public expenditures which maximizes the sum of individual utilities. It is, in effect, primarily an application of partial and general welfare economics to the public sector.

The fundamental notion which underlies the pure theory of public finance is that one of the most basic economic distinctions separates those goods whose consumption by one individual precludes consumption by another from those for which this exclusiveness of consumption does not hold. The former category comprises the familiar and conventional private goods. The latter category has been called collective, public, or social goods by various authors.[2] In the context of the pure theory this group of goods has the property that "each individual's consumption of such a good leads to no subtraction from any other individual's consumption of that good" (Samuelson, 1954, p. 387) or, in Musgrave's words, they "must be consumed in equal amounts by all."

From this distinction between private and public goods discussion of the public sector proceeds to both partial and general analysis. The partial analysis proceeds from the conventional set of ceteris paribus assumptions and focuses on the significance of the unique characteristics of public goods for an equilibrium solution. Here, then, primary concern lies with questions of conceptualization, revelation of preferences, and dynamic adjustment of demand and supply for public goods, with additional concern for the welfare implications of the analysis. In essence, interest centers on comparison of the usual partial equilibrium analysis for private goods with the application of this technique to public goods. When attention turns to the context of general equilibrium, emphasis shifts to the mutual accommodation of private and public goods. Here, one pertinent issue concerns the existence and properties of an equilibrium solution which conforms to underlying preferences and cost conditions for both public and private goods. Another concerns the character of the welfare optimizing solution to resource allocation, pricing, and distribution when public as well as private goods are included in the analysis.

This chapter first develops the distinction between public and private goods. Then it turns to the framework within which the economic theory of public expenditures has been developed and the limitations of this framework. Finally, the details of the partial equilibrium analysis are presented. Chapter 3 analyses the general equilibrium approach. Both of these chapters deal with "pure" theory, that is, with goods which are at either extreme in terms of privateness or publicness. Chapter 4 removes this restriction, and the study

2. These terms are used interchangeably throughout this book.

turns from pure theory to consideration of a wide range of sources of failure of decentralized markets and the implications of these failures for public policy.

The Concept of Public Goods

As noted above the foundation of the pure theory rests on the distinction between public and private goods. It is essential to understand the implications for economic organization and resource allocation of this distinction. The concept of a public or social good, defined so that one person's consumption does not reduce another's, does not in itself necessarily imply government organization of its production or the necessity to abjure market pricing. Yet these implications generally emerge from closer analysis of pure public goods. What are the essential features of such goods viewed from the perspective of economic analysis?

One way in which public goods have been characterized is that they are jointly supplied because, "once produced, any given unit of the good can be made equally available to all" (Head, 1962, p. 201). This feature provides the basis for the conventional partial equilibrium analysis of public goods. The solution of private-good joint supply is applied to public goods. The resulting equilibrium solution, however, is not one which would ensue from any feasible market arrangement. It is argued that for goods which are essentially similar to polar public goods a solution approximating the equilibrium position requires public intervention.

PUBLIC AND PRIVATE JOINT SUPPLY

Samuelson recently (1969) has reviewed the contrast between public and private joint supply. Figure 2.1 shows the standard private joint-supply analysis, using Marshall's illustration of wool and mutton for two consumers. The top row of the figure depicts the horizontal summation of the demands by the two men for mutton, yielding the demand curve dm-dm, while the middle row shows the similar addition of demands by the same men for wool, giving the demand curve dw-dw. The graph at the bottom shows the vertical addition of dm-dm and dw-dw into a demand curve for sheep; this curve, when juxtaposed with the supply curve for sheep (assumed equal to a constant marginal cost), determines the equilibrium price and quantity of sheep. Note that in this solution the prices for mutton and wool, given the equilibrium quantity of sheep (and, therefore, specified quantities of wool and mutton under the assumption of fixed proportions) sum exactly to the marginal cost of sheep. At these prices each will have consumed mutton and wool up to the point where

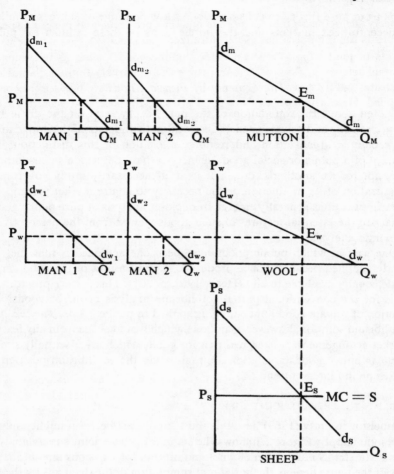

Figure 2.1. Private Goods Joint Products (both Horizontal and Vertical Summing of Demands)

his respective marginal valuation is equal to the price.[3] Since these prices are the same to each man, at equilibrium they each attach the same value to the last unit of wool or of mutton purchased, and, hence, to the last sheep produced. The market solution for private joint products, thus, is in all essential

3. The term "marginal valuation" as used in this book is defined as the marginal rate of substitution of money (or income) for a unit of a good. It is a monetary measure of the subjective valuation of a marginal unit of a commodity or service. See Tibor Scitovsky, *Welfare and Competition* (Homewood, Illinois: Richard D. Irwin, Inc., 1951), pp. 38–39, for further discussion.

respects analogous to that for private nonjoint products, and raises no special problems for the operation of decentralized markets.

Acts of joint supply which provide "public goods" such as television or national defense do, however, create problems for market solutions. Samuelson illustrates public goods joint supply by Figure 2.2, where television is being supplied. Here, the nature of the good produced is such that each man consumes whatever amount is produced so that there is no possibility for individual variation in quantity taken. The demand of each man must, therefore, be summed vertically to obtain an aggregate demand for television, as in the bottom diagram. Juxtaposition of this aggregated demand with a supply curve determines the equilibrium quantity and price. At this equilibrium quantity the valuation placed on the marginal unit of output differs among the consumers, but, in line with the requisites for optimality, the sum of their marginal valuations is equal to the supply price.

The crucial point, of course, is that in this instance there is a fatal difficulty for decentralized markets. Usually, this difficulty is referred to as the "inability to exclude," and is added to the characteristic of joint supply to take into account that aspect of public goods which prevents application of the Marshallian solution to joint supply. Careful examination reveals that it is not the literal impossibility of exclusion of nonpayers from consumption of public goods which vitiates the relevance of the private goods joint supply solution. Rather, it is the absence of a mechanism for full preference revelation.

Suppose, for example, that a technology were developed which permitted exclusion of those who did not pay from consumption of a "public good." That is, assume a good like Samuelson's TV whose use by one individual does not reduce the amount available to others. Exclusion still would not yield a solution analogous to the private good joint supply where for each consumer, prices, marginal valuation, and marginal cost are equated. In the public goods case, only one commonly consumed quantity would be produced, and there is no reason to expect each consumer's marginal valuation for this quantity to equal its uniform exclusion price. It is the consumer's inability to adjust quantity taken in response to his preferences, rather than technical difficulties of exclusion, which account for the failure of decentralized markets in the area of public goods. The obvious solution to a fixed quantity is to vary the prices charged to individual consumers, in order to bring the prices into equality with marginal valuations at the given amount. It is precisely this which cannot be done in the absence of knowledge of preference. Unlike private goods where variation in quantities demanded at different exclusion prices serves to reveal preferences, the inability to vary quantity eliminates the possibility of preference revelation through market processes for public goods.

The nature of this failure can easily be seen in the small-number case where the relative shares in the costs of a jointly supplied commodity will, within the

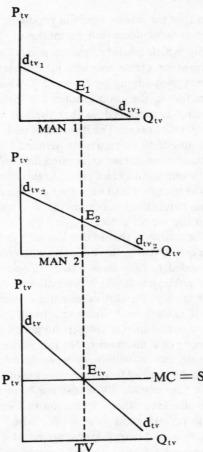

Figure 2.2. Public Goods Joint Products
(Vertical Summation over All People)

limits of offer curves, depend upon bargaining. In the Marshallian case of joint supply the introduction of large numbers leads to optimal output and prices because price exclusion induces each consumer to adjust quantity so that his marginal valuation is equated to the market price. In the public goods case of joint supply, price exclusion, even if feasible, would not permit consumers to equate marginal valuation to price since there is no way to achieve individual adjustment in quantity for goods with "public good jointness." A further problem, which arises when exclusion is not feasible, is that the larger the number of joint consumers the greater the incentive for dissembling and for enjoying the benefits of being a free rider.

The problem now is clear. A quasi-competitive solution for public goods can be developed along the lines of the joint supply analysis if preferences are assumed to be revealed. If such an assumption is not made, the appropriate analytical approach is in terms of a bargaining model, with the usual distinction made between large and small numbers, perfect and imperfect knowledge, and strategies employed by the various parties. These considerations lead Samuelson to conclude, "The theory of public goods is not simply an extension of Mangoldt-Marshall joint supply or of joint demand. In general public goods involve consumption externality with a game theoretic or bi-lateral monopoly element of indeterminancy of the sort that may not be removable by use of an 'exclusion' device or that cannot *optimally* be handled by such a device" (1969a, p. 110).

It is important to note here that the two characteristics of polar social goods have different implications. The "joint supply" or nonrival element is the feature which necessitates modification of the conventional pricing rule of marginal cost equals price equals marginal valuation for the achievement of a welfare maximizing solution when social goods are involved. If more than one individual "consumes" the same unit of a commodity, efficiency requires that output be extended to the point where the sum of the marginal rates of substitution (or marginal valuations) of all consumers are equal to the commodity's marginal cost. This modified price rule is appropriate when joint supply prevails regardless of whether it is possible to exclude nonpayers from consuming. If such exclusion is feasible, as in Marshall's classic illustration of wool and mutton, or in the theater or at sporting events, consumers or potential consumers can be made to reveal all or at least a portion of their preferences through market arrangements.

In the complete absence of price exclusion, private producers would not be able to limit consumption of their products to those who pay for them. No one would have to buy in order to consume, and producers would have no way of covering their costs. As has been shown above, due to the inability of individuals to vary quantity taken, the application of arrangements which permit the employment of price exclusion for nonrival goods does not ensure that market provision of such goods will produce an optimum analogous to that reached by market provision of pure private (rival) goods. What such arrangements do permit is the *feasibility* of private provision, since revenues can be obtained by private producers through price exclusion.

The assumption that polar social goods are more like national defense than baseball, and, thus, are not at all subject to price exclusion eliminates the possibility of private (nongovernment) provision of public (nonrival) goods. As a result, in the pure theory, the problem of optimal choice between private and social goods becomes at the same time a question of market versus public provision. That is, it involves determination of government versus private organization of production. Hence, it raises the question of public supply of goods and services rather than that of modification of the operation of decentralized markets through taxation, subsidy, regulation, or other policies as indicated by welfare considerations. It is extremely important to note that when, in Chapter 4, concern shifts from the pure theory and its restrictive double-polar conditions of joint supply and inability to exclude, to consideration of the problems of public economic policy in the context of far less restrictive assumptions, this neat identity between public goods and public supply no longer holds.

SOME FURTHER ASPECTS OF EXCLUSION

The distinction between joint supply and inability to exclude is approached in another way by Carl Shoup, who contrasts items of group and collective consumption (1969, pp. 65 – 77). Group consumption goods are distinguished from marketable goods on the basis that the "cost of charging prices" of certain kinds of goods is so high that it is appropriate that they be provided by government free of direct charge. For collective goods, on the other hand, costs of exclusion need not be excessive, but total costs are such that they do not rise as the number served increases. As a result, exclusion pricing, even if feasible, would not yield an economically optimal solution. Shoup suggests that police protection is a group consumption good that is not, at the same time, an item of collective consumption, while theater performances are collective consumption but not group consumption. Mosquito abatement measures and television, however, embody both group and collective consumption.

There are a variety of circumstances which give rise to the condition of "inability to exclude" as defined here (Musgrave, 1969, pp. 134 – 42). There is the situation where essentially the same commodity or service can be consumed by many individuals at the same time with little or no reduction in the amount available to each with the addition of more consumers. Television and overseas military operations are examples. In terms of utility functions this condition may be defined as: $U_A = U(X_A, Y); U_B = U(X_B, Y)$, Where X_A and X_B are amounts of a private good separately consumed by A and B and Y represents a social good all of whose quantity is available to both A and B. This circumstance may be distinguished from a quite different situation where the good involved is the same for both parties, but the "inability to exclude" operates only in one direction. An illustration would be water pollution abatement which would benefit those downstream but not those upstream. If Y_A is the pollution abatement undertaken by A and Y_B abatement by B, then in utility terms:

$$U_A \text{ (upstream)} = U_A (X_A, Y_A)$$
$$U_B \text{ (downstream)} = U_B (X_B, Y_A, Y_B)$$

Situations where exclusion may or may not be reciprocal but where the joint product is essentially the same for both parties must be distinguished from cases where the product received by the various parties is fundamentally different. For example, the provision of specific educational services may enter the utility function of both the student and other members of the community. The product or service received by the student who attends class is, however, vastly different from that received by others whose benefits accrue as the result of direct or indirect interaction with the "educated" person.

The polar concept of a pure social or public good incorporates the idea that exclusion is literally impossible. This idea has caused great confusion, since for virtually all real world public goods some form of exclusion is in fact possible. If "impossibility of exclusion" is interpreted as implying less than perfect ability by consumers to adjust quantity taken to price paid, then private markets employing perfect discrimination would provide a basis for an optimum solution to the provision and financing of public goods. Each consumer then would pay an amount equal to his total valuation of the given quantity of a jointly supplied commodity, and for the marginal unit he would pay a price equal to its marginal valuation (Buchanan, 1967, p. 195). In effect, the assumption of perfect discrimination restores the link between price and quantity. This conclusion does not, however, imply the practicality of a market rather than a budgetary solution to the supply of public goods because the essential nature of these goods is such that market arrangements do not provide the information necessary for perfect discriminators (Samuelson, 1967, pp. 199–204). The issues involved in deciding whether in practice market or quasi-market institutions, such as private clubs, can obtain and utilize information with regard to public goods in a more efficient manner than government decision-makers is discussed below in Chapters 4 and 5.

FURTHER ASSUMPTIONS OF THE PURE THEORY

In addition to the contrast between public and private goods a second element of the pure theory is that all public expenditures are assumed to be for final goods and services. One reason for this assumption is the avoidance of the complexities introduced into welfare analysis by the imputation of values of intermediate goods. Since it has been shown that no additional conceptual problems arise from the inclusion of intermediate goods in the identification of welfare solutions, the essential treatment of the welfare problem need deal only with outputs of final goods and inputs of original factors of production (Scitovsky, pp. 167–70). The analysis of the pure theory of public expenditures follows this approach.

More significant is the limitation of the pure theory to resource-using expenditures. Transfer payments (positive or negative) for stabilization objectives are excluded on the grounds that analysis of the factors which determine whether an economy reaches the production-possibility curve is essentially different from analysis of the optimum or general equilibrium point along this curve, and that only the latter is a relevant concern for a pure theory of public finance. Although some economists view underemployment as the inability of the private sector to internalize the full benefits of increased consumer and producer expenditure and thus conceive of the reasons for government stabilization outlays as analogous to those for resource-using expenditures,[4] the exposition in this chapter follows the usual convention of assuming full employment and, hence, excludes explanation of compensatory expenditures as an element of the pure theory.

Treatment of redistributive transfers is a more fundamental issue, and various views of the proper treatment of income distribution in a pure theory of public finance are discussed at length in Chapter 3. At this point it is necessary only to indicate that alternative versions of the pure theory follow the dual treatment of income distribution found in contemporary normative economic analysis. That is, one approach takes the distribution of income (defined in terms of purchasing power, claims against goods, or factor endowments, rather than as quantities of commodities actually taken) as given and is concerned with the conditions that define the unique Pareto optimum consistent with that distribution. The other posits a social welfare function, thereby permitting selection from among the infinity of alternative income distributions of that one which is consistent with the highest attainable point on the given social welfare function. Significant here is that even in the latter approach, where redistributive transfers are necessary for the achievement of the welfare maximizing distribution of income, the need for such transfers stems from the inherent nature of the welfare analysis and is also relevant when only private goods are under consideration. Thus, it seems appropriate for the pure theory of public finance to deal only with those special aspects of income redistribution which arise as essentially endogenous elements of the allocation of resources between private and social goods.

A final sense in which the theory is "pure" is related to the underlying values or preferences which serve as the normative goals of the model. As in traditional economic analysis, individuals are assumed to have preference orderings such that they can rank alternative bundles of goods. In an individualistic theory of public expenditures, preference orderings of this kind constitute the basis for choices among public goods and between private and public goods.

---

4. This view is forcefully argued in John G. Head, "Public Goods and Public Policy," *Public Finance,* No. 3, 1962, especially pp. 217–19.

Such literal translation of the framework of individual values, designed to reflect preference mappings for private goods, into the realm of public goods raises several problems. What meaning can be attached to the notion of individual preferences for those public goods of which individuals have neither the knowledge nor experience to form subjective valuations? This question has been raised with regard to such infrequently purchased private goods as private residences, but concerns of this sort become pervasive rather than exceptional elements in a theory of public expenditures derived from individual preferences (Johansen, 1955, p. 128). Despite these considerations, the pure theory accepts the legitimacy of a conception of preference mappings for the full range of public goods which is strictly analogous to those for private goods.

The range or comprehensiveness of preferences relevant for the theory of public expenditures is an even more troublesome aspect of the purity of the theory. Although in normative economic analysis the goal of economic activity is generally referred to as the maximization of welfare, or even of social welfare, it is implicitly understood that *economic* welfare is under consideration and that human welfare encompasses far more than those realms of human satisfaction which are influenced by alternative uses of scarce resources. The distinction of economic and noneconomic aspects of welfare cogently stated in I. M. D. Little's *Critique of Welfare Economics* (1950, p. 51) is reflected by economists' use of the term "consumer sovereignty" in reference to those aspects of individual preferences relevant for economic analysis, and by the inclusion in economic welfare or utility functions only quantities of commodities consumed and labor services provided. Thus Bergson (1966, pp. 5–6) distinguishes between a general welfare function which includes elements "other than the amounts of commodities, the amounts of work of each type, and the amounts of the non-labor factors in each of the production units, affecting the welfare of the community," and a partial analysis which takes these other factors as given and is, therefore, called the economic welfare function.

The element which distinguishes welfare economics from more general concepts of social welfare is its restriction of concern to conformance with consumer sovereignty conceived of in Marshall's sense as those aspects of preferences subject to the measuring rod of money. This limited foundation may be a satisfactory basis for evaluation of the efficient provision of private goods since the consequences of consumption of such goods are defined as narrowly circumscribed to those units whose decisions give rise to the consumption. The value basis for a theory of the public sector cannot be resolved so easily. Public policies involving governmental outlays are precisely the mechanism for expression of many noneconomic preferences of individuals, and a theory which aims at an explanation of optimum public expenditures either must deal with the influence on such expenditures of political, social, cultural, religious, and other values, or, by limiting itself only to those values which can be termed consumer preferences, be accordingly reduced in comprehensiveness and relevance. Following Musgrave, one may include as relevant the full range of individual values conceptualized as an all-encompassing preference field which ranks not only alternative public and private consumption patterns, but other public policies which "have no immediate opportunity costs in terms of private wants" (1959, p. 88). The implications of this approach are, to say the least, disquieting since a similarly wide-ranging conception of the value basis of preferences for private goods would obliterate distinctions among behavioral sciences by the erection of a unified theory of social choice.

The outstanding contribution to such a unified theory is, of course, Kenneth Arrow's *Social Choice and Individual Values* (1963). Here the crucial issue turns upon the development of a method of aggregation of individual values which is consistent with a predetermined set of conditions derived as the minimal set necessary for an aggregate not to violate the individual preferences upon which it is based. This approach transcends the classic problem of welfare economics by dealing with the ordering of entire "social states," thus presuming knowledge of "trade-offs" among economic and other aspects of social welfare. The ultimate difficulty with which Arrow attempts to deal is not scarcity of resources but the logical contradictions that arise when individual values are aggregated through voting or some other procedure in accordance with certain reasonable conditions. One important aspect of the general problem of social choice is that once the range of relevant choices is extended beyond those that deal with alternative uses of scarce resources, the problem takes on an entirely different cast since certain choices no longer imply the impossibility of others. The constraint which determines the essential character of economic analysis — the principle of opportunity cost — is not uniformly binding in a unified approach to social choice where within wide limits the establishment of certain political or cultural arrangements does not restrict the number of similar arrangements which can simultaneously exist.

Perhaps a unified approach to social choice and social policy is the wave of the future, but its acceptance implies rejection of a special concern for the unique characteristics of choice under conditions of a hierarchy of infinite ends and relatively scarce means. It appears that the logical consequence of acceptance of an all-encompassing conception of preferences in the pure theory of public expenditures is the abandonment of normative and, perhaps, positive economics as a discrete subject of inquiry.

The alternative is to limit the conception of preference to the realm of economic welfare; that is, to employ only that portion of the preference field relevant to the partial welfare function suggested by Bergson, a function which includes only commodities and services. This procedure retains for the pure theory of public expenditures the conception of preferences generally applied to the analysis of private expenditures, but it further diminishes the relevance of the theory since those public expenditures undertaken to satisfy noneconomic preferences are excluded from consideration. This omission is quite serious, and its implications are nowhere better expressed than in Julius Margolis's comment on the original Samuelson article:

> it is . . . likely that there is a structure of existential social values, differentiated according to range, levels of legitimation, logical connectedness, and so forth, which are the bases of alternative public activities. Genetically one might argue that these values are the results of compromises among competing groups where each tries to maximize its tastes, but this is not a sufficiently interesting statement. The values, whatever their origins, are existential and are instrumental to controlling group behavior.
>
> What relation would this positive theory of the budget have to a normative theory which was the concern of the Samuelson note? Not only are the rules of behavior of individuals different according to whether they are operating in the everyday individualistic activities or as a conscious part of a social group but also the criteria that are applicable to these two situations are different. To explain the existence of public activities and to evaluate the efficiency of an allocation of the public budget we must refer to the structure of *social values*. (1955, p. 349, emphasis added)

Acceptance of a narrowly economic conception of relevant preferences reduces both the predictive and the normative content of the pure theory of public expenditures far more than such a conception affects theories of private economic behavior. Nonetheless, there remains considerable interest in the characteristics of a pure theory of public expenditures founded on the same notion of preferences as is traditional economic theory.

A final troublesome aspect of preferences is the treatment of altruism. Welfare theory distinguishes between utility functions in which only the individual's own consumption appears and those which include the consumption of others. Bergson suggests that the latter could be present either because one gains satisfaction when others are happy (altruism) or because there is an element of joint consumption, as in the pleasure of viewing a neighbor's garden. Benefits of joint consumption are easily incorporated into the concept of the narrow economic preference function already discussed. If, however, public expenditures are to take account of altruistic motives, efficiency might be thought to require that the donor know the benefits which accrue to recipients as a result of altruistically provided public services. Since the basis of the entire normative economic problem is the assumption of the impossibility of interpersonal utility comparison, such knowledge is clearly ruled out. Perhaps this requirement is too strict. The apparent difficulty can be averted by viewing efficiency with regard to voluntary transfers only from the standpoint of the donor whose optimum policy should be to extend donations to the point where satisfactions from altruism are equivalent at the margin to those from other uses of income. It is, however, rather strange to conceive of efficiency in altruism without regard for the effects of beneficence upon the recipients. It is by no means clear that this often-raised argument against a completely preference-based approach to the public sector is so easily disposed of.[5]

SUMMARY

In the attempt to derive a pure theory of public expenditures, several fundamental issues have to be resolved. The framework which has emerged consists of a theory which focuses upon final resource-using government expenditures of a polar type such that all goods are completely consumed jointly and are not at all subject to the exclusion principle. Furthermore, the given preference functions against which public and private expenditures are valued and compared are solely those which pertain to the valuation of commodities and productive services, so that the effects of government expenditures on aspects of social welfare other than the economic are not taken into consideration. Within this setting the theory attempts to explicate: (1) the composition of public expenditures among various programs and projects; (2) the distribution of tax payments among various citizens; (3) the overall mix of public and private use of resources; and, in certain versions, (4) the distribution of the public and private goods that insure the maximization of economic welfare. The theory thus encompasses the entire allocation of final product. Since factor inputs can be treated as negative goods, they are implicitly covered in the theory, although, unlike the collective consumption aspect of public goods, the production of public goods is not considered sufficiently different from that of private goods to warrant special consideration in the development of the pure theory.

Partial Equilibrium Approach

Within the framework set forth above, a partial equilibrium analysis of pure public goods encompasses two essential aspects. First, under the usual ceteris paribus assumptions of partial analysis, and assuming revelation of preferences, the analysis develops the characteristics of an equilibrium solution and the normative significance of such a solution. The method used is essentially the Marshall joint supply analysis. Second, the analysis explores the question of the effects which exclusion difficulties have on the attainment of this equilib-

5. The treatment of altruism in the theory of public expenditures is further discussed in Chapter 4. See Gerhard Colm, *Essays in Public Finance and Fiscal Policy* (New York: Oxford University Press, 1955), pp. 33 – 34, for an attempt to establish a distinction between the nature of preferences as they operate in private and public spheres, and Musgrave's rejoinder in *The Theory of Public Finance* (New York: McGraw-Hill, 1959), pp. 87 – 88.

rium solution. This second concern arises for pure public goods because the inapplicability of the exclusion principle (whether interpreted as a technical inability to exclude or as the inability of consumers to vary quantity consumed at an administered uniform exclusion price) prevents full preference revelation through market behavior. The conventional mechanisms that operate in perfect and, to some extent, even in imperfect markets to produce an equilibrium solution are more or less inoperative here. As a result, the partial analysis of public goods is heavily concerned with the adjustment process, where participation in consumption of a good is possible without the necessity of revelation of preferences. Issues associated with attainment of the solution for public goods are most analogous to the introduction of reaction curves of bilateral monopolists and oligopolists into partial equilibrium analysis of private goods.

REQUISITES OF A PARTIAL EQUILIBRIUM SOLUTION

A partial equilibrium analysis of pure public goods probably should, insofar as possible, follow the conventional method developed for analysis of private goods. That is, it should take as given, incomes, preferences, technology, and the prices of factors and of other final commodities,[6] and by juxtaposing industry or product group demand and supply indicate equilibrium price and quantity. Conventional partial equilibrium analysis for a commodity derives these overall supply and demand curves from the aggregation of actions of the fundamental behavioral units of the economy: households and production units. Finally, it is recognized that the behavior of these units takes place over time, and this temporal element, especially important in the analysis of production, is reflected in the classic division of the "length of the run" into market, short-run, and long-run periods. The task of a comprehensive partial equilibrium analysis of public goods would be to show for each of the time periods the derivation of individual demands for public goods and their aggregation; the derivation of quantities supplied by individual production units and their aggregation; and, finally, the determination of equilibrium price and quantity and the dynamic properties of this equilibrium. A most important, but extremely difficult, extension would involve integration of spatial aspects into the partial equilibrium analysis. The deplored neglect of spatial elements in traditional equilibrium analysis of private goods is at least equally serious in the analysis of public goods. In addition, application of partial equilibrium analysis

---

6. There is controversy regarding the last two items. When a particular commodity requires use of a "substantial" proportion of available quantities of specific factors, prices of these inputs may in a partial analysis be treated as varying with levels of industry output. Milton Friedman has championed the view that only the prices of close substitutes should be treated as being constant in partial equilibrium, allowing all other prices to fluctuate just enough to offset the income effect of the change in the price of the good under analysis. See Milton Friedman, *Price Theory* (Chicago: Aldine · Atherton, 1962), pp. 23 – 30.

to public goods ought to involve consideration of such details as specification of units for the measurement of the quantity of public goods and analysis of any unusual aspects of demand for and supply of these goods.

The state of partial equilibrium analysis of public goods falls far short of the complete analysis described above. For obvious reasons, analysts of public goods wish to emphasize their unusual characteristics and have, therefore, presented only such elements. As a consequence, time-period distinctions, so important to partial equilibrium analysis of private goods, are not singled out in the treatment of public goods and, hence, the analysis is presented only in terms of long-run equilibrium. Further, probably on the implicit grounds that the "laws of return" are the same for public as for private goods, the theoretical development has ignored entirely the matter of the optimum-size plant and production unit for the provision of public goods. There is, therefore, nothing in this theory that corresponds to the aggregation of firm cost schedules into commodity-wide cost and supply curves. In effect, the theory treats government units as single-plant monopolists. Thus, there is presented directly an aggregated long-run supply curve for the public good which, while usually drawn to show constant costs, can also encompass increasing or even decreasing costs. Omission of analysis of the short-run period and of the individual production unit results in exclusion from the pure theory of public finance of the difficult but highly important questions of the nature of production and cost functions for public goods and the mechanisms of adjustment of quantities supplied in response to changes in demand.

While it is easy to understand why public finance theorists have wished to separate the analysis of efficient technological and administrative aspects of the production of public goods from the analysis of proper pricing and output policy, given such efficiency, it should be recognized that conventional partial equilibrium analysis is concerned with the former as well as the latter. If the partial equilibrium analysis of public goods is to result in as embracing a theoretical apparatus as that for private goods, it will ultimately have to incorporate in an integral way those unique aspects of cost and production functions that characterize governmental units. At present, only scant empirical findings or logical analyses are available as a basis for such incorporation.[7] It must, of course, be recognized that the primary value of so comprehensive and wide-ranging a conception of the requisites of a partial equilibrium analysis of pure public goods lies in setting forth the totality of relevant considerations and permitting classification of specific contributions, not in the establishment of a standard for pointing out the shortcomings of theoretical endeavors in this area.

7. See Chapter 9 for a discussion of cost and production functions for governmental units.

THE STANDARD SOLUTIONS

The partial equilibrium solution, when preferences are treated as if they were revealed completely, has taken two alternative forms: those of Eric Lindahl (Musgrave and Peacock 1958, pp. 168–76) and of Howard Bowen (1948). Both approaches rely on a vertical aggregation of demand for public goods analogous to the aggregation of supply of jointly-produced private goods. The difference, as developed below, is that Bowen's method derives a conventional demand curve which relates price to quantity demanded while Lindahl relates quantities demanded by each individual to the share of the total cost of the public good the individual is assigned to bear.

Derivation of Individual Demand Curves. The derivation of conventional or Lindahl-type individual demand schedules for public goods under the assumption of an income constraint and given preferences, as well as prices of other commodities, is in principle quite straightforward. An issue which arises at the outset is the definition of the unit of public goods to use in the explication of the pure theory.[8] In the literature, the Lindahl-type demand curve generally has been associated with the use of amounts of public expenditures as the measure of the quantity of public goods, and the conventional price-quantity demand curve has been employed when units of public goods are measured on the quantity axis. So long as constant costs are assumed for the good in question, no essential difference arises in the formal derivation of individual demand curves and Lindahl-type relative share demand schedules.

In order to maintain as close a parallel as possible to partial equilibrium analysis of private goods the convention of measuring units of public goods on the X axis is employed here in the derivation of both Bowen and Lindahl-type demand curves. Thus, in Figure 2.3 money income is measured on the Y axis, quantities of a single homogeneous public good on the X axis, and preferences are represented by the indifference curves. It should be noted that the shape of these indifference curves depends not only upon preferences, but also upon the assumed structure of relative prices for other public and private goods, which along with preferences determine the marginal valuation of money income. A conventional price-consumption curve for the public good can now be generated by varying the slope of the price lines from Y, the assumed level of income. Points of tangency of these price lines and indifference curves give the utility maximizing quantities of public goods taken and income retained at various prices. Plotting these points on a price-quantity axis yields the usual individual demand curve, which is shown in Figure 2.4, using the scale for the Y axis under the heading "Bowen Scale." This demand curve is viewed as a

---

8. Measurement of actual outputs of the public sector is discussed in Chapter 9.

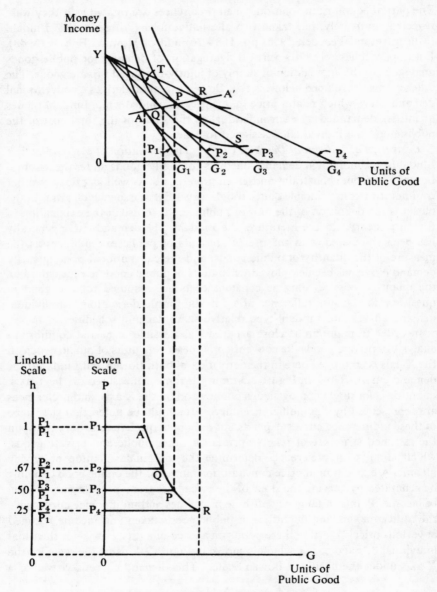

Figure 2.3. *Price Consumption Curve For a Public Good*

Figure 2.4. *Individual Demand For a Public Good*

long-run one, and the subtle issues regarding temporal aspects of adjustment of quantity taken to changes in prices or incomes are ignored. Vertical addition of these individual demand curves yields the total demand curve for the public good which is a counterpart to the horizontally aggregated industry or product-group demand curve of traditional partial equilibrium analysis.

When the long-run supply curve, which is assumed to be the long-run marginal cost curve, is specified, a Lindahl-type demand curve can also be derived from Figure 2.3. This type of demand curve shows for different shares of a given unit cost the quantity of the public good which would maximize the consumer's utility.[9] Under the assumption of constant unit costs, variations in the share of such costs borne by a taxpayer are analogous to variations in the price of the commodity, and Lindahl-type curves can be derived directly from the specification of the preferences and income constraints of each individual (Johansen, 1963, pp. 346–48).[10] Figure 2.3 can be interpreted to show this if the slope of the price line YG_1 represents the constant cost of the public good and therefore indicates the options between purchasing G and retaining income open to the individual when he bears the full share of costs. YG_2 and YG_3 represent similar options at successively lower shares of costs. The locus of tangencies to those price lines traces a share-consumption curve which can also be mapped into the diagram of Figure 2.4 but with the Y axis transformed into shares of the constant unit cost, as shown under the heading, "Lindahl Scale."

Aggregation of Demand and Its Relation to Supply. As has been said above, the truly unique feature of the analysis of demand for public goods is the vertical addition of individual demands. In the Bowen model individual demands are so aggregated, and then juxtaposed in traditional fashion with a supply curve to reveal the equilibrium price and quantity. The Lindahl approach juxtaposes the shares of total costs which each party would be willing to pay and derives the equilibrium at that quantity where total shares equal 100 percent. Figures 2.5 and 2.6, taken from Musgrave (1959, p. 75), illustrate for a two-party case the alternative models and the identity of their solutions. The underlying preferences and incomes for the demand curves of Figure 2.5 are, of course, presumed to be identical to those for Figure 2.6, so that they

9. This interpretation of the Lindahl curve, suggested by Johansen, seems superior to Musgrave's view that Lindahl curves show for each quantity the share of unit cost which a particular demander is willing to pay.

10. Consideration of increasing or decreasing costs complicates the derivation of Lindahl-type demand curves if measurement is in units of public goods, since the share of costs paid in this case depends both on demand price for a specific quantity and the unit cost of this quantity. Under these conditions, specification of preferences and incomes is insufficient to derive Lindahl-type demand curves; the cost curve also must be given.

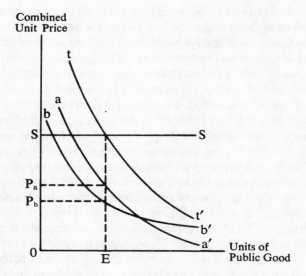

Figure 2.5. Partial Equilibrium Solution: Bowen Model

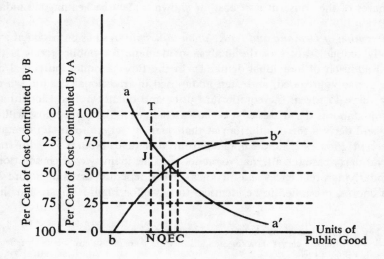

Figure 2.6. Partial Equilibrium Solution: Lindahl Model

are alternative depictions of the same situation. In Figure 2.5, it is the vertical aggregation of aa′ and bb′, shown as tt′, and its intersection with marginal cost, SS, which determines the equilibrium quantity of the social good as OE. At this quantity, the sum of the individual prices Pa and Pb, which measure the respective marginal valuations of A and B, are just equal to marginal cost. In Figure 2.6, aa′ and bb′ show the quantities of public goods which A and B would be willing to take at various shares of unit cost (assumed to be equal to OE in Figure 2.5); only at quantity OE do these shares sum to 100 percent.

Buchanan's Solution. James Buchanan also has examined the problem of equilibrium provision and cost sharing of public goods (1968). With characteristic thoroughness he begins with exchange among two identical parties or persons who both produce and consume a single public and private good, and then introduces, step by step, differences in tastes between the two parties, additional public and private goods, and finally, additional parties. Buchanan's simple graphic presentation of the equilibrium for public goods covers all the cases mentioned above save that of many persons; there, he argues, bargaining and strategy must enter.

The advantage of Buchanan's approach lies in its depiction of the dependence of the costs of public goods to one party on the demands of others (Buchanan, 1968, pp. 29 – 32). In Figure 2.7, let Et and Ec represent demand curves for units of public goods by T and C respectively. The constant marginal cost of the public good is shown by the horizontal line MC. In the simplest case of exchange among two persons and one public and private good Buchanan measures the cost of the public good and demanders' valuation of it in terms of units of the private good foregone. As the framework is expanded to be more like that of conventional partial equilibrium, so that concern is with one public good in the context of a great many other public and private goods, the price of any private good or money may be used as numeraire.

If C acts independently he will purchase OX_c of public goods. But, at this quantity T is willing to subsidize the purchase of additional units in accordance with that portion of his demand curve to the right of OX_c. The cost to C of additional units of the public good is obtained by vertical subtraction of Et from MC. The curve St, which results from this subtraction, shows the marginal cost at which T is willing to supply additional units of the public good. This curve is a true reaction curve only if C is assumed to contribute in accordance with his actual preferences and to engage in no strategic behavior.

The intersection of St and Ec at B′ marks the equilibrium quantity OX_0 of public goods. At this point, each individual is contributing to the cost of the marginal unit of the public good an amount equal to his marginal valuation of that good, and the sum of these marginal valuations is just equal to the marginal cost. Reversal of the procedure for determination of equilibrium yields the identical result as shown by the intersection of Sc, C's marginal supply curve with T's demand curve at B. As expected, consistent with the Bowen solution, vertical aggregation of Et and Ec gives a curve which intersects marginal cost at OX_0, the equilibrium quantity.

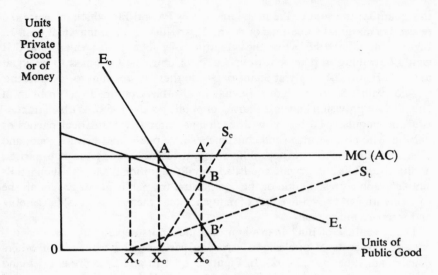

Figure 2.7. Partial Equilibrium Solution: Buchanan Model

Interpretation of the Solution. The virtue of the Bowen formulation is that it reveals the allocative efficiency of the solution in a fashion similar to that of the partial equilibrium solution for private goods. At the equilibrium quantity, the sum of the individuals' marginal valuations of the public good are just equal to its supply price (marginal cost). If the measure of cost reflects the value of foregone alternatives, then at this equilibrium the members of society value the satisfactions received from the last unit of the public good precisely as much as they would the most highly-valued alternative product which could have been produced with those resources which were used for the public good. Provision of any more or less would lower total welfare. Further, if preferences were to be revealed, a voluntary exchange basis for taxation would establish each taxpayer's contribution to costs as equal to his marginal valuation of the equilibrium quantity.[11] By regarding such payment as a price or pseudo-price[12] for value received rather than a compulsory payment, this conception depicts the equality of price and marginal valuation necessary for economic

11. Of course, under the assumptions of complete joint supply and nonexclusion, revelation of preferences could not be expected. It is this feature of public goods which prevents a general benefit solution to taxation and public expenditures. See below, pp. 52 – 62, for further discussion of the problems introduced by the failure of preferences to be revealed.

12. Samuelson in J. Margolis and H. Guitton, eds., *Public Economics* (New York: St. Martin's Press, 1969), uses this term as a surrogate for the demand price of public goods which would be paid if preferences were fully revealed.

efficiency. The partial equilibrium solution to the provision and pricing of pure public goods equates price and marginal valuation for each consumer by varying the price paid for an equivalent quantity available to all. This is in contrast to the solution for private goods where an identical price for all is brought into equality with marginal valuation through variations in quantities taken by different consumers.

While the Bowen approach reveals similarities and differences in the partial equilibrium solutions for public and private goods, Johansen has shown how the Lindahl formulation can be used to provide a clear demonstration of the Pareto optimal nature of the solution and the importance of the initial distribution of income in determining the apportionment of gains from the provision of public goods (1963). The derivation of a Lindahl-type demand curve from specification of indifference curves, price or cost share curves, and money income has already been presented. The curve AA′ in Figure 2.8 is identical with that in Figure 2.4, as derived from Figure 2.3. Within the dimensions of this figure it is possible to depict a family of indifference curves which show rates of substitution between an increased share in the cost of the public good and the increased quantity available of this good. Such a family of indifference curves is shown in Figure 2.8. Note that the Lindahl demand curve is the locus of points of tangency of these indifference curves and given expenditure shares.

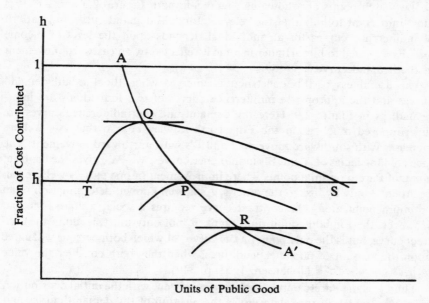

Figure 2.8. Indifference Curve for Public Goods in Relation to Cost Shares

This is not surprising because a horizontal movement in Figure 2.8 corresponds to a movement along a price line in Figure 2.3. Points A, Q, P, and R in Figure 2.8 correspond to similar points in Figures 2.3 and 2.4.

The derivation of the indifference curves in share-quantity space warrants further explanation. Their general shape is the consequence of utility always rising as the share of unit cost falls with a constant quantity of public goods, and rising up to a point as the quantity of public goods increases at a constant share. In share-quantity space higher indifference curves are always encountered moving vertically from top to bottom, while utility rises and then falls with horizontal movements. The relation of these indifference curves to those in conventional commodity or money-commodity space is easily illustrated. Start, for example, with the indifference curve in Figure 2.3 which is tangent to the price-ratio line at Q. This point maps into Figure 2.8 as point Q with the quantity the same as in Figure 2.3, but with the point on the Y axis converted from the amount of unspent money income to the appropriate share of constant unit cost. To derive another point on the same indifference curve of Figure 2.8, select another price-ratio (share) and determine, from the indifference curve tangent to P_2 of Figure 2.3, the two quantities of public goods that leave the individual on the same indifference curve. Plotting the new share and quantity on Figure 2.8 gives other points on the indifference curve through Q. Two such points are shown as T and S in both Figures 2.3 and 2.8. It is most important to note that the relevant Lindahl demand curve and pattern of indifference curves for an individual depends upon the level of income initially assigned to him. Higher income is reflected by an eastward movement of the demand curve.

The usefulness of this construction emerges when the Lindahl demand curves and the appropriate indifference curves of two individuals are inter-related, as in Figure 2.9. Here the demand and the indifference curves are superimposed much as in the Edgeworth-Bowley box so that A's welfare increases with southward movement and B's with northward movement. The locus of tangencies of A and B's indifference curves, $W - W'$, gives the contract curve of Pareto optimal points where improvement of one party's welfare can be attained only by loss to the other's. As is well known, determination of an optimum point along the contract curve requires a social welfare function. However, the Lindahl equilibrium point, P, not only must lie along the contract curve, but is the only point on the curve "at which both persons will agree upon the amount of public expenditures, when they both consider the value of h as given. . . ."[13] (Johansen, 1963, p. 349).

Thus, P is the Pareto optimal solution consistent with the initial distribution of income, which in turn determines the position of the demand curves and

13. See below, Chapter 3, pp. 79 – 80, for a further interpretation of the WW´curve.

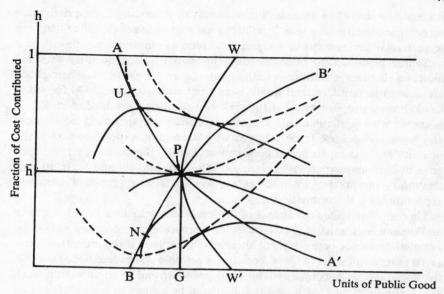

Figure 2.9. Lindhahl Model Supplemented by Indifference Curves (derivation) of Contact Curve with Public Good)

the utility levels that could be attained. This analysis, then, is a counterpart for public goods to the Bowley-box technique employed to show the efficiency of a competitive market-clearing price in the theory of distribution of private goods. There is no reason, however, why of all points along WW′, P should maximize the social welfare function. If it does not, redistribution of income appears in order, but as we shall see, redistribution raises serious problems when the analysis is broadened from partial to general equilibrium.

SOME FURTHER ISSUES IN THE PARTIAL EQUILIBRIUM SOLUTION

Before turning to the implications of abandoning the assumption of necessarily revealed preferences, a few complexities of the analysis under the revealed preference assumption merit brief elaboration.

Measurement of the Quantity of Public Goods. In his presentation of the partial equilibrium analysis of public goods, Musgrave defines the measure of the quantity axis as "units of social goods." Yet the question of what constitutes an appropriate measure of output, and indeed what is being measured, requires further explanation. Samuelson (1954 and 1955) avoids this concern by reference to a single, presumably homogeneous, public consumption good which can be varied only in quantity. Perhaps assuming away this problem is not an unwarranted prerogative in the formulation of a pure theory. Bowen, however, is keenly aware of the difficulties of selecting an inherently appropriate measure of the quantity of a social (public) good and suggests that the quantities of particular components of social goods, such as buildings, equipment, and personnel be conceived of as the units measured on the quantity axis. He indicates that this is analogous to the treatment of private goods where goods are defined in terms of their qualities and not their function.[14] On the other hand, Bowen proposes that "if the scale of priorities is established so that it is known what particular services are to be added with increased expenditure and what services are to be dropped with decreasing expenditure, then the quantity of the complex social good can be usefully measured in terms of the amount of money expended" (1948, pp. 175 – 76). Lindahl and his main contemporary interpreter, Lief Johansen, employ this latter approach of indicating expenditure on the ordinate.

The fact that under conditions of constant cost, measures of expenditures and measures of units of goods are exactly proportionate does not vitiate the essential difference between these alternative measures. If the ordinate is measured in terms of units of social goods, it is possible and indeed necessary that the social goods encompassed be homogeneous, and that, therefore, each essentially different type of social good could be subject to a separate partial analysis in a manner analogous to the separate analyses of various industries or product-groups. On the other hand, if the ordinate can indicate levels of public expenditures, all kinds of social goods can be encompassed in a single "partial" analysis.

Measurement in money or other terms of the *totality* of social goods along the quantity axis converts the analysis into something very close to general rather than partial equilibrium. Under such conditions, the price axis in effect shows public/private price relatives and the solution, therefore, gives the relative price ratios between public and private goods and the equilibrium quantity or expenditures on all public goods. Subtraction of this total from the set of production possibilities would yield the amount of private goods. Only the determination of income distribution remains outside the purview of such a conception. Such conclusions are rather far removed from the usual implications of partial analysis in which the solution yields the price of a specific commodity relative to a numeraire (money) and the quantity taken. Aside from the problems introduced because of the enormously increased importance of income effects in the wider conception, it seems hardly productive to approach the development of an analogy to the partial equilibrium analysis of private goods within such a more encompassing framework. It is surely more

---

14. For an elaboration of the consequences of treating consumption goods in terms of their characteristics, see Kelvin Lancaster, "Change and Innovation in the Technology of Consumption," *American Economic Review,* May 1966, pp. 14 – 23.

suitable for the portrayal of a partial equilibrium analysis of social goods to measure only one such good along the quantity axis, or only one component. This procedure may be objected to, however, on the grounds of being too disaggregated. Thus the problem of how to group outputs for useful partial equilibrium analysis, so familiar to value theory, arises in an even more fundamental manner in the pure theory of public expenditures.

Treatment of the Income Effect. A small discrepancy among versions of the partial equilibrium analysis has its basis in some fundamental issues in the treatment of income in demand analysis. Since, in the pure theory, preferences for social goods are treated as analogous to those for private goods they can be represented by indifference curves, and, given the level of income, for any individual there can be derived a schedule which relates price to quantity taken or expenditures made. In the derivation of a demand schedule there are alternative ways of holding income constant to avoid confounding the effects on quantity of changes in prices with variation in income. The approach followed by Musgrave and used in the analysis presented above is to employ Hicks' technique of holding money income constant so that the demand curve includes those variations in real income that occur as the price of the commodity is varied. Samuelson and Bowen refer not to individual demand curves, but to marginal rate of substitution curves in which real income is held constant. The schedule derived under this assumption shows, for a given quantity, the prices of the marginal unit which, if paid, would leave utility unchanged. Unless the marginal utility of money is constant (that is, indifference curves are vertically parallel) the shape of the marginal rate of substitution curve will vary with the level of real income, and will be less elastic than conventional demand curves.

Choice among alternative methods of holding income constant depends upon the objectives of the analysis. Use of demand curves for estimation of responses to price changes of individual commodities appears to favor holding money income constant while concern for the normative implications of alternative resource use seems to favor an approach which yields prices as measures of marginal valuations of different quantities. Consideration of the objectives of the analysis indicates that the conception of the schedules relating prices and quantities of social goods for various individuals should be thought of as marginal rate of substitution or marginal valuation schedules rather than conventional demand curves. Of course, these two approaches converge as the portion of income spent for the commodity decreases.

Buchanan (1968, pp. 37–47) also is strongly concerned about the treatment of the income effect. His concern is not with the normative aspects of the problem, but with the difficulty encountered if, for public goods, it is possible for price to vary in such a way that marginal and average price diverge. Under such circumstances, akin to price discrimination, the conventional conception of a demand curve becomes meaningless in a manner analogous to the disappearance of the supply curve for a monopolist. In this situation the appropriate demand function is the marginal evaluation curve derived by measuring the marginal rate of substitution of successive indifference curves as they intersect a given price ratio or offer curve. Since there is a different marginal evaluation curve for each price ratio, knowledge of the equilibrium price is necessary to select the price ratio relevant to a particular analysis. As a way out of the indeterminacy posed by the "proper" conception of demand, Buchanan accepts for analytic convenience the "convention that tax-prices per unit of the good are to be uniform over various quantities for each person, although, of course, these need not be uniform as among separate persons. This step allows us to derive demand curves for the public good in the orthodox fashion. Conceptually, we simply confront each individual with the opportunity to 'purchase' or to 'vote for' a most preferred quantity at each price (marginal = average)" (Buchanan, 1968, p. 44).

The significance of the assumption of uniform tax prices is not only that it permits determinancy, but also that it apportions the division of the gains from trade that result from the production of public goods. Buchanan points out that the uniformity of tax prices is analogous to conventional market prices, but that, in the absence of resale possibilities for public goods, such uniformity, in practice, requires arbitrary introduction or "constitutional" agreement.

Attainment of the Equilibrium Solution

All of the various formulations of the normative or competitive-like partial equilibrium solution for pure public goods presented above indicate the way in which unit costs and individuals' demands determine an equilibrium price and quantity for a particular public good. At the same time they show how a variable tax or pseudo-price based on individual demands can, in effect, equate price with marginal valuation for each consumer, thus achieving efficiency in consumption. In an effort to maintain the closest possible similarily to partial equilibrium analysis of private goods, the problem of public goods has been presented in a market-like setting in which the assumption that no strategic behavior occurs serves as a substitute for competitive markets. While this approach seems appropriate for the elaboration of a normative partial equilibrium solution for nonrival goods, it is unsatisfactory for the development of the positive or dynamic properties of the analysis of pure public goods. The issue here is: given the nature of the normative or competitive-like equilibrium solution for a public good, are there elements inherent in the conception of such a good which preclude attainment of that equilibrium? Another way of putting the problem is to ask whether the normative optimum level of output of public goods can be achieved through a voluntary solution when such a solution is defined "as a situation: (a) in which all members of the collectivity simultaneously agree to both the amount of public goods and the distribution of its cost, (b) that is reached through a mechanism of offers and counter-offers concerning at the same time the amount of public goods and the distribution of its cost" (Campa, 1961, p. 403).

The distinction drawn between the competitive-like solution and other solutions may be thought of either as a normative-positive dichotomy or as one based on different behavioral rules. In the later interpretation, the solution which emerges at the point where the Lindahl curves cross or when, in Bowen's treatment, the sum of the demand prices equals marginal cost results when it is assumed that all parties fully and honestly reveal their preferences. The condition of a solution is defined when, with given cost-shares or ratios of psuedo-prices, all parties choose the same quantity of public goods, so there is no incentive for further adjustment of price or quantity. This solution is similar to that of a competitive market in which buyers and sellers maximize their positions under given terms of exchange. In markets for pure private goods, buyers or sellers frequently are able to influence terms of exchange; with pure public goods, their very nature assures that in virtually all circumstances the actions of one participant will influence the prices which others must pay. Behavior with respect to public goods is unlikely to resemble that found in competitive markets, and other solutions, especially those analogous to duopoly and bilateral monopoly, must be considered.

The interpretation of solutions in terms of normative and positive aspects has similar implications. A normative solution for pure public goods is one where "the utility of the last unit of public good produced is simultaneously equal to the tax-price for each and every member" (Head, 1964, p. 426). Such a condition implies that the quantity of public goods supplied and the distribution of cost shares is such that no alternative output or sharing arrangement could increase one individual's welfare without decreasing another's. The normative solution, however, is by no means a necessary outcome. Partial analysis encompasses description of underlying motivations and institutional arrangements relevant to decisions, in order to provide the basis for positive theory. As a result, discussion of normative outcomes must be supplemented by a positive analysis for comprehensive treatment.

THE INFLUENCE OF NUMBERS OF PARTICIPANTS

Lindahl's original formulation of the positive solution to the public goods problem was not presented in the form of a partial equilibrium market analysis with large numbers of demanders, but rather was framed in a bargaining context.[15] He develops the analysis within the framework of two categories or

15. John C. Head in "Lindahl's Theory of the Budget," *Finanzarchiv,* October 1964, in

groups of taxpayers, one relatively well-to-do and the other relatively poor. This situation is likened not to competitive markets but to isolated exchange because "in both cases supply and demand are monopolistic, and equilibrium is reached by agreement between the two protagonists rather than by free competition. Theoretical economics generally regards price formation in the case of isolated exchange as an indeterminate problem" (Musgrave and Peacock, p. 168). Instead of thinking of the solution to the problem of public goods as similar to competitive market equilibrium, Lindahl recognized the need for an approach which could take into account the elements of bargaining implicit in a situation where preferences need not be revealed in order for benefits to be received.

As a consequence, in his discussion of the partial equilibrium solution, Lindahl does not assume that preferences for public goods are necessarily revealed. Instead, he examines the conditions which determine the extent to which revelation is to the advantage of an individual or a homogeneous group. The pertinent issue is whether for pure social goods there are mechanisms inherent in assumptions regarding the numbers of participants and their behavioral responses which lead to the achievement of the normative equilibrium position or, if not, to some other determinate solution. Lindahl considers this question in the context of bargaining among representatives of a few political parties, each of which has a distinct preference function. In contrast, a large-numbers case can be envisioned with as many different demand schedules as there are household decision-making units. The difficulty with both of these alternatives, as Musgrave points out, is that neither contains, logically, an implicit dynamic that leads to the normative partial equilibrium solution.

The main problem with the static normative partial equilibrium solution is that the presence of moderately or extremely large numbers, which usually implies one or more stable dynamic processes corresponding to the static analysis, fails to provide such a dynamic in the case of pure social goods, where it is to the advantage of participants to conceal their preferences.[16] The small-numbers case characterized by interaction among participants is analogous to bilateral monopoly or oligopoly. Lindahl suggests that the equilibrium solution will in fact ensue if there is "equal bargaining power" among the parties. By

interpreting Lindahl's objectives writes, "his approach is first of all to set up a stylized model of the democratic political mechanism under which his fiscal optimum will necessarily be established. Then, by comparing the characteristics of the model with those of actual parliamentary democracies, he proceeds to indicate the nature of the departures from the optimum, which must be expected in practice" (p. 439).

16. See William Baumol, *Economic Dynamics* (New York: Macmillan, 1959), pp. 122–23, 373–78, for a discussion of the correspondence principle and the implicit dynamics in any stable static equilibrium model.

interpreting bargaining power as the ability to enforce one's own preferences, Lindahl is, in effect, simply restating the conclusion that the equilibrium solution emerges when preferences are fully revealed, so that each party stands ready to contribute up to the point where marginal outlay is equal to marginal valuation of the public good.

Consider, first, the case where a public good can be provided only in indivisible units so large (costly) that any individual's financial contribution has an infinitesimal effect on the quantity. Under these circumstances an individual well might be inclined to deny whatever preferences he has for the good since revelation will not gain him any greater quantity. If, with preferences fully revealed, the community would be willing to finance some quantity of the good in question, then denial of preferences by all is self-defeating. Nevertheless, despite the possibility that complete denial and consequent nonprovision of the public good could be worse than revelation of preferences, voluntary revelation when there is no direct effect on quantity received seems highly unlikely behavior. On the other hand, if unit costs are such that by bearing a share of costs a household can increase the amount of goods available to it by a measurable amount, it may be in a position to augment its economic welfare (consumer surplus) by making known some, but not necessarily all, of its preferences. In this latter case, the crucial element is whether numbers are sufficiently large so that to an individual his actions appear to have no effect on the actions of others or whether numbers are small enough so that each participant expects his behavior to influence that of others. Analysis of the process of adjustment varies significantly depending upon whether large or small numbers of participants are assumed. From the standpoint of positive application, the question of numbers turns on whether the context of the analysis is thought of as individual voting behavior by citizens, decision-making by members of a club, or political interaction among representatives of a few (monolithic) political parties.

Large Numbers. Musgrave distinguishes moderately large from very large numbers (Musgrave, 1959, pp. 78 – 80). In the former, he imagines efforts to form coalitions to extract better terms from those outside the coalition, and recognizes the usual problems of strategy and instability that arise in such situations. His conclusion is that under these circumstances the optimum solution will not result. If numbers are even larger, so as to preclude the possibility of strategic behavior, Musgrave concludes that an individual will understate his preferences because such action "will have no significant effect on the total supply but result in a smaller assessment on himself." Musgrave simply dismisses the possibility of large numbers providing a mechanism to reach the revealed preference equilibrium, and does not attempt to develop an analysis of what the actual solution might be in the large-numbers case.

If this case is treated as one in which any single individual knows the aggregated demand curve of all others, taking it as given and, therefore, unresponsive to his actions, it is possible to derive an optimum strategy which maximizes the utility of the particular individual in question.[17] Lindahl, with an acknowledgment to Wicksell, solves this problem for a simplified two-party case in which the utility functions for the two are identical. (Musgrave-Peacock, 1958, p. 171 – 72). Lindahl's solution is developed within the framework of his cost-shares demand curves, but the issues can be brought out more clearly by means of traditional demand schedules. In fact, Sharp and Escarraz have analyzed the problem in just this way (1964, pp. 134 – 35). Their argument is that, given a nonoptimal position, it *may* be advantageous for one who has understated his preference to reveal it more fully. The reason they give for such behavior is that, as the previous concealer of true preferences for a public good reveals them, collective demand shifts to the right, encouraging a greater quantity since, at the existing quantity, price now is above marginal cost. This rationalization, however, is inadequate since once the possibility of dissembling is admitted, the equation of price and marginal valuation is no longer the condition of maximum welfare for any individual. Still, it is highly probable that it will pay any individual to reveal some preferences for collective goods under the assumption that others will maintain their contribution in accordance with their demands.

Figure 2.10, adapted from Sharp and Escarraz, serves to indicate the issues. Let aa′ represent the demand curve as perceived by B of all members of the community except B, and bb′ the demand curve of B. The curve aa′ may be thought of as the aggregation of the true preferences of all other individuals or as that presented to B by a single individual or one particular coalition in a two-party situation. (See note 17 below.) Assume constant costs of OP. If, despite actual preferences for the public good as shown by bb′, B fails to reveal any of them, quantity OQ_1 will be provided and B, paying a zero price, will obtain a consumer's surplus of $ObZQ_1$. Since at a zero price B actually desires OQ_2 of X and is only getting OQ_1, Sharp and Escarraz conclude: "Taxpayer B may have a strong inclination to reveal at least some of his preference." The relevant issues are: should he, and if so, how much? The answer of course, hinges on whether he can increase his consumer's surplus by so doing. Revelation of all or part of his preferences tends to lessen B's welfare because he now must pay a portion of the costs of all units of collective goods supplied; on the

17. Head, op. cit., pp. 442 – 44, analyzes this situation by means of a figure essentially similar to that of Figure 2.10. He contends that it is an illustration of the small group analysis model called "leadership equilibria." However, he finds it difficult to accept the lack of response of one party in the small group setting. Thus, it appears more reasonable to view this situation as depicting a large-numbers model in which the absence of response is attributable to the minute effect of the behavior of any single participant. The formalities of the analysis, of course, are the same regardless of the explanation for the absence of interaction.

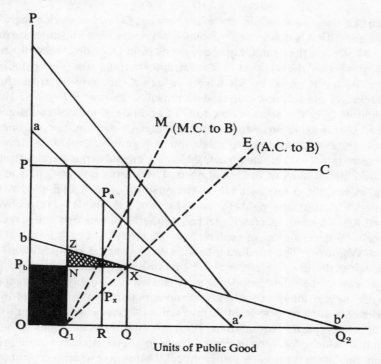

Figure 2.10. Preference Revelation With Large Numbers

other hand his welfare is increased because he gains additional utility from every increase in quantity for which he pays a price less than his marginal valuation.

In Figure 2.10 full revelation of preferences by B requires B to pay a price of OP_b for the quantity OQ and costs him the consumer surplus measured by the shaded area, OP_bNQ_1, since for OQ_1 which he formerly got for nothing he now must pay a price of OP_b. On the other hand, he gains the cross-hatched area, ZNX, the consumer surplus associated with the increased consumption of the collective good. There is no a priori reason for ZNX always to be greater than OP_bNQ_1, and furthermore, no certainty that any movement away from OQ_1 will improve B's position. If the elasticity of A's demand curve is great, a small contribution by B, since it is equivalent to a fall in the price paid by A, will move A substantially along his demand curve. At the same time the increase in B's welfare, which results from the increased quantity of the social good, measured in terms of consumer surplus, will be larger the greater his elasticity of demand.

Given A's demand schedule, there lies between Q_1 and Z a price share for B consistent with A's demand curve, which maximizes B's consumer surplus. One could increase the quantity of social goods from OQ_1 and observe for each increment whether the addition to B's consumer surplus was greater than the marginal outlay required by B's having to pay a successively larger share. Geometrically, the solution can be determined as shown in Figure 2.10 by derivation of Q_1E, the average cost to B of additional units of social goods (obtained by the same procedure of subtracting A's demand curve from the constant cost as described above in relation to Figure 2.7), and then drawing the curve marginal to Q_1E, shown as Q_1M, which measures the marginal outlay to B of additonal units of the social good. The intersection of Q_1M and B's demand curve, bb´, determines OR as the quantity of the social good which maximizes B's utility and yields the cost shares of RP_x and RP_a, respectively, to B and A. This solution, clearly, reflects neither complete preference revelation nor total concealment of preferences.

Small Numbers. The small-numbers case has marked similarities to the situation just discussed. Here, however, numbers are small enough so that there is present the interdependence associated with duopoly and oligopoly. There are a great many possible assumptions regarding the nature of interdependence in such situations. Musgrave sensibly considers as relevant to the question of the partial equilibrium solution of pure public goods only the assumption which, for private goods, leads to the competitive equilibrium solution: the Cournot price-constancy model.[18] Musgrave interprets this model as requiring for public goods the assumption "that A and B both disregard the effect of their votes (share of cost) upon the other's cost share." By use of Lindahl-type demand curves Musgrave demonstrates that under this behavioral rule, if the initially assumed cost shares — which each treats as fixed — are not those associated with the equilibrium, the actual solution will fall short of the optimum quantity (1959, p. 79).[19] This can be demonstrated either with the Lindahl- or Bowen-type analysis.

Assume an initial output of public goods of ON and prices of P_a and P_b paid

---

18. A survey of duopoly models is found in Edward Chamberlain, *The Theory of Monopolistic Competition* (Cambridge: Harvard University Press, 1935). Cournot is known mainly for his duopoly solution under the assumption that quantity is held constant. This assumption, however, yields a solution which is not equivalent to that of competitive markets. Cournot also develops a price-constant analysis of duopoly in which the solution does coincide with competitive results. It is this model against which Musgrave tests public goods on the grounds that if its assumptions with regard to behavioral reactions do not lead to results congruent with competitive conditions no other assumptions with regard to interactive behavior will.

19. It is important to note that in this analysis cost shares are given and assumed fixed, so the problem is solely the determination of output, while in the model illustrated in Figure 2.10 both cost shares and output are variable.

by A and B, respectively, as indicated in Figure 2.11. Given constant costs, this situation can also be depicted in terms of the Lindahl model of Figure 2.6 with the relative prices transformed into the relative costs shares $NJ/TJ = (P_a/P_b)$ and output shown identically as ON. At these given prices or cost shares A wishes to expand consumption to OQ and B to OC. These amounts are shown on both diagrams. A's wishes can be achieved since B's marginal valuation of quantity OQ, equal to OP'_b (Figure 2.11) is more than sufficient to induce him to pay the difference between OS (marginal cost) and P_a. On the other hand, B's preferred position cannot be achieved, because at OC A's marginal valuation is too low to cover the difference between P_b and OS. Explanation of the behavioral dynamics leading to this outcome hinges on recognition that, under the Cournot assumptions, A presumes that P_b is given and fixed so that with unit costs also given there is a constant price A must pay to obtain additional units of the good. Given this price, welfare maximization for A implies the usual behavior of consuming up to the point where price equals marginal valuation, which is achieved at quantity OQ where P_a intersects A's demand curve. As has been said, this is a feasible solution. Reversing the argument leads to B's maximum, OC, but at this output costs are not covered. Since of the two outcomes consistent with the assumptions only one is feasible, it is the logical outcome which follows from the initial prices or

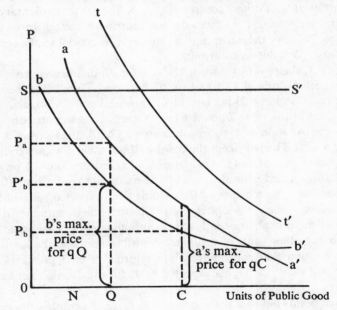

Figure 2.11. Solution under Assumption of Fixed Price Ratios

share ratios. Other initial price ratios would lead to different quantities as the solution.

ANOTHER VIEW OF THE EFFECTS OF SMALL AND LARGE NUMBERS

The foregoing discussion of the effects of numbers on the outcomes of the partial equilibrium approach attempts to differentiate the preference revelation difficulties of large numbers from the strategic elements of small numbers. Buchanan ingeniously uses game theory to provide a most revealing insight into this distinction (1968, pp. 88 – 91).

To illustrate the essentials of large numbers Buchanan assumes that in a community of 1,000 members, the provision of a pure public good costing $5,000 will yield benefits valued at $10 per person. Each individual, because of the relatively large number of participants, assumes his contribution has no effect on the probability that the public good will be provided. Under these circumstances if an individual "predicts that others in the group will contribute an amount sufficient to finance the facility, he can obviously gain from not contributing. If he predicts that others in the group will not contribute, he gains nothing by contributing himself because of the indivisibility of the benefits" (pp. 88 – 89). In order to illustrate this situation with a matrix Buchanan assumes (1) that voluntary payments of $5 per person are solicited, (2) that the probability of others contributing is .5, and (3) that voluntary contributions are not returned if others do not contribute enough to finance the public good. None of these assumption, however, is crucial to the conclusion that it always pays not to contribute.

In Table 2.1, the payoffs shown in the row for "Individual contributes" are positive expected gains of $2.50 when "Others contribute" ($10 benefit – $5 voluntary contribution = $5 net benefit x .5 probability = $2.50), and negative expected gains of the same amount when "Others do not contribute" (– $5 voluntary contribution lost x .5 probability = – $2.50), thus giving a net expected value of 0. The payoffs in the row for "Individual does not contribute" are an expected gain of $5 ($10 net benefit – 0 contribution x .5 probability = $5) and an expected gain of 0 when "Others do not contribute" (0 benefit – 0 contribution x .5 probability = 0), yielding a net expected value of $5. The higher expected value for a strategy of not contributing continues to prevail regardless of the probabilities assigned because they remain the same in both rows. Also any other value of voluntary contribution up to the limit of $10, or the assumption that contributions are returned if enough others do not contribute still yields the higher expected value for the decision not to contribute.

Buchanan points out that the conclusion in favor of complete noncontribution in the large-numbers case is a consequence of the indivisibility of the size of the public good. Assumption of divisible units would probably lead to some

Table 2.1. Payoff Matrix for Contribution to Public Good: Large Number of Participants

	Others contribute	Others do not contribute	Expected value
Individual contributes	$ 5 (.5)	– $5 (.5)	0
Individual does not contribute	$10 (.5)	0 (.5)	$ 5

contribution but in amounts far below optimal output. Such an outcome is consistent with the analysis developed above.

Contrast with the small-numbers case is achieved by reducing the number of participants to ten. Now, each person expects a benefit valued at $1,000 and the pro rata cost becomes $500. The key assumption that provides different results is that each person recognizes that his action will influence the probability of the public good being provided. Buchanan's illustration of this situation assumes that when an individual does contribute he believes there is a probability of .8 that the facility will be provided, while he believes that this probability falls to .2 if he does not contribute. Under these assumptions, as Table 2.2 shows, the individual maximizes his expected value by contributing.

Table 2.2. Payoff Matrix for Contribution to Public Good: Small Number of Participants

	Others contribute	Others do not contribute	Expected value
Individual contributes	$ 500 (.8)	- $500 (.2)	$ 300
Individual does not contribute	$1000 (.2)	0 (.8)	$ 200

In this illustration, if the assumed probabilities when the individual contributes were .6 and .4 the expected values would shift to where the choice not to contribute would yield a higher expected value. Buchanan mentions the possibility of a "negative charisma" such that one person's contribution would lower the probability of others contributing, in which case, of course, his strategy is not to contribute.

Buchanan's conclusions are:

The probabilistic approach makes the distinction between individual behavior in the large-number and the small-number setting clear. There is, of course, no *a priori* means of determining just what size a group must be in order to bring about the basic shift in any individual's behavior pattern. This will vary from one individual to another, even for members of the same group. The critical limit is imposed by the personal relationships that the individual feels with his fellows in negotiation. (p. 91)

It is of interest to note that considerations very similar to these are involved in the determination of when an industry's behavior turns from oligopolistic to competitive or vice versa.

Partial analysis lends itself to enormous potentialities for alternative treatments. Despite a great many possibilities for further variations, attention must now turn from partial to general analysis.

THREE

The Pure Theory of Public Expenditure: General Equilibrium

The preceding chapter has shown how the characteristic features of pure public goods, joint supply and the inability to exclude, can be encompassed by partial equilibrium analysis. An important conclusion of the partial analysis of public goods is that while the properties of a normative, competitive-like equilibrium solution can be known, no reasonable assumptions about motives of, and interactions among, individuals ensures that it will be reached. Nonetheless, the nature of the partial equilibrium analysis and the issues that arise in the determination of a solution are significant because they indicate the fundamental similarities and differences between public and private goods. But, as has been demonstrated in so many other areas of economic analysis, partial equilibrium takes as given many of the factors which are in fact variables in an overall system. A comprehensive pure theory of public finance must, therefore, be cast in general rather than partial equilibrium terms.

From Partial to General Equilibrium

There are many possibilities for generalizing the partial analysis presented above which deals with a single public good, given preferences, technology, income distribution, prices of private and other public goods, and prices of factors. The major alternatives for such generalization encompass consideration of more than a single public good, removal of the assumption that the prices of private goods are given, and, finally, elimination of the specification of income distribution or factor endowments. It is useful to distinguish the following cases.

1. Retain all the assumptions of the foregoing partial analysis and add a second social good. Interest in this case arises because its solution shows that for an efficient outcome individual shares in the finance of social goods must vary from one social good to another, thereby raising further complexities for an operational tax policy. Johansen (1965, pp. 138 – 40) analyses this problem, and it is not discussed further in the present study.

2. Retain preferences, technology, and factor endowments as given, but let price and quantity of private as well as social goods be determined within the system. This case is, in effect, traditional general equilibrium with public goods added. As such, primary focus would involve the usual issues of the conditions for the existence and stability of a general equilibrium for an entire economy. Applications of this mode of analysis, which is concerned with the internal consistency of reactions of decentralized decision-makers to a system which includes public goods, seems scarcely appropriate. The very nature of public goods is that preferences for them are not fully reflected in effective demand, which makes them unsuited to an analysis which explores the consistency of prices and quantities mutually determined by preferences, technology, and the assumption of maximizing behavior by participants.

Despite the practical problems of nonrevelation of preferences for public goods it is useful to know whether a general equilibrium solution emerges from a system which contains both public and private goods. Also, if a solution emerges, its properties may prove pertinent to public policy-making. As a consequence of these considerations, another approach to generalization of the treatment of public goods is to engage in a positive general equilibrium analysis of a system which contains both pure private and pure public goods. The objective is to determine whether one or more solutions emerge and, if solutions do occur, to examine their stability and other characteristics.

3. Another alternative extends the previous case to a general equilibrium welfare analysis. Here, the same assumptions as in 2 above prevail, including the distribution of income (more properly the distribution of factor endowments) as given. The questions raised, however, deal with the conditions under which an equilibrium solution is or is not optimal according to the Pareto or other welfare criteria.

4. Finally, it is possible to apply to a system inclusive of public goods the general equilibrium welfare approach which utilizes a social welfare function. Preferences and technology remain given. The social welfare function serves to determine mutually the income distribution and the prices and quantities of social and private goods which maximize total welfare. This is a variant of the "bliss point" solution for private goods (Bator, 1957), and, unlike the other alternatives, involves interpersonal utility comparisons.

General equilibrium analysis has tended to be conducted largely by formal mathematical techniques for the obvious reason that since mathematics provides the best means for generalization of analysis, it is ideally suited for the study of general equilibrium. A few ingenious graphic devices have been developed to illustrate the essential nature of general equilibrium solutions which often is not obvious from mathematical analysis. In this chapter, where major concern is with contrasts between the nature of general equilibrium with and without public goods and between general and partial analysis with public goods, the more intuitive, if less rigorous, graphic approach is used. The normative or welfare aspects of the general equilibrium solution are considered first. These issues have received most attention and have spurred a great deal of controversy. Demonstrations and discussion of positive solutions then follow.

Normative Solutions

Samuelson in his two classic articles (1954, 1955) sets forth a social welfare general equilibrium solution for a system with public goods. His approach is that described as alternative 4 above. The demonstration, as will be shown, applies the device of the social welfare function to the infinite number of alternative mixes of public and private goods and their distribution among participants to select the one which maximizes social welfare. Musgrave, who had long been concerned with normative aspects of public goods, abjured the artifact of the social welfare function, no doubt due to its purely formal character, in his treatment of the matter in *The Theory of Public Finance* (1959). Instead, he follows the Paretian welfare approach of defining an optimum in terms of the impossibility of improvement without making some one worse off, given a specified income distribution. To specify the "proper" distribution Musgrave assumes a "distribution branch" which determines, in terms of private goods only, a just or equitable distribution of income. An "allocations branch" provides public goods up to the point where further increase in public goods, however the costs were distributed, could not occur without making some one worse off.

The alternative normative solutions of Musgrave and Samuelson have been widely debated. Musgrave's effort to maintain a distinction between distribution and allocation has been attacked on the grounds that the proper distribution of income cannot be defined without taking into account public as well as private goods. Also, as a result of defining income distribution in terms of shares of private goods rather than as factor endowments in a general equilibrium context, Musgrave's analysis yields a dual rather than a single solution. He erroneously interprets this outcome as a consequence of the inclusion of public goods instead of as the result of his unusual method of specification and treatment of the distribution of income. Despite these shortcomings, the attempt to distinguish distributional from allocational considerations remains essential, since failure to accomplish such separation is a further damaging blow to the operationalism of the theory. To add the need for a social welfare function to the requirement of preference revelation is virtually fatal to the policy relevance of the analysis. No wonder, then, that so much of the discussion of the pure theory centers on the issue of separation.

The Basic General Equilibrium Welfare Analysis

Musgrave's version of Samuelson's diagrammatic depiction of the welfare maximization solution appears most useful for illustration of the basic issues. The framework of the analysis is that there is a single social and a single private good, given quantities of resource inputs and two consumers. Figure 3.1 shows the transformation or production possibility schedule between social and private goods as curve PQ. Each point on this curve indicates the maximum possible production of one good given the output of the other. The distance of the curve from the origin depends upon the assumed quantity of resources available and the technical efficiency of production. Its slope has the usual property of increasing marginal costs, with the rate of increase dependent upon the degree to which the various given resource endowments are substitutes in the production of the two commodities and upon differences in factor intensities.[1]

Figures 3.2 and 3.3 are constructed to show the consumption possibilities for each of the two consumers given the production possibility curve and the consumption of the other. If B's consumption is established at those quantities which will maintain his utility at the level given by B's indifference curve UB_I in Figure 3.1, then curve CN in Figure 3.2 gives A's consumption possibilities. Similarly, if A's utility is held constant at the level indicated by $UA_{1/2}$ in 3.1, B's consumption possibilities are as given by VW in Figure 3.3. By lining up the vertical axes of these figures, the property of equal quantities of social goods available to all consumers is conveniently represented.

Movement toward the selection of a point on the transformation schedule and a distribution of the resulting private goods among the two consumers (whatever the outcome, both parties will, of course, receive equal amounts of

1. The transformation curve can be derived graphically from a Bowley-Edgeworth box diagram in which the resource availabilities determine the size of the box and production isoquants reflect technological possibilities. Isoqants which represent the factor combinations necessary to produce varying quantities of the different goods are drawn from opposite corners. Their points of tangency constitute the locus of points of maximum output, since a movement to the contract curve from any point off the curve results in an increase in one or both goods. See Tibor Scitovsky, *Welfare and Competition* (Homewood, Illinois: Richard D. Irwin, Inc., 1951), pp. 173–77, for a demonstration of this method of derivation of the transformation curve.

the social good) can proceed in accordance with two essentially different methods. One, analogous to the conventional general equilibrium approach, requires specification of an initial distribution of factor endowments or purchasing power among participants so as to assign relative weights to the preferences of the different parties and by so doing to determine the solution consistent with such a weighting. In the application of this sort of general equilibrium analysis to an economy composed solely of purely private goods, the assumption of perfect markets is the mechanism that leads to weighting preferences of various individuals in accordance with their incomes. For a similar analysis, which includes pure public goods, it is necessary to introduce the proviso that preferences for such goods are revealed without market transactions in order for specification of the income distribution to determine the relative weights to be given to the preferences of various participants.

The other approach, based on the maximization of welfare, derives the utility possibility frontier, or a portion of it, by determination of the production combinations and their distributions which maximize one party's welfare subject to given levels of welfare for the other. Specification of a social welfare function permits the choice of the most favored of these possibilities.

THE SOCIAL WELFARE MAXIMUM APPROACH

Select at random a level of utility for individual B and indicate it on Figure 3.1 by the indifference curve UB_1 which shows the combination of social and private goods for which utility is constant at this level. Unless there are unusually strong complementarities between the social and private goods in question, the curve UB_1 will intersect the X axis which represents private goods, but it is unlikely that it will intersect the social good axis since man (probably) cannot live by social goods alone. Musgrave suggests that the intersection of an indifference curve with the private goods axis can serve to define the distribution of income since, with a given transformation schedule, such an intersection defines the relative shares of private goods going to each person. However, as Sharp and Escarraz have shown, this relative distribution of private goods changes as one individual moves along a specified indifference curve and the other consumes the residual from the transformation curve (pp. 136 – 38).

Subtraction of the arbitrarily selected constant utility curve of individual B (UB_1) from the transformation curve gives a schedule of combinations of social and private goods available to A while B's utility remains fixed at the initial level. The optimum along this now familiar construct of consumption possibilities shown as NC in Figure 3.2 is determined at that point which is tangent to A's highest attainable indifference curve. In Figure 3.2 this is shown at point X, where A's indifference curve UA_2 is tangent to NC.

This procedure yields one point on the utility possibility frontier, since it

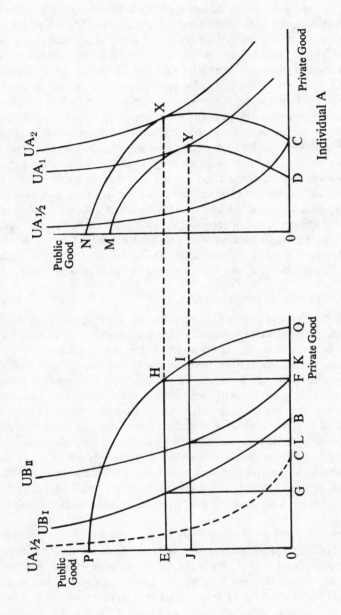

*Figure 3.2. Indifference Curves and Consumption
Possibilities of A*

*Figure 3.1. Transformation Curve Between Public
and Private Goods*

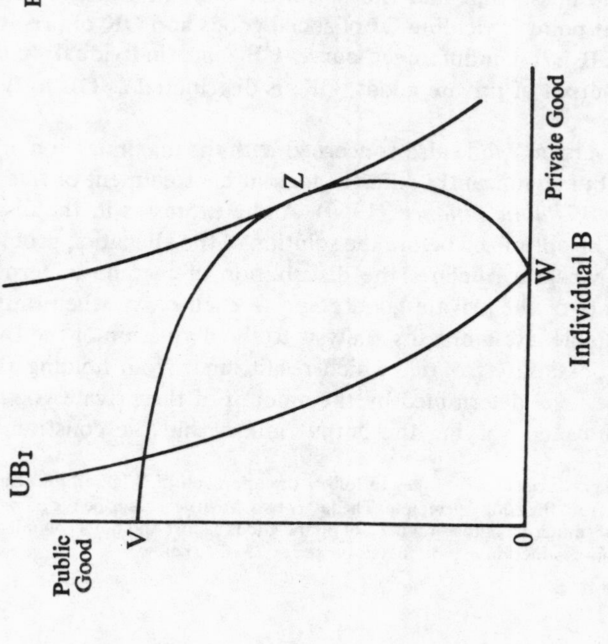

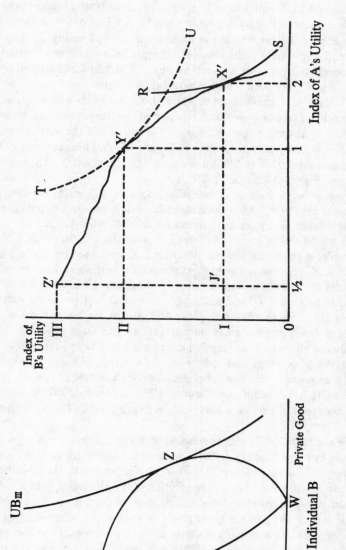

Figure 3.4. Utility Possibility Frontier

Figure 3.3. Indifference Curves and Consumption Possibilities of B

shows that for specified utility level UB_I for individual B, the highest possible utility which can be reached by A is utility level UA_2. This outcome maps into point X´ on Figure 3.4, in which the axes are indices of utility for the two individuals and imply only ordinal scales. The procedure can be repeated for all relevant levels of utility for B. Such an analysis would lead, ultimately, to the specification of the entire utility possibility frontier, and hence would provide the full range of alternatives to which the social welfare function would have to be applied. For example, the derivation of an alternative point is shown by use of B's indifference curve, UB_{II}, in Figure 3.1, the corresponding consumption possibility curve MD of A in Figure 3.2, and the tangency of MD with A's highest attainable indifference curve, UA_1, at point Y. These conditions map into Figure 3.4 as point Y´.

The analysis presented above is essentially Samuelson's path-breaking diagramatic treatment (1955). All attainable utility levels are considered, and the social welfare function by its determination of the "bliss point" implicitly indicates on which utility level (indifference curve) the solution places A and B. For example, if the social welfare function is as indicated by RS in Figure 3.4, then point X´ represents the highest attainable welfare and the optimum solution involves: (1) production at point H along transformation curve PQ, where there is produced OE of public goods and OF of private goods; (2) placement of B on his indifference curve UB_I and A on his curve UA_2; (3) distribution of total private good output OF as OG to B and GF to A. However, should the social welfare function look like TU in Figure 3.4, then Y´ becomes the bliss point and the optimum solution changes so that: (a) production is at point I, yielding OJ of social goods and OK of private goods; (b) individual B is on indifference curve UB_{II} and individual A on curve UA_1, and (c) output of private goods, OK, is distributed as OL to B and LK to A.

Musgrave's version, while also concerned with the maximization of welfare, takes a subtly but significantly different tack in his treatment of this problem in *The Theory of Public Finance* (1959). As he expresses it, the distribution of income is to be optimized before the solution of the allocation problem.[2] For this purpose, Musgrave defines the distribution of income in terms of the relative amounts of the private good going to each party when only private goods are available. He limits his analysis to the derivation of the two points on the utility possibility frontier which result, first, from holding B's utility constant at the level determined by the amount of the private good initially allocated to him and varying the output mix within the constraints of the

2. Here Musgrave obviously wishes to follow the approach of Wicksell and Lindahl, who separate the fiscal from the equity principle. The latter two, however, describe the income distribution before the determination of the provision of public goods as *just* and not as *optimum*. Possible implications of this distinction are discussed on pages 73–74, below.

transformation curve so as to maximize A's welfare, and then from reversing the procedure to obtain B's highest utility given A's utility level.

Point X in Figure 3.2 and point X′ in Figure 3.4 correspond to the first of these points under the condition that the initial distribution of private goods was OB going to B and BQ to A (Figure 3.1). The second point is derived from the identical procedure but, this time, maintaining A's utility at the level associated with the amount of private goods initially allocated to him. In Figure 3.1, A's initial endowment of private goods is shown as OC (BQ), and the associated utility by the dashed indifference curve $UA_{1/2}$. Subtraction of this constant utility schedule from the production possibility schedule gives the locus of B's consumption possibility curve VW, in Figure 3.3, and the tangency of UB_{III} to VW at Z represents the position of highest attainable welfare for B given the maintenance of A's initial utility level. This point maps into Figure 3.4 as point Z′. Musgrave concludes that the two points, X′ and Z′, set the limit to feasible exchange.[3] Without a social welfare function it is impossible to select a particular point within these limits, but any point within them is superior to J′, which shows the distribution of utility in the absence of provision of social goods.

SEPARATION OF DISTRIBUTION AND ALLOCATION

It is apparent that there are two interrelated differences between the Samuelson and Musgrave treatments. First, by placing no special significance on those levels of utility associated with a particular initial distribution of private goods Samuelson is able to identify the entire utility possibility frontier rather than only two points on it. Second, as a consequence of specification of a social welfare function Samuelson's analysis determines a unique optimum point on the utility frontier. Of course, if the social welfare function selects the welfare-maximizing distribution of final goods, it implicitly also selects the welfare optimizing utility levels for the two participants which, at the same time, can indicate an equivalent utility yielding initial distribution of private goods. Acceptance of a social welfare function obviates any welfare optimization implications attached to an initial specification of the distribution of private goods or of factor endowments, since the social welfare solution uniquely determines these distributions.

Musgrave, in *The Theory of Public Finance,* recognizes that the separation of optimum distribution from optimum allocation has serious analytic shortcomings. He asks: "can we determine the proper state of distribution independent of the effects on real incomes of the particular pattern by which social

3. Musgrave also concludes, erroneously, that X′ and Z′ represent dual solutions to a positive general equilibrium analysis with a specified distribution of income. This interpretation is discussed below in the section on the positive approach, pp. 84–94.

wants are satisfied?" (p. 84). Most commentators have answered this question in the negative. For example, Gordon R. Sparks writes:

> Without a social welfare function which permits interpersonal utility comparisons, no optimum distribution of income can be defined regardless of whether or not there is a public sector. If, as in Musgrave's discussion, it is assumed that there is no criterion for choosing among the Paretian optima when social goods are produced, it is a contradiction to assume such a criterion does exist when only private goods are produced. . . . Without a social welfare function, both the optimum distribution of income and the allocation of resources between public and private uses are indeterminate. Moreover, if we postulate a social welfare function, both the distribution of income and the allocation of resources are determined simultaneously. (pp. 592–93)

Despite recognition that Samuelson's comprehensive treatment of distribution and allocation "meets the test of theoretical rigor and sweeping elegance and ranks among the great contributions to the theory of welfare economics as applied to public finance," Musgrave, in a more recent discussion (1969), remains concerned that practical implementation of the principles of the pure theory will have to treat income distribution objectives as determined separately from taxation and expenditure policies to achieve efficient public provision of goods and services. As he puts it, "unless a basis for separation is established, we are left with a theory of public expenditures, or better resource use in which the tax problem has no conceptual place" (p. 133). That is, without separation, there is no basis for distinguishing taxation for welfare redistribution from taxation as a price surrogate for public goods.

Musgrave's attempt at restoration of the "fiscal principle" is to point out that even under the social welfare approach it is still possible to separate the issues of optimal income distribution and optimal pricing rules. The former can be drived from the "bliss point" (the tangency of the utility frontier and the social welfare function) by "work[ing] back to a distribution of resource endowments which corresponds to this point, provided that a specific pricing rule is followed." The appropriate pricing rule where pure social goods are concerned is that marginal cost equals the sum of the marginal valuations. The problem again is split into distributive and allocative segments, although Musgrave now recognizes that the optimum distribution of income cannot be defined independently of the distribution of public goods.

The shortcoming of Musgrave's present position is that in accepting the income distribution indicated by the social welfare function he abandons the aspect of his original analysis which is relevant for public policy. As will be shown below in the section on the positive approach, Musgrave's version, with income distribution conceived as the distribution of factor endowments, rather than as quantities of private goods, yields a unique solution, which is Pareto optimal under the application of appropriate pricing rules for the two types of goods. Since there is no conceivable way of estimating the parameters of a social welfare function, the application of efficient pricing rules to the public sector without regard for whether income distribution is economically optimal, is the type of second-best solution economists traditionally urge policy-makers to accept. Granted that there are considerable difficulties in the implementation of pricing rules for public goods where political mechanisms must substitute for prices as means of revelation of valuation, further addition of the need for interpersonal utility comparisons enormously diminishes any operational potentialities for the pure theory. This nihilistic position is the logical outcome of Samuelson's posture, but Musgrave, who has steadfastly fought against such a conclusion, seems now to have accepted it by allowing the social welfare function to determine the income distribution.

If optimum income distribution derived from the bliss point solution of the social welfare function approach is ruled out on the grounds of nonfeasibility, what can be salvaged of the separation of distribution and allocation? In one sense the very concept of predetermined distribution of income is not subject to precise specification because, whatever may be the initial distribution of money income or purchasing power, the distribution of real income depends on the ultimate emergent prices in relation to individual preferences. With or without consideration of public goods, the distribution of real income, except in the case of a one-commodity economy, cannot be specified independently of knowledge of ensuing prices or of the mix of final goods. An operational approach to distribution must confront this problem, and while the presence of public goods introduces an added complication, it does not add a difficulty where none existed before. To the extent that the community is willing, through its political processes, to employ rules of thumb for setting standards of equity for the distribution of money income for purchase of private goods, so also can it take account of the use of such income for tax payments for the provision of public goods.

Surely it is in the general sense of social justice that Wicksell and Lindahl refer to the initial distribution of income as required to be "proper" or "just." As used in the Swedish tradition these terms are not intended to portray the welfare maximizing distribution of income as contemporary welfare economics defines it. Rather "proper" and "just" mean equitable or fair in terms of general social standards which are operationally manifested through political policies and in social and cultural traditions and institutions. This is the only sense in which distributional considerations can become operational. Insistence on standards for distribution which are truly welfare maximizing imposes a paralysis on decision-making which simply will not be tolerated in practice.

The pragmatic issue which emerges, then, is that an operational approach requires separation, but a strict welfare maximization approach necessitates joint consideration of distribution and allocation. Definition of an equitable or just income distribution in terms of generalized purchasing power not only is an unsatisfactory conceptual approximation to the welfare maximizing distribution, but excludes the variations in real income which arise out of the particular mix of public goods. Still, adjusted money income may be a sufficiently good approximation to permit separation in the practice of public sector policy. With respect to private goods, the question of whether or not money income is a satisfactory proxy for real income hinges on the distribution of preferences among members of the economy in relation to relative prices. So also the question of how similar in welfare terms a distribution of private goods only is to a distribution inclusive of public goods depends on the dispersion of preferences for private and public goods. In general, the greater the variation in preferences for goods, the less well does money income indicate real income.

The crucial question for the relevance of the theory of public expenditures as a guide to resource allocation is whether the introduction of public goods raises difficulties beyond those pertinent to private goods. As has been demonstrated, there does exist, analytically, the further necessity that before proceeding to efficiency considerations, the income distribution in terms of public as well as private goods must be considered. The logical implication of this conclusion for policy with respect to public goods would appear to be that the convention of adjusting the income distribution to attain greater justice or equity through changes in money income or purchasing power is incomplete, and that the achievement of desired equity in distribution requires knowledge of the ensuing mix of public goods. As a practical matter this conclusion seems overly strong. The same problem arises in the context of an economy composed only of private goods in the impossibility of defining real income in monetary terms until prices are known. A reasonable operational resolution, under these circumstances, would appear to involve hypothetical variation of the income distribution, and then, under established pricing rules, which include rules for the distribution of tax shares, to estimate the resultant pattern of consumption of public and private goods. Then, by means of acceptable political processes, judgments are made as to which among the various income distributions leads to more preferred outcomes.

A FORMAL TREATMENT OF THE SEPARATION OF DISTRIBUTION AND ALLOCATION

The general issues raised in the preceding discussion concern operational aspects of the separation of distribution and allocation in a setting where preferences are not revealed through decentralized market behavior. What of the conceptual but nonoperational question of whether separate distribution and allocation branches equipped, as it were, with perfect knowledge of preferences could act so that a decision on distribution of private goods could be made which, in concert with the achievement of allocational efficiency by the allocations branch, would lead to the full Pareto optimum with respect to all goods, both public and private? What is needed is analytic clarification of how income distribution, efficient allocation, and the relative distribution of welfare interact in the case of public goods. An effort to explicate precisely this by McGuire and Aaron (1969) leads to some important further insights and helps to show the relations among various versions of the normative approach to the pure theory.

McGuire and Aaron assume an arrangement for public sector decisions in which there are independent distribution and allocation branches. Under these conditions the authors distinguish three situations: (1) the distribution branch determines distribution without regard for the actions of the allocation branch, which then, taking both this distribution and an arbitrary division of cost shares as given, determines the quantity of public goods; (2) the distribution branch again independently determines the income distribution, and the allocation branch sets cost shares and the quantity of public goods so as to achieve a kind of partial Pareto efficiency; and (3) the distribution branch determines income distribution anticipating that the allocation branch will act to achieve Pareto optimality through its determination of cost shares and quantity of public goods.

Case 1. Initial Income and Cost Shares Both Fixed. The geometric presentation of the analysis is based on a simple, but highly useful, diagram. The usual two persons are encompassed in the graphic treatment, although the authors also present a general mathematical treatment. In Figure 3.5, the incomes of the two individuals in terms of private goods are measured on the Y axis, with A's income measured from south to north and B's from north to south. Point D, therefore, represents the distribution of income, which is set by the distribution branch. Quantities of public goods are measured on the X axis. Cost shares are indicated by the relative slopes of rays emanating from D. The angle between rays for A and B's cost share is determined by the unit cost of the public good, which is assumed to be constant. Differences in relative cost shares are indicated by pivoting the cone formed by the cost rays around point D, differences in unit costs by the angle between the rays, and differences in income distribution by movement of point D along the Y axis.

Given an income distribution, as indicated by point D and cost shares as shown in Figure 3.5, each participant can determine the quantity of public goods which would maximize his utility. For A this quantity is AE, where A's highest attainable indifference curve, U_α, is tangent to his cost-share line; for B it is BH, determined in a similar manner. Clearly, a cone of different shape emanating from D, or an alternative income distribution, locating D at a

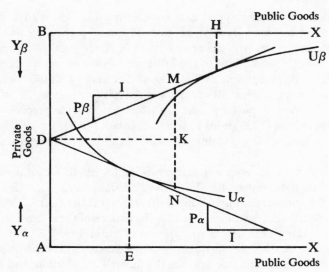

*Figure 3.5. Equilibrium of Public and Private Goods
With Income and Cost Shares Fixed*

different point along the Y axis would yield different results. As for the choice between AE and BH, utility for both parties would be reduced if less than AE or more than BH were provided, while amounts between these limits increase the utility of one party at the expense of the other. Given the income distribution and cost shares, any quantity between AE and BH is "efficient" and the choice among such quantities is "ethical" in that it requires a judgment on interpersonal levels of welfare. As McGuire and Aaron state, the distinction between allocation and distribution in this situation is without substance, since by assumption cost shares cannot be altered to accommodate differences between payments and marginal evaluation.

This model has close similarities to that already presented above in Figure 2.11 of Chapter 2, where the amounts desired by A and B, OQ and OC, respectively, correspond to AE and BH in Figure 3.5. The difference is that Figure 2.11 is intended to depict a voluntary determination of public goods such that at the given cost shares neither party will agree to purchase more public goods than the quantity which maximizes his welfare. Therefore, output of public goods will never be extended beyond the point where, for either party, marginal cost exceeds marginal valuation. In the situation under analysis here, it is assumed that the parties will contribute in accordance with the assigned cost shares for the quantity determined by the allocations branch, even if at this quantity consumer surplus for one or the other is less than at a smaller quantity, so long as the surplus is positive. That is, each will contribute so long as the indifference curve which he attains when public goods are acquired is above the one passing through point D, where he takes no public goods.

McGuire and Aaron conclude that, although the solution in this situation has no normative significance since it is unlikely to·be Pareto optimal, it is of practical importance. In practice, taxation is such that cost shares are fixed and, thus, given different preferences for public goods, distributions of real income and welfare are to a significant degree determined as a result of the quantity of public goods provided.

Case 2. Initial Income Fixed: Cost Shares Variable. If, now, cost shares are allowed to vary, and income distribution is still defined in terms of private goods, the allocation branch can act so as to achieve a Pareto optimality with regard to levels of welfare that are attainable through the allocation of private goods. Such optimality, as the next section shows, is not fully general, first, because it omits the effects on welfare of the provision of public goods and, second, because at the resultant quantity and price shares one or the other party would prefer to change his position.

Analysis of this situation as depicted in Figure 3.6 again takes income distribution as at Point D. This time an arbitrary utility level for A is established and depicted as U^*_α. Given that A's utility is fixed at U^*_α, it is possible to derive the locus of B's attainable consumption possibilities. This is accomplished by observing the price ratio which is consistent with a particular quantity of public goods on U^*_α, measured by the slope of a line from D to the point on U^*_α, and then determining the cost (or pseudo-price) to B for this same quantity by subtracting A's price ratio from the unit cost. Curve R shows this set of possibilities with A's utility determined at U^*_α. B's utility is maximized at T, where R is tangent to U^*_β, the highest indifference curve attainable from the available possibilities. AQ of public goods is the quantity at which B's utility is at a maximum, subject to A's utility being fixed at U^*_α, thus, one point on the utility possibility frontier is determined, along with its corresponding cost share or tax price ratio. As levels of A's utility are varied, a series of different pairs of cost shares and quantities of public goods emerge, each with the property that utility is maximized. In this manner the entire utility possibility frontier can be established.

In this case of variable cost shares the set of solutions does not provide for equality between individual marginal rates of substitution (marginal valuations) and tax prices paid, but only that the sum of the marginal valuations equals marginal cost (that is, the cost-shares sum to one) and, of course, that no increase is one party's welfare can be obtained without a decrease in that of the other party. For example, in Figure 3.6, A would prefer quantity AS at a price of P^*_α, and B quantity BV at P^*_β; these are the quantities at which

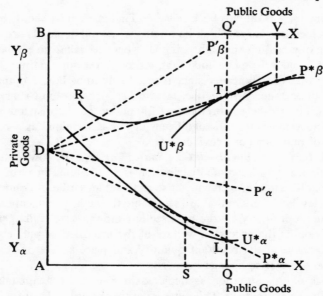

*Figure 3.6. Equilibrium of Public and Private Goods with
Income Fixed and Cost Shares Variable*

relative marginal rates of substitution are equal to relative tax prices. But
public goods must be consumed in equal amounts by all, and if quantity AQ
is provided at the relative cost share $P^{*}_{\alpha} / P^{*}_{\beta}$, B's utility is at a maximum,
subject to A's being at utility level U^{*}_{α}. Failure of the parties to desire the
same quantity of the public goods at the established price ratio, as they do at
the "Lindahl point," does not, however, rule out this solution. As the authors
write:

An objection might be raised that every non-Lindahl Pareto-optimal solution (as in
Figure 3.6) suffers from the drawback that, at the derived cost shares, the consumers
do not agree on the quantity, x, to be bought. In Figure 3.6, A prefers AS and B
prefers BV. This objection is misplaced, for, as Samuelson points out, selection of
AS and BV by A and B, respectively, does not represent market behavior at all.
Individuals have no incentive to move to the point of tangency where $P_a = MRS_a$. The
incentives are to pay as little as possible, and shift the cost burden on others, a
strategy by which each household seeks to consume the public good for nothing.
(P. 34)[4]

4. Chapter 2 above discusses the error in the view that utility maximization for pure public
goods necessarily implies payment of as little as possible. Under a variety of strategies it is
advantageous to reveal (and pay for) a lesser or greater share of preferences for public goods.
Individuals, therefore, have some incentives to move to the point where pa = MRSa, but as
Chapter 2 also showed such a point is unlikely to be attained in a voluntary setting regardless of
whether the number of participants is large or small.

McGuire and Aaron's analysis of the variable cost-shares situation serves to clarify Johansen's version of the Lindahl solution presented above, especially as in Figure 2.9, which is reproduced here as Figure 3.7. Johansen's WW′ curve is precisely the locus of points like AQ in Figure 3.6, where utility levels are maximized for jointly determined quantities and cost shares. That is, if both the quantity of public goods and relative cost shares are simultaneously determined, a series of Pareto optimal points emerge which can be illustrated graphically either as the WW′ curve in Figure 3.7, where the indifference curves of the various parties are tangent, or as a series of points like AQ which maximize one party's utility for given levels of the other. These points represent the limits to mutually beneficial accommodation, and indicate optimal solutions. Johansen recognizes this explicitly when he rejects Lindahl's assertion that the locus of "voluntary" solutions lies along U-P-N in Figure 3.7, thought of as a contract curve. He rightly insists that, if cost shares and quantities are simultaneously determined, the contract curve corresponds to WW′. If, however, cost shares and quantities are separately determined, as in McGuire and Aaron's Case I, then U-P-N corresponds to the locus of points like E in Figure 3.5 or Q in Figure 2.11. Such points depict the quantity desired by the participant who takes the least amount at the given ratio of cost shares.

Thus, the allocation branch can take distribution as given and through joint determination of cost shares and quantities achieve an infinite variety of Pareto

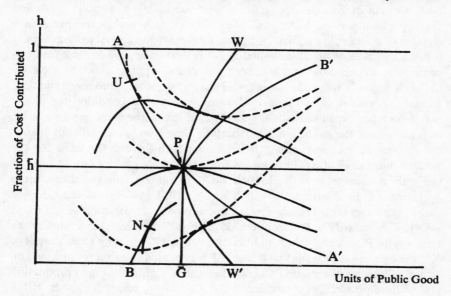

Figure 3.7. Lindahl Model Supplemented by Indifference Curves (Derivation of Contract Curve with Public Goods)

optimal outcomes. With the exception of the one which corresponds to the Lindahl solution, however, these outcomes will not be such that each individual's marginal valuation and his tax price will be equal. Still, they are Pareto optimal in the sense that the utility of one party is at a maximum subject to the utility of the other. That is, for any given cost share, except that at the Lindahl point, there is a point along the WW′ curve which is superior to the corresponding point on the U-P-N curve. It is only when cost shares are fixed, and quantity is the only variable, that U-P-N is the locus for voluntary solutions.

However, the range of possible Pareto optimal outcomes is still circumscribed by the given distribution of private income. That is, although there is only one point like P on a WW′ curve, each different distribution of income determines another such curve. As long as the distribution branch makes its determination without regard for contributions to welfare which the provision of public goods can make, the separation of distribution and allocation is not consistent with economic efficiency. It is with the removal of this constraint of a given income distribution that the next case deals.

Case 3. Both Initial Income and Cost Shares Variable. In this situation the distribution branch acts to coordinate its decision with that of the allocation branch. The issue is whether a distribution of private goods can be established which is consistent with a judgment on the final distribution of welfare that takes account of the influence on utility of the availability of public goods and the apportionment of their costs. The difficulty with such a comprehensive concept of distribution is that for public, unlike private goods, price generally is not a measure of marginal valuation. If it were, marginal income (money) compensation could be compared with quantities of public goods as it can be for private goods where prices measure marginal income (money) valuation. Lindahl's solution, however, provides precisely such a condition for public goods because: "each individual would pay a tax in the same amount as his income value of the public good, [so that] the allocation branch will not disrupt the income distribution among individuals which formed the basis for the welfare judgments" (McGuire and Aaron, p. 35).

Figure 3.8 shows how the Lindahl solution can be achieved through the operations of the distribution branch acting with knowledge of the behavior rule of the allocations branch. Let the initial income distribution be at D, and utility of A set at U^*_a. B's optimum position is determined, as before, by the tangency of R and his highest indifference curve, U^*_β, leading to an output of X^*. Cost shares here would be P^*_a and P^*_β, but this solution is not based on an initial income distribution which takes account of the changed production and welfare possibilities introduced by the provision of public goods. If the distribution branch chooses U_a^* and U_β^* as the appropriate welfare distribution when the full range of possibilities is considered, it can redistribute income to point C. Then, when the allocations branch, following the rule for Pareto optimality, sets output at X* to maximize B's utility subject to U_a^*, the Lindahl solution emerges, so that at X* the marginal valuations for A and B are equal respectively to their tax prices. Thus X* is the quantity desired by both at P_a' and P_β', given income distribution as at C.

Thus, distribution can be separated from allocation, as Musgrave suggested (see above pp. 71–72), by working backward, in effect, from the chosen point on the utility possibility frontier. The allocation branch would not have to be concerned with distribution, only with achieving a solution in which each individual's marginal valuation was equal to his tax price. Conceptually this separation permits the allocations branch to function much as free competitive markets do in the welfare analysis of private goods. In fact, as has been emphasized above, this approach yields only a formal solution because the absence of a mechanism to assure preference revelation prevents such operation in practice. McGuire and Aaron conclude, "*This* [absence of a means for revelation of preference] *is the sole reason for a necessary breakdown of the allocation-distribution distinction in public goods supply*" (p. 36).

As a matter of economic analysis, however, it is now clear that distribution

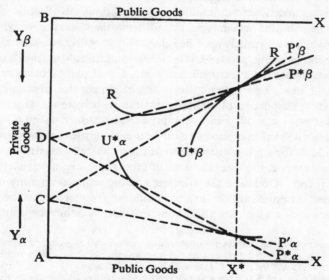

Figure 3.8. Equilibrium of Public and Private Goods with
Income and Cost Shares Variable

and allocation can be separated conceptually in the theory of public goods provided the connection between the valuation of public goods and money income is established through a Lindahl solution, and the distribution branch takes cognizance of the welfare implication of different quantities of public goods and the sharing of their costs. Unfortunately, little is gained for the practice of public policy by this conclusion, since the required connection calls for knowledge of valuation, available only when markets function perfectly.

Positive Solutions

Up to this point the discussion has proceeded on the assumption that a unique general equilibrium solution exists when preferences are revealed, the relevant pricing rules are employed, and an initial distribution of income is specified. That is, concern in this chapter has centered on the normative character of the general equilibrium solution. It still remains to be demonstrated whether, under the assumed conditions, a unique general equilibrium solution exists and is stable, whatever may be its normative properties.

A REINTERPRETATION OF MUSGRAVE'S APPROACH

Sparks, in the article quoted above, suggests, as an alternative interpretation of Musgrave's original treatment of income distribution, that the initial allocation of private goods not be thought of as an optimal distribution of income but as the distribution which would result from the operation of competitive markets given an arbitrarily specified distribution of factor endowments and no production of public goods.[5] Under these conditions Musgrave's two-point solution establishes the Pareto efficient limits for a bilateral bargaining situation in which neither party would be willing to accept the substitution of any social goods for a portion of his initially attained private goods unless it left him at least no worse off than in the private-goods-only position.

Musgrave's definition of income distribution in terms of utility levels of the two individuals for a given distribution of the technically maximum output of private goods serves to define the area of mutually acceptable substitution of social for private goods and the allocation of the reduced quantity of private goods. The two points on the utility possibility frontier define the limits of those substitutions which are also Pareto optimal. Whether the utility frontier

5. Musgrave assumes that the distribution of factor incomes is given and remains constant regardless of the mix of final products. As has been pointed out above, Sharp and Escarraz (p. 136), have shown that in the context of this analysis constant factor incomes do not imply constant shares of final products. Musgrave's assumptions are, however, an attempt to eliminate any distinction between income distribution as factor endowments or factor earnings or as command over final product. He wishes to assume that income distribution in all three of these senses is the same and is optimal.

will be reached, and which particular point on or off it is selected, depend upon the static and dynamic properties of the behavioral system. It has been clearly demonstrated for similar problems in other areas of economics that although in the case of small numbers the actual solution is indeterminate, depending upon the bargaining abilities of the participants, if numbers become sufficiently great so that competitive conditions emerge, the bargaining area contracts until a unique solution is determined. This solution is the conventional general equilibrium solution which, if the functions are "well behaved," results in a unique and mutually consistent set of prices and quantities for products and factors. If it is assumed that preferences are revealed, a similar unique outcome should ensue even if social as well as private goods are included in the analysis. This interpretation supports the notion that the fundamental explanation for Musgrave's dual solution lies in the unusual method chosen for specification of the distribution of incomes and the limitation of the analysis to two partici-pants, not in any inherent characteristic of social goods.

The foregoing discussion can be used to help clear up a persistent ambiguity in the literature on the pure theory of public finance. Musgrave has argued that there is a fundamental difference in the general equilibrium with and without social goods because his analysis yields a two-point solution for the social goods case when the income distribution in terms of private goods is given. The case of private goods only, Musgrave contends, would yield a single such point. As was pointed out above, Sharp and Escarrez (1964) have shown that Musgrave's procedure applied to two private goods also yields two points on the utility possibility frontier. What has not been demonstrated is that, al-though Musgrave's general equilibrium procedure does yield two points re-gardless of the kinds of final goods considered, only one such point results, again regardless of the kinds of final goods, if the given distribution of income is defined in terms of initial factor endowments.

The explanation of the dual solution, as has been said above, lies not in the characteristics of social goods but in the conceptualization of a given income distribution as meaning a constant level of utility.[6] Of course, if one party's utility is held constant, the other is in a position to select from the residual consumption possibilities those which maximize his utility, and there is every reason for the resulting product mix and distribution to be quite different from that which would prevail if the tables were turned and the second individual's utility were held constant. If, however, income distribution is specified in terms

6. Donald R. Escarraz, *The Price Theory of Value in Public Finance* (Gainesville: University of Florida Press, 1966), reaches the same conclusion. He writes: "The existence of the public good in the model modified the analysis but does not affect the nature of the conclusions. The arbitrary statement of the second man's utility is the cause of the large number of solutions in the model, and not the nature of the goods used in the model" (p. 34).

not of constant utility, but of given factor endowments and in addition preferences are specified, and the relevant functions "well behaved," a single, unique set of prices and quantities emerges whether social goods are included or not. Further, the assumptions that the usual marginal equalities prevail for private goods and that the special marginal conditions prevail for public goods lead to the conclusion that this unique set of prices and quantities is Pareto optimal; that is, the set is represented by a point on the utility frontier.

A DEMONSTRATION OF THE POSITIVE GENERAL EQUILIBRIUM SOLUTION

It is frequently stated that the prevalence of the marginal equality conditions with a given distribution of income leads to a unique point on the utility possibility frontier, which is Pareto optimal. The classic nonmathematical treatment of welfare economics, Francis Bator's "The Simple Analytics of Welfare Economics" (1957), assumes a social welfare function and does not, therefore, demonstrate this proposition directly. Donald R. Escarraz (1966, pp. 35 – 47) does, however, provide such a demonstration for both the private-goods-only case and the mixed social and private goods case.[7] His approach is essentially similar to that presented below, but is elaborated somewhat more fully. Escarraz develops in detail a graphic depiction of the interactions among a given pattern of factor endowments, transformation possibilities, and preferences which determine a unique mutually consistent set of factor and product prices, output mix, and income distribution. This approach is applied first to two private goods and then to a private and a social good. Comparison of the two results shows that while there are differences in the way in which preferences and factor endowments influence the equilibrium output mix and its distribution, depending on whether social or private goods are involved, in either case specification of preferences, factor endowments, and technical coefficients of production are sufficient for the determination of a single general equilibrium solution. Escarraz's ingenious analysis is not reproduced here, partly because it is available in his book, but primarily because Harry Johnson's approach presented below is more general; it does not require, as Escarraz's does, the assignment of ownership of all of each kind of factor input to only one of the individuals in order to specify the distribution of income.

Certain simplifications greatly facilitate illustration of the essential aspects of the general equilibrium solution with public goods. First of all, as is conventional in most treatments of general equilibrium analysis, the supply of factors is taken as perfectly inelastic. This assumption in no way changes the equilibrium nature of the solution, but from the standpoint of economic efficiency it

7. Gordon R. Sparks, "Professor Musgrave's Theory of Public Expenditures," *Canadian Journal of Economics and Political Science*, November 1964, p. 592 presents a formal mathematical definition of the Paretian optimum conditions for an economy which contains social as well as private goods.

eliminates concern for the efficient rate of production. Second, the establishment of equilibrium prices for factors and the efficient combination of factors is assumed to be no different in the production of social than of private goods. The reason for making these assumptions is to bypass the need for inclusion of a demonstration of the full general equilibrium character of the model so as to focus attention on the special features introduced by incorporation of social goods.

Acceptance of these assumptions permits concentration on the essential issue of the efficient combination of products. Equilibrium among products requires that the price and quantities of products be such as to clear product markets and to be consistent with assumed factor prices and endowments. Conditions for a Pareto optimum further require that the equilibrium solution be such that no other combination of products could make anyone better off without making someone else worse off. For this condition to prevail, marginal rates of transformation (the slopes of the production possibility curve) must be equal to marginal rates of substitution for all consumers.

Scitovsky in *Welfare and Competition* (1961) demonstrates graphically and without the use of any type of aggregated indifference curves that, given preferences, transformation possibilities, and the distribution of income, there exists an equilibrium combination of products which is also Pareto optimum when consumers and producers are price takers. This demonstration can be modified to yield a similar conclusion for public and private goods. Following Scitovsky, it is assumed that perfect competition prevails in factor markets and that private and public producers are efficient so that relative marginal costs are equated with marginal rates of transformation. Also, it is assumed that perfect competition prevails in product markets for private goods so that the marginal valuations of such goods by each individual is brought into equality with prices and that prices are equal to marginal costs. With regard to public goods, the unrealistic but analytically essential assumption of preference revelation is maintained so that for each consumer there exists for any specified quantity of a social good (available in equal amounts to all) a pseudo-price equal to his marginal valuation of that quantity. The equilibrium quantity of a social good is that amount for which the sum of these pseudo-prices is equal to the marginal cost of the social good.

In Figure 3.9 let a single public good be measured on the X axis, and a single private good on the Y axis, and let DE represent the transformation curve between them, drawn with the conventional increasing cost assumption. The problem is to demonstrate that there exists a unique price ratio which, at one and the same time, is equal to the relative marginal costs of the public and private goods at a specified production point on the transformation curve and which, given income distribution and preferences, leads consumers to demand just that mix of public and private goods consonant with the production point.

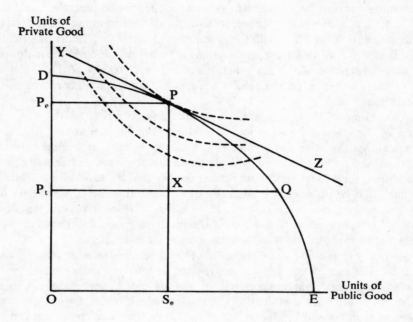

Figure 3.9. Transformation Curve and Consumption by N-1 Individuals

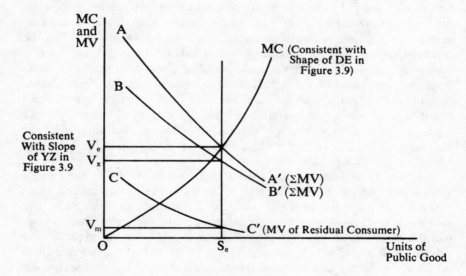

Figure 3.10. Marginal Valuation of Public Good by N-1 and Nth Individuals

Let YZ tentatively represent such an equilibrium price ratio. Then, P in Figure 3.9 represents the point on the transformation curve for which the marginal rate of transformation (the ratio of the marginal costs) is equal to the price ratio. This point is associated with the production of P_e of the private good and S_e of the public good. Now, if this combination represents an equilibrium mix of outputs, it is necessary that at the assumed price ratio consumers demand the actual quantities provided (that is, P_e and S_e).

Demands for the public and private goods will, of course, depend upon the distribution of income and consumer preferences as well as upon relative prices. The distribution of income becomes determinate, in this setting, since it is assumed that there is a given distribution of factor ownership and that the supply of factors is completely inelastic. Given transformation possibilities, the tentative price ratio and the output mix it implies are sufficient to determine factor prices as inelastic factor supplies interact with derived demands for factors. Application of factor prices to the assumed factor endowments yields a unique income distribution.

On the basis of this income distribution and the assumed preferences of consumers it is possible to determine the quantities of the public and private goods demanded by all but one individual. Let point X in Figure 3.9 represent this situation, so that N-1 consumers demand P_t of the private good at the given price ratio YZ and are provided S_e of the public good. There is nothing unusual about the determination of the quantity of the private good; it is simply the sum of the various quantities demanded by each of the N-1 individuals (given their incomes and preferences) at the assumed price for the private good. The quantity demanded of the public good does, however, require further explanation.

As has been shown above, when preferences are revealed the quantities of a pure public good demanded can be indicated by the vertical summation of individual demands at different (pseudo) prices which represent marginal valuations. Figure 3.10 depicts hypothetical demand for the public good in the present illustration. Curve AA′ is the vertically aggregated demand for the public good by all consumers, while BB′ shows demand by N-1 consumers. Thus, CC′ is the demand curve for the residual consumer. Since it is the essence of a pure public good that it be consumed in equal quantities by all consumers, the quantity of the public good provided to the N-1 consumers must be the same quantity as that provided at the tentative equilibrium, S_e. Figure 3.10 shows that for the quantity S_e the sum of the marginal valuations of the N-1 consumers is equal to V_x (V for valuation), an amount which is less than the marginal cost of the S_eth unit of the public good.

Another way of depicting the situation for the N-1 consumers is that given the tentative equilibrium price and quantity of the private good, P_t of it is taken, leaving P_e-P_t for the Nth consumer. For the public good, the N-1 consumers contribute V_x to the cost of the tentative equilibrium marginal unit (that is, the S_eth unit) leaving V_e-V_x to be contributed by the Nth consumer. It is important to note that at point X each of the N-1 consumers has maximized his position given the tentative relative prices, the income distribution, and preferences, since each has consumed both public and private goods to the point where the price (or pseudo-price) is equal to marginal valuation of the last unit taken.

The general equilibrium character of point P can be seen most clearly by examination of the incremental consumption of the Nth consumer. In order for the tentative price ratio to prove an equilibrium one, given point X and production consistent with the tentative price ratio YZ, the final consumer has to take P_e-P_t of the private good and also contribute V_e-V_x for his share of the commonly supplied quantity, S_{e_1}, of the public good. If, when confronted by the potential production possibility arc, PQ, the residual consumer maximizes his utility by moving to point P, then the tentative price ratio is indeed a Pareto optimizing general equilibrium solution. This follows because given the choices open to him the marginal rate of substitution between the two commodities which prevails at the most preferred attainable position for the ultimate consumer is exactly equal to the price ratio at which all other individuals maximize their positions. The market has been cleared and there is no possibility for making any consumer better off without making someone else worse off. The result is perfectly general because exchange of the Nth consumer with any other consumer would displace point X in Figure 3.9 and curve CC′ in Figure 3.10 by just those amounts necessary for the new ultimate consumer's preferences and incomes to lead him to choose point P as the most preferred locus on his arc of attainable positions.

From another viewpoint, if the tentative price ratio were not consistent with the assumed preferences and income distribution, the ultimate consumer would not maximize his welfare by consuming the residual quantity of the private good nor would he value the marginal unit of the public good at an amount just equal to the difference between its marginal cost and the sum of all others' marginal valuations. If, for example, at the tentative price the residual consumer wished more of the private good than P_e-P_t, this would indicate that too low a relative price was placed on the private good, given the income distribution and preferences of other consumers, and that a rise in its relative price would move the system toward equilibrium by lowering the demand for the private good while permitting a movement along the production possibility curve toward a larger output of this good. On the other hand, if he valued the S_eth unit of the public good at an amount greater than V_m (equal to V_e-V_x), so that the sum of the marginal valuations at that quantity of public good exceeded its marginal cost, it would indicate too low a relative price for the public good and a corresponding adjustment would constitute a move toward equilibrium.

While the foregoing analysis does not constitute a rigorous demonstration of the existence of a unique Pareto optimal general equilibrium solution to the case of a pure public-private dual commodity economy, it establishes the essential outlines for such a proof. It does show that the introduction of pure public goods into general equilibrium analysis influences the character of the equilibrium condition, but does not upset conventional conclusions with regard to the existence of a unique and Pareto optimal equilibrium. The essential problem of public goods is the absence of any mechanism for revelation of preferences, rather than the prevalence of an area of indeterminance even when preferences are revealed.

JOHNSON'S GRAPHIC GENERAL SOLUTION

The depiction of the positive general equilibrium solution with public goods presented above abjures explicit consideration of factor distribution and stability conditions in order to emphasize the way in which quantity and price of public goods are made consistent with the requirements of a general solution.

Harry Johnson, bringing the techniques of international trade analysis of general equilibrium to bear on the problem of equilibrium with public goods has produced an elegant, complete, and rigorous graphic analysis, which clearly shows both the conditions for equilibrium and the determinants of stability (Johnson, 1971, Appendix C).

Johnson develops a graphic technique for portrayal of the general equilibrium analysis for private goods by means of a two-factor, two-commodity, two-person model. He then applies this technique to the case of one public and one private good. As usual, a transformation curve depicts technology and total factor supplies as shown by TT′ in Figure 3.11. To depict factor ownership and income distribution between the two persons, Johnson introduces the highly useful device of income determination curves which are shown as $W_1W_1′$ and $W_2W_2′$. These curves depict the unique relationship between a point on the transformation curve (which sets relative prices for the two products), the factor proportions implicit in the particular mix of outputs at this point, the value of the marginal products of the factors and their unit prices (which are determinate in view of the already given relative product prices), and, finally, the incomes received by each of the two parties given the quantities of factors assigned to each. Thus, at point Po, relative marginal costs and product prices are shown by MM′, which also measures total income.

The distribution of income between the two persons for a given production point along TT′ such as Po is given by the points on $W_1W_1′$, and $W_2W_2′$, (P10 and P20 respectively) which are intersected by a ray from the origin to the

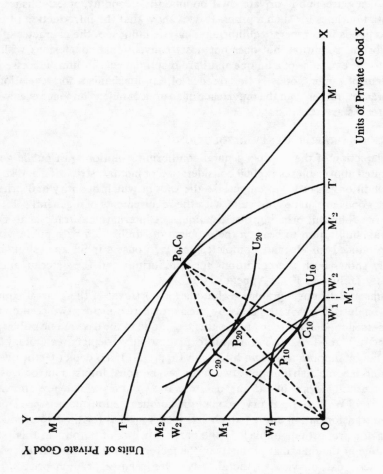

Figure 3.11. General Equilibrium for Private Goods

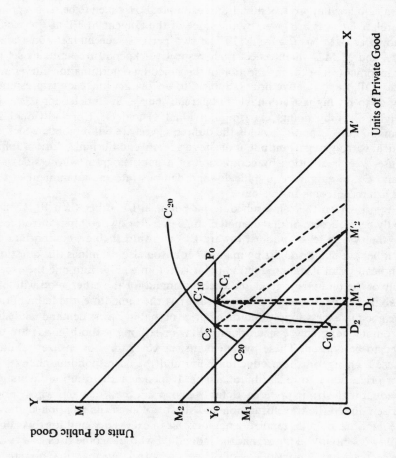

Figure 3.12. General Equilibrium for Public and Private Goods

point on the transformation curve. Selection of another point on TT′ changes relative product prices and factor intensities and, hence, marginal productivities and factor prices would change, leading to a new income distribution. W_1W_1' and W_2W_2' trace out the effects of such movements on the income of each of the persons given his initial factor endowments.

Two Private Goods. The analysis of the case of two private goods begins with the selection of a point on the transformation curve as yielding a potential general equilibrium product mix. If, for example, Po is taken to be such a point, then relative prices are given by the slope of the tangent to TT at Po, which is shown as MM′ in Figure 3.11. The two persons face budget constraints M_1M_1' and M_2M_2' which reflect their respective expenditure limits as set by their incomes (set at the intersection of their income-determination curves and the ray OP_O) and relative prices. Subject to his budget line each is presumed to move to his highest attainable indifference curve. Such behavior is shown in Figure 3.11 by points C_{10} (for individual 1) and C_{20} (for individual 2). Summation of C_{10} and C_{20} yields the desired aggregate bill of goods which, if identical with aggregate output, indicates a general equilibrium solution. Johnson uses vector addition by completion of a parallelogram whose sides are C_{10} and C_{20} to aggregate graphically and demonstrate the attainment of the equilibrium outcome in this case.

Suppose, given the same schedules, a point on TT′ other than P_0, C_0 had initially been chosen, or that a small change in factor ownership is introduced. Does the system tend to adjust toward P_0 or toward the new equilibrium, or does it behave in a distabilizing manner? Johnson also examines this question. He indicates that if the production point is not an equilibrium one the excess supply of the redundant good and excess demand for the other good will lead to stablizing adjustments in relative prices. At the same time, the falling price of the good in excess supply and rising price of that in excess demand tend also to promote stabilizing consumption behavior so long as both goods are assumed to be normal. These two elements, however, do not ensure stability, because a change in the production point and the corresponding changes in factor prices serve to redistribute income. If income redistribution favors the individual with strong preferences for the good in excess demand whose price has risen due to the transformation and substitution effects mentioned above, there might result a destabilizing net increase in excess demand for this good. Stability essentially requires that the individual whose income rises as a result of an increase in the price of one of the goods has relative marginal preference for the other good.

A Public and a Private Good. The application of this general equilibrium framework to encompass public goods requires that one axis depict a public good whose quantity is available to both persons. Income determination curves, budget lines, and the optimizing behavior of each individual are as before, but the aggregation of demand for the public goods requires vertical rather than horizontal summation to allow for cost sharing by the two persons. Johnson develops the graphic analysis of this case as in Figure 3.12 by taking the Y axis to represent the public good and showing the possibilities for cost sharing by rotating the budget line for each individual from its intersection with the X axis over the range of equality with the unit cost of the public good (where its slope is equal to MM') to a cost of zero where its slope is completely vertical. The locus of points of intersection of the rotating budget lines (M_1M_1' and M_2M_2') with the highest attainable indifference curves generates the demand curves for the public good by the two persons ($C_{10}C_{10}'$ and $C_{20}C_{20}'$), consistent with the income distribution that follows from production point P_0. The demand price for public goods of an individual has here the usual interpretation of indicating the price which the individual would pay for a marginal unit of goods; therefore, for a public good, these prices can be taken to show how the costs of the public good can be shared among the participants.

As the schedules are drawn in Figure 3.12, neither party alone is willing to provide the tentative equilibrium quantity of public goods, OY_0, consistent with the production point P_0. A cost-sharing arrangement does exist, however, by which both parties together would be willing to pay for the equilibrium quantity. The question for a general solution is whether that arrangement also is consistent with an aggregate demand for the private good equal to its supply at the production point. In Figure 3.12 the demand curves for the public good by the two persons are $C_{10}C_{10}'$ and $C_{20}C_{20}'$, and C_1 and C_2 are the points where these demand curves intersect the quantity of public goods. The cost shares consistent with OY_0 of public goods are, in effect, the relative price which each individual would be willing to pay for the OYoth unit of public goods. Johnson depicts these relative prices on Figure 3.12 by dropping perpendiculars from C_1 and C_2 to the X axis (D_1 and D_2 respectively) and then connecting C_1 and C_2 to the respective intersections of their budget lines with the X axis at M_1' and M_2'. Slopes C_1M_1' and C_2M_2' represent the prices at which the two individuals value the OY_0th unit of public goods. If the sum of these prices equals the unit cost of the public good at the production point, general equilibrium is achieved. Graphic addition of these slopes involves addition to the slope of C_1M_1' (which represents C_1's valuation of the OY_0th unit of the public good) the slope C_2M_2' (which represents C_2's valuation of this same unit). Such summation is accomplished by addition of the distance D_2M_2' to the point M_1', giving point D_3, and then drawing the slope from C_1 to D_3. If this line, C_1D_3, which measures the sum of the prices which the two individuals are willing to pay for the OY_0th unit of the public good, has a slope equal to M_2M_2', aggregate consumption is consistent with the output of the production point and general equilibrium is achieved. If the line from C_1 to D_3 has a steeper slope than M_2M_2', then the sum of the demand prices at quantity OY_0 is less than the marginal cost of this quantity; the reverse holds if the line from C_1 is less steep than M_2M_2'.

Here, as for two private goods, unstable solutions are possible. If an adjustment of the production point toward increasing the output of the good in excess demand redistributes income in favor of an individual with strong enough marginal preferences for that good, the substitution effect may be overcome. For example, if it is the public good which is in excess demand (that is, the sum of the demand prices exceeds the marginal cost), instability arises if income redistribution results in an increase in the marginal valuation of the increased quantity of the public good by the individual whose income has risen greater than the corresponding decrease in marginal valuation by the other person.

Summary

The context of the pure theory of public expenditures at one and the same time consists of a highly abstract exercise in normative economic analysis and a discussion of the most realistic problems of preference revelation under extreme economic interdependence. The theory is almost exclusively concerned with the analysis of resource-using expenditures for a polar concept of public goods characterized by complete joint supply and the impossibility of exclusion. The theory treats public goods as final products for which consumers have transitive preferences and essentially ignores the production of public goods and noneconomic motivations for public spending.

The partial equilibrium solution for pure public goods appears to be essentially similar to the standard Marshallian joint supply case. However, the formal similarity of the equilibrium solutions masks intractable problems of preference revelation for public goods such that no market mechanism exists by which this solution can be attained. Small numbers lead to partial revelation of preferences, but strategic considerations prevent achievement of the equilibrium at the optimum, except by chance. Large numbers provide an incentive for the "free rider" to enjoy the same benefits from pure public goods without payment that he would with payment in accordance with his marginal valuation. Only under the highly unrealistic assumption of full preference revelation is the outcome of partial equilibrium analysis of public goods analogous to the conventional joint supply solution, such that at equilibrium the sum of the marginal valuations, viewed as pseudo-prices, is equated to the marginal cost of the good. Because of the inability to exclude, however, this analysis is essentially irrelevant as an approximation to any viable decentralized voluntary solution. At the same time, it does provide a normative guide for the evaluation of those political arrangements which endeavor to simulate a consumer-preference-directed solution to the provision of public goods.

Analysis of general equilibrium with pure public goods ignores the problems of preference revelation and concentrates on the mutual determination of optimum quantities of public and private goods. The analysis is especially concerned with the treatment of income distribution and the heuristic value of the concept of a social welfare function, issues which also predominate in conventional general equilibrium analysis where only private goods are considered.

If income distribution is to be taken as given, comparability with general equilibrium analysis of private goods dictates that this distribution be defined in terms of initial factor endowments. Under such interpretation, the usual "optimum conditions" (that is, the extended set of marginal equalities and the assumption of "well-behaved" functions) for private goods, combined with the special condition for public goods (that is, that marginal cost equals the sum of the marginal valuations), lead to a unique general equilibrium Pareto optimum solution. This, along with underlying stability conditions, is best shown by Johnson's analysis. Musgrave's "two point" solution turns out to be the special result of defining income in terms of utility levels rather than factor endowments.

The social welfare function approach to general equilibrium in a setting that includes public goods remains the conventional one of mutual determination of that output mix and its distribution which maximizes social welfare. By an ingenious diagramatic, as well as a formal mathematical demonstration, Samuelson shows that by application of the special condition of equality of the sum of marginal valuations to marginal cost for the public goods the "bliss point" solution, familiar to analyses of general equilibrium for private goods, can be extended to include public goods. Such extension in no way vitiates the potent criticism of any and all welfare analysis based on the social welfare function that there is no acceptable way of formulating an operational version of such a function.

Within the highly rarified atmosphere of a theory of pure public goods which assumes that preferences are revealed, there may be advantages to avoidance of the further ascent to the stratosphere implied by the social welfare approach. In this regard, McGuire and Aaron verify Musgrave's notion that if the conception of income distribution is broadened to encompass the benefits of public as well as private goods the formal distinction between distribution and allocation can still be preserved. This is accomplished, in effect, by lump-sum transfers which adjust the income distribution so that it leads to the optimum outcome, as determined by the social welfare function, for the full system inclusive of public goods. Such a conclusion has slim practical consequence, however, since in the absence of any operational content to the social welfare function it is not meaningful to attempt to determine this welfare maximizing income distribution as a matter of policy.

The relevant questions for public policy pertaining to social goods concern the effects of various nonoptimal income distributions on the ensuing mix of public and private goods, and on the influence, given the distribution of income, of alternative arrangements and regulations for the determination of this mix.

These issues comprise the subject matter of the next two chapters. Chapter 4 develops approaches to public policies for the attainment of equity and efficiency under the assumption that wherever possible decentralized decision-making will be accorded a primary role. Chapter 5 considers the same issues from the viewpoint of political solutions.

FOUR

Market Failure, Public Policy, and Public Expenditure

Analysis of the pure theory of public expenditures reveals a pathological case of market failure. That is, goods with the "double polar" characteristics of joint supply and the impossibility of exclusion are such that their production will occur only under public organization (collective supply). Yet, in itself, the pure theory of public finance constitutes neither an economic rationale for the state nor an adequate economic theory of government expenditure. An economic theory of the state, consistent with the traditions of individualistic economics, may be developed around the assumption that the state aims to maximize societal economic welfare defined in terms of conformance with individual preferences.[1] If market-determined prices are presumed to be the primary way in which preferences are manifest, such a theory requires a thoroughgoing description of all sources of failure of decentralized markets coupled with an analysis of the potentialities of various government policies to deal with these failures. The analogous economic theory of public expenditure must elucidate the specific role of government budgetary outlays as one among various state actions intended to deal with market failure. Further, it must distinguish public expenditures whose purpose is to subsidize households and private market organizations from those government expenditures for goods and services which then are either provided through collective organization and supply or are sold by the state.

1. See the section on merit goods, below in this chapter, for a detailed discussion of the meaning of conformance with individual preferences and the relation of preferences and welfare.

The Economic Framework of Public Expenditure

From its inception as a discrete subject of inquiry economics has been concerned with state public policy, and one of the most pervasive traditions of economics is the effort to define the role of the state in economic life. In this chapter, emphasis shifts from the depiction of the most extreme case of market failure, where government organization of production is the only way to satisfy individual wants, to the consideration of all sources of market failure and their implications for public policy, especially government expenditures. While it is assumed that the relevant objective function continues to be defined in terms of individual preferences, the special conditions of the pure theory no longer hold. Among the major assumptions discarded are that all goods are either polar public or private, preferences are necessarily revealed, and competition is perfect. This chapter reviews and analyzes issues relevant to the question: In what economic activities should the state engage and how should it operate?[2]

The overall objective here is to examine the role of public expenditures in an efficiency-oriented economic theory of the state. The chapter begins with a brief overview of the historical development and refinement of the notion of economic efficiency, or social economy, and of the economic role of the state as inferred from discrepancies between the actual situation and the ideal. With this review as background, the concept of public goods, defined in far less restrictive terms than in the previous chapter, is shown to be an integral, yet distinct, element in a comprehensive conception of causes of market failure. Recognition of alternative sources of market failure does not permit delineation of a set of articulated public policies, however, and the chapter goes on to review the wide-ranging difficulties that beset any attempt to link particular public economic policies, especially government expenditures, to specific distortions of the conditions for economic efficiency.

Among the issues discussed with regard to the proper role for government expenditures are the theory of second best, the establishment of a market in externalities and other forms of private agreements, the costs of information and agreement necessary for public policy, and the significance of merit goods. In conclusion, it is argued that there emerges no simple or unitary principle

2. Extensive surveys of the literature on external effects are contained in Julius Margolis and Philip E. Vincent, *External Economic Effects — An Analysis and Survey* (Stanford, California: Institute in Engineering-Economic Systems, 1966), and E. J. Mishan, "Reflections on Recent Developments in the Concept of External Effects," *Canadian Journal of Economics and Political Science,* February 1965, pp. 3 – 34. In many respects these surveys cover the same ground as the present chapter, but here the focus is on implications for public expenditures and public organization of supply while the primary interest of Margolis and Vincent is the nature of the concept of externality and its relevance to project analysis, especially water resources projects; Mishan's interest is also in the concept itself.

for determination of when a public rather than private solution is appropriate nor whether government organization of supply is superior to such other public policies as subsidy, taxation, or regulation. Instead, situations must be judged on their own merits, and, most important, distributional as well as efficiency considerations and noneconomic as well as economic values must be considered in choosing among policies. Appropriate modifications of the operation of decentralized markets cannot be satisfactorily determined by rule-of-thumb public policies. They require instead resolution through the mechanism by which major issues of conflicting values are dealt with in democratic societies — the political process.

An Historical Overview of Economic Efficiency and Public Policy

During the long prehistory of economic thought from Aristotle to Adam Smith, there was little recognition of the self-regulating features of markets. It was generally held that, in the absence of traditional or ritualistic economic behavior, state control was essential to the performance of economic functions. The revolution in understanding economic relationships embodied in the theories of laissez-faire, which were carried to their extreme by the "harmony economists," removed the state from economic affairs as fully as the former conception had involved it. The initial criticism of the divorce of political authority from economic affairs was largely an attack on the institution of private property as leading to widespread social injustice and to the creation of antagonistic social classes. While these concerns are still a major objection to economic systems based on market institutions, the development of value theory provided a source of criticism which was not grounded in rejection of the principle of private property as the cause of intolerable inequities, but on the failure of the unregulated market to achieve the efficiencies claimed for it.

The aspects of value theory relevant to the role of the state, codified in the writings of Alfred Marshall, were what have come to be called the "old" welfare economics. In this view the theory of value is more than a positive theory which describes how prices come to be established under specified technological, preference, and market conditions. This theory has also a normative component which explains how the economic welfare of society is maximized when demand prices, as measures of the marginal utilities of commodities, are equated with supply prices, as measures of marginal opportunity costs. Marshall and his successors (especially Pigou) argued that if, under market arrangements, prices fail to indicate true social marginal utilities or social marginal costs, the decentralized maximizing behavior of consumers and producers would not promote the social optimum. At the same time, the followers of the "old" welfare economics held the view that all individuals had roughly the same capacities for satisfaction so that interpersonal comparisons of well-being were possible. They also believed that the marginal utility of income diminished with increments in income. These propositions led to a conception of a dual economic role for the state: the adjustment of resource allocation distortions resulting from failures of prices as accurate measures of social utilities, and the redistribution of income to increase social welfare in accordance with interpersonal utility comparisons.

It took several decades to clarify the issues raised by Marshall and his neoclassical followers regarding the conditions under which market-deter-mined prices fail to be proper signals to decentralized decision-makers. The essential idea, that of a discrepancy between private and social valuation, has survived, however, and is today a cornerstone of the economic theory of the state. On the other hand, the neoclassical doctrine of state redistribution of income based on interpersonal utility comparisons among individuals pos-sessed of equal capacities for satisfaction never was widely accepted, even among economists, because its major implication, post-redistributive income equality, raises virtually insuperable problems for incentives. This practical objection was reinforced by Lionel Robbins's (1932) devastating attack on the notion of interpersonal utility comparison. Despite an imposing array of in-genious efforts to provide an economic rationale for income redistribution policies, it now appears clear that such policies cannot be derived as a result of the maximization of an objective function but must be an integral element in such a function. (See the discussion of income distribution in Chapter 3 above.) The issue is that of choice among the different outcomes implicit in alternative income distributions; preferences among such outcomes are essen-tial components of ultimate values.

In the "new" welfare economics, built on the corpse of interpersonal utility comparisons, the conditions for a welfare optimum are spelled out in detail subject to any given income distribution. The analysis of the necessary condi-tions that must prevail in product and factor markets in order for it to be impossible to make any person better off without making someone else worse off has been treated as a basis for an economic theory of the state which avoids interpersonal comparisons. The implicit position taken is that there is a role for the state whenever one of the optimum conditions is violated. This ap-proach to defining the operational role of government in the economy was initially developed by such liberal socialists as Oskar Lange (1964) and Enrico Barone (1935) and Lerner (1944) who attempted to show how a decentralized socialist economy operating on the basis of prices adjusted for externalities and other distortions could achieve the social optimum which the private market economy found so elusive.

While formalization and analysis of the optimum conditions have contri-buted to an understanding of the relationships between economic institutions and social welfare, they have not contributed greatly to resolution of the problems of policy. At one level the criterion for efficiency embodied in the optimum conditions imposes too restrictive a standard for policy evaluation. These conditions which define the Pareto optimum justify only those actions which improve the position of some while leaving no one worse off. Since virtually all practical policy actions do, in fact, make some worse off, there have been weaker criteria proposed, such as that of potential compensation, which do accept policies that leave some in a less favored position. Acceptance of any of these criteria would justify state action ruled out under the Pareto criterion. At another level, however, it is argued that even violations of the Pareto optimal conditions by the operations of decentralized markets are not sufficient basis for state intervention. For example, certain departures from optimum conditions may be accommodated by voluntary agreements involving compensatory payments; even when such arrangements are not forthcoming there is no assurance that state intervention will, on balance, increase welfare. The arguments for this last assertion range from consideration of the costs of gaining information to establish the details of public policy to the conclusion of the theory of second best — there is no reason to believe that an improvement in one element of a generally imperfect system will, necessarily, increase welfare.

These and other arguments on the suitability of public action to improve welfare even when optimum conditions are violated have led Buchanan and some of his supporters close to the position of the "harmony economists" in which the market is endorsed for its intrinsic noncoercive qualities and not for its welfare achievements. This view gives the appearance of a bald defense of the status quo. Instead, it is suggested that the consequences of alternative public policies, including the absence of public action, can be evaluated by the body politic. It is one of the major tenets of this book that choice between what are essentially market solutions and those substantially influenced by actions of the state can and should be based on an evaluation of outcomes and not on predispositions regarding the intrinsic values of particular institutional arrangements. The extended discussion of market failure, public goods, and externalities that follows presents and attempts to clarify the economic issues which must be taken into account in making such choices.

Static and Dynamic Efficiency

Before proceeding to this discussion, however, a further element in the development of the rationale for public economic policy needs to be mentioned. The ideas whose development has been sketched out above are set in a static framework. That is, they take preferences, resources, and technology as given and attempt to show how public policy can increase levels of welfare in relation to the results of purely private markets. Yet, historically and practically, another important rationale for public economic policy evolves from what Margolis and Vincent (1966, p. 45) call "dynamic development externalities." Here cost reductions or investment outlays are stimulated or accelerated by a coordinated set of actions — in effect, economic planning of one form or another — which serve to promote economies of scale, new technologies, and other sources of productivity increase (Rosenstein-Rodan 1943).

The question of whether it is proper to extend the concept of external economies to encompass the variety of reasons adduced for public economic development planning or policy appears to be essentially a matter of convenience. Most of the arguments for public policies to foster economic development derive from recognition of the external benefits of expansion of markets and the size of producing units. Regardless of whether such benefits of economic growth are essentially similar to the traditional static externalities, most of them can be assumed to have been realized for products where national markets prevail in industrialized economies. Here, many of the "dynamic externality" arguments for government economic policy do not apply. However, even, or perhaps especially, in such economies the dynamic aspects of urban and regional growth and decay lead to both external economies and diseconomies, and the advantages of some form of coordinated public policy at this level appear virtually unquestionable. At the same time, quite independently of the external benefits of coordinated growth policy, a great deal of concern in the study of industrial economies does stem, as it should, from the external effects of changes in resource availabilities and new technologies.

Any realistic discussion of the sources of market failure must, then, go beyond static efficiency into the area of policies toward activities which promote change in those parameters which static analysis takes as constant. Important as this matter is for contemporary policy, a history of the concept of dynamic development externalities parallel to that for static considerations is not presented here. Although policy issues raised by growth and development are touched upon in the discussion which follows, this volume does not attempt to deal systematically with public expenditures in the context of economic development planning. Instead, it follows the tradition in public finance of deriving the role of public policies, including government expenditures, out of a comprehensive analysis of the shortcomings of private markets.

Public Goods and Market Failure

The theory of market failure deals with the fundamental factors which account for the inability of decentralized private markets to attain economic efficiency. Its primary usefulness lies in the attempt to reduce a variety of conditions to their basic common elements and then to determine if such exposure reveals a simplified pattern of remedies. Two distinct approaches characterize examination of the sources of market failure. One attempts to reduce all instances of market imperfections to a single essential concept. For example, for Arrow (1970) this concept is "transaction cost" and for Head (1962, 1965) it is "non-appropriability." The other approach segregates the determinants of market failure into a few distinct categories. Bator (1958) distinguishes ownership, technical, and public good externalities while Scitovsky (1954) separates externalities into pecuniary and technical and Meade (1952) contrasts "unpaid factors" and "atmosphere" as separate categories of market failure. The concept of public goods plays a crucial role in the theory of market failure. Regardless of whether public goods are a distinct category in a taxonomy of sources of market failure, or an especially clear-cut illustration of a single basic attribute in a unified concept, no approach to the evaluation of the functioning of a decentralized economy fails to recognize the difficulties that result from the presence of goods with a substantial degree of "publicness" or "collectiveness."

When the focus shifts from pure to "impure" public goods, where complete joint supply and the impossibility of exclusion are not fully in force, the conclusion that collective supply is the only operational solution to the provision of public goods no longer holds. Instead, potential responses to market failure which stem from problems of partial joint supply and exclusion may also encompass private agreements, the formation of clubs and other private organizations, and government tax and subsidization policies. Further, it is conceivable that factors relevant to nonmarket solutions, such as costs of information and agreement, may be so substantial that private markets, even if they fall short of an optimum solution, may remain the most efficient arrangement for provision, distribution, and finance of the commodity in question. The task of a normative, yet realistic, economic theory of the public sector is to disentangle issues relevant to determination of the propriety of such forms of public intervention as public enterprise, collective supply, and subsidization and taxation, in relation to alternative sources of market failure.

At the same time, it is essential to recognize the related, although different, concern of a positive economic theory of government which acknowledges the public good characteristic of virtually all economic actions of governments. Government economic and other policies are such that they affect jointly all members of the society, so that from the standpoint of a positive conception of the public sector, it is not the characteristics of the goods themselves which makes them public or collective but the fact that many items are provided by government to all citizens and cannot be rejected (Olson, 1965, pp. 9 – 16; Breton, 1966, pp. 458 – 59). The task of a positive approach to public finance, according to Buchanan, is first to develop a "logical theory of individual choice among alternative institutions . . . through which certain goods and services will be supplied publicly," and second, to explain empirically and to predict the consequences for public good provision of various "real world fiscal structures" (Buchanan, 1968, pp. 200 – 1). Others see the positive theory grounded less in individual choice and more in conceptions of political groups and notions of the public interest. These matters are the substance of Chapter 5. The present chapter deals mainly with the normative question of what public policies are appropriate for what sources of market failure. It is important, however, to keep in mind the ultimate need for positive as well as normative theory.

Joint Supply, Externalities, Exclusion, and Market Failure

There can be no doubt that the existence of goods with public or social elements inhibits the achievement of Pareto optimality in a market-organized economy regardless of the state of competition or the convexity of production functions. That is, as shown in Chapter 2, market failure results when individuals or firms cannot adjust quantity taken, and information necessary for price discrimination is not revealed. It is a "fact of nature" that these conditions are fulfilled for certain goods. Market failure, however, is a concept intended to embrace, within a set of mutually exclusive and exhaustive categories, the full range of factors which prevent an economy organized on the basis of decentralized markets from achieving the utility possibility frontier. What then are the relations among the phenomena of joint supply, externalities, exclusion, and the generalized concept of market failure?

These relations are explored in this section. No single dominant interpretation has emerged from the extensive literature on the subject. The custom has been to discuss external effects without any great rigor in their definition. As a result, a number of alternate definitions of externality and related concepts have emerged (Baumol, 1965a, p. 24). Mishan's provision (1969) of a rigorous taxonomy of definitions based on common notation is, therefore, most welcome. In order, however, to give the flavor of the substantive debate over the relations among the fundamental concepts in the theories of market failure and of public economic policy a brief review of major viewpoints is presented first, followed by a summary of Mishan's comprehensive analysis.

UNIFIED APPROACHES

Nonappropriability. John Head has advanced the view that exclusion difficulties and externalities refer to essentially the same phenomena. He defines, traditionally, the presence of external economies as a condition such "that a change in the production and/or consumption of [a] good will affect the utility and/or production functions for other goods." The condition arises as a result of "the divorce of scarcity from effective ownership" such that it is "impossible for private firms and individuals, through ordinary private pricing to appropriate the full social benefits (or to be charged the full social costs) arising directly from their production and/or consumption of certain goods" (Head, 1962, pp. 203 – 4). Head finds this conventional notion of externality identical to the concept of "impossibility of exclusion" as used by Musgrave and Bowen.

According to Head's analysis, which has great similarities to Shoup's views (1969) as presented in Chapter 2 above, externality is equivalent to less than perfect exclusion and is a phenomenon separate from jointness or joint supply since many manifestations of this latter condition, such as those found in trains and concerts, raise no price-exclusion difficulties. These are what Shoup calls collective consumption goods. At the same time, there are exclusion difficulties or externalities which arise for products whose total can be divided among individuals so that more for one implies less for the other. Head mentions the extraction of oil as an illustration of an activity where externalities are imposed as a consequence of drilling a new well in the vicinity of existing wells, yet where no elements of joint supply are involved. Shoup, it will be remembered, calls these group consumption goods.

Head's position is that joint supply, in effect, is one among several causes of decreasing cost, and that at bottom both decreasing cost and externalities are accounted for by nonappropriability. According to Head, nonappropriability explains not only the problems of public goods joint supply but also such interferences with optimality as technological indivisibilities, underemployment, suboptimal growth, and barriers to international trade. In all of these cases, the failure of the decision-maker to appropriate the full benefits (or absorb the full costs) of his action leads to less than optimum behavior. Although Head distinguishes between joint supply and exclusion-externality, in his final synthesis he links them, through the notion of nonappropriability, to a unified conception of the basis for a theory of market failure.

Buchanan's Identification of Externality with Joint Supply. Buchanan, perhaps the most authoritative student of the concept of externalities, reaches a far different conclusion. In his view "any externality becomes a joint-supply relationship" because "an individual's act of consuming or producing a good or service is, at the same time, *jointly* supplying at least one other person with a 'good' (or a 'bad')" (Buchanan, 1966, p. 408). The converse, however, does not apply; all joint products do not create externalities, as analysis of Marshallian-type joint supply conditions demonstrates. Buchanan thus eliminates the distinction between externality and what has generally been called public good joint supply. That is, his approach would classify as an externality yielding joint supply relationship, the contribution of the bees to the pollination of the apple blossoms, even though it is possible, by adjusting the number of the bees, to vary the quantity of their service to apple-growers in response to payments received. The issue raised by extension of the concept of externality to encompass aspects of joint supply is whether the gains from this more comprehensive approach outweigh the usefulness of distinguishing between resource allocation problems which arise because no decision-maker can adjust the quantity available to him (that is, conventional public goods joint supply) and those that result when activities under the control of one decision-maker affect the production or utility functions of another (conventional externalities).

It is interesting to note that in the matter of a unified approach to externalities and joint supply the usual antagonists, Buchanan and Samuelson, appear to agree. Samuelson has written recently, "A public good . . . is simply one with the property of involving a 'consumption externality' in the sense of entering into two or more persons' preference functions simultaneously" (Samuelson, 1969, p. 102). In contrast to Musgrave's effort to distinguish among different conditions which might lead to the simultaneous presence of a good in several preference functions (Musgrave, 1969, pp. 134 – 42, and below, pp. 136 – 38), Samuelson suggests that "the useful terminology in this field should be: pure private goods, and possibly close approximations to them, versus the whole field of consumption — externalities or public goods" (1969a, p. 109).

Arrow's Synthesis in Terms of Transactions Costs. Kenneth Arrow recently has turned his attention to the question of market failure (1970). He views this concept as more general than externality, but still not sufficiently general, because market failure seldom is absolute. Like Bator (see next section) he distinguishes externalities which arise as a result of the mode of economic organization from increasing returns which are a technological phenomenon and would present difficulties regardless of the form of organization. The broadest concept pertinent to choice of economic organization on efficiency grounds is, according to Arrow, that of transaction cost. Despite the contrary assumption in value theory, the formation and maintenance of markets involves greater or lesser costs. The relative success or failure of markets depends on the magnitude of these costs and the willingness and ability of participants to bear them.

Transaction costs take many forms. One such form, the costs of exclusion of nonpayers, has already been discussed. When such costs become infinite, exclusion becomes impossible and private markets inoperable. At finite exclusion cost arrangements other than conventional markets enter into consideration. These range from market-like organizations such as clubs to informal agreements and trust among individuals and to such nonmarket solutions as public supply. Another kind of transaction cost is the "costliness of the information needed to enter and participate in any market." Arrow points out that "information is closely related . . . to communication and . . . to uncertainty." These factors weigh heavily in the arguments for bypassing the market in the provision of certain commodities sometimes termed "merit goods" (see below in this chapter).

Transaction costs exist in all modes of economic organization. Market failure for Arrow arises where "transaction costs are so high that the existence of the market is no longer worthwhile." In certain areas of economic activity a price system provides information and communication far more cheaply than alternative mechanisms. Where information, communication, and exclusion are highly costly under the market mode, alternative systems may reduce welfare loss; but before any conclusions can be drawn it is necessary to balance market transaction costs with those of the alternative systems under consideration.

MULTIPLE CAUSES OF MARKET FAILURE

The heuristic value of a unified theory of market failure must be set against the usefulness of a multiple approach which attempts to characterize sources of market failure in order to illuminate potential remedies. The most ambitious undertaking of this sort is Francis Bator's effort to distinguish five modes or conditions of market failure, which he classifies into three fundamental types (Bator, 1958, pp. 351–79). Bator is skeptical of the usefulness of the generalized concept of externalities or nonappropriability as the basis for a theory of market failure. He prefers the term direct interaction for the concept of externalities, and recognizes that:

> Such interaction, whether it involves producer-producer, consumer-consumer, producer-consumer, or employer-employee relations, consists in interdependences that are external to the price system, hence unaccounted for by market valuations. Analytically, it implies the nonindependence of various preference and production functions. Its effect is to cause divergence between private and social cost-benefit calculation. (P. 358).

Granted that such divergence is the essence of market failure, the fundamental question remains: "What is it that gives rise to 'direct interaction', to short circuit, as it were, of the signaling system?" (p. 361).

There can be no doubt that "the divorce of ownership from effective scarcity" or "nonappropriability" or "unpaid factors" is a cause of divergence of social and private benefits and/or costs. The standard example of the interactions between apple and honey production, where the quantity of honey produced is a function not only of resources applied to honey but also of those applied to apple blossoms and vice versa shows clearly how unpaid factors will not be supplied in optimum amounts — in this case because neither apple-growers nor beekeepers appropriate the value of certain of their outputs to the other. The problem here, essentially, is that legal or feasibility considerations prevent certain factors which contribute to output or utility from being included in the relevant function of the decision-making unit. However, these inputs are finely divisible and rationable, in that the amounts used by particu-

lar users can be specified. Further, there are no difficulties with "total conditions."[3] Bator suggests that the failure here is "by enforcement," in the sense
that, while a set of Pareto optimum prices exists and, if established, would raise
no incentive problems, monopoly, legal, institutional, or bookkeeping difficulties preclude the enforcement of such prices. The problem here is the one most
commonly referred to as the "divorce of scarcity from effective ownership";
Bator, therefore, denotes "ownership externalities" as one type in his threefold
typology of of externalities.

Is this sort of difficulty the only explanation for externalities? Suppose there
are no "unpaid factors," but in one form or another indivisibilities are present.
Conditions of increasing returns imply marginal costs below average costs and
losses to producers. Under these circumstances marginal conditions as contained in price-quantity information do not provide the relevant guides to
efficiency; comparison of total benefits and total costs and/or of consumers'
and producers' surpluses is necessary here. Decentralized prices fail in this case
either "by incentive" where prices are determined at marginal costs by administrative fiat and imply losses to producers, or "by structure" where private
market operation implies monopoly and the consequent inefficiencies. In contrast to ownership externalities, the presence of these technical externalities
arises not because of difficulties of appropriation or exclusion which stem from
the inherent character of decentralized markets, but from the nonconvexities
in transformation curves created by the technological phenemenon of increasing returns. Put another way, with regard to ownership externalities a set of
prices exists which, if only means could be found for their enforcement, would
provide the efficient configuration of inputs and outputs; whereas with regard
to technical externalities, problems of incentive and structure would prevent
decentralized decision-makers from reaching the appropriate configuration of
inputs and outputs even if the proper set of prices were established.

How does the concept of social or public goods relate to these sources of
market failure? According to Bator, "public good externalities" are a third
basic type and stem from considerations quite distinct from those for the other
two types. Here the characteristic of joint supply or joint consumption raises
insuperable problems for decentralized pricing because "no single set of relative prices will efficiently ration any fixed bill of goods so as to place the system
on its contract locus" (p. 371). This difficulty arises for public goods even if
there are no technical externalities (nonconvexities) in their production, al-

3. This term is used to denote all the conditions that must be fulfilled to ensure the attainment of a global maximum. Situations may arise when fulfillment of the marginal (first order)
conditions and even of the second order conditions produce only a local maximum such that a
movement away from this maximum reduces welfare but leads eventually to a point higher than
the initial one. The caveat that there are no difficulties with total conditions has the effect of
eliminating this possibility.

though, generally, goods which have substantial joint supply elements also are lumpy (lighthouses, TV networks). Moreover, and most important, the problem of public goods cannot be reduced to another illustration of ownership externalities because the issue is not failure to enforce payment for a known or knowable set of "unpaid factors" but the absence of any mechanism for discerning the valuation of public goods. The mode of failure for public goods is "by existence," that is, by the absence of a set of efficiency prices,[4] rather than "by enforcement," that is, the inability to impose a set of knowable efficiency prices. Bator's conclusion here reinforces the viewpoint, presented earlier (in Chapter 2), that literal inability to exclude is not an essential aspect of public goods. Difficulties of exclusion are associated with problems of enforcement as manifested by nonappropriability of benefits, while the fundamental difficulty of public goods lies in the inability of decentralized markets to reveal the preferences necessary for establishment of optimal prices. The problem is one of existence rather than enforcement.

A FORMAL TAXONOMY OF JOINT SUPPLY, EXTERNAL EFFECTS, AND PUBLIC GOODS

Mishan (1969) distinguishes among the four situations of private goods with and without externalities and collective (public) goods with and without externalities. Also, for each of these pairs he further distinguishes joint from single supply. For each category he sets out a description of the good in formal terminology and presents the equation for optimal conditions in terms of Pareto efficiency.

The framework for the definitions is the general term in which $v_k{}_h^i{}^j$ represents "the increment in value to person j arising from person i's marginal purchase or use of the hth good of activity k." Joint supply is indicated by the use of subscripts to indicate that more than one good (h goods) result from a single activity (k). An activity which produces only one good is represented by a single subscript (for example v_k). External effects are reflected by the superscripts which show that one individual's purchase or use of a good (j) may influence the value received by another (i). A good without externality is, therefore, characterized by a superscript such as 11, 22, or jj to show that no one except the purchaser or user receives any value. An illustration of a jointly

---

4. Application of the notion of failure by "existence" to public goods refers to the inability of any decentralized arrangement to provide a series of prices that are correlates to preferences in a manner analogous to the relation between market prices and quantities taken for private goods. In his application of failure by existence to public goods, Bator does not mean to imply that underlying preferences for public goods do not exist in the same sense as preferences for private goods. Unlike Colm, for example, Bator does not distinguish in any way the nature of preferences for goods that do or do not present problems for market algorithms.

supplied good without externality is $v_k{}^j{}_h{}^j$ and one with externality $v_k{}^i{}_h{}^j$, while a single good without externality is $v_k{}^{ij}$ and with externality $v_k{}^{ij}$.

In this approach, the distinction between private and collective goods does not depend upon jointness or presence of externality and, therefore, cannot be shown by variation in subscripts or superscripts. This distinction hinges, rather, on the nature of the conditions for a social optimum with respect to the two types of goods.

For private goods the optimum condition is that the marginal value of the goods which result from a particular activity be equal for each individual and that these marginal values also equal the marginal cost of the activity. In the simplest case of an activity which produces a single good with no external effects the optimal condition is given by:

$$v_k^{11} = v_k^{22} = \ldots\ldots = v_k^{ss} = c_k \ldots , \tag{1}$$

If joint products prevail, the condition becomes:

$$\sum_{h=1}^{m} v_{kh}^{11} = \sum_{h=1}^{m} v_{kh}^{22} = \ldots = \sum_{h=1}^{m} v_{kh}^{ss} = c_k \ldots , \tag{2}$$

where m equals the number of joint products, s the number of individuals, and the subscript kh indicates that activity k yields more than one good. Summation indicates that the marginal values of all of the h goods produced by activity k must be considered.

Collective goods, in contrast, are such that the optimum condition necessitates that the sum of the marginal values of the kth activity be equal to its marginal cost. A further complication arises for collective goods in that, depending on the nature of the good, the individual who receives the value may or may not be able to adjust quantity taken. For an activity that yields a single collective good with adjustment possible the optimal conditions are:

$$v_k^{11} + v_k^{22} + \ldots\ldots\ldots + v_k^{ss} = c_k \ldots \tag{3}$$

If adjustment is not possible and each individual must take whatever quantity of the collective good which is provided, the condition becomes:

$$v_k^{01} + v_k^{02} + \ldots\ldots + v_k^{os} = c_k \ldots \tag{3'}$$

The superscript 01 in contrast to the superscript 11 of equation (3) shows that individual 1 cannot himself adjust the quantity of collective goods which he takes. The 0 in the superscript is to indicate that the amount of k provided to any individual is not dependent upon the purchase or use of k by any other particular individual but upon the amount of the collective good which all must consume in equal quantities. Finally, joint collective goods can be introduced into this scheme by adding the appropriate subscripts:

optional quantity:

$$\sum_{h=1}^{m} v_{kh}^{11} + \sum_{h=1}^{m} v_{kh}^{22} + \ldots\ldots\ldots + \sum_{h=1}^{m} v_{kh}^{ss} = c_k \ldots \quad (4)$$

nonoptional quantity:

$$\sum_{h=1}^{m} v_{kh}^{01} + \sum_{h=1}^{m} v_{kh}^{02} + \ldots\ldots\ldots + \sum_{h=1}^{m} v_{kh}^{os} = c_k \ldots \quad (4')$$

This formulation, then, clearly distinguishes joint supply, externalities, and private and collective goods. Private and collective goods are distinguished by different optimal conditions and each may entail joint supply or externality or both or neither. The optimum condition for joint private goods with externality is:

$$\left(\sum_{h=1}^{g} v_{kh}^{11} + \sum_{h=g+1}^{m} v_{kh}^{oj} \right) = \left(\sum_{h=1}^{g} v_{kh}^{22} + \sum_{g+1}^{m} v_{kh}^{oj} \right) = \ldots \quad (5)$$

$$\left(\sum_{h=1}^{g} v_{kh}^{ss} + \sum_{h=g+1}^{m} v_{kh}^{oj} \right) = c_k \ldots$$

The first of each pair of terms indicates the marginal value of an individual's chosen purchase or use of the g private goods produced by activity k. The second term reflects the value (positive or negative) of the m-g external effects of activity k, each of which is assumed to have the same effect on valuation regardless of the particular individual whose consumption is responsible for it. The optimum condition requires equality of the sum of the two components of value for each individual and equality of each to the marginal cost of activity k.

Depiction of externality with collective goods depends heavily on assumptions regarding adjustment of quantity. The case where such adjustment is not possible, which conforms to the usual definition of pure public goods, inherently embodies consideration of externalities because the amount of goods taken is not dependent upon the individual's decision to purchase or use. Rather, value depends upon the quantity of the good collectively provided (that is, the appropriate superscript for a particular individual is os and not ss). If, on the other hand, quantities of the collective good are optional, so that individuals do determine the amount of good taken, another term must be added to that which shows the valuation of nonexternality aspects of the good to reflect the presence of externalities. The optimal condition for an optional joint collective good with externalities is:

$$\left(\sum_{h=1}^{g} v_{kh}^{11} + \sum_{g+1}^{m} v_{kh}^{01} \right) + \left(\sum_{h=1}^{g} v_{kh}^{22} + \sum_{g+1}^{m} v_{kh}^{02} \right) + \ldots + \quad (6)$$

$$\left(\sum_{h=1}^{g} v_{kh}^{ss} + \sum_{g+1}^{m} v_{kh}^{os} \right) = c_k \ldots$$

Here, the first term in the parentheses reflects the direct benefits to the individual of his optional consumption of the joint collective goods which result from activity k. The second term represents the value to the same individual of the external effects of these same collective goods. At the same time, this second term also may be interpreted as showing the value of those aspects of collective goods for which quantity adjustment is not possible.

The basic reason for the confusion over the relation of collective goods and externality emerges clearly in this approach. It is a consequence of the identity of the formal definition of nonoptional collective goods with and without external effects. That is, if collective goods are assumed, as they usually are, to be incapable of quantity adjustment by individuals a situation arises where the value of an activity or good to a particular individual depends upon the quantity which others purchase or use. It is formally impossible to distinguish the two; they both are depicted for individual j as $v_k{}^o{}_h{}^j$.

Market Failure and Public Policies

With this discussion of the underlying concepts as background, it is now appropriate to turn to analysis of alternate policies to deal with market failure. Development of an economic theory of the state based on conceptualization of sources of market failure requires identification of the various sources with alternative public policies. Attempts to draw such a theory have met with great difficulties, and although recent developments in linear programming, benefit-cost analysis, and voting solutions have led Baumol to recant somewhat on the negative conclusions he reached in the first edition of *Welfare Economics and the Theory of the State* (1965a), a host of new problems appear to arise for every contribution to the solution of known difficulties.

THE NAIVE APPROACH

Until recently welfare analysis of public policies has tended to follow a rather simplistic notion of the relation between market failure and government economic policy. One aspect of this tendency has been that virtually all sources of market failure were considered ripe for public action of one sort or another without any attempt to compare conceptually, much less empirically, the extent and significance of departures from optimum conditions with the costs, benefits, and incidental distortions resulting from proposed public policies. Another manifestation of the oversimplified approach has been the unnecessarily strict identification of particular sources of market failure with specific policy remedies. As Arrow writes with regard to the theory of externalities: "The best developed part of the theory relates to only a single question: the statement of a set of conditions, as weak as possible, which insure that a competitive equilibrium exists and is Pareto-efficient. Then the denial of any of these hypotheses is presumably a sufficient condition for considering resort to nonmarket channels of resources allocation — usually thought of as government expenditures, taxes, and subsidies" (1970, p. 59).

Problems primarily attributable to ownership externalities as, for example, those which arise with respect to smoke nuisance, common use of an oil pool or fishing bank, training in labor skills, or immunization injections, which could not be internalized through mergers, private clubs, or other means, were to be dealt with by taxes or subsidies designed to reflect the divergence between private cost (or price) and social cost (or valuation). Taxes on tobacco and liquor may be interpreted as attempting to perform such a function, as might the provision of subsidies to firms engaged in on-the-job training. Externalities that originate in technical nonconvexities (decreasing cost) were handled by one or another mechanism of public control to permit marginal cost pricing, such as government ownership or some subsidy arrangement for regulated or unregulated private firms. For public good externalities, the indicated policy was public provision, free of direct charge, financed out of taxation. Ideally, it was argued, such taxation should be of the benefit variety, but problems of preference revelation and administrative considerations led generally to acceptance of general taxation.

COMPLEXITIES INTRODUCED

There is an impressive array of objections, qualifications, and disavowals of the simple, straightforward conception sketched above. The discussion which follows begins with the most general considerations and then moves to more technical specific issues.

The Theory of Second Best. Most proposed applications of the principles of the new welfare economics embodied in such policies as taxation, subsidies, and regulation are attempts to bring about conformance of a small portion of the economy with the optimum conditions for Pareto efficiency. As Baumol says, "It is easy to fall into the temptation to view each marginal rate of substitution that can be brought into line with its price ratio as an improvement and to argue that the more marginal optimality conditions that can be satisfied the better off the world must be" (Baumol, 1965a, p. 17). As specific proposals along these lines came under analytic scrutiny, the conclusion became clear that if optimality conditions in other spheres of the economy are not fulfilled, movement of a small segment toward one of the required marginal equalities might reduce rather than increase welfare. For example, the substitution of an income tax of equal yield for an excise tax might remove the distortion in relative prices caused by the excise, but would not necessarily increase welfare if relative prices in the absence of the excise tax reflect imperfections in factor or product markets in favor of the formerly taxed commodity (Friedman, 1962, pp. 56 – 67). Or, to cite Little's illustration, although an income tax avoids the distortions in relative prices of goods subject to excise taxes it imposes distortions in the relative prices of work and leisure. Judgment in favor of one or the other of these alternatives cannot be made on the basis of superior fulfillment of optimal conditions since either policy leaves some necessary condition unsatisfied (Little, 1959, pp. 123 – 31).

The "theory of second best" is a generalization of these criticisms of partial optimization (Lipsey and Lancaster, 1956 – 57). That is, for any system with a set of specified constraints there exists "necessary conditions" for an optimum; as constraints are expanded, these conditions become more extensive. Fulfillment of the necessary conditions for a more restrictive set of constraints does not imply closer approximation to the optimum for a system with a more extensive set of constraints.

While the logic of this argument is unquestionably correct and introduces a most important caution as regards the need to consider all the relevant constraints in the formulation of optimal rules, its effects on the usefulness of the familiar rules as guides to efficiency may not be so devastating as they appear. Baumol concludes that while the theory of the second best rightly emphasizes the inappropriateness of a few isolated correctives through taxation and subsidies, it "does not require us to stand back helplessly and say that nothing can be done about any externalities problems until they are each and all conquered in one gigantic sweep" (Baumol, 1965a, p. 30).

Mishan (1962) points out that second-best solutions to problems of exchange are likely to be as optimal as first-best solutions, because of the usual assumption that consumers maximize utility subject to whatever constraints they may face. He further argues that producers attempt to maximize profits, and so also will themselves find the second-best solution which achieves this purpose. The major difficulty arises with regard to the top-level optimum in which the optimization rule is that the "subjective rate of substitution between each pair of goods is equal to their technological rate of substitution." Mishan concludes that in such a situation,

> it would seem very reasonable to believe that (i) the smaller are the constrained sectors relative to the remaining ones, and (ii) the larger are the initial discrepancies in the price-marginal cost ratios of the free sectors compared with the constrained sectors, the surer we are to improve matters by optimizing in the free sectors alone than by standing by and sadly sucking our thumbs under the sign of second best. We shall not improve matters quite as much as we might have done if we could but have alighted on the complex of exact second-best rules and could have applied them at no greater cost. But by adopting the simple and familiar rules for the free sectors we may not be very far from this hypothetically ideal position. (P. 214)

Furthermore, in practice there may be sectors or geographic areas of an economy which have little interaction with other sectors or areas. Application of optimal conditions to such segments will increase welfare without the possibility of (significant) off-setting effects elsewhere.

Mishan's conclusions here are quite strong:

> Much of the recent disillusion with welfare economics has arisen from the rather depressing spectacle of familiar universal propositions being tripped up by facile possibility theorems of [the second best] sort. But though it is fashionable to wallow in scepticism about welfare propositions we can and must do better. We can turn our ingenuity to more constructive purpose by attempting to determine the range of conditions under which welfare propositions hold, or hold approximately, and to discover methods that enable us to come within satisfactory distance of an ideal position whose attainment is not practicable. (P. 217)

FURTHER SOURCES OF DIFFICULTIES

A moderate interpretation of the implications of the theory of second best might conclude that it permits retention as meaningful social policy of Pigovian-type tax subsidy schemes for equating social marginal costs and social marginal benefits provided such schemes are scrutinized for concomitant distorting effects. This conclusion, however, has been challenged on several grounds. At the broadest conceptual level, recognition of motives for private bargains and agreements among parties to externalities have led Coase, Buchanan, Olson, and others to question the need for public policy intervention as a general response to externality. Another line of criticism focuses on the costs of tax subsidy systems not only from the standpoint of administration but, more importantly, with regard to the costs of estimating the scope, magnitude, and incidence of the externalities necessary for determination of policy details. Achievement of this latter requirement for tax subsidy systems involves estimation in value terms of nonmarket consequences of economic activities. A technical criticism, potentially even more destructive of the rationale for Pigovian-type policy, is the contention that no theoretical solution exists for so-called nonseparable externalities where mutual interaction raises problems usually associated with oligopolistic markets.[5] A related set of difficulties with regard to Pigovian policy-rules arises from the tendency of externalities to cause violation of the second-order conditions for a maximum. This happens, for example, as a consequence of interdependencies among activities such that expansion of one activity yields increased utility directly but decreases the

5. Nonseparable externalities or, as they also are called, inseparable and reciprocal externalities, arise when the marginal effects of A's activities on A are dependent not only upon his actions but on B's actions as well, and vice versa. A's behavior cannot be determined independently of knowledge of B's actions, but B's actions in turn depend upon those of A. See, in this regard, Otto A. Davis and Andrew Whinston, "Externalities, Welfare and the Theory of Games," *Journal of Political Economy,* June 1962, pp. 241 – 62. This problem is of far less concern in competitive-like markets where behavior units assume themselves to be isolated decision-makers.

utility derived from another activity. Achievement of the global optimum is not accomplished in such a situation by policies which approach "local" maxima. Finally, the issues raised by the concept of merit goods, where consumer preferences are not taken to be the ultimate standard for evaluation of economic activity, suggest that policies should not even aim at equalizing margins derived from individual preferences.

Superimposed on these considerations, of course, is the question of income distribution which is assumed to be "given." Furthermore, the entire discussion of welfare or normative analysis is presented in a static framework. The transition from theoretical propositions to policy is, as we have seen, difficult enough in a static frame which accepts a given income distribution, but policy prescriptions must be relevant to the real world and its constantly changing parameters. When dynamic considerations are introduced and the problem is recast in terms of dynamic efficiency, where trade-offs among growth, distribution, and static optimality in allocation became pertinent, the implications for policy of the analysis of static optimum conditions seem far removed indeed.

This overall review of difficulties and objections to the classic Pigovian policy-remedies for externalities serves to set forth the general framework for discussion. Several of the specific issues, however, are worthy of more detailed treatment.

A MARKET IN EXTERNALITIES

The presence of an "allocationally significant" or Pareto-relevant externality implies the existence of a situation in which there exists uncompensated interdependence with regard to costs or benefits.[6] Put another way, externality signifies that "the extent of the activity may be modified in such a way that the externally affected party, A, can be made better off without the acting party, B, being made worse off" (Buchanan and Stubblebine, 1962, p. 374). If such a situation exists, cannot and will not the party standing to gain from an alteration in the extent of the activity offer to compensate the acting party to effect such an alteration? This line of thought has led to the proposition that in many situations involving externalities public policies such as taxation and subsidy are inappropriate and that, instead, opportunities for private markets in externalities should be encouraged.

6. Among others, James M. Buchanan and William Craig Stubblebine, in "Externality," *Economica,* November 1962, pp. 371 – 84, have shown that such means of dealing with externality as payment of compensation do not eliminate it. Rather these measures attempt to equate social costs and benefits at the margin so that the externality no longer prevents a Pareto optimum from being reached and loses its allocational significance or Pareto relevance. Rational policy calls not for the elimination of all externality but for that outcome which maximizes net benefits or, in other words, leaves in effect the optimum amount of externality. In this regard, see F. Trenery Dolbear, Jr., "On the Theory of Optimum Externality," *American Economic Review,* March 1967, pp. 90 – 103.

The essential argument for a contractual rather than administrative solution to "the problem of social cost" is found in Ronald Coase's article on that subject (Coase, 1960). After an extensive review of the legal history of social cost, Coase develops a numerical illustration of a standard external diseconomy involving smoke from a railroad which damages farm crops. He shows that although a Pigovian policy of forced compensation by the railroad might lead to an optimum solution it would not do so if farmers were induced by compensation to intensify production. Wellisz summarizes Coase's argument here:

> According to Coase, "if the railway could make a bargain with everyone having property adjoining the railway line and there were no costs involved in making such bargains, it would not matter whether the railway was liable for damage caused by fires or not." If the damage suffered by the landowners is greater than the benefits reaped by the railway, the landowners will be able to pay a sum sufficient to induce the railway to curtail operations. If the damage is less than the benefit, it would be unwarranted to prevent the railway from operating because total product would thereby be diminished. (Wellisz, 1964, p. 348)

Coase's illustration is not so simple as it appears and his conclusions depend to a great extent on the market setting within which bargaining leading to contractual compensation takes place. In his example, the railroad gains $20 (equal to social product) by operation of a marginal train but farmers lose $25 (equal to social cost) in crop damage from the operation. A bargain can be struck, it would appear, somewhere between these amounts which will stop the Pareto-inefficient train from running. Generalization of this particular voluntary resolution, however, requires as necessary conditions that (1) bargaining concerns only the marginal unit, (2) bargaining limits are well defined, (3) each party to the bargain knows how much it pays him to offer for a change in the output of another party, and (4) the number of parties involved in the bargain are not so large as to raise the possibility of a "free ride." Achievement of the optimal solution becomes far less likely upon recognition that bargaining probably will involve total rather than marginal quantities. The limits of the bargain thus become the optimal position of each party before any activity takes place. This is the framework traditionally employed in analysis of such other essentially similar bargaining solutions as labor-management negotiations. When these considerations are specified, Coase's explicit assumption of costless bargaining becomes questionable, since the costs of establishing voluntary contracts for situations involving externalities rise as the various conditions are violated. A further difficulty with voluntary agreements arises because the third assumption is not likely to be satisfied if there are reciprocal or nonseparable externalities present. In this case, the value or cost of an externality to any one party depends upon the behavior of other parties, thereby making it extremely difficult if not impossible for any party to establish an estimate of the benefit to it, or the cost of, a marginal unit of the commodity or discommodity in question.

Wellisz's conclusion on the relevance of private bargains as a solution to the problem of social cost is harsh. The conditions under which private markets and voluntary agreements accommodate social costs apply only to exceptional cases which are of little interest to the policy-maker. Judicial or administrative actions are necessary for the frequent situations in which,

> "payment cannot be extracted from the benefited parties or compensation enforced on behalf of the injured parties " [Pigou], that is, with situations where private bargains fail. Moreover, the policy maker cannot be restricted to perfect competition but must also deal with monopolies, and private bargains involving monopolies **may** . . .aggravate resource misallocation instead of achieving a social optimum. (P. 354)

While Wellisz's dissatisfaction with the range of possibilities for private bargains seems well taken, he does not consider another most important aspect of Coase's critique of the Pigovian tax subsidy remedy for externalities. In his extended review of the legal history of compensation for externalities, Coase shows that there is no a priori single correct way of valuation and assignment of external costs. The external effects of an industrial smokestack, for example, may be dealt with by a variety of policies. One general policy might involve installation of a smoke baffle financed by sufferers, consumers of the product, owners of the firm or factors used by the firm, or some combination of these. Another policy could levy taxes on the firm or the commodity (which might or might not be shifted), the proceeds of which could be used to restore the damage done (where physically possible) or to pay compensation related to disutilities incurred. A tax set at an amount to cover damages from smoke, measured in such terms as costs of repainting, laundry, and medical services might be in excess of the amount necessary to compensate those affected for moving away or accepting dirty clothes, walls, and increased illness (Turvey, 1963).

Despite the apparent validity of Wellisz's contention that Coase is too sanguine in his treatment of private bargains, Coase's insistence that a Pigovian tax-subsidy arrangement cannot resolve the fundamental problem of the optimum externality also appears valid. The problem is not simply one of technical difficulties such as determination of an equilibrium tax or subsidy in the presence of externalities. Wellisz has shown (pp. 354 – 61) that a Pigovian system of taxes can be designed for nonseparable as well as separable externalities. The practical question, however, remains of the proper measurement of externalities and establishment of who should legally bear the burden or receive the benefit of the tax or subsidy. Except by accident the welfare maximizing solution will require neither the complete elimination of the externality nor its promulgation at the nonmodified market level. Analysis of the solution to the determination of the optimum externality (Dolbear, 1967) verifies Coase's insistence that no tax subsidy system can ensure the maximization of net product.

If bargaining solutions are impracticable and tax subsidy schemes inefficient, what is the proper role of policy? A negative conclusion is that the existence of uncompensated externalities does not automatically call for government intervention. Decisions regarding such intervention require comparison of costs and benefits. Coase's conclusion that, in general, economists have insufficient grounds for proposing intervention in situations which involve externalities is not based on the results of such comparisions, but on the argument that they cannot be carried out with sufficient objectivity and concern for legal rights. Yet the most pressing economic issues of the day devolve from external effects, broadly conceived. Are we, then, to abjure, in principle, intervention in ecological deterioration, unemployment, inflation, growth, education, and urban decay because economists cannot develop a completely unambiguous and value-free framework for evaluation of externalities? The problems are too vital and the chances of solution through private self-interest too slight to permit default by those intellectually committed to these concerns (Baumol, 1965a, pp. 29 – 30).

INFORMATION, AGREEMENT, AND COSTS

Most of the literature on public policies toward externalities, increasing returns, and public goods accepts the convention in value theory of treating transactions as costless. That is, it is assumed that the acts of selection and implementation of policies impose no significant resource or opportunity costs. If, however, it is recognized that the establishment and maintenance of both private market arrangements and public policies are costly, then it is appropriate that such costs figure in the determination of situations consistent with Pareto optimality.

The relevance of the concept of cost to the establishment of public policies regarding externalities is most complex. There is no question that the creation of public bodies to enact and then implement decisions about taxation, subsidies, transfer payments, and public provision of goods and services is a costly affair. Granted that the overhead expenses of such an establishment are substantial, the administrative costs of making marginal decisions would appear sufficiently minute to be virtually irrelevant to the choice between imposition of alternative public policies or maintenance of a purely market decision. On the other hand, the costs of efforts to apply market mechanisms where externalities are not easily internalized may be inordinately large. As McKean writes, "One reason external effects exist is that the cost of defining, exchanging, and policing rights to benefits or rights not to be afflicted with damages, sometimes exceed the gains to private groups 'internalizing' these effects " (1968, p. 65). Shoup, it will be recalled, uses the term "group consumption" to characterize goods with these properties, and illustrates them by such government services as crime and fire protection, flood control, and highway and street construction and maintenance.

These considerations introduce a further basis for public provision of such goods and services. Not only does price exclusion fail to equate the sum of marginal valuations with marginal cost for these goods but efforts to exclude add to the real resource costs of the goods in question. On the other hand, incremental costs attributable to a public policy solution appear to be only those associated with marginal decisions by an already existing duly constituted body politic with established operating agencies.

Costs of Information. The issue, however, is not this simple when account is taken of the need for information regarding consumer preferences and producer possibilities by the decision-making public body. The concept of costs appropriate for public policy decisions is not the cost of making one more decision no matter what, but of making a "good" decision in terms of the objective function and available means. Regardless of the specifics of the objective function there can be no doubt that information about the consequences of alternative policies is essential to rational decisions (McKean and Minasian, 1966).

For a great many goods, decentralized markets provide at very low cost an enormous amount of information regarding the valuation of goods and services by citizens. Private decision-makers act on the basis of this market information to allocate resources presumably so as to maximize utilities and profits. Their decisions are more or less efficient depending on such factors as market structure, prevalence of externalities, rationality of decision-making, and their knowledge of relevant options. When private decentralized markets are modified by taxes or subsidies or are replaced by public supply, much of the information that markets normally generate is lost or at least distorted. Instead, the body politic must either spend large amounts in an effort to obtain, through interviews, experiments, and other means reliable information about consumer valuations or make decisions in the absence of the more or less perfect information which market decision-makers would have at their disposal were the outcome left in the hands of private markets.[7]

7. To some extent the political counterpart to the interaction of buyers and sellers in the market is the interplay of interest groups. These groups provide information on valuations of alternative policies to political decision-makers that some have likened to the market information provided by prices. The limitations of this analogy have been again pointed out most tellingly by Mancur Olson, Jr., *The Logic of Collective Action* (Cambridge: Harvard University Press, 1965), especially Chapter 5. Discussion of the role of interest groups is found here in Chapter 5 below, which deals with political solutions to public expenditure determination. For the present discus-

Viewed in this context, the question of costs involves a balance between "inefficient" decisions (that is, externality-omitting) reached by decentralized markets on the basis of cheaply obtained, extensive information, and "efficient" decisions (that is, externality-encompassing) reached by public authorities on the basis of less complete, expensively acquired information. McKean and Minasian call this latter procedure "achieving Pareto optimality regardless of cost." Here cost is the opportunity cost of information foregone when, in the interest of taking account of externalities, market imperfections, and other sources of market failure, public policy eschews or so grossly modifies market solutions that it fails to obtain the information which market pricing would provide.

Public policy cannot, in fact, achieve Pareto or any other kind of optimality if relevant information is omitted from consideration. An optimum determined without regard for a relevant cost is not a true optimum. The fundamental issue is the need to balance the costs of a policy of pricing with the costs of substitution for pricing of alternate means of obtaining information on consumers' evaluations. The logic of the position of McKean and Minasian appears unassailable if it is interpreted simply as a reminder that an optimum strategy of decision-making must pay attention to this balance between the anticipated benefits of decisions grounded on information which encompasses externalities and other elements not reflected by markets and the costs of obtaining such information. The issue is quite different if their view is taken as an argument for the general superiority of market information and market solutions over the information generated by political or administrative decision processes, and public solutions. To the distortions of market data and outcomes emanating from unpriced externalities and the host of imperfections that characterize real world markets must be added the information on nonmarket values that the political process encompasses; political leaders and elected representative introduce, at relatively low marginal costs, considerations ranging from attitudes on income redistribution to social, political, and cultural preferences into the determination of government economic policy. It is within a context that recognizes these positive informational elements of political solutions (as well as their defects, of course) that an optimal decision strategy should choose between private market and public policy solutions.

Costs of Agreement. The discussion of cost as an element in dealing with market failure has so far recognized the costs of decision-making, exclusion, and information, but has not yet touched on the most significant aspect of such costs: the external costs of public policies. At this point a brief review of the

---

sion the activities of such groups are irrelevant since they do not provide information about valuations of public policies by specific individuals. Instead, through group behavior, they may indicate the intensity of commonly held attitudes.

context of the issues under discussion can serve to depict the nature and significance of these external costs.

The approach to market failure thus far presented is grounded on an extended concept of externalities in which the criterion for economic efficiency against which markets and public policies are judged is conformance with Pareto optimality. While many other standards for the evaluation of alternative economic situations have been proposed, Pareto optimality is the most restrictive of these criteria, and any policy or position which satisfies the Pareto criterion will at the same time satisfy any of the others.[8]

In the context of the Pareto criterion, any public policy (for example, taxation) not unanimously approved by those legally bound by it produces an external cost of its own which must be compared with the external costs generated by the private market solution to the same problem. The external costs of private market solutions are those discussed earlier in this chapter. The external costs of nonunanimously approved public policies are the costs imposed on the citizen by tax and/or expenditure decisions to which he is legally bound despite the absence of his consent. Since the absence of unanimity is associated with the presence of external costs, the implication follows that only policies approved by all members of a community are acceptable under the Pareto criterion. Recognition of this condition led Wicksell to his renowned unanimity principle, but awareness of the strategic possibilities for withholding consent under a rule of unanimity induced him to moderate this rule in the interest of viable democratic political arrangements.

Of course, it is not impossible to conceive of tax subsidy schemes or tax-financed public good provisions of which all members might approve. Such policies would touch only a trivial portion of the sources of market failure. Efforts to press further encounter the well-known dilemma of toleration of inefficiencies because of an unwillingness or inability to make impersonal comparisons with regard to relative burdens of the incidence of externalities under alternative policies or the abandonment of the Pareto criterion for one of the other less strict alternative criteria for welfare judgments.

Buchanan and Tullock attempt to resolve this dilemma by development of a rationale for political decisions that neither violates Pareto optimality, nor requires the veto power. Their solution emerges from consideration, for any particular individual, of the relation between the potential costs to him of public policies and the proportions of favorable votes which he deems necessary for the approval of such policies. Total costs in this framework emerge as a U-shaped curve which results from the summation of a negatively sloped

8. William J. Baumol, *Economic Theory and Operations Analysis,* 2d ed. (Englewood Cliffs: Prentice-Hall, 1965), Chapter 16, contains a description of the main criteria for welfare judgments developed by economists.

external cost function and a positively sloped decision cost function each of which is dependent on the number of favorable votes required. In Figure 4.1, CN shows the reduction in expected external costs as the requirement for approval of collective action increases from any single individual to all persons. On the other hand, OD shows the rising costs of reaching agreement as collective action must take a form acceptable to an ever greater number of individuals. The lowest point on C+D, the total cost function, indicates that proportion of favorable votes which minimizes expected costs and hence becomes the optimum voting rule. In Figure 4.1, this proportion is OK/ON. For these cost relationships to be valid for each and every individual and, therefore, relevant to a decision to consent to the voting rule, Buchanan and Tullock contend that it is necessary to assume that a particular individual, "cannot predict with any degree of certainty whether he is more likely to be in a winning or a losing coalition on any specific issue." He chooses the rule that most generally will maximize utility in the face of uncertainty regarding particular outcomes. Efforts to maximize utility in this context lead to the acceptance of a rule of less than unanimity with regard to collective action without the need for interpersonal comparisons. Buchanan and Tullock summarize their conclusions:

> If the constitutional decision is a rational one, the external costs imposed by "nonoptimal" choices because of the operation of a less-than-unanimity voting rule will be more than offset by the reduction in the expected costs of the decision-making. . . . An interpersonal comparison of utilities, of a sort, does enter into the analysis here, but note that the individual is not required to compare the utilities of A and B. He is required only to compare his own anticipated gains in utility in those situations in which he is in the decisive group with his anticipated losses in situations in which he is in the losing coalition. This calculus is made possible by the chain of separate choices that is anticipated. Moreover, since this calculus is possible for each individual, constitutional decisions to allow departures from unanimity at the level of specific collective choices may command unanimous consent. (Pp. 94 – 95)

There can be no doubt that the concept of external costs of collective action is highly relevant for the evaluation of public policies aimed at improving economic efficiency. At its most negative this notion is an alternative statement of the compensation approach to the Pareto criterion where no policy can be accepted which does not actually, rather than potentially, compensate all those who lose by it. Only provision of veto power to all individuals ensures conformance with the Pareto criterion and avoids the possibility that the external costs borne by a dissenting party may outweigh the benefits to all others. Consideration of the difficulties of unanimity as a principle of collective action, long recognized by Wicksell and his followers, has led away from the Pareto criterion into a search for viable alternative operational guides to the evaluation of public policies which at the same time eschew interpersonal compari-

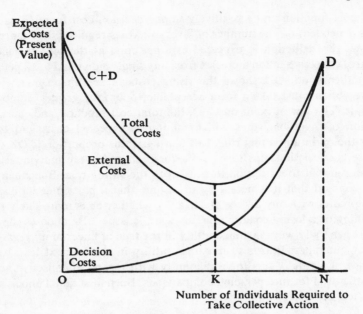

Figure 4.1. External and Decision Costs

sons.[9] Nevertheless, at an operational level the contemporary approach to evaluation of potential policy continues to stress separate evaluation of resource allocation and income redistribution. Choice among policies by balancing these aggregates clearly involves an unknown element of interpersonal gains and losses.

Buchanan and Tullock attempt to salvage the Pareto criterion by introducing the concept of decision-cost and making a distinction between a rule for constitutional choice (which still must be unanimity) and a rule for approval of particular policies (which need be neither unanimity nor majority rule). The key to individual acceptance of a nonunanimity rule for approval of policies is the assumption that each individual is uncertain with regard to his income, class, or other dimensions relevant to the anticipated effects of approved policies. This assumption, along with that of sharply increasing costs of agreement, as the proportion necessary for approval rises, yields a cost-minimizing decision rule other than unanimity. Thus Buchanan and Tullock claim to have divorced Pareto optimality, with its tremendous advantage of the absence of interpersonal welfare comparisons for policy evaluation, from the nonopera-

9. *Ibid.*

tional rule of unanimity. In place of unanimity they propose decision by that proportion of the electorate for which decision-costs are minimized. This proportion, as is shown by the shapes of the functions for external and agreement costs in Figure 4.1, may approach unanimity and is almost certain to be greater than that required under majority rule.

Criticism of this effort to restore to grace the Pareto criterion centers on the issue of the decision rule. First, the basic assumption of individual uncertainty with regard to policy outcomes is highly unrealistic for a functioning society. It is subject to the well-known sociological objections to the concept of the social contract. Second, with respect to the specific rule, a rule of near unanimity permits a small minority to block a policy that would remove existing external costs borne by a large portion of the population as well as preventing imposition of external costs by the majority on the minority. Baumol (1965a, pp.43 – 44) points out that "the obverse of a unanimity rule is the veto power which it gives to any one person if an arrangement is not initially optimal. . . . A unanimity rule is the ideal instrument for the preservation of externalities and inequities which are already extant." In this context majority rule is not simply one arbitrary rule among others. "It is the rule which may be said to minimize the tyranny of a conservative minority while not at the same time offering any minority the unilateral power to institute change. . . . Power resides both in the group which can impose and the one which can prevent. Majority rule is the one arrangement which makes the smaller of these groups as large as possible" (Baumol, 1965a, p. 44).

With the exception of some brief remarks in Chapter 2, the presentation to this point has accepted uncritically the notion of a preference-based criterion for evaluation of economic states and policies. The precise meaning of a "preference-based approach" has received considerable attention in discussions of the appropriate specification of welfare functions. The next section addresses itself to these issues as they relate to public expenditures.

Merit Goods

The term "merit goods" was introduced into public finance literature by Musgrave (1959, pp. 13 – 15) in contrast to the concept of social goods. The latter are, of course, those goods which, because they entail exclusion difficulties and jointness of supply, present problems for decentralized markets but whose optimal supply depends, ultimately, on the preferences of consumers. Merit goods, as Musgrave defines them, present no special problems with respect to exclusion or jointness, but do embody some characteristic or characteristics which make them more or less unsuited to private market provision.

Musgrave's explanation of the feature of merit goods which indicates public rather than private provision is far from clear. His most direct statement on this point is that merit wants[10] are considered, "so meritorious that their satisfaction is provided for through the public budget, over and above what is provided for through the market and paid for by private buyers. . . . The satisfaction of merit wants, by its very nature, involves interference with consumer preferences" (p. 13).

What then are these mysterious goods which, according to Musgrave, have a part in a theory of the public sector based on individual values? One explanation for their inclusion is realism. That is, government does influence the provision of some goods and services which display no special "social" aspects. Entirely to leave such goods out of the theory of public finance would be a serious omission. To include them one simply infers that those in control of the government act with regard to these goods because they believe them to be of some special merit (or demerit) not reflected in market behavior. These aspects of government policy remain, however, outside of a normative model based on individual economic preferences (Musgrave, 1969, p. 125).

Another explanation is that many publicly supplied goods which, at first glance, appear not to entail "social" aspects do, in fact, involve substantial elements of externality, interdependence, or exclusion difficulties which convert them from merit to social goods. Here, public intervention which seems based on imposed preferences is explicable in terms of conventional theories of market failure or their extension, and, therefore, policy turns out not to be in violation of preferences. It is also argued that many goods and services provided by government to the poor, apparently because these things have some merit which redistributive transfers do not possess, turn out on closer inspection to encompass features of social goods. This rationalization for government redistribution in real rather than money terms is less than fully satisfactory. It fails to answer why, if such goods incorporate substantial social benefits, they are provided by government only to the poor.

Finally, however, a third possibility emerges in which a distinction is drawn between individual preferences and individual welfare. That is, the "overt" or revealed preferences of individuals manifested through their market behavior may not lead them to maximize their own welfare. If individual preferences can be "distorted," in the sense of not being conducive to individual welfare,

10. The term "wants" is used by Musgrave in the broad sense of preferences. Although he subsequently disavows the usefulness of distinguishing among types of wants rather than of goods ("Provision for Social Goods," in J. Margolis and H. Guitton, eds., *Public Economics* [New York: St. Martin's Press, 1969], pp. 125–26), in the *Theory of Public Finance* he suggests that social, private, and merit goods are manifestations of essentially different sorts of preferences that he terms social, private, and merit wants (pp. 8–9).

a potential role of government arises to correct the effects of distorted preferences.

The question of the validity of this argument for public intervention hinges on the precise definition of preferences and introduces the more fundamental issues of the meaning of such other basic notions as consumer sovereignty, choice, satisfaction, utility, and welfare. This range of concerns, which Bergson terms "meta-welfare economics" (1966, p. 62), has proved to be extremely complex. The central issue for the theory of economic policy, however, is relatively straightforward. What exactly does it mean to define the normative standard, and hence the basis for policy prescription, as resting on the underlying preferences of the members of the economy or society? Put differently, is there any middle ground between authoritarianism and individual preferences such that one may justify policies with "interfere with" or "violate" preferences as nonetheless consistent with democratic values? The ultimate issue here is nothing less than specification of the fundamental standard in the normative approach to economic analysis.

The literature on merit goods is, in effect, an extension of the discussion of the appropriate arguments (factors, elements) in a social or individual welfare function. If the view is taken that individual preferences, whatever they may be, are the single relevant item in the welfare function, then the issue is, by definition, resolved. The normative standard of an economy is welfare, and welfare is a function, solely, of preferences. There is no place in such a normative theory for "interference" with preferences (McLure, 1968). On the other hand, if distinctions can be drawn among choice, preferences, satisfactions, utility, and welfare, as in the discussions of the content of welfare functions, a far wider range of issues is opened. It then becomes appropriate to inquire whether factors in addition to those associated with market failure should interpose between preference-based behavior and normative evaluation on the basis of individual values. Several possible sources of discrepancy between what Bergson calls "overt" preferences and economic welfare have been suggested: (1) ignorance, (2) uncertainty, (3) interdependencies, (4) evaluation difficulties, and (5) household inefficiency and irrationality.

PREFERENCES, SATISFACTIONS, AND RELATED NOTIONS

Bergson has explored, more carefully than anyone else, the issues involved in the selection of the appropriate arguments in welfare functions. He concludes that "each welfare economist, then, must finally decide for himself how to represent the criterion" (1966, p. 57). Bergson suggests that the relations among preferences, satisfaction, and welfare are, at bottom, empirical questions, but that they may, in principle, be distinguished. His illustration of the distinction is:

Should the individual buy cigarettes in ignorance of injurious effects on health, and yet somehow learn of such effects while smoking, overt preferences would diverge from satisfactions, but the latter might still be indicative of welfare. Should the individual remain in ignorance of the injurious effects, overt preferences might conform to satisfactions, but these might diverge from welfare. Should the individual continue to buy cigarettes after learning of the injurious effects, one might still have misgivings about the relation of his overt preferences to welfare, though admittedly the individual might feel that they were as satisfying as any might be. (P. 54)

INTERFERENCE WITH CONSUMER PREFERENCES

If by overt consumer preferences is meant actual market choices (or the hypothetical choices which in this study have been referred to in terms of preferences for public goods) then there are several reasons adduced for interference in the interest of attainment of higher levels of individual welfare. The issue, essentially, is that the normative standard for the economy is welfare and not overt preferences and that these may diverge. This question is entirely separate from the matter of preference aggregation and the derivation of a social welfare function. The point is that individual welfare and individual preferences are not necessarily identical. In some of the situations where they are not, the state may be in a position to enhance individual welfare by correction of "distorted" preferences; that is, those that are not consonant with welfare. In this case, it is maintained that interference with preferences is neither authoritarian nor a violation of the conventional individualistic norms for evaluation of economic situations.

Ignorance of alternatives is perhaps the clearest case for interference with preference-based behavior. If an individual is unaware of the consequences of his economic actions or lacks knowledge of viable alternatives then he will not attain the maximum level of welfare which his constrained situation would permit. One can argue that apparent ignorance may, on closer inspection, prove to be a preference for satisfactions derived from activities alternative to conquest of ignorance. This argument may have merit up to a point — the costs of acquisition of knowledge must be included in determination of whether welfare is at a maximum — but carried to the tautological conclusion that extant ignorance is always the result of an optimum pursuit of knowledge to the margin it is nonsensical.

Extensive implications for public policy emerge as a consequence of acceptance that ignorance can provide a legitimate rationale for interference with preferences. As Head (1966) has argued, ignorance of consequences broadly defined can encompass the effects of drugs, feeblemindedness, and other apparent causes of irrational behavior, of advertising, of the hard-to-evaluate products and services of the public sector such as the national defense establishment, and even of uncertainty with respect, for example, to future employment prospects or occupational choice. Once the idea is accepted that individuals' preferences do not always reflect what is good for them (by their own standards, not those of "experts") almost any interference becomes hypothetically justifiable as still falling within an individualistic framework.

In addition to the broad concept of ignorance, the other major basis for correction of individual preferences is interdependent utilities. Here the issue is not the tangible interdependence usually associated with externalities. What is involved is a psychic interdependence such that the economic status of others appears in an individual's utility function. In this case, it is not tangible effects on me of your behavior, such as noise or smoke, that reduces my welfare, or your flower garden that increases it. Rather, it is the psychic effect of your smoking marijuana or wearing your hair long which reduces my satisfactions, and the fact that you go to church which increases them. As a result, any policy which curtails certain of your acts and promotes others benefits me and all those who share my values. Since I benefit from such policies whether or not I pay any of the costs incurred, there is an incentive for me not to reveal my preference and to "free-ride."

MERIT GOODS AND PUBLIC POLICY

It is difficult to distinguish between distorted preferences due to ignorance and irrationality and the genuine absence of superior alternatives in the face of risk and uncertainty. For some goods uncertainty, unfamiliarity, ignorance, or interpersonal interdependencies may drive a wedge between individual preferences and individual welfare. At the same time, these conditions may also give rise to tangible or psychic external effects. Both situations present the opportunity for public intervention to improve total social welfare.

Public measures to deal with ignorance, uncertainty, and risk range from pure food and drug laws to regulations regarding industrial safety, social insurance, and unemployment compensation. Lack of information and inability to evaluate the quality of commodities may serve to strengthen monopolistic tendencies, and government policies to inform and educate consumers can be interpreted as attempts to improve the efficiency by which consumers effectively spend their incomes. Such policies do not undermine the preference basis for public programs, and it may be argued further that public policies such as unemployment compensation and even direct redistributive transfers to low income families provide for preference-based arrangements to reduce the risk inherent in a market-organized economy. What appear to be goods provided outside preferences quite frequently are goods demanded on the basis of individual preferences for avoidance of some of the most distressing consequences of the uncertainty and risk inherent in a market system. Some policies intended to avoid personal disaster consequent upon risk, such as fire and life insurance, are efficiently organized under private markets, but many policies for dealing with risk and uncertainty involve substantial external benefits and may be most efficiently provided through the public sector (Head, 1966, pp. 10 – 12).

Attribution of a preference basis for the public provision of certain apparent merit goods does not fully encompass the motives for the provision of merit goods that are responses to irrationality and other sources of divergence of welfare from preferences, but it narrows the relevance of this concern. The previous paragraph suggests that public policies to dispel ignorance or to eliminate or reduce risk and uncertainty need not be thought of as providing merit goods. Treatment of the feebleminded, mentally ill, or those under the influence of drugs scarcely raises fundamental problems for economic policy, as it does for social policy. A remaining ground for merit goods is the provision of goods for one group by another "simply" because such philanthropy appears in the grantors' preference functions.

The phenomenon of interdependent utility functions where external effects arise because one individual's welfare is influenced by another's consumption raises serious problems for normative economic analysis. The phenomenon has been used to justify public rather than private redistribution schemes. The argument is that when *one* individual makes a unilateral transfer to the "poor" *all* those whose utility functions are positively influenced by a reduction in poverty gain; these external benefits cannot be appropriated by the single individual but are relevant to the optimal amount of redistribution which a public policy might achieve through compulsory transfers. Here again, an apparent interference with preferences turns out to be a redistributive externality. Acceptance of interdependent utilities, however, carries with it the further implication that preference-directed behaviors of individuals or groups which reduce the utility of other individuals or groups may be curtailed, again, not on grounds of authoritarian interference, but on externality considerations. In this case, those whose sensibilities are offended may term the offensive behavior irrational, while, in fact, it merely enters as a negative argument in their utility functions.

Acceptance of the legitimacy of psychic interpersonal dependencies introduces a potential for justification of the most outrageous public and private policies on the grounds of such psychic interpersonal dependencies in utility functions. It then becomes possible to rationalize as consistent with consumer preferences such depersonalizing practices as slavery and racial and ethnic discrimination. On the other hand, these considerations also provide a way of introducing altruistic and humanitarian considerations and the concept of extended sympathy into the usually narrow, hedonistic behavior of the utility maximizer.

The major element which appears to distinguish so-called merit goods from social or private goods is that consumers are assumed to have a set of preferences for the latter two which are based on complete knowledge and which do not involve psychic interpersonal utilities. On the other hand, the problems raised in the literature on merit goods are those which arise in relation to goods or services for which, in Bergson's terminology, individual preferences, due to uncertainty, unfamiliarity, ignorance, or interdependent utilities, are not closely linked to individual welfare. At the same time, goods characterized by such difficulties in preference evaluation also tend to be those which entail conventional externalities and jointness. Much of the confusion in the merit goods controversy lies in the difficulty in separation of these elements commonly found together.

A final word is in order on the relation of preferences to dimensions of social welfare other than the economic. When public policies allocate resources in a manner which appears inconsistent with consumer sovereignty, individual preferences are not necessarily being violated. Consumer sovereignty deals only with "economic" preferences and public policy deals with the full range of individual tastes. It is possible, although of course, not necessary that such actions reflect conformance with the noneconomic dimensions of individual preferences.[11]

AN EXISTENTIAL VIEW OF PREFERENCES

A quite different approach to analysis of the normative values which underlie public policy is found in the works of those who take what might be called an existential view of preferences. Both Rothenberg and Lindblom, for example, appear to believe that preferences for alternative social states are manifested only through observable and accepted public policies (Lindblom, 1961; Rothenberg, 1961, pp. 317 – 29). This view recognizes the impossibility, in practice, of distinguishing economic from noneconomic preferences for public activities and of separating merit from social wants in the public sector. The resultant of all relevant preferences is manifest in the ensuing public policies if these actions are accepted. As is shown in the discussion in Chapter 5, where this argument is developed in detail, the essential ingredient for the effective revelation of preferences relevant to public policy is a procedure for the preparation and approval of policies in which all groups with important interests at issue have an appropriate influence. Failure of policy to conform to preferences results in reactions ranging from electoral defeat to revolt. This approach

11. Abram Bergson, *Essays in Normative Economics* (Cambridge: Harvard University Press, 1966), p. 65, writes on this matter: "The scope of welfare economics is conventional, but the relevant convention concerns the nature of the causes of social welfare rather than the nature of the states of mind to be considered. Thus, reference is to welfare as this is affected by economic causes, and to economic welfare only in this sense rather than as a category that is necessarily psychologically distinct from noneconomic welfare. And rather than presume that economic causes are not offset by noneconomic causes, it would seem reasonable to consider this as a matter to be evaluated in each case."

undermines the elaborate policy guides that follow from efforts to modify the system in accordance with conditions for Pareto optimality. Instead, policy-makers seek consent and consensus. The operational content of this approach lies in developing a positive theory of political agreement. Unlike the economic approach in which the political mechanism is seen as an unsatisfactory but necessary substitute for the market as an indicator of preferences in certain areas, the existential view accepts the political process as distinct from the market and as the legitimate mechanism for the revelation of social preferences.

Intriguing as this approach may be, as a normative rather than positive standard, it appears to fall on a crucial issue: legitimation by consent is not equivalant to optimization. This criticism is not intended to be one that can be met by the assertion that legitimation may be a "second-best" solution because full optimization is too costly a decision criterion. Rather what is meant is that popular acceptance or even endorsement of a particular policy does not imply that alternative policies with equivalent or even lower decision-costs might not provide higher levels of welfare. For example, securing consent for one policy rather than another may be entirely a consequence of the accepted policy being presented first. While the political process provides for periodic elections and legislative sessions, this is not analogous to recontracting, which in perfect private markets ensures that, of all acceptable bargains, the equilibrium solution is the one for which utility is maximized. Existence of gains from trade to all parties at one price does not prove that at another price the sum of the gains might not be greater. Put differently, Arrow's possibility theorem implies that there is no *logical* way to infer from a pattern of observed public policies either a unique set of individual preferences or a unique social welfare function which is consistent with the observed policies. It is, of course, possible simply to define or identify observed social states as points on a social welfare function, but there is no way to be sure that, given the constraints, attainable social states other than those observed would not have occasioned even higher levels of social welfare.

This discussion of merit goods reveals some of the serious difficulties in specification of a normative basis for public economic policy. Inclusion of a concept of merit wants which encompasses the notion of authoritarian interference with preferences destroys any theory of public policy based on consumer preferences, the traditional lodestone of economic efficiency. Extension of the concept of externalities reduces the extent of nominal interference with preferences but fails to resolve the difficult problems of those situations where conformance with preferences does not maximize welfare. Also the extended externality concept applied to interdependent utilities introduces possibilities for public policies based on individuals' attitudes towards the behavior of others. Finally, an existential approach which substitutes the political process for an economic calculus resolves the entire problem of preference aggregation but at the expense of any objective criteria for efficiency.

Which Goods Should Be Public?

Perhaps the salient conclusion, thus far, is that theories of market failure and analysis of conditions for optimum resource allocation are not sufficient to determine the ideal organization of economic activities. If, for example, analysis indicates that policy for correction of a particular instance of market failure requires expansion of output beyond the quantity which private markets would provide, choices remain among such organizational arrangements as: (1) public provision free of direct charge with production by private firms, (2) public provision free of direct charge with production by public enterprises, (3) public subsidization of private producers, (4) direct public subsidies to consumers applicable only to specified privately produced goods, and (5) public production with sale at prices below cost. To this partial list of organizational arrangements which involve public participation of one sort or another in pursuit of more optimal allocation of resources must be added private arrangements such as clubs and other conventions for collective voluntary organization of the provision of goods or services. Thus, recognition of the existence of significant externalities does not necessarily imply public organization of production or even public expenditures. The issue is, what criteria, if any, provide the basis for an economic determination of the "publicness" of particular goods?

BUCHANAN'S APPROACH

Buchanan's statement of this problem is: "Under what circumstances will collective-governmental supply be more efficient than private or noncollective supply?" His answer is that "the results that may be predicted to emerge from publicly-organized supply must, in each case, be compared with those that may be predicted to emerge from noncollective, voluntarily organized market supply" (Buchanan, 1968, p. 172). Such comparison is best carried out by comparison of the costs and benefits of public and of private organization with respect to the distribution, allocation, and financing of those goods for which the market solution is other than Pareto optimal. Buchanan's approach is, first, to classify goods in accordance with the extent and character of their externalities and, then, to evaluate the appropriateness of private or public organization of their provision.

Starting with the assumption that externalities or spillovers are the major obstacle to an optimal allocation of resources by private markets, Buchanan classifies goods in accordance with their degree of indivisibility or jointness. He argues, however, that the size of the interacting group is highly relevant to the classification of a good in terms of divisibility or indivisibility. There are goods such as swimming pools that are highly indivisible among rather small groups while others, like national defense, are highly indivisible among very large groups. On the other hand, some goods may be moderately divisible among small groups (Buchanan suggests portable fire extinguishers as an illustration) and others also moderately divisible, but among larger groups, as, for example, innoculation against communicable diseases.

From this twofold classification Buchanan derives five categories of goods and services: (1) pure private goods and services — all goods fully divisible; (2) partially divisible goods and services — interactions limited to groups of critically small size; (3) partially divisible goods and services — interactions extend over groups of critically large size; (4) fully indivisible goods and services — interactions limited to groups of critically small size; (5) pure public goods and services — all goods fully indivisible over groups of all sizes. Buchanan recognizes that "small" and "large" are relative terms and that the size of the political decision-making unit determines whether an indivisibility will encompass all or only a few members of the group. What may be a small-number indivisibility for a nation may be a large-number indivisibility for a school district.

The efficiency of alternative arrangements for the provision of each of these five categories of goods and services must be evaluated on the basis of each of the relevent dimensions of distribution, allocation, and finance. Distributional efficiency refers to the effectiveness by which collective or private organization would distribute quantities of each of the five types of goods if they were provided, like manna from heaven, in fixed amounts. Buchanan's conclusion is that for goods and services in both categories 1 and 2 there "will arise a pricing-structure out of the ordinary utility-maximizing behavior of individuals." True, case 2 involves indivisibilities which would not be taken into account in a pricing-structure based on individual utilities. However, since spillovers in this case are limited, "we should expect small groups to form and to bid among themselves and among individuals for the scarce quantity. This will take place until some distribution is achieved that does take the benefit spillovers into account" (p. 180). Category 3 where indivisibilities are extensive, may appear to require a mechanism for distribution other than the market, but this turns out not to be so. Although spillovers are not taken into account by the market distribution, Buchanan's assumption that all persons secure identical spillovers ensures that no alternative distributional arrangement will increase the benefits derived from the spillovers. The market solution to distribution is as good as any other. Distribution of those goods which are completely indivisible over small groups (category 4) will take place as "sharing clubs" emerge equal in size to the group over which the good is indivisible. These clubs will bid for the available quantity of such goods and the clubs containing those members who most strongly desire the good will win out.

Only in category 5, the case of pure public goods, will a market distribution fail to be efficient. Here, distribution can hardly be said to exist, since there is no way of dividing the commodities among individual members of the group. Any effort to impose user charges, therefore, will introduce distributional inefficiency by excluding some members while offering no gains whatsoever to other members.

Comprehensive evaluation of alternative organizational arrangements involves replacement of the assumption that goods arise manna-like by assumptions regarding production and costs. Introduction of production possibilities requires performance of both allocation and financing functions. Buchanan contends that for categories 1, 2, and 4 those market prices which resolve the distribution problem also solve, efficiently, the functions of allocation and finance. The prices which serve to distribute these kinds of goods and services in accordance with the utilities placed upon them by the members of the group also function to signal producers with regard to quantities to be produced and provide adequate revenues to cover the costs of such levels of production. If, therefore, market organization were not the arrangement for the provision of such goods, efficiency criteria would indicate a governmental arrangement virtually identical with that of the market.

While efficient distribution of goods falling into category 3 proves amenable to a purely market solution, efficient production and finance of goods with extensive spillovers may well require departure from market pricing. In this category, which includes goods and services traditionally viewed as encompassing significant externalities, such as education, direct user pricing is feasible but private marginal valuations or marginal costs diverge from social valuations and costs leading to under or overproduction. Buchanan recognizes, here, a case for tax pricing which requires collectivization of finance, but does not imply public provision. Individuals still purchase goods on a quid pro quo basis but at prices influenced by collective action.

Does this approach reserve for collective provision category 5, the pure public goods? Not necessarily, according to Buchanan, because the distributional inefficiencies of a quid pro quo solution to pure public goods must be weighed against the allocational and financial inefficiences of collective supply. From the standpoint of finance the inefficiencies of collective supply are the traditional excess burdens of taxation where, because taxes are compulsory payments which cannot always be levied on economic surplus, they distort at the margin. With regard to allocation, the indivisible character of the goods in question implies equivalent quantities provided to all, making it impossible for each individual to equate marginal valuations with his tax charges. For any given tax scheme some individuals would desire more, and others less of publicly provided goods, so that all allocational inefficiency prevails. Ultimate determination of whether provision of a good of category 5 should be privately or collectively organized depends on an analysis of the relative net benefits from exclusion devices which permit user prices to be charged in contrast to collective supply.

EVALUATION OF BUCHANAN'S ANALYSIS

Buchanan's effort to disentangle collective supply from public finance involves a method of classifying goods and services and an analysis of the emergent categories. Both aspects are worth detailed examination.

Categorization of Spillovers (Musgrave versus Buchanan). Musgrave as well as Buchanan sees value in a taxonomy of spillovers. In regard to the usefulness of such classifications both stand in opposition to Samuelson, who proposes distinction only between purely private goods and all other goods involving some degree of externality. Yet Samuelson in the same article in which he rejects a taxonomy of goods suggests "serious analytical studies of cases where public goods situations can be solved by algorithms immune to bilateral-monopoly or game-theoretic objections" (1969a, p. 110). Attempts at categorization of externalities or spillovers may provide a useful basis for just such analysis.

The approach followed by Musgrave (1969, pp. 134 – 42) is similar to that of Buchanan in that their polar cases are pure private and pure public goods. Musgrave, however, chooses to reflect the extensiveness of spillovers (or indivisibilities) in terms of a continuous coefficient rather than by means of the twofold classification of degree of indivisibility and size of interacting group used by Buchanan. Lesser degrees of spillovers, which in Buchanan's framework may be the consequence either of a good of generally greater divisibility or of the consideration of a more extended group, are in Musgrave's approach reflected by a discount factor which applies to the utility received by one person from a commodity provided by or possessed by another. At the same time that Musgrave compresses into a single measure Buchanan's distinction between degree and extent of divisibility, he adds the possibility of asymmetrical spillovers such that B may gain from A's provision of a commodity but not vice versa. Further, Musgrave distinguishes spillovers where goods provided by A are essentially substitutes for own consumption by B (A's insect-spraying is to some extent a substitute for neighbor B's spraying), from nonsubstitute spillovers where A's provision of a good yields B a consumption quite different in kind from that of A (education of A may increase B's consumption of good conversation from talking with better educated A).

Possible categories of spillovers for "substitute externalities" which emerge from Musgrave's classification are:

I. *Pure Private:* $\quad U_A = U_A (Y_A); U_B = U_B (Y_B)$ $\hfill (7)$

Utilities of each individual depend solely upon own consumption.

II. *Symmetrical Substitute Externalities:* $\quad U_A = U_A \ (Y_A + \beta Y_B);$ $\qquad$ (8)

$$U_B = U_B \ (Y_B + \gamma Y_A)$$

Utilities of each depend on own consumption plus other's consumption, with β and γ being the discount applied to the consumption by others. If β and γ are equal to one for each party there is "full and reciprocal spillover" which defines a pure social good. Under these circumstances:

$$U_A = U_A \ (Y_A + Y_B); U_B = U_B \ (Y_B + Y_A) \qquad (8')$$

III. *Asymmetrical Substitute Externalities:* $\quad U_A = U_A \ (Y_A + \beta Y_B);$

$$U_B = U_B \ (Y_B) \text{ or } U_A = U_A \ (Y_A); U_B = U_B \ (Y_B + Y_A) \qquad (9)$$

Utility of one party depends on the other's consumption but not vice versa. Nonsubstitute externality also can be shown as follows:

IV. *Symmetrical Nonsubstitute Externalities:* $\quad U_A = U_A(Y_A, Y_B);$

$$U_B = U_B \ (Y_A, Y_B) \qquad (10)$$

The absence of the plus sign between the arguments of the utility functions indicates that Y_A and Y_B are not substitutes but rather entirely different and hence rival goods. Education of A (Y_A) may be an argument in B's utility function, but B's own demand for education (Y_B) is not diminished by A's schooling.

It is, of course, possible to have a mixture of substitute and nonsubstitute externalities. An illustration of such a combination gives:

V. *Symmetrical Mixed Externalities:* $\quad U_A = U_A \ (Y_A, Y_A + \beta Y_B);$

$$U_B = U_B \ (Y_B, Y_B + \gamma Y_A) \qquad (11)$$

As Musgrave points out in this case "outside" consumption cannot substitute for all aspects of "own" consumption.

The use to which Musgrave puts his taxonomy of spillovers is most illuminating. He does not attempt to deduce principles for determining when collective organization of the provision of one or another category of spillovers is called for. Instead he suggests that the "attraction of the present formulation is that it neatly transforms the all-or-nothing case of the pure social good into a generalized theory of public subsidy" (Musgrave, 1969, p. 139). That is, the presence of spillins is an indication of willingness to pay subsidies to originators of spillouts, and the specification of discount factors and asymmetries permits estimation of the optimum rate of subsidy and location of input. Musgrave's graphic illustration of the determination of the optimum solution is well worth examination (pp. 138 – 42) but, since it is not essential for the question at issue here, it is not shown. What is relevant is that Musgrave's conclusions relate to the matter of optimum rates of subsidy and not to optimum organizational arrangements:

> The fact that governments typically provide social goods where a 100 percent subsidy is called for, but rarely where a lesser rate is indicated, shows a rigidity in social behavior which leads to inefficient results. If many goods are indeed of the mixed type, an extensive set of subsidies at varying rates would be called for.
>
> Determination of the proper subsidy rate is undertaken through the budget process and poses precisely the same difficulties (including non-revelation of preferences, choice of point on Johansen's WW´ curve, etc.) already familiar from the polar case of social goods. (P. 141 – 42)

Unfortunately, this provocative and otherwise illuminating effort to characterize spillovers appears to yield little guidance to those concerned with the choice between private and public organization of supply.

An Evaluation of Buchanan's Schema. What can be said with regard to which goods should be public if so profound a student of the public sector as Musgrave is able, on economic grounds, to derive only a theory of public subsidy and not one of public organization? Buchanan's analysis of this matter, it will be recalled, left only the case of goods with substantial indivisibilities extending over large groups as qualifying for public provision, and even here problems of excess burdens associated with allocation and finance might balance the scales in favor of a market solution. Buchanan's provocative dissection of the externality basis for public organization, however, appears to go a bit too far. While in principle one can agree that even for his category 5, that of pure public goods, it is possible that the distributional inefficiencies of a quid pro quo approach may be counterbalanced by failures of public organization to ascertain preferences and to establish tax liabilities that operate as pseudo-prices, the great likelihood is that the balance will go in the other direction. That is, where goods are provided under conditions of substantial joint supply with difficulties of quantity adjustment by individual consumers the strategic elements that prevent revelation of preferences will operate to preclude or at least seriously impair the establishment of satisfactory user prices essential to the feasibility of a market solution. It must be recognized, as noted in Chapter 2, that the exclusion devices which in some cases may permit private organization also incorporate excess burdens. The probabilities of achieving efficiency seem considerably greater under public organization of essentially pure public goods.

In addition, Buchanan's ingenious argument for rescuing from public operation category 3 goods, where externalities are significant over a relatively large group, hinges on the assumption of completely symmetrical spillovers. The reason there is no problem with regard to the location of inputs in Buchanan's category 3 is because all parties benefit equally so that no particular distribution is preferable to any other. Subsidies or taxes are required in this case to adjust for discrepancies between private and social valuation, but under Buchanan's assumptions these can be accomplished without regard to the distribution of inputs. If, however, this rather unrealistic limiting case, which according to Musgrave's formula is

$$Y_A = U_A (Y_A + \beta Y_B) \text{ and } Y_B = U_B (Y_B + \gamma Y_A)$$

(where β and γ both equal one) is replaced by the more usual condition of less than complete symmetry of spillovers, benefits then do depend on the location of consumption (or input). In consequence, distribution does matter and a strong case for public organization arises. The issue here is that when location (in either the geographical or personal sense) of a good does yield significant spillovers whose benefits are unevenly distributed among the members of the (relatively large) group, efficiency requires that the distribution of benefits be taken into account in the decision regarding location. Since, however, these benefits are external, market arrangements cannot reflect them satisfactorily and public organization well may be the most efficient solution. Of course, as Buchanan insists, the distribution gains (and losses) of public organization must be compared with the allocational and financial costs, but, clearly, abandonment of the assumption of complete symmetry of spillovers reintroduces this case to relevancy for public supply.

A BROADER FRAMEWORK

Despite these criticisms of Buchanan's ever-vigilant efforts to prevent conceptual overextension of the economic rationale for public supply, the fact remains that it is indeed difficult logically to take the final step from public finance to public supply. The thrust of this chapter can be described as an effort to mark out a path from the market principle (private supply) to the budget principle (public supply) using only the tools of economics. What has emerged is a depiction of the thickets that envelop not only this long path but those shorter paths between market organization and tax and subsidy schemes, regulation, and other forms of public control and policy. However, resolution of the problems which preclude the establishment of ideal tax and subsidy arrangements or those which prevent the establishment of rules for public utilities and other regulated industries still would not provide a basis *in principle* for determination of whether provision of a good should be organized publicly. Resolution of these issues would provide the basis for calculations in terms of benefits and costs relevant to such determination. But each situation would have to be decided on its own merits. The conclusion which follows from this extensive review of the economic considerations underlying the choice between public and private organization of supply is that little if anything can be said in principle on the basis of economic considerations. This is in marked contrast to the question of public finance, where a good deal more can be said, although contemporary analysis has revealed that even here efficient public policy must be based on detailed investigation of individual situations.

Efforts to develop a more satisfactory foundation for the analysis of public supply take as their point of departure recognition that economic values and objectives are not the only criteria for public organization of economic activity. Decisions with regard to the mode of organization of economic activity influence social, political, cultural, and other aspects of human life, and these considerations as well as economic efficiency rightly have a place in a normative theory of economic organization. The chapters which follow develop in detail theories of the behavior and objectives of the public sector which incorporate policital and other perspectives. A most useful transition to these chapters is an attempt by Francesco Forte, the Italian economist, to develop a conceptual basis for the public sector based on a few essential principles of economics and democratic government (Forte, 1967, pp. 39 – 46).

Forte agrees that externality and jointness provide the basis for a theory of subsidy, or transfer as he calls it, but do not explain public organization of supply. He suggests that the explanation for the choice of public rather than private economic organization lies in characteristics of goods other than externality or jointness. Among these characteristics Forte lists (p. 41):

(a)   the possibility that only the government as a public institution is able to provide a service of the required standard;

(b)   the possibility that entrusting some services to private organizations might increase their political power so that a general loss of independence for other private and public entities would result;

(c)   the possibility that only governmental units would be large enough to provide the service efficiently;

(d)   the possibility that business firms of sufficiently large scale, even if economically possible, would be so large as to threaten the freedom of the others;

(e)   the existence of as yet unexploited economies of scale in governmental institutions already justified by other reasons, which therefore may be charged with additional services of a given nature without much marginal cost.

For identification, these characteristics may be simplified as:

(a)   maintenance of required standards
(b)   avoidance of excess political power
(c)   scale efficiences
(d)   avoidance of excessive economic power
(e)   advantages of overhead facilities

The clear advantage of this approach is that it combines economic and sociopolitical considerations. A particular function such as education, that involves externalities, is considered for public organization also on grounds such as the need for required standards, the avoidance of undue political influence from a narrow class-based private system, and perhaps scale efficiencies. This schema can provide a rationale for public organization of education in response to the purely economic argument in favor of public subsidy but private operation of schools. The range of applications of this framework is quite broad. Forte mentions, among other illustrations, police services that can to a degree be provided privately with subsidy arrangements to take account of the external benefits — for example, of patrol. Some police services, however, would also have to be organized publicly to ensure that standards with regard to private freedom and private secrecy were maintained and that there was no undue political influence exerted. Only a police force responsible to public authority should have the right to arrest citizens, and only a public prison system should have responsibility for carrying out sentences of the courts, even if the Hilton chain could provide more efficiently operated jails.

Forte's approach proves highly useful only if the political or social principles that underlie points (a) and (b) are accepted. Clearly (c), (d), and (e) are rather conventional principles of economic efficiency; and (e) even requires the existence of a substantial organization for public supply before it becomes relevant for still further government distribution. This way of looking at Forte's schema reveals the fact, perhaps self-evident to all but the welfare economist, that a normative theory of public organization of scarce resources must include an element to represent preferences for political as well as economic outcomes.

The failure of normative economics to produce a set of principles for determination between public and private organization of economic activities is, at bottom, not due to its analytic shortcomings or even the inability to make interpersonal comparisons. It is instead a necessary consequence of the impossibility of deriving a meaningful normative model of organizational choice on the grounds of economic considerations alone.

References for Chapters 2, 3, and 4

Arrow, Kenneth. *Social Choice and Individual Values.* New York: Wiley, 1963.
————. "The Organization of Economic Activity: Issues Pertinent to the Choice of Market versus Nonmarket Allocation," in J. Margolis and R. H. Haveman, eds. *Public Expenditures and Policy Analysis.* Chicago: Markham, 1970, pp. 59 – 73.
Barone, Enrico. "The Ministry of Production in a Socialist State," in Friedrich A. von Hayek, ed. *Collectivist Economic Planning.* London: Routledge and Sons, 1935, pp. 245 – 290.
Bator, Francis M. "The Simple Analytics of Welfare Maximization." *American Economic Review,* March 1957, pp. 22 – 59.
————. "The Anatomy of Market Failure." *Quarterly Journal of Economics,* August 1958, pp. 351 – 79.

Baumol, William. *Economic Dynamics.* 2d ed. New York: MacMillan, 1959.
———. *Economic Theory and Operations Analysis.* 2d ed. Englewood Cliffs: Prentice-Hall, 1965.
———. *Welfare Economics and The Theory of The State.* 2d ed. Cambridge: Harvard University Press, 1965a.
Bergson, Abram. *Essays in Normative Economics.* Cambridge: Harvard University Press, 1966.
Bowen, Howard R. *Toward Social Economy.* New York: Rinehart & Company, Inc., 1948.
Breton, Albert. "A Theory of the Demand for Public Goods." *Canadian Journal of Economics and Political Science,* November 1966, pp. 455 – 67.
Buchanan, James M. "Joint Supply, Externality, and Optimality." *Journal of Political Economy,* November 1966, pp. 404 – 15.
———. "Public Goods in Theory and Practice: A Note on the Minasian-Samuelson Discussion." *Journal of Law and Economics,* 1967, pp. 193 – 97.
———. *The Supply and Demand for Public Goods.* Chicago: Rand McNally, 1968.
Buchanan, James M., and William Craig Stubblebine. "Externality." *Economica,* November 1962, pp. 371 – 84.
Buchanan, James M., and Gordon Tullock. *The Calculus of Consent.* Ann Arbor: University of Michigan Press, 1962.
Campa, Giuseppe. "On the Pure Theory of Public Goods." *Public Finance,* No. 4, 1967, pp. 401 – 16.
Chamberlain, Edward. *The Theory of Monopolistic Competition.* Cambridge: Harvard University Press, 1935.
Coase, Ronald. "The Problem of Social Cost." *Journal of Law and Economics,* October 1960, pp. 1 – 44.
Colm, Gerhard. *Essays in Public Finance and Fiscal Policy.* New York: Oxford University Press, 1955.
Dolbear, F. Trenery Jr. "On the Theory of Optimum Externality." *American Economic Review,* March 1967, pp. 90 – 103.
Escarraz, Donald R. *The Price Theory of Value in Public Finance.* Gainesville: University of Florida Press, 1966.
Friedman, Milton. *Price Theory.* Chicago: Aldine • Atherton, 1962.
Forte, Francesco. "Should 'Public Goods' Be Public." *Papers on Non-Market Decision-Making,* Fall 1967, pp. 39 – 46.
Head, John G. "Public Goods and Public Policy." *Public Finance,* no. 3, 1962, pp. 197 – 221.
———. "Lindahl's Theory of the Budget." *Finanzarchiv,* October 1964, pp. 421 – 54.
———. "The Welfare Foundations of Public Finance Theory." *Revista di Diulto Finanziario e Scienza delta Finanze,* May 1965, pp. 379 – 428.
———. "On Merit Goods." *Finanzarchiv,* March 1966, pp. 1 – 29.
———. "Merit Goods Revisited." *Finanzarchiv,* March 1969, pp. 214 – 25.
Johansen, Lief. "Some Notes on the Lindahl Theory of Determination of Public Expenditures." *International Economic Review,* September 1963, pp. 346 – 58.
———. *Public Economics,* Chicago: Rand McNally, 1965.
Johnson, Harry G. *The Two Sector Model of General Equilibrium.* London: Allen and Unwin, 1971.
Lancaster, Kelvin. "Change and Innovation in the Technology of Consumption." *American Economic Review,* May 1966, pp. 14 – 23.
Lange, Oskar. "On the Economic Theory of Socialism," in O. Lange and F. M. Taylor,

On the Economic Theory of Socialism. New York: McGraw-Hill, 1964.

Lindblom, Charles E. "Decision-Making in Taxation and Expenditures," in *Public Finances: Needs, Sources, and Utilization.* Princeton: Princeton University Press, 1961, pp. 295 – 329.

Lipsey, R. G., and Kelvin Lancaster. "The General Theory of Second Best." *Review of Economic Studies,* no. 63, 1956 – 57, pp. 11 – 32.

Little, I. M. D. *A Critique of Welfare Economics.* London: Oxford University Press, 1950.

————."Direct Versus Indirect Taxes," in Musgrave and Shoup, eds. *Readings in The Economics of Taxation.* Homewood, Ill.: Richard D. Irwin, Inc., 1959, pp. 123 – 31.

Margolis, Julius. "A Comment on the Pure Theory of Public Expenditure." *Review of Economics and Statistics,* November 1955, pp. 347 – 49.

Margolis, Julius, and Phillip E. Vincent. *External Economic Effects — An Analysis and Survey.* Stanford: Institute in Engineering-Economic Systems, 1966.

McGuire, Martin C. and Henry Aaron. "Efficiency and Equity in the Optimal Supply of a Public Good." *Review of Economics and Statistics,* February 1969, pp. 31 – 39.

McKean, Roland N. *Public Spending.* New York: McGraw-Hill, 1968.

McKean, Roland N., and Jora R. Minasian. "On Achieving Pareto Optimality — Regardless of Cost." *Western Economic Journal,* December 1966, pp. 14 – 23.

McLure, Charles E, Jr. "Merit Wants: A Normatively Empty Box." *Finanzarchiv,* June 1968, pp. 474 – 83.

Meade, J. E. "External Economies and Diseconomies in a Competive Situation." *Economic Journal.* March 1952, pp. 54 – 67.

Mishan, E. J. "Second Thoughts on Second Best." *Oxford Economic Papers,* 1962, pp. 206 – 17.

————. "The Relationship between Joint Products, Collective Goods, and External Effects.," *Journal of Political Economy,* May/June, 1969, pp. 329 – 48.

Musgrave, Richard A. "The Voluntary Exchange Theory of Public Economy." *Quarterly Journal of Economics,* February 1938, pp. 213 – 37.

————. *The Theory of Public Finance.* New York: McGraw-Hill, 1959.

————. "Provision for Social Goods," in J. Margolis and H. Guitton, eds. *Public Economics.* New York: St. Martin's Press, 1969, pp. 124 – 44.

Musgrave, Richard A., and Alan T. Peacock. *Classics in the Theory of Public Finance.* London: Macmillan, 1958.

Olson, Mancur, Jr. *The Logic of Collective Action.* Cambridge: Harvard University Press, 1965.

Robbins, Lionel. *An Essay on the Nature and Significance of Economic Science.* London: Macmillan, 1932.

Rosenstein-Rodan, P. N. "Problems of Industrialization of Eastern and South-Eastern Europe." *Economic Journal,* September 1943, pp. 202 – 11.

Rothenberg, Jerome. *The Measurement of Social Welfare.* Englewood Cliffs: Prentice-Hall, 1961.

Samuelson, Paul A. "The Pure Theory of Public Expenditures." *Review of Economics and Statistics,* November 1954, pp. 387 – 89.

————. "Diagramatic Exposition of a Theory of Public Expenditures." *Review of Economics and Statistics,* November 1955, pp. 350 – 56.

————. "Public Goods and Subscription TV: Correction of the Record." *Journal of Law and Economics,* October 1964, pp. 81 – 84.

————. "Pitfalls in the Analysis of Public Goods." *Journal of Law and Economics,*

October, 1967, pp. 199–204.

———. "Contrast between Welfare Conditions for Joint Supply and for Public Goods." *Review of Economics and Statistics,* February 1969, pp. 26–30.

———. "Pure Theory of Public Expenditure and Taxation," in J. Margolis and H. Guitton, eds. *Public Economics.* New York: St. Martin's Press, 1969a, pp. 98–123.

Scitovsky, Tibor. "Two Concepts of External Economies." *Journal of Political Economy,* April, 1954, pp. 143–51.

———. *Welfare and Competition.* Homewood, Ill.: Richard D. Irwin, Inc., 1961.

Sharp, Ansel M., and Donald R. Escarraz. "A Reconsideration of the Price or Exchange Theory of Public Finance." *Southern Economic Journal,* October 1964, pp. 132–39.

Shoup, Carl. *Public Finance.* Chicago: Aldine · Atherton, 1969.

Sparks, Gordon R. "Professor Musgrave's Theory of Public Expenditures." *Canadian Journal of Economics and Political Science,* November 1964, pp. 591–94.

Turvey, Ralph. "On Divergencies Between Social Cost and Private Cost." *Economica,* August, 1963, pp. 309–13.

Wellisz, Stanislaw. "On External Diseconomies and the Government Assisted Invisible Hand." *Economica,* November 1964, pp. 345–62.

FIVE

The Politics of Collective Choice

The framework for public expenditure decisions explored in Chapters 2 to 4 is grounded on individualistic assumptions. The satisfaction of social wants, in this approach, must rest on the preferences of sovereign consumers. Optimality for the public sector is conceived of in terms of conformity with individual preferences in a manner strictly analogous to the conformity with preferences that defines Pareto optimality in the private sector.

The strength of this approach to public sector decisions is that it involves essentially the same set of behavioral and technological assumptions as those employed to analyze and evaluate private economic activity. The individualistic approach to the public sector stands on all fours with conventional assumptions about private economic behavior — assumptions that go back at least as far as Adam Smith's initial elaborations: goods are scarce and man is rational. Individuals prefer more goods to fewer goods, and will order their conduct so as consistently to choose more rather than less. There is a choice among competing demands, public and private, for the use of limited resources. Individuals' choices for social wants respond to the same maximizing assumptions as choices for private wants, and a general theory and a general optimum can be described.

It is the purpose of this chapter to explore formulations of the theory of collective choice that are alternative to those resting on individualistic assumptions. As was pointed out in Chapters 2 to 4, an individualistic theory of public goods encounters difficulty in dealing with "free rider" problem. Individuals in the large-number case have no incentive to reveal their preferences for public goods since such goods, once provided, will be made available to all. Where there are relatively few individuals involved, tactics of strategy and bargaining emerge and the results are indeterminate.

The alternative formulations examined here fall into two general approaches or types of theory. One approach accepts the existing political framework of decision-making and describes the processes by which public sector decisions are reached. In this view, public sector decisions may not conform to the preferences of the individuals who comprise the collectivity, but such decisions may, nonetheless, exhibit a collective rationality. This approach is associated with the writings of Colm, Lindblom, and Wildavsky and will be called here the "public interest" approach (Steiner, 1969, pp. 29 – 48).

The second approach is concerned with organizational and political processes, but is generally and ideologically much closer to individualistic theory. In this approach public organization is viewed as an extension of individual utility maximizing functions, with objectives that are identical with those of citizen-voters. Collective organization and its behavior is judged in terms of its ability to maximize individual authority, power, prestige, or some other variant of utility or self-interest. It is implicitly postulated that only in individualism can there be an expression of democracy. This approach is associated with the writings of Downs, Buchanan, Tullock, and McKean and will be called here the "self-interest" approach.[1]

In both approaches the political order is an independent variable in the determination of collective choice, but in the first it exists somewhat apart from the consumer-voters who bring it into existence. Here, collective rationality differs from a simple aggregation of individual values. In the second approach the political order is a direct projection of individual preferences. Individual maximization occurs and collective rationality emerges from the interplay among individual maximizers within a political framework which responds solely to individual preferences and which ignores considerations that do not yield personally appropriable utilities. There are no group preferences as such. But the public interest approach assumes that a resource allocation process that is ultimately controlled and guided by votes is and should be a different allocation process than one that is controlled directly by dollars. It may be less individualistic, but it is not less democratic.

There is a third approach to the institutions of collective decision-making which will not be examined in detail here. This is the approach that is concerned with the definition and derivation of a social welfare function. One line of inquiry within this framework is the exploration of the conditions under which it may be possible to move from an ordering of individual preferences to a consistent ordering of social preferences — the inquiry associated with Arrow and the possibility theorem.[2] The studies of committee voting as a

1. That which is termed the "self-interest" approach is described as the "political approach" in Otto A. Davis and George H. Haines, Jr., "A Political Approach to a Theory of Public Expenditure: The Case of Municipalities," *National Tax Journal,* September 1966, pp. 259 – 75.

2. Kenneth J. Arrow, *Social Choice and Individual Values,* 2d ed. (New York: Wiley 1963).

technique for individual preference ordering and the examination of coalitions are the political science counterpart of this inquiry.[3] A second line of inquiry is directed to the definition and content of a social welfare function, as well as to the condititions under which it can be logically derived. Rothenberg's writings are representative of this concern.[4] In general, the attempt to formulate the conditions necessary for a consistent social welfare function rests on individualistic assumptions.

Although a number of the problems examined by the social welfare theorists are identical with those examined by the public interest and self-interest approaches, the context is different. The social welfare theorists are concerned primarily with the internal logic of collective choice and not with the institutional setting nor, except to a very limited degree, with outcomes. The public interest and self-interest theorists are very much concerned with the outcomes; the implicit assumption of these theorists is that it may be possible to have a consistent set of decisions without a consistent social welfare function.

There are important philosophic differences between the public interest approach on the one hand and the individualistic and self-interest approaches on the other. The proponents of individualistic approaches, for example, have urged that an examination of the public sector by way of group needs and group feelings is not consonant with a theory of public finance in a democratic setting (Musgrave, 1959, pp. 86–9). Since the group as such cannot speak, there is no way to reveal group feelings and preferences. Therefore, all such approaches are labelled "organic," with the unhappy implication that group theories of political behavior are authoritarian. This is an unproductive view, both of the nature of the political and economic order and of the types of approaches that incorporate political variables.

Such a view is unproductive on two counts — first because of the inadequacy of the postulates of the individualistic and self-interest approaches, and secondly because of the operational nature of complex economic and political mechanisms in modern society. Collective choice is not synonymous with authoritarian choice.

The several-decade struggle with the intricacies of welfare economics has at least served an educational function for economists. It is now understood that not all of economic activity can be encompassed within the preference functions of individuals and not all of social welfare can be encompassed within definitions of economic welfare. As I.M.D. Little has said, "Most

3. See Duncan Black, *The Theory of Committees and Elections* (Cambridge: Cambridge University Press, 1958); William H. Riker, *The Theory of Political Coalitions* (New Haven: Yale University Press, 1962).

4. Jerome Rothenberg, *The Measurement of Social Welfare* (Englewood Cliffs: Prentice-Hall, 1961).

people who consider the welfare of society do not, I am sure, think of it as a logical construction from the welfares of individuals. They think rather in terms of social or economic groups, or in terms of average, or representative, men."[5]

The narrowness of the hedonistic calculus has been pointed out since its refinement by Jeremy Bentham in the eighteenth century. But its narrowness is particularly damaging in application to contemporary problems of public finances. A complex economic order generates widespread concern about both consumer and producer externalities and a recognition that costs and benefits must be broadly defined, to include a wider range of social costs and benefits. Increasingly, fiscal theory, initially concerned with efficiency values, has come to be equally concerned with distribution values.

Neither the individualistic nor the self-interest approaches provide satisfactory solutions for externalities or distributional concerns. In fact, the recognition of this condition has led to the introduction in individualistic theory of such constructs as "extended sympathy" or "altruism," which are intended to describe the individual's concern for others in society. The concept of merit wants, as defined by Musgrave, is a further effort to recognize the social content of individual economic behavior (Musgrave, 1959, pp. 13 – 14). These concepts are a recognition of the complexity of the problem, but their operational content is most limited. Concepts such as "extended sympathy," "altruism," and "merit wants" have no more operational content than the traditional efforts to define a social welfare function.[6] It should be stressed that the impossibility of excluding consumers from enjoying the benefits of public goods means that preferences will not be revealed and alternative mechanisms for collective choice must therefore be utilized.

The principal difficulty with the individualistic and self-interest approaches, however, is that they start with the individual and not with the society, and therefore not with the mechanisms or organizations for collective choice. Public interest theories, on the other hand, make no assumptions about individual maximizing behavior or the importance of consumer sovereignty and, instead, postulate simply that there are in existence institutions and organizations for the expression of social ethics and for the implementation of social actions. These social ethics and social actions are assumed to be different from individual values and actions. The individual is as rational with respect to his maximization behavior in public economic activity as in private economic activity, but the expressions of this rationality are necessarily different, because

5. I. M. D. Little, *A Critique of Welfare Economics* (London: Oxford University Press, 1950), p. 49.

6. For a comprehensive review of the concept of merit wants in relation to public goods see John G. Head, "On Merit Goods," *Finanzarchiv,* March 1966, pp. 1 – 29.

they must be implemented through collective institutions. The individual may be motivated by class interests, by social interests, by occupational interests, by philanthropic interests. However he is motivated, his activities become group activities, not individual activities, and are directed, in his concerns for public programs, to those who are in charge of existing institutions of public decision-making — legislators, bureaucrats, political executives. The behavior of groups and classes is thus as "objective" as the behavior of individuals in a market economy.

The public interest approach to public sector decisions lacks the elegance and rigor of individualistic solutions. It does attempt to describe a kind of general equilibrium solution, but it does not seek a general theory of behavior. Rather, it postulates that man may act quite rationally to maximize his consumer satisfactions in a market economy, and at the same time be rational when, in a social context, he acts to maximize his public or political satisfactions. What is irrational is to assume that the individuals are consistently motivated in terms of maximizing their own individually appropriable economic welfare.

In summary, the public interest approach is grounded on the assumption that the collectivity has concerns that are in no way encompassed in individual preferences or values. The individualistic approach can be narrowly conceived in terms of consumer preference. It can be broadened to include individually-held values such as sympathy and altruism. The self-interest approach may include social and political values held by individuals that require collective action and may be broadened still further to embrace some elements of collective policy that are not perceived by individuals, such as the values that attach to the heritage of future generations.

The Public Interest Approach

An essay by Harry Eckstein suggests that one of the intellectual precursors of the public interest approach was Max Weber.[7] Weber searched, both in his personal life and in his writings and teachings, for "a symbiosis of free, creative moral responsibility and technical mastery, either being senseless without the other. This necessarily implied a symbiosis between politics, the preeminent realm of the first, and science, the chief source of the second."[8] This symbiosis did not mean simply a combination of science and politics, or of objective knowledge and moral behavior, nor a dichotomy between the two — but an interaction and a partial compartmentalization of duties and responsibilities.

7. Harry Eckstein, "Political Science and Public Policy," in Ithiel de Sola Pool, ed., *Contemporary Political Science* (New York: McGraw-Hill, 1967), pp. 121 – 65.

8. *Ibid.*, p. 155.

For Weber there was no science of politics; at best there could be a mutual enlightenment between these two realms of discourse.

A second, and peculiarly American, source of intellectual stimulus to the public interest approach is the reality of organized interest groups on the American political scene and their examination as a fruitful source of understanding of political phenomena. Here the strands of theorizing go back to James Madison and his concern in the Federalist papers with factions. Much later, a volume by Arthur Bentley at the turn of the century is credited with redirecting the attention of American political scientists to interest-group behavior.[9] Investigations in this area have had their intellectual fluctuations since that time, but the examination of the relationship of interest groups to the formulation of public policy has continued to be an important area for study.[10]

Among economists the public interest approach to government decisions has been most fully elaborated by Charles E. Lindblom; his contribution will be examined in some detail. Other economists have also adopted this approach. Gerhard Colm, in particular, in a Weberian view of the public sector, has urged that there are two sectors of a mixed economy, a budget sector and a market sector. Citizen preferences are expressed differently with respect to the activities of these sectors. Individual preferences for public and private goods may be conceptualized by means of a single all-encompassing preference function, but the means for translating such preferences are necessarily different since there is no way by which demands at the margin in the two sectors can be equated in monetary terms. It follows that the public sector operates on different rules than the private sector. In the latter, conventional maximizing assumptions are appropriate, but for the public sector attention must be directed to such concepts as the public interest and the public welfare. The collectivity has concerns that extend beyond the values that characterize individual self-interest (Colm, 1955, pp. 3–43; 1956, pp. 408–12; 1965, pp. 209–16; 1966, pp. 115–28).

In general, the public interest approach urges that the collectivity does have an independent existence and objectives that differ from the aggregation of the preferences of individual citizens. The collectivity does not exist simply to translate individual preference functions, but assumes, through executive lead-

---

9. Arthur F. Bentley, *The Process of Government* (Chicago: University of Chicago Press, 1908).

10. The documentation is voluminous. The leading textbook is David B. Truman, *The Governmental Process* (New York: Knopf, 1960). The dominant view, taken by Truman, is that interest groups are an essential party of the pluralism of American political processes. For a less complacent view see Grant McConnell, *Private Power and American Democracy* (New York: Knopf, 1966). And for an even less complacent view see C. Wright Mills, *The Power Elite* (New York: Oxford University Press, 1957).

ership, the legislature, and the operating programs of departments and agencies, an independent role. What, then, is maximized? What is the objective function? If not the welfare of individual citizens, it may be the power, prestige, and authority of the bureaucracy itself. Or it may be a kind of social welfare that transcends individual welfares and is expressed in the amalgam called the public welfare. The failure to specify clearly the nature of the objective function is one of the serious deficiencies in the public interest approach.

For Lindblom, who has made the most important contributions to public interest approaches, it would appear that what is maximized is simply agreement. Public policy is viewed, not in terms of welfare maximization, either individual or group, but in terms of agreement maximization. The proper concern of policy-making is the process of reaching agreement. The organizations, procedures, strategies, and tactics that are employed for this purpose must be examined (Lindblom, 1959, pp. 79 – 88; 1959a, pp. 160 – 79; 1961, pp. 295 – 336; 1963; 1965; 1968).

Lindblom's approach to policy analysis proceeds in three stages. The first is a criticism of classical decision-making — the so-called synoptic or rational-comprehensive method. The second is an examination of the procedures and processes of real world decision-making, which he finds differ sharply from the classical model. The third is the conceptualization of the reality — the provision of theoretical or philosophic underpinnings for the resulting pragmatic incrementalism.

THE SYNOPTIC METHOD

The logical-deductive methods of the natural sciences, according to Lindblom, are the traditional basis for systematic analysis of social science policies. In this approach rationality requires an initial clarification of goals and objectives, with an ordering of their relative importance. All possible policies that are available for the attainment of these goals are then analyzed, with their costs and consequences. This permits an ordering of policies in relation to goals and an efficiency choice among alternatives. This method — classical decision-making — is both rational and comprehensive.

But the synoptic method, Lindblom argues, cannot be pursued for any but the most trivial of economic and social problems. The specification of goals and objectives implies the specification of values, but values and analysis are intertwined. Values, in fact, are discovered only in the process of analysis. To carefully postulate, in advance, the values that are to be sought will serve as a barrier to policy analysis. The conflicts among values will become more evident and agreement more difficult to secure. In practice the final decision is always a choice among value mixes.

Furthermore, for large and complex policies the synoptic method is simply unattainable. The human mind cannot grasp all of the alternatives that are available in major choices between, for example, expenditure on national defense and on welfare programs. Therefore we always value a restricted set of alternatives that are only incrementally different, one from another. We simplify our problems by accepting constraints, political, administrative, or fiscal. The process of analysis and decision becomes as important as the outcome. This is a social and political process, not, primarily, an analytical exercise.

THE REALITY OF POLICY ANALYSIS

Because of the inablity to attain the synoptic ideal in the real world it becomes necessary to employ alternative strategies for policy analysis. Rather than maximizing to attain a specified objective it may be desirable to "satisfice," to use Herbert Simon's word. An acceptable level of accomplishment is sought, rather than the maximum that might be attained. Attention may be directed to those resources that are critically scarce, as in "bottleneck" planning. For Lindblom the most significant alternative to the synoptic method is and must be incrementalism. Since goal specification, in complex problems, may be impossible it will be necessary in some circumstances to determine the direction of policy change and move along that path. Policies may be adopted that will give a maximum of feedback, to provide additional information to assist in the next round of decision. Most complex problems persist; there are second and third chances for analysis. Both objectives and analysis change from month to month and year to year in such areas as foreign aid, social security, or national defense.

The strategy of policy analysis is, above all, incremental. This year's budget shows only marginal change from last year's budget. It is not humanly or procedurally possible to start over, afresh, on each year's budget policy. And in all areas attention will necessarily be devoted to the new problems, to the changes, and not to the comparison of "total" policies. Moreover, the incrementalism is "disjointed." Not all marginal values are examined at any one time. The strategy of decision consists of a selection process — of choices among the values to be costed out, the alternatives that can be looked at, and the goals that can be discovered or modified. In Lindblom's words:

> Man has had to be devilishly inventive to cope with the staggering difficulties he faces. His analytical methods cannot be restricted to tidy scholarly procedures. The piecemealing, remedial incrementalist or satisficer may not look like an heroic figure. He is nevertheless a shrewd, resourceful problem-solver who is wrestling bravely with a universe that he is wise enough to know is too big for him. (Lindblom, 1968, p. 27)

For complex public programs neither policy analysis nor decision-making is centralized. Instead, it is fragmented — among levels of government, among different departments and agencies, among legislators and administrators. The fragmentation is a necessary corollary of a pluralistic government that serves diverse and conflicting goals (Wildavsky, 1964, pp. 1 – 62).

The fragmentation of the analysis and of the decision process and the absence of agreed-upon values and goals requires the continued presence of partisan mutual adjustment, which consists of the interpersonal and decentralized interplay among the participants in the process. Partisan mutual adjustment describes the process of value discovery and reconciliation. Since values cannot be specified in advance, but must be searched out, partisan mutual adjustment, in effect, weights and aggregates the emergent values of the participants in the process and the external influences that are brought to bear.

PRAGMATIC INCREMENTALISM

The philosophic underpinnings for disjointed incrementalism lie in a rehabilitated utilitarianism (Lindblom, 1963, Chapters 9 – 10). The felicific calculus must be rejected; there is no possibility for rehabilitating simplistic concepts of the greatest good to the greatest number. But a general utilitarian approach can be utilized by efforts to index group "happiness" in terms of, for example, improved material welfare which results from reduced disease rates or improved housing. Presumably no effort would be made to attach values to one component of the index as against another; the values would emerge implicitly from the policy deliberations. It may be noted that additional economic content could be added to this process by costing out the alternative improvements that are possible and thus establishing trade-offs. The explicit introduction of decision costs attached to the alternatives would also add a useful element of quantification.

Peremptory rules that will be honored on most, if not all, occasions must be established. For example, even if one person has a superior capacity for happiness it would not be appropriate to reduce the remainder of the community to misery in order to increase that superior happiness. The strategy of disjointed incrementalism handles, as well as possible, both meliorative and distributional concerns by designing policies that satisfy multiple objectives and by assigning, through bargaining and compromise, a measurement of the priority of values.

Policy analysis is not an analytical process; it is a political process. The policy-maker does not search out underlying citizen preferences and attempt to attain an optimum that reflects these preferences. On the contrary, the policy-maker is engaged continuously in reconstructive leadership. This means that he does not take preferences as given, but that instead he attempts to re-mold these preferences. He will not attempt to persuade all participants on all issues, but some participants on some issues. The policy-maker's task is to shift preferences, to remove some of the existing constraints on new courses of action. He is engaged in a continuous and dynamic process of interplay between his own views and those of the constituency. The reconstructive leader is not simply a compromiser or just killed negotiator among powerful constituent forces. He can and does influence the outcome by introducing new preferences and strengthening the existing preferences of individuals for particular policies.

It may be noted that this conception of the role of leadership in influencing preference patterns and policy outcomes assumes a good deal. The legitimacy of leadership must be pre-established and it must be responsive and responsible. Leadership must be possessed of or willing to secure substantial information on social and economic issues and to use this information effectively and honestly in its attempts at influence. And it must be assumed that leadership is, in fact, conducting its affairs in ways that are basically approved by the citizenry. In the absence of these conditions the leadership role can obviously be manipulative and authoritarian.

Public decision processes, in the Lindblom view, must therefore be viewed as a "play of power" in which policy analysis is one of the instruments or weapons in the game. The analysis influences the nature of the game, and the outcome, but it is not the game itself. The play of power is a process and a continuous one. The analysis of trade-offs is a technique of bargaining, not the policy itself.

In the short run pragmatic incrementalism seeks to maximize agreement, to establish consensus, and to enable the leadership to remain in power. In the long run pragmatic incrementalism can be judged to be a success or failure only in terms of organizational survival — which, in Chester Barnard's phrase, is the ultimate test of efficiency.[11] It may be hoped that organizational agreement will lend to organizational survival, but, of course, there is no assurance that this will be the case.

INCREMENTALISM EVALUATED

The great strength of Lindblom's analysis is its relevance to the operating reality of government. He has described the process of decision-making in terms that are meaningful to participants. It is a description that gives aid and comfort to the legislator or the administrator who discovers that there is a rationality in what he does and that his necessarily incremental activities are, in fact, the process of governance.

It is even possible that a kind of optimizing occurs in terms other than agreement. As Margolis states, "There are social processes by which public decisions are guided . . . political bargaining, bureaucratic myopia, professional self-interest; it is likely that outcomes of each process considered indepen-

---

11. Chester I. Barnard, *The Functions of the Executive* (Cambridge: Harvard University Press, 1946), pp. 40–44.

dently would be far from socially optimal, but this does not mean that the total set of processes are not optimal" (1970, p. 320).

But in rationalizing what is, pragmatic incrementalism leaves insufficient room for what might be. The synoptic ideal may be unattainable in the real world, but the emphasis on the tactics of bargaining and compromise necessarily encourages agreement for its own sake and for the specification of extant goals, but not for the drastic shifts in public policy that may, from time to time, be necessary.

This means that pragmatic incrementalism is necessarily conservative in its approach to decision processes (Dror, 1964, pp. 153–57; Dror, 1968, pp. 143–47). Lindblom himself points out that incremental changes are usually accompanied by a high understanding and high predictability of the consequences of change, but large changes are typically accompanied by a low understanding and low predictability. Large changes may occur, but they are of the nature of a gamble for the policy-maker and are not susceptible to analysis because they fall outside the conventional processes of government decision (Braybrooke and Lindblom, 1963, pp. 66–71).

The fundmental criticism of the theory of pragmatic incrementalism turns on whether there is a conflict between the synoptic method and incrementalism. Lindblom himself is highly eclectic in these matters. He has no objection to synoptic approaches where they can be used, but he feels that their use is operationally limited. But if this view is assumed, policy analysis is in danger of degenerating into a "science" of tactics with an emphasis on bargaining and compromise and with little attention paid to the possibilities for extending the range of analytical content, for quantifying values and lifting the constraints and for the measurement of progress toward specific societal goals. The responsibility of the policy analyst is to remove constraints, not to accept them.

The pitfalls of incrementalism are nowhere better illustrated than in the plight of the nation's central cities. Public policy in urban America is and has been characterized by pragmatic incrementalism. The interplay of market forces, governmental agencies, and political parties has produced, not policy goals for land use, transportation, housing, and education, but a series of bargains and compromises that have generated a very large volume of external costs.[12] A somewhat larger content of synoptic method for all aspects of urban policy could certainly have avoided some of the crises that now beset the nation's urban regions. The fragmentation of governmental and political party authority in the metropolitan area facilitates the incrementalism and prevents the establishment of appropriate planning mechanisms.

12. For an exploration of this theme, see Alan K. Campbell and Jesse Burkhead, "Public Policy for Urban America," in Harvey S. Perloff and Lowdon Wingo, Jr., eds., *Issues in Urban Economics* (Baltimore: The Johns Hopkins Press, 1968), pp. 577-649.

It should also be pointed out that the description of incremental decision processes can never be comprehensive, and has very limited predictive value. Decision processes in a complex government are themselves infinitely complex. Case studies of prior decisions may reveal the crucial elements in the interplay among constituents and leaders, among market forces and public power, the interaction of analysis and outcome, the importance of information flows, and of all other elements that might enter into a specific case. But the next act will be different, with a different script, stage, lights, music, producer, director, actors, and audience.

As a description of actual public decision processes pragmatic incrementalism is realistic and insightful. As a method of analysis of the consequences of public decisions it is much less useful.

THE NATURE OF THE PUBLIC INTEREST

Pragmatic incrementalism approaches public decision-making by starting with the body politic, its institutions, procedures, and processes. It is assumed, without discussion, that there are public interests that differ from any simple aggregation of private self-interests. Lindblom and Wildavsky, for example, do not explore the nature of the public interest that emerges from the process of incrementalism other than to argue that the process of reaching agreement is, in and of itself, necessary to establish the public-interest values.

It would appear, however, that this approach should have some philosophic underpinnings at least to the extent of defining outcomes as optimal or nonoptimal. In the literature of political science, for several decades, there have been struggles for such underpinnings in the development of the concept of the public interest. This concept has been beset with difficulties, however, and as things now stand there is certainly no consensus as to the conceptual or operational validity of "the public interest" (Friedrich, 1966; Price, 1962, pp. 141 – 59).

The concept of the public interest, in its philosophic dimensions, has an intellectual history that runs from Plato to Walter Lippman. It became an important concept in American jurisprudence in the last quarter of the nineteenth century when governmental regulation of public utilities was established, both in the states and nationally. Its emergence was synonymous with the growth of independent regulatory commissions. In recent decades most of the concern with its definition and content is a product of the writings of the theorists of public administration within the discipline of political science. For many years it was employed without careful attention to its definition. In most contexts it appeared to be vaguely equivalent to a transcendent political welfare.

By the mid-1950s a number of political scientists had come to be uneasy about both the conceptual validity and the operational vitality of public interest doctrines. Schubert, for example, explored in detail the history, philosophy, and applicability of various concepts of the public interest and found them all seriously wanting (Schubert, 1957, pp. 346–68; 1961; 1966, pp. 162–76.) He discovered that there are three general classes of public interest theorists: the rationalists, the idealists, and the realists. The rationalists postulate the existence of a common good, which finds expression in a popular will. It is the responsibility of public officials to interpret this common will. The instrumentalities for this interpretation may be organized political parties or presidential authority — the rationalists differ as to the appropriate instrumentality. But there is agreement that instrumentalities other than existing interest groups must be utilized for the interpretation of the popular will. The rationalists usually conclude that these existing instrumentalities are inadequate and should be strengthened

The idealists find that the public interest resides in a kind of natural law. The public interest is described as a matter of substance, independent of any specific procedure or decision process. This approach, Schubert points out, quickly degenerates into a defense of despotism.[13]

The realists depend on the interplay of interest groups to achieve a kind of consensus; the public interest is that which emerges when the full range of interest group influences are taken into consideration. The role of the decision-maker may vary greatly (as will be discussed below); he may simply serve to reconcile diverse interests, or he may be an influential participant in the decision process.

From this brief description of differing approaches to the concept of the public interest it is evident that there are grounds for dissatisfaction. The rationalists are engaged in a search for new instrumentalities to develop a central expression of the "public will" in a political world that is dominated by disparate group interests. The idealists have acquired an aura of authoritarianism. The realists have served up no guidelines. As noted above, pragmatic incrementalism is a description of experience.

If the concept of the public interest is to have meaning and its emotive content is to be reduced, the concept must be reestablished through some variant of the realist approach. That variant must be procedural, not substantive. It must be related to the complex interplay among interest groups, administrators, legislators, and citizen-voters. It must reside in a recognition that public policy is the expression of something other than individual self-interest.

In administrative law it is usually impossible to define substantive due

---

13. The reality of the misuse of the "public interest" has been well documented by Charles A. Reich, "The New Property," *Yale Law Journal,* April 1964, pp. 733–87.

process, but it is not as difficult to define procedural due process. If this analogy is appropriate it should be possible to define a procedural public interest, even though its content cannot be specified. A procedural public interest would consist of an assurance, in the decision process, that the widest possible range of interests will be consulted. This consultation will assure that the intensities of preferences are revealed, even if these cannot be measured with precision. The esthetic cost of destroying a scenic wilderness cannot be compared with the value of power and water to be produced from a reservoir, but the intensity of reaction of affected groups can at least be assessed. A procedural public interest would both establish the values that underlie the public interest and reveal the consequences of alternative policies. The rules of the game are important, not just the specific, isolated outcomes.

This approach makes for a complicated set of relationships between the rules and procedures on the one hand and the values or outcomes on the other. Rules and procedures may be accepted because of a belief, that, in the long run, outcomes will be favorable to the great majority of participants. Or, there may be values in participation in the decision process that are quite independent of the outcomes at any point in time. In any event procedures and outcomes are at least partially independent; both are a reflection of values that are important to the citizenry.

A procedural public interest may be roughly equivalent to the economist's concern that the widest possible range of externalities be reviewed in decisions about resource allocation. If this condition is observed, it is probably unimportant whether such frequently empty phrases as "the public interest" or "the public welfare" are retained. Their operational content, as the critics have pointed out, will never be high.[14] The terms themselves can perhaps be retained as symbols that are a reminder to recognize and consult interests that might otherwise be "forgotten or overlooked in the pressure of political combat" (Sorauf, 1957, p. 639).

Economists have devoted relatively little attention to the struggle over the definition of the public interest, unless one wishes to identify the whole of contemporary welfare economics with the problem. This, however, would be an inappropriate identification, since welfare economics is essentially individualistic, and the public interest concept is societally oriented.

Occasionally those economists who have been dissatisfied with individualistic solutions for the public sector decisions have appealed to "social values" (Margolis, 1955, pp. 347–49). But most of the effort to put economic flesh on the public interest concept has come from Gerhard Colm.

14. The classic attack on these empty boxes is contained in E. Pendleton Herring, "The Politics of Fiscal Policy," *Yale Law Journal,* March 1938, pp. 724–45, where it is argued that conflicts over the distribution of income are at the basis of all public finance and that these cannot be resolved except through the interplay of interest groups in the political arena.

Colm argues, as noted above, that individuals are motivated by more than immediate pecuniary self-interest. Individuals and groups of individuals express a concern for the next generation by their willingness to reduce their present consumption in favor of higher living standards for the future. Individuals are motivated by a concern for less fortunate citizens — those of their own nation and of other nations. They may be motivated, for good or ill, by a desire for national prestige, and will devote additional resources to achieving such prestige. But the public interest does not consist solely of noneconomic concerns — these are recognized and can be incorporated into the individualistic approaches. The public interest expresses a different set of motivations: those values and concerns that are held collectively and translated through group institutions.

Colm suggests that there is nothing undemocratic about recognizing extrapersonal motivations or the importance of institutions in influencing such motivations. The role of leadership in a democracy is a particularly legitimate function which is played out by means of persuasion, analysis, and information, not coercion. Political leadership obviously changes and influences individual motivations.

Economic content can be injected into the concept of the public interest by national economic budgets that measure the performance of an economy in relation to goals that have been outlined by the democratic process. In addition, Colm says, there are achievement goals that "refer to the specific content of the public-interest concept, such as an adequate standard of living for the people, adequate education, defense, conservation and development of resources, a proper contribution to underdeveloped countries" (Colm, 1966, p. 124).

From another body of writing — the socialist tradition — it is also possible to define a collective preference function that differs from individualistic self-interest. Drewnowski, for example, has proposed that in socialist theory there should be a middle ground between the Pareto-Barone centralized decision approach and the decentralized consumer sovereignty approach of Lerner and Lange (Drewnowski, 1961, pp. 341 – 54). There are, in fact, in contemporary socialist countries, two systems of valuation — the multiple system of individual preference functions and the state preference function. The latter determines those actions taken by the state to satisfy the collective wants of the population. The degree of sensitivity of the state to collective interests and aspirations is a measure of the degree of democracy. Political decisions thus consist of electing a government that corresponds with the general notions of individuals with respect to collective wants. The details are then formulated by the state, and out of this emerges a "state preference function" which is a reflection of individual preferences for collective action.

This approach is applicable to a capitalist economy as well as to a socialist economy if one will agree that every economic system, as Drewnowski argues, has three "zones" — a state zone, an individual zone, and a dual influence zone. The state zone is larger in a socialist economy; it is smaller in a capitalist economy. There will always be controversy, in any economic system, about the relative size of the zones and about the character of the dual interest zone.

Again, it is a matter of the starting point. If wants are to be conceptualized only in terms of individual welfare and self-interest then social valuations must be ruled out. But if wants can be conceptualized as possessing a dual character — both social and individual — then it would seem that collective wants are as valid as individual wants and that it is quite appropriate to examine their determination by processes of social decision, not by processes that are appropriate only for the maximization of individual self-interest.

INTEREST GROUPS

The approaches to public sector decision-making that have been described here under the general rubric of "public interest" incorporate and legitimate the role of interest groups. Interest groups are not regarded as wholly "selfish" or "evil" but are viewed as representing authentic group values that are the expression of something other than individual self-interest. In pragmatic incrementalism, for example, the interests that are reconciled are group interests, including those of formally organized lobbies. Among American political scientists interest groups are generally viewed as a reflection of the pluralism that characterizes political life.

In the older literature, developed largely before 1955, there are two general views that may be distinguished.[15] These may be designated as the "group process" view and the "reconciliation" view. Both are concerned primarily with the interplay between the public official who is responsible for the decision and the organized and unorganized interest groups that wish to influence the decision.

In the group process approach, exemplified in the writings of Herring and Latham, the public official is responsible primarily for providing the arena and the ground rules under which the combatants engage in the contest for the control of public policy. The official may not be quite a helpless pawn in the interplay of forces, but his major responsibility is to judge the strength of the contending forces, to declare the winner, and to stamp as official the final decision (Herring, 1936; Latham, 1952).

In the reconciliation theory, which has been the traditionally dominant theory among political scientists, the role of the public official is far more important (Key, 1954; Redford, 1952). He is in a position, as in pragmatic

15. The description here is necessarily a cursory one. For a more extended treatment see Truman, op. cit., and references contained therein.

incrementalism, to play one interest group off against another, to structure the outcome by changing the ground rules, and to impose on the outcome his own concept of appropriate policy. Interest groups can express the intensity of concern of those who may be affected, positively or negatively, by a proposed public policy. In this sense their participation in the political process is a reflection of the presence of externalities in public policy and their presence is necessary if these externalities are to be reviewed as part of the decision process. Interest groups are essential to an expression of diverse values.

In recent years there have come to be a number of dissents from these traditional views of the role of interest groups in the formulation of public policy. A significant study by Bauer, de Sola Pool, and Dexter of U.S. tariff policy in the years 1953 to 1962, utilizing behavioral analysis techniques to study patterns of communication among the parties at interest, concluded that interest groups were far less significant in the legislative process than had hitherto been supposed. (Bauer et al., 1963). Individual Congressmen, for example, tended to utilize lobbies to promote their view of public policy, rather than the reverse. However, the authors of the study chose an unfortunate case for their detailed examination. From 1953 to 1962, American tariff policy was structured by an aggressive foreign policy, in both economic and military dimensions. Tariffs must be reduced if investment and trade are to expand. The case study may show no more than that local protectionist interests will yield before strong international expansionist interests.

Other political scientists who have continued to study interest groups in recent years have found them to be both highly effective in public policy and by no means wholly benevolent.[16] McConnell, in examinations of regulatory policy and natural resources, found that interest groups may express a legitimate pluralism but that very often they are subject to no countervailing power at the regional level (McConnell, 1966). They tend to dilute and pervert the national interest and establish a narrow local control over national policy.

Other writers continue to discover nonbenevolence in the impact of interest groups on public policy. Kariel, for example, feels that the concept of pluralism has become a fashionable myth in American political life, and that public policy is, in reality, dominated by bureaucratic organization, public and private, leaving few avenues open for influence by the outsiders (Kariel, 1961). Lowi has carried this attack further (1967, pp. 5–24). He characterizes the working model of modern political science as that of the "interest group liberal." This model rests on three assumptions. The first is that organized interests are homogeneous, easy to define, and possess representative spokes-

16. An attack by an economist on what he finds to be logical inconsistencies in the position of the "analytical pluralists" is contained in Mancur Olson, Jr., *The Logic of Collective Action* (Cambridge: Harvard University Press, 1965), pp. 125–31.

men. The second is that organized interest groups adequately represent most
of the sectors of our lives. The third is that the role of government is to assure
access to the most effectively organized groups and to ratify the adjustments
that must be worked out among competing claimants.

Lowi points out that interest group liberalism has historically been defined
as the essence of pluralistic democracy. If, however, that was once an adequate
rationalization, it is no longer so. Interest group liberalism is now a degenerate
solution in the sense that it justifies the sharing of public power with private
groups, and a consequent dilution of public authority. Decisions that should
be public are turned over to private groups; decisions that should be made are
blocked by private groups. Neither is it a self-correcting system; countervailing
powers do not emerge. Political alienation sets in and confrontation politics
replaces the traditional mechanisms for orderly interest-group representation
and electoral activity. Lowi's proposals for recovery, however, are not impressive. He would have us change the ideology and return to Madison's prescription to regulate factions rather than legitimate them. Congress should be asked
to spell out the standards for implementing legislation since vague legislation
invites the excesses of shared power.

The relationships among interest groups and government decision processes
will continue to be most complicated and to defy any simple taxonomy. There
are many instances where it is uneconomic for groups to organize, as when the
costs of organization exceed the benefits. In other cases the group, once organized, will fail to attain an optimal supply of group oriented action because
rewards are small or do not accrue uniformly to members who bear the cost
(Olson, 1965, pp. 5 – 52).

There are instances, as in water resource project areas, where groups appear
to reflect an adequate expression of the preferences of affected parties and
where these preferences must be taken into account in public decisions if
external costs and benefits are to be revealed. There are cases where interest
groups capture government bureaucracies, as in the regulatory field, and the
agency becomes an extension of private groups. There are cases where the
government agency assumes a role almost independent of private interests, and
acquires its own dynamic, as the military is often charged with doing. In some
instances, as in the COMSAT case noted in Chapter 1, public and private
interests are merged in a new institutional form.

Furthermore, the rules of the game differ from one area of decision to
another. In the federal government the administration's stabilization policy is
developed by the Council of Economic Advisers, in consultation with the
president, in a framework that is largely insulated from the influence of the
organized parties at interest, such as labor, agriculture, finance, and industry.
The Office of Management and Budget is largely isolated from direct contacts

with interest groups, large or small. But this is not the case with departments and agencies, whose programs, budgetary and otherwise, are continuously subject to interest group scrutiny.

In this welter of complex reality and divergent perceptions thereof, one thing seems certain — interest groups will persist. They will not be replaced by technological solutions for complex public problems. We are not on the verge of an end of ideology, at least as far as interest groups are concerned.[17]

The concept of the public interest and the role of interest groups in forging that public interest are central to what has been described here as the public interest approach to political decision theory. This approach does not constitute a neat analytic scheme, in the way that individualistic approaches describe a self-contained Pareto optimal solution. But as it loses in elegant analytics, the public interest approach gains in realism; there is the conventional trade-off between rigor and relevance.

It is hardly surprising, as we move from the formal constructs of welfare economics to the political economics of the public sector, that concepts should become more vague and diffuse. This development is inherent in the subject matter. It is, unfortunately, not possible to define "political behavior" or to measure units of political power, or to maximize a political objective function.

Whether collective choice is approached by way of individualistic solutions or by way of public interest solutions there are common problems that must be dealt with: the revelation of preferences for public goods, the inclusion of the full range of economic and noneconomic values, and the aggregation of the full range of values. The crucial difference between the individualistic and public interest approach is the insistence of the latter that collective choice is not expressed as an aggregate of individual choice, but that it may nevertheless be rational.

The Self-Interest Approach

In recent years political science, formerly prescriptive and descriptive, is said to have undergone a revolution. The revolution is described as behavioralism, and has come to embrace a number of diverse approaches, generally quantitative and generally concerned with maximizing models (Easton, 1962, pp. 1 – 25). Some of the stimulus to behavioralism has come as economists and their techniques have invaded the analysis of political behavior; often, as in international warfare, the invader has been absorbed and those who have been invaded

---

17. For a contrary view, see Daniel Bell, "The Adequacy of our Concepts," in Bertram M. Gross, ed., *A Great Society?* (New York: Basic Books, 1968), pp. 127 – 61.

have adopted his methods. The analysis of political phenomena by means of multivariate techniques, for example, is now commonplace in political science. And the Robbinsian distinction between positive and normative now dominates this area as much as it has, until recently, dominated economics.

An important contributor to the invasion of political science by economics is Anthony Downs and his 1957 study, *An Economic Theory of Democracy.* In this volume political behavior was looked at, for perhaps the first time, in the way that economists have traditionally looked at the maximization of net revenue.

Downs hypothesized a political world of two major components: political parties who controlled the government but were subject to periodic election or reelection, and citizen-voters. Political parties in power wish to stay in power and, therefore, formulate policies that will win elections. Citizens will vote for the party that appears to offer the greatest utility income for the forthcoming period. The budget becomes the central focus of the struggle for election. The government in power attempts to increase expenditures for various public services until the vote gain from the marginal expenditure is just equal to the vote loss from the marginal tax. Downs concluded, perhaps not surprisingly, that as politcans seek to maximize their chances for reelection they will not necessarily maximize the economic efficiency of the public sector.[18]

The Downs model is, of course, a narrow one. Political parties may be interested in other objectives than winning votes and retaining office. Parties may wish to avoid the responsibilities of office but retain sufficient organizational viability to hold some patronage, or to preserve a minimum organization with secure positions for party leaders; or political parties may obtain pay-offs by not undertaking aggressive campaigns (Wilson, 1961, pp. 369 – 80). As usual, in a political model where units of political power cannot be quantified, there is difficulty in specifying the objective function.

The self-interest approach to collective action, however, has been most fully developed by James M. Buchanan. (Buchanan, 1960; Buchanan and Tullock, 1962; Buchanan, 1967; Buchanan, 1968.) It should be stressed that Buchanan's objective is not to search for an individualistic Pareto optimum for public expenditure in the manner of Samuelson and Musgrave. The task is not to start and stop with the conditions for individual utility maximization. Collective activity exists and must be recognized to influence individual choice. Public finance is the economics of politics. We must, therefore, explore the economics

---

18. Downs has applied this approach to an equally provocative study of the internal workings of public and private bureaucracy. See Anthony Downs, *Inside Bureaucracy* (Boston: Little, Brown, 1967). In this same tradition see Gordon Tullock, *The Politics of Bureaucracy* (Washington: Public Affairs Press, 1965), and Olson, op. cit., 1965, Chapters 1 – 2, where the self-interest approach is applied to the analysis of interest groups.

of fiscal choice, but always in a positive setting; and we must take, as the basic behavioral unit of politics, the individual and his motivating self-interest. The central proposition is that individuals, not groups, make fiscal choices.

For Buchanan there are two basic political models. One is the authoritarian or ruling class model, where a dominant elite makes decisions in behalf of the citizenry. The second is the democratic model, where the individual controls the decisions of the collectivity. Buchanan suggests that "if the analyst chooses to work within the confines of the democratic model, he must commence at the level of the individual citizen-voter, and he is obligated to explain how the choices of this citizen-voter are translated into collective decisions" (1967, pp. 174 – 5). It follows that group interests, or pluralistic approaches are outside this framework: "Political scientists, and others, often refer to the "public interest" as something that exists independently of the separate personal or private interests of the individual members of a community. The approach taken here does not recognize the existence of such a "public interest," and individuals are presumed to act simply as utility-maximizers, although utility functions need not be narrowly defined" (Buchanan, 1967, p. 219). It likewise follows that there is no point in searching for an "independent" social welfare function. Welfare must always be defined as a aggregate of individual self-interest.

This approach places the theory of markets and not the theory of resource allocation at the center of economic analysis.[19] Adam Smith's propensity to "truck, barter and exchange" — the continued pursuit of gains from trade — is the dynamic element in economic analysis, not the examination of choices among alternative resource allocation patterns. Therefore, "Economics is the study of the whole system of exchange relationships. Politics is the study of the whole system of coercive or potentially coercive relationships."[20]

For Buchanan, then, there is an essential polarity between market processes, which are noncoercive, and in which individuals freely associate to pursue gains from trade, and political processes, which are basically coercive and compulsory. For Buchanan, the most renowned statement in Adam Smith is, "It is not from the benevolence of the butcher, the brewer, or the baker, that we expect our dinner, but from their regard to their own interest."[21] It may also be noted in passing that another quotation from Smith is equally well-known: "People of the same trade seldom meet together, even for merriment and diversion, but the conversation ends in a conspiracy against the public, or in some contrivance to raise prices."[22] Or, equally appropriate: "The capricious

---

19. James M. Buchanan, "What Should Economists Do?" *Southern Economic Journal,* January 1964, pp. 213 – 22

20. Ibid., p. 220.

21. Buchanan, in foreword to Tullock, op. cit., p. 1.

22. Adam Smith, *The Wealth of Nations* (New York: The Modern Library, 1937), p. 128.

ambition of kings and ministers has not, during the present and preceding century, been more fatal to the repose of Europe, than the impertinent jealousy of merchants and manufacturers."[23]

The point is that such strongly worded concepts as "coercion" are not meaningful in distinguishing between private and public economic activity. A definition of coercion in terms of the power of the state is not a satisfactory basis for distinguishing among institutional arrangements. Such a definition is a tautology, and establishes a dichotomy between the state and all other organizations. The concept, then, is neither analytically nor descriptively useful.

For example, private markets where one party to the gains from trade possesses monopoly power are obviously coercive. Gains from trade will be disbursed evenly only when there is some kind of equality of resources in the hands of the parties to the exchange before the exchange commences. An imperfect distribution of resources imparts a bargaining advantage, and market coercion results. As Wicksell observed, there can be justice only among equals. Conversely, in the public sector "one man, one vote" is as noncoercive a behavior rule as can be imagined. But in the political world some votes seem to count more than others, and no one would deny that there are coercive elements in political decisions even as in market decisions.

It is true, of course, that public decisions always involve, at the time when they are reflected in public budgets, an authoritarian allocation of resources and the imposition of tax liabilities, however much "free" interplay may be involved in the process. Once the budget decision is made, taxes are collected by legal authority for expenditures on legislated programs. But this consideration neglects the outcomes of the budget program itself. A particular budget program, may, on balance, as pointed out in Chapter 1, reduce the total amount of "coercion" that is present in the existing political and economic order.

Buchanan's quest is for a mechanism of public choice that approximates as closely as possible the "noncoercive" nature of market choice. He urges that Wicksell's approach to fiscal choice be recognized as the logical equivalent, for the public sector, of Pareto optimal solutions in the market sector. Starting from an original position, if no change may be made in the budget by unanimous consent of all parties, then the original position is optimal. If a change is proposed and adopted by all parties, the original budget position was nonoptimal. But, Buchanan points out, in order to secure a change the parties to the bargaining are led to invest in resources to gain the support of others. This may lead to wasteful social behavior and the final results may only approximate optimality.

There are two additional difficulties with Wicksellian unanimity solutions.

23. Ibid., p. 460.

The first, as Wicksell himself recognized, is that there cannot be a "just" share of taxes and expenditures when there is an "unjust" distribution of income and wealth. "It is clear that justice in taxation tacitly presupposes justice in the existing distribution of property and income" (Wicksell, 1964, p. 108). And, "The attempt to base a just tax system upon an unjust property system is an attempt to take a fair share out of an unfair whole."[24] But since there are no economic efficiency rules for establishing a proper distribution of income, noneconomic or sociopolitical solutions must be found.

The second difficulty is in the operation of the rule of unanimity, or "relative unanimity" as Wicksell modified it. The budget in the first year, reached under conditions of relative unanimity, might represent an optimal allocation. But in the second year exogenous or nonbudget factors may enter to disturb the equilibrium. Such factors, as is customary in these matters, will advantage some and disadvantage others. Those who are advantaged, by exercising their veto power, can perpetuate the misallocation.[25] In short, the Wicksellian solution does not satisfactorily resolve, in economic terms, the determination of an appropriate distribution of income. Neither does it assure, over time, an allocational optimum.

Even with these underlying conceptual infirmities Buchanan's analysis of fiscal institutions provides a number of provocative insights. The examination of such institutions in their impact on individuals' choice patterns permits the analysis of specific institutional arrangements in a behavorial context. The earmarking of taxes, for example, can be looked at in terms of taxpayer attitudes toward the fisc when budget revenues are specifically assigned, as compared with general fund financing. Similarly, taxpayer attitudes toward collective goods will be influenced by the degree of progressivity in the tax structure and by the use of specific and general excises. By examining the impact of fiscal institutions, it is possible to broaden the self-interest approaches to embrace three questions: How will the individual pay for collective goods? How much should the collectivity provide? How will the individual react to the resulting change in market conditions? (Buchanan, 1967, Chapters 3 – 7, 14 – 16).

The individual may also desire, appropriately and rationally, institutions for fiscal choice that differ from collective institutions for purposes other than fiscal choice. A constitution, for example, typically prescribes special patterns of rules and procedures for fiscal affairs. Specific objects of taxation may

24. Quoted by Gunnar Myrdal in *The Political Element in the Development of Economic Theory,* trans. Paul Streeten (Cambridge: Harvard University Press, 1954), pp. 178 – 79. Myrdal's major cirticism of Wicksell is that the distribution of property and income cannot be separated from the purely fiscal problem of exchange (allocations). Ibid., pp. 176 – 90.

25. See William J. Baumol, *Welfare Economics and the Theory of the State,* 2d ed. (Cambridge: Harvard University Press, 1965), pp. 43 – 44.

be precluded from the decision authority of the legislature. Tax or debt limits may be established to restrict the range of fiscal choice available in annual budget decisions. Buchanan finds such restrictions to be an expression of efforts to retain the essential properties of Wicksellian unanimity with the necessary real world modifications. Such restrictions, that is, different institutions for fiscal choice than for other collective choices, can usually be understood as a consequence of the exorbitant costs of obtaining agreement when there is frequent recurrence of choice. Fiscal decisions are not made once, but annually. The repetition of choice runs over a series of time periods.

In private markets, no matter how frequent the choice, the individual's decision cost is minimal and imposes no external burden on others. Such costs generally need not be taken into account. But in the public sector the costs of reaching agreement may be substantial. A separate set of rules for fiscal institutions may be necessary to minimize agreement costs (Buchanan, 1968, pp. 151 – 202.) Likewise, information costs may be onerous. To secure an accurate assessment of citizen preferences would, in most cases, be costly and in some cases impossible.[26] Therefore, it may be desirable to establish institutions for fiscal choice that operate, within specified limits, in terms of simple majoritarian rule. The sequential character of the decisions will be helpful in achieving a kind of long run reflection of citizen preferences.

Buchanan has also provided major insights into the conditions under which individuals will choose to satisfy their wants by undertaking collective action. Much of this analysis is contained in *The Calculus of Consent* (Buchanan and Tullock, 1962, Chapters 8-17). Starting again from the assumption of self-interest maximization, Buchanan and Tullock explore the conditions under which collective action will emerge, the costs and gains of collective action as compared with market behavior, and the institutional patterns of collective action that are most likely to maximize the individual's want satisfaction. A summary and necessarily cursory account of this analysis will indicate something of its contribution in the context of collective choice.

The market and public activity are both devices for assuring cooperation among individuals. A citizen will participate in either market or collective activity for the same reason — to increase his utility. Therefore, individual rationality may be examined but not social rationality; the individual will rank bundles of collective goods transitively, "in the same way" that he ranks bundles of private goods. The individual will thus enter into collective action

---

26. The relationship of information costs to fiscal choice is most fully developed in Roland N. McKean, *Public Spending* (New York: McGraw-Hill, 1968), esp. Chapters 2, 3, 5. McKean's view is a generally pessimistic one: information costs are typically so high that accurate preference determinations are impossible and anything resembling either a Pareto optimum or a Wicksellian optimum is consequently most difficult to attain.

to gain external benefits or to reduce the external costs that are imposed by the alternative of purely private action. These external costs must be weighed against decision costs; if the reduction in external costs exceeds decision costs, collective action will be undertaken. Decision costs will include the expenses of establishing an organization for collective action, and the information and agreement costs that may be incurred in reaching a decision. In general, the larger the number of individuals required to reach agreement the larger the costs. The conditions for agreement will vary in accordance with the kind of action contemplated. Decisions to modify or restrict established property rights are expensive because near-unanimity is required.

When a large proportion of the members of the collectivity are required for a decision the expected external costs of decision are reduced, since fewer individuals are likely to be disadvantaged by the outcome. Under a rule of unanimity these costs are reduced to zero since the group cannot impose burdens on the individual against his will.

The expected external costs resulting from collective action and the expected decision costs are both, therefore, a function of the number of individuals required for collective action. The first is a decreasing function, the second an increasing function of numbers. The two together will give a U-shaped curve; C + D is the summation of expected external costs and expected decision costs. The lowest point on the curve defines the optimum. This relationship was explored above in Chapter 4 and can be set forth in a simplified fashion (Buchanan and Tullock, 1962, p. 71).

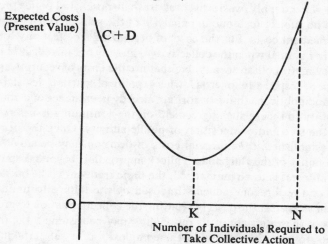

Figure 5.1. External and Decision Costs

The costs of securing agreement are dependent on the communication network that exists, and hence on incremental information and leadership costs. Since most collective decisions are sequential it is often possible to adopt decision rules that simplify agreement and reduce the volume of bargaining costs. Individuals are quite willing to choose decision rules on different bases than they would choose specific resource allocations, once their economic position has been established. One of the ways for reducing agreement costs is to decentralize decision mechanisms and minimize the size of the collective unit. Vote trading (logrolling) in sequential decisions and side payments to secure agreement provide partial means to indicate the intensity of preference and are necessary concomitants of efforts to reduce agreement costs; such practices make the collectivity behave more like a market, and reduce the possibilities that resources will be misallocated for the benefit of minorities. Vote trading is particularly useful and may achieve Wicksellian unanimity.

The Buchanan-Tullock analysis of collective decision-making is most relevant to the examination of developments in an economy as it moves from a primitive Robinson Crusoe structure to a more complex pattern of trading and exchange. When there is no established mechanism for making collective decisions in an individualistic Crusoe economy, the decision to establish such a mechanism is an economic decision that ought to be undertaken on efficiency grounds, with a rational analysis of the costs and gains thereof. The Buchanan-Tullock analysis is also interesting in the individualistic world of contemporary exurbia, where decisions to collectivize or not to collectivize public services in such matters as water supply, waste disposal, trash disposal, and police protection may again be subject to economic analysis of the self-interest type, with attention to agreement costs. But the costs of organizing a collectivity for the next decision are minimal when the collectivity is already organized, as in most of contemporary metropolitan society. Neither are the costs of securing agreement likely to be especially onerous where political parties, legislatures, bureaucracies and political administrators are already in existence and charged with responsibility to secure such agreement on the continuing issues related to changes in the size and composition of public activity. Once the decision unit has been established, the marginal costs of decision may be small.

But the rationality of the Buchanan-Tullock approach is beyond dispute. If individual self-interest is to be maximized, the basic trade-off is the burden of external costs or the foregone benefits imposed by the failure to undertake collective action as against the costs of securing the collective action to prevent the imposition of the externalities. If rationality may be assumed, the public sector continues to grow in size and in the complexity of its undertakings in an advanced industrial economy, precisely because external costs imposed by that society and the benefits of potential public programs are increasing more rapidly than the costs of reaching collective decisions. This, however, merely states a tautology; the more interesting questions center on the distribution of the costs and benefits.

Public Interest versus Private Interest

The theories of collective choice that have been examined in this chapter differ sharply from those examined in Chapters 2 to 4. In the pure theory of public goods the economists' traditional approach is to define the conditions for individual welfare maximization in terms of Pareto optimal solutions and to explore the possibilities for attaining such an optimum. When externalities are examined, as in Chapter 4, the complexities of the analysis are increased, but the objective function is unchanged; an efficient allocation of resources is the goal of the inquiry.

In the politics of collective choice it is necessary to explore a different range of inquiry. Here the institutions of fiscal choice must be explicitly examined. They may no longer be assumed to exist as a simple reflection or aggregation of individual preferences. This examination requires a fundamental specification at the outset — that of the objective function. Those who are concerned with the maximization of individual welfare, called here the self-interest approach, will explore the relations between institutions of fiscal choice and individuals' welfare. Those who are concerned directly with the achievement of agreement, called here the public interest approach, will start the analysis with the institutions themselves and the nature of the public interest that is to be attained.

It is evident that the public interest approaches are much less satisfying, definitionally and analytically, than the others. Their strength resides in their reasonably high content of descriptive and operational reality. It is also evident that the self-interest approaches, such as those of Downs and Buchanan, are substantial simplifications of the complexity of real world decisions, although their analytic content is more satisfying. This is not surprising. The continued currency of such phrases as "politics is the art of compromise," or "politics is an art and not a science," suggests that economic welfare, viewed individualistically, is at least a partially different world than political welfare, viewed in terms of society as a whole or in terms of the groups and classes that make up a society.

References

Bauer, Raymond A., Ithiel de Sola Pool, and Lewis A. Dexter. *American Business and Public Policy.* New York: Aldine · Atherton, 1963.

Braybrooke, David, and Charles E. Lindblom, *A Strategy of Decision.* New York: The Free Press, 1963.

Buchanan, James M. *Fiscal Theory and Political Economy.* Chapel Hill: University of North Carolina Press, 1960.

————. *Public Finance in Democratic Process.* Chapel Hill: University of North Carolina Press, 1967.

————. *The Demand and Supply of Public Goods.* Chicago: Rand McNally, 1968.

Buchanan, James M., and Gordon Tullock. *The Calculus of Consent.* Ann Arbor: University of Michigan Press, 1962.

Colm, Gerhard. *Essays in Public Finance and Fiscal Policy.* New York: Oxford University Press, 1955, esp. pp. 3 – 43.

————. "Comments on Samuelson's Theory of Public Finance." *Review of Economics and Statistics,* November 1956, pp. 408 – 12.

————. "National Goals Analysis and Marginal Utility Economics." *Finanzarchiv,* July 1965, pp. 209 – 24.

————. "The Public Interest: Essential Key to Public Policy," in Friedrich, ed., *The Public Interest,* pp. 115 – 28.

Downs, Anthony. *An Economic Theory of Democracy.* New York: Harper and Row, 1957.

Drewnowski, Jan. "The Economic Theory of Socialism: A Suggestion for Reconsideration." *The Journal of Political Economy,* August 1961, pp. 341 – 54.

Dror, Yehezkel. "Muddling Through — 'Science' or Inertia?" *Public Administration Review,* September 1964, pp. 153 – 57.

————. *Public Policymaking Reexamined.* San Francisco: Chandler, 1968.

Easton, David. "The Current Meaning of 'Behavioralism' in Political Science," in James C. Charlesworth, ed., *The Limits of Behavioralism in Political Science.* Philadelphia: American Academy of Political and Social Science, 1962, pp. 1 – 25.

Friedrich, Carl J., ed., *The Public Interest.* New York: Aldine • Atherton, 1966.

Herring, E. Pendleton. *Public Administration and the Public Interest.* New York: McGraw Hill, 1936.

Kariel, Henry S. *The Decline of American Pluralism.* Stanford: Stanford University Press, 1961.

Key, V. O., Jr. *Politics, Parties, and Pressure Groups.* New York: Crowell, 1954.

Latham, Earl. *The Group Basis of Politics.* Ithaca: Cornell University Press, 1952.

Lindblom, Charles E. "The Science of Muddling Through." *Public Administration Review.* Spring 1959, pp. 79 – 88.

————. "The Handling of Norms in Policy Analysis," in Moses Abramovitz, ed., *The Allocation of Economic Resources.* Stanford: Stanford University Press, 1959a, pp. 160 – 79.

————. "Decision-Making in Taxation and Expenditures," in *Public Finances: Needs, Sources and Utilization.* Princeton: National Bureau of Economic Research, Princeton University Press, 1961, pp. 296 – 336.

————. *The Intelligence of Democracy.* New York: The Free Press, 1965.

————. *The Policy-Making Process.* Englewood Cliffs: Prentice-Hall, 1968.

Lowi, Theodore. "The Public Philosophy: Interest-Group Liberalism." *American Political Science Review,* March 1967, pp. 5 – 24.

Margolis, Julius. "A Comment on the Pure Theory of Public Expenditure." *Review of Economics and Statistics,* November 1955, pp. 347 – 49.

————. "Shadow Prices for Incorrect or Nonexistent Market Values," in Robert H. Haveman and Julius Margolis, eds., *Public Expenditures and Policy Analysis.* Chicago: Markham, 1970, pp. 314 – 29.

McConnell, Grant. *Private Power and American Democracy.* New York: Knopf, 1966.

Musgrave, Richard A. *The Theory of Public Finance.* New York: McGraw Hill, 1959.

Olson, Mancur, Jr. *The Logic of Collective Action.* Cambridge: Harvard University Press, 1965.

Price, Douglas. "Theories of the Public Interest." in Lynton K. Caldwell, ed., *Politics and Public Affairs.* Bloomington, Ind: Institute of Training for Public Service, Indiana University, 1962, pp. 141–59.

Redford, Emmette S. *Administration of National Economic Control.* New York: Macmillan, 1952.

Schubert, Glendon A. " 'The Public Interest' in Administrative Decision-Making: Theorem, Theosophy, or Theory?" *American Political Science Review,* June 1957, pp. 346–68.

————. *The Public Interest: A Critique of the Theory of a Political Concept.* New York: The Free Press, 1961.

————. "Is There a Public Interest Theory?" in Friedrich, ed., *The Public Interest,* pp. 162–76.

Sorauf, Frank J. "The Public Interest Reconsidered." *Journal of Politics,* November 1957, pp. 616–39.

Steiner, Peter O. *Public Expenditure Budgeting.* Washington: The Brookings Institution, 1969. An excellent summary is contained in Peter O. Steiner, "The Public Sector and the Public Interest," in Robert H. Haveman and Julius Margolis, eds., *Public Expenditures and Policy Analysis.* Chicago: Markham, 1970, pp. 21–58.

Wicksell, Knut. "A New Principle of Just Taxation," in Richard A. Musgrave and Alan T. Peacock, eds., *Classics in the Theory of Public Finance.* London: Macmillan, 1964, pp. 72–118.

Wildavsky, Aaron. *The Politics of the Budgetary Process.* Boston: Little, Brown, 1964.

Wilson, James Q. "The Economy of Patronage." *Journal of Political Economy,* August 1961, pp. 369–80.

SIX

Program Budgeting

The preceding chapters have explored the state of contemporary fiscal theory, to examine the conceptual bases that are available for analyzing the appropriate level and composition of public economic activity. Program budgeting, examined in this chapter, and benefit-cost analysis (Chapter 7) are the operational side of fiscal theory.

Program budgeting is a relatively recent development in a long history of efforts to quantify and evaluate the output of the public sector. It is the product of two general strands of influences — the continued efforts of budget examiners and central budget offices to improve their techniques of evaluation, and the introduction into contemporary budget-making of the concepts and methods of economic analysis, along with the latter's offspring, systems analysis.

Program budgeting, in its recent evolution, has three partially separable objectives. The first is taxonomic — the classification of government activity by goals and objectives. The second is analytical — the comparison of costs with outcomes and the exploration of alternative means of achieving outcomes. The third is projective — the long-range planning of government programs.

Benefit-cost analysis is concerned only with the second of these objectives — the comparison of costs and outcomes for specific projects. Nor is benefit-cost the only analytical technique that is available for such purposes, although it is certainly the most important one. Benefit-cost can be viewed as an integral part of government budgeting. But it also has interest and significance for public sector decisions in ways that are not immediately linked with the budgetary process, as will be examined in Chapter 7.[1]

1. Terminology in this area is far from standardized. "Systems analysis," "benefit-cost," "cost effectiveness," "cost utility," "operations research," and "operational research" are all used

The significance of program budgeting, and its distinguishing characteristics as compared with conventional government budgeting, requires some definitions and a brief historical perspective.

Traditionally government budgets have been prepared, reviewed, adopted, and executed in terms of what is known as a line item classification. The expenditure side of the budget has described the things that government buys (Burkhead, 1956, pp. 127–32). This line item or object classification was developed primarily in the interests of management control and accountability. The classification was based on the types of inputs that were purchased or hired, such as personnel, usually specified in considerable detail, office supplies and expense, printing, travel expenses, and the like. Each of these classes of expenditures was supported by established procedures for warrants and vouchers; accounts were maintained and audited in this classification.

The object classification continues to be necessary in all governments for accountability — financial control and audit. It is also important for program management, which must be directed to the control of inputs. However, object classification is necessarily restricted to the measurement of inputs. It will not describe either the activities of government agencies or their outputs.

Activities are the implementing link between inputs and outputs; they are the intermediate step in the sequence inputs — activities — outputs. The activities of a government agency are the things that it does. For an educational institution, for example, inputs consist of the factors that are hired or purchased — teachers and supervisory personnel, materials and supplies, buildings and equipment. The activities consist of the number of classes taught or the number of student-hours of instruction. The outputs are the end results, the accomplishments — or the outcomes. In education these should be measured in terms of student acquisition of skills and wisdom, or by whatever goals are established by educational administrators as a reflection of community values (Burkhead, Fox, and Holland, 1967).

Activity schedules are significant and useful, again for purposes of program management. But for many government programs, it may not be possible to move from activity schedules to measures of output. This, however, is the mission of program budgeting: to attempt to measure, in systems terms, the relationship between inputs and outputs. This measurement, ideally, must be related to the organization that manages the program.

The conception of output relevant to program budgeting is one which encompasses the full range of objectives of the operating agency. Concern for program outputs or outcomes extends to consequences even when the linkage between activities and consequences is a tenuous one. A narrower view would

---

in a variety of contexts, sometimes as synonyms and sometimes to describe rather different analytical techniques. For an attempt at definitional clarity see Chapter 7.

treat as output only the activities themselves, and then view the consequences or outcomes as mutually determined by the activities and the factors that establish the environment in which the activities take place. This latter view seems appropriate for the study of empirical cost and production functions for governmental services since it permits a separation of relations between services provided (activities) and inputs used, and services provided (activities) and consequences (see Chapter 9).

The difficulty with the concept of output in a program budget context may be illustrated with reference to linear programming. In a typical linear programming problem for a business firm, inputs and the production function are given, and the objective function is to maximize profit. The solution will establish the appropriate activity levels and these activity levels will determine the output. For the business firm activities and outputs are distinct. But in program budgeting in the public sector the relationship between activities and outputs is less clear-cut. If output is defined broadly in terms of consequences, such as crime prevention, then identical policing activities may yield very different outputs in different cities or in the same city at different points in time. On the other hand, it will be difficult to distinguish a narrower definition of output in terms of services provided from a description of the activities themselves. The difficulties with the concept of output for program budgeting may be described as the absence of an invariant relationship between activities and outputs.

Down the years a great many governmental bodies in the United States have experimented with budget classifications that attempted to measure government output and relate that output to the costs of inputs. The most recent major step was taken by the federal government in 1965; this step has been followed by parallel efforts on the part of some states and local governments. In the federal government this reform is known as the Planning-Programming-Budgeting System — PPBS, or simply PPB. The generic term is program budgeting; this in turn is related to classification efforts in the early 1950s that were more commonly called performance budgeting.[2]

Program budgeting could be viewed simply as an additional system of expenditure classification of a type that many governments have attempted. But program budgeting, as it is currently practiced, raises a number of fundamental issues that go far beyond its role as a classificatory system. Program budgeting requires a restructuring of decision-making within a government. It alters relationships affecting the power and authority of bureaus, departments, the chief executive, and the legislature. Program budgeting raises further issues

---

2. The terms "program" and "performance" are often used interchangeably. "Program budget" seems to have found recent favor as the most widely accepted term.

in the relationship of analysis to policy and thus in the relationship of economics to politics.

The Historical Dimensions

As early as 1912 the federal government's Taft Commission on Economy and Efficiency stressed the importance of budgeting in accordance with the subjects of work to be accomplished. The first operational applications of this approach came at the local level with the work of the New York Bureau of Municipal Research in the years 1913 – 15 (Burkhead, 1956, pp. 133 – 34). The bureau devised a budget for the Borough of Richmond, New York City, for the years 1913 – 15 that applied performance concepts to three public works functions — street cleaning, sewerage, and street maintenance. Physical units of work to be accomplished, unit costs and total costs, with appropriate subclassifications, were set forth in the budget document and written into appropriation acts by the Board of Aldermen. This approach, however, turned out to be too detailed and inflexible and was soon abandoned.

During the 1920s there were occasional discussions of an output approach to budgeting for the federal or for state and local governments, but no new innovations were undertaken until the program budget approaches of the U.S. Department of Agriculture and the Tennessee Valley Authority in the mid-1930s. In both cases an effort was made to devise a program classification within existing agency organizational patterns and to measure work accomplishment within these programs. At the end of World War II the Navy Department began to present its budget along both object and program lines. These developments in the federal government were encouraged by the report of the first Hoover Commission in 1949. The commission recommended that "the whole budgetary concept of the Federal Government should be refashioned" (Commission on Organization of the Executive Branch of the Government, 1949, p. 8). The commision's report also contributed to a popularization of the term "performance budget."

There were other developments in the federal government at this time. Amendments to the National Security Act in 1949 required the Department of Defense to report the cost of performance of programs and activities. The Budget and Accounting Procedures Act of 1950 also encouraged extension of performance concepts throughout the whole of the federal government (Mosher, 1954, pp. 37 – 42).

In the 1950s a number of American cities also introduced budgetary innovations under the heading of program and performance. A few states, including Maryland, New York, Michigan, Connecticut, Illinois, California, and Oregon likewise utilized performance concepts in one or more departments and agencies (Burkhead, 1956, pp. 136 – 38).[3] These developments have not been confined to the United States. The Philippine government introduced a comprehensive system of performance budgeting in the mid-1950s (Yoingco and Casem, 1969, pp. 166 – 84), and there has been considerable international interest in this area. The Department of Economic and Social Affairs of the United Nations has sponsored a series of budget workshops with attention to program and performance concepts and has encouraged innovations in a number of countries.[4]

An output orientation to budgeting has, however, been subject to fluctuations in enthusiasm. During the 1950s much of the animation that had surrounded performance budgeting gradually diminished. The U.S. Bureau of the Budget during these years continued to encourage agencies and departments to improve their activity schedules and to develop cost-type budgets based on work measurement. This encouragement contributed to a continuous improvement in the quality of budget justifications and budget presentation. But it did not appear to have dramatic consequences.

The setting changed, however, in the spring of 1961 when Robert S. McNamara became Secretary of the Department of Defense. Charles J. Hitch was appointed Comptroller of the Department, and was charged with responsibility for refashioning the budget structure of DOD in program terms and with introducing systematic analysis of alternatives as a basis for budget formulation.

The successful experience of the Department of Defense with this approach to budgeting led to its adoption on a government-wide basis in August, 1965, first as a memorandum from the president to the heads of all federal departments and agencies, and then, in October of that year, as a directive from the Bureau of the Budget (Schick, 1966a, pp. 243 – 58).[5] The first budget to reflect the impact of PPBS was submitted to the Congress in January, 1967. The system has been gradually extended and refined since that time, to the point where almost all major federal departments and agencies have undertaken program classifications and have developed, to a greater or lesser extent, an improved analysis of program outcomes.

Requirements for PPB-type project justifications have been written into the statutes affecting such agencies as the Department of Housing and Urban

---

3. See the symposium in *Public Administration Review,* Spring 1960, pp. 63 – 85. Wisconsin initiated a revised and expanded approach to program budgeting in 1960, New York in 1964, and California in 1966.

4. See United Nations, *A Manual for Programme and Performance Budgeting* (New York: United Nations, 1965); idem, *Report to the Fourth Workshop on Problems of Budget Reclassification and Management* (New York: United Nations, 1967).

5. Bureau of the Budget, Bulletin No. 66 – 3, October 12, 1965. The Bureau of the Budget became the Office of Management and Budget in 1970.

Development and the Office of Economic Opportunity; a number of congressional committees have shown interest in the area of output measurement. A foundation-sponsored project has supported states and local governments in their program budgeting innovations. Five states, five counties, and five cities have received special encouragement and assistance.[6] Other cities have undertaken program budget innovations, usually in areas that are eligible for federal grant assistance (Mushkin, 1969, pp. 167–78).

Before turning to the conceptual and other issues that are posed by program budgeting, it would be useful to review briefly the experience of the Department of Defense, since it is this experience that provided the 1965 stimulus to the extension of PPB in the federal establishment.

The Experience of the Department of Defense

The success of program budgeting in the Department of Defense must be viewed in an organizational context, against a fourteen-year background of difficulties with attempts to establish unified central direction over the whole of the defense establishment (Novick, 1965, pp. 81–91). In the National Security Act of 1947, Congress created the Office of Secretary of Defense (OSD) with general authority over the Army, Navy, and Air Force. The Office of the Secretary was further strengthened by legislative amendments in 1949 and by a reorganization in 1958. Nevertheless, as of 1961, the budget and planning system in the department suffered from some serious shortcomings.

Prior to this time planning proceeded independently of budgeting and was generally oriented toward the development of new weapons systems. Programming, that is, the time phasing of installations, was separated from both planning and budgeting (Hammond, 1968, pp. 57–69). There was, moreover, no systematic evaluation of costs, and, in particular, no articulation of the relationship among research and development, installation and operating cost requirements. The budget, on the other hand, consisted of fitting the requests of the separate branches of the armed services into the appropriations structure of predetermined defense expenditure ceilings imposed by the administration. Military planning was undertaken by each of the services, frequently with emphasis on new projects that could lay the basis for future expansion. Budget decisions were made by civilian staff of the Office of the Secretary, and when

6. The State-Local Finances Project of The George Washington University, supported by the Ford Foundation and directed by Selma J. Mushkin. The Project's publications, which examine conceptual, measurement, and organizational aspects of program budgeting, include *Criteria for Evaluation in Planning State and Local Programs*, a series of PPB Notes, *Planning, Programming, Budgeting for City, State, County Objectives*, and Harry P. Hatry and John F. Cotton, *Program Planning for State, County, City*. See also Joint Economic Committee, *Innovations in Planning, Programing, and Budgeting in State and Local Governments*, (Washington, 1969).

there were budget reductions these were often imposed arbitrarily without careful evaluation of their impact on military plans. The planning and operations of the three branches of the service remained substantially uncoordinated.

From 1948 to 1961 there was developed at the RAND Corporation a substantial body of research on economics and budgeting for defense. Staff members of RAND acquired considerable skill in the operating problems of the Department of Defense.[7] Therefore, in developing a new philosophy and procedure for centralized management in the Department of Defense, RAND experience and RAND personnel could be utilized.

Novick has pointed out that the new system had two primary aims. First, "to permit analysis of total force structures for all of the services in terms of common missions or national objectives," and second, "to project the resource impact (or financial requirements) of the proposed force structures over an extended period of years" (Novick, 1965, p. 87).

There are three phases in the DOD system (Hitch, 1965, pp. 21 – 39; Niskanen, 1967, pp. 3 – 22). The first is military planning and requirements determination; here the starting point is the political determination of national security objectives by the President and the Secretary of State (McNamara, 1966, p. 27). In the next step the Joint Chiefs of Staff prepare the predetermined political objectives. This plan also indicates, from the viewpoint of the military, the forces and programs that should be supported over the next five to eight years, but without linkages to specific resource costs. The plan is reviewed annually, in the spring of each year, by the Secretary of Defense, in relation to the major cost effectiveness studies that are related to the proposals. The Secretary then issues a Tentative Force Guidance that serves as a baseline for program changes in the five-year plan. The Tentative Force Guidance is transmitted to the services and is followed by a series of draft memoranda on each major mission area and support activity, prepared by OSD (see below). These memoranda are reviewed by the JCS and serve as the basis for the evaluation of issues on force levels between JCS and OSD.

The second phase — programming — consists of a definition of program structure in terms of missions, forces, and weapon and support systems, and analytical comparisons of alternatives.

The major program structure of DOD has been redefined several times since 1961. As of fiscal year 1972 the structure consisted of:

    I. Strategic forces

---

7. See papers by David Novick: *Efficiency and Economy in Government Through New Budgeting Procedures* (1953), *A New Approach to the Military Budget* (1956), *Which Program Do We Mean in "Program Budgeting"?* (1961) (Santa Monica: RAND Corporation). The most extensive treatment is Charles J. Hitch and Roland N. McKean, *The Economics of Defense in the Nuclear Age* (Cambridge: Harvard University Press, 1960).

II. General purpose forces
III. Intelligence and communications
IV. Airlift and sealift
V. Guard and Reserve forces
VI. Research and development
VII. Central supply and maintenance
VIII. Training, medical and other general personnel activities
IX. Administration and associated activities
X. Support to other nations
(Bureau of the Budget, *Special Analyses,* 1971, p. 273)

Within the major programs, program elements are defined where possible in terms of the forces or weapons system that contribute to the ten major programs. About 1,000 such program elements have been designated for the whole of the Department of Defense. Program elements are defined in terms of an "integrated force or activity." A B-52 bomber, together with the related manpower and equipment required to keep the bomber operational, is a program element. Other examples of program elements are attack carriers, F-4 fighter wings and the Manned Orbiting Laboratory. The approach to the costs of a program element is comprehensive — all directly supporting costs are intended to be counted. In addition, program packages, made up of all the program elements related to a larger mission, such as missile defense, are designated for examination and analysis. Where possible, research and development program elements are associated with major programs, such as strategic forces. However major R & D activities that cannot be so associated are defined as program elements within the general R & D program.

The basic document that emerges from this planning effort is the Five-Year Defense Plan (FYDP). This incorporates a set of planning assumptions and a projection of the implications of past decisions. Force projections are for an eight-year period; cost projections for a five-year period (Enthoven and Smith, 1970, p. 487). The FYDP is thus the official source of planning assumptions and permits each of the services to ascertain what is needed for common missions.

Within this classification of program and program elements the Office of Comptroller of DOD has initiated studies of the cost-effectiveness or cost-utility of specific weapons systems (Enthoven, 1963; Enthoven and Smith, 1970; Fisher, 1965). These analyses are generally undertaken to estimate the relative costs of achieving specified levels of deterrent strength or force structure with a careful examination of the alternative means that are available for attaining stated objectives.

The cost effectiveness studies which have characterized the analytical aspects of defense budgeting since the first work at RAND are important vehicles for the analysis and debate on policy issues within DOD. The results of such studies are reflected in a series of memoranda; each is known as a Draft Presidential Memorandum, is addressed to major functional areas, and is prepared annually by the Office of the Secretary of Defense. These lay down the basis for preliminary discussion within each of the services. In addition, the cost effectiveness studies are reflected in Development Concept Papers, an approach introduced in 1967, and directed toward new programs (Enthoven and Smith, 1970, pp. 490 – 91).

The third phase is budgeting, which is conducted jointly by the Comptroller's Office and the Bureau of the Budget (Since 1970 the Office of Management and Budget) and is required in order to link programs and costs to the appropriation structure. Basically the budget is the financial implementation of the first year of the five-year plan (FYDP). The preparation of the budget requires attention to "procurement lists, production schedules, lead times, prices, [and] status of funds" (Hitch, 1965, p. 39). The budget must show financial requirements in terms of inputs; military plans are oriented to outputs.

The budget justifications of the Department of Defense, prepared in terms of the program format, are primarily for internal decisions and for the Office of Management and Budget. The "program packages" are made available to the Congress, and congressional review of the DOD budget has directed increased attention to program objectives and costs. However, the DOD has not realigned its appropriation structure to conform with the program structure; budget authorizations continue in terms of such traditional categories as procurement, military personnel, and operation and maintenance — categories that cut across program lines.

The lack of congruence in program structure and appropriation structure and the lack of congruence between program structure and the organizational structure of the Department of Defense has required the development of the "crosswalk." This is the term that has been applied to the informational pattern that is intended to link together the program structure and the budget (appropriations) structure. The crosswalk is the coding and cross-classification system that permits the review of DOD activities from either perspective (Schick, 1966, pp. 14 – 21).

The program budget system of the Department of Defense was intended to, and did, concentrate decision authority in the Office of the Secretary of Defense. Program packages are defined here; the statistical information that is required for cross-walking is developed centrally. The budgetary authority of the bureaus within the service departments and of the departments themselves has been greatly diminished.

As a part of the expanded pattern of central control, the Office of the Secretary also introduced a system for Program Change Proposals (PCP). This system requires prior approval by OSD for any cost variances that occur during the execution of the budget (Novick, 1965, pp. 98-100). At the same time the PCP system is intended to assure flexibility within the budget year; changes may be proposed and approved at any time. This provides a continuous updating of the five-year projections. When there are several hundred program changes each year, however, actions on individual instances may be isolated from the overview provided by the annual budget process. Conversely, a decision on a single PCP may structure a budget decision that is to be made later in time.

Finally, six years after the initial introduction of the PPB system, the Comptroller of the Department of Defense initiated a revision in cost accounting procedures to assure a uniform DOD-wide approach and to link cost accounts and budget accounts.

As a system of financial management, program budgeting in the Department of Defense has brought three major advances. The first is better costing. The authorization of a research and development proposal for a weapons system is accompanied by at least some rough calculations of the prospective future installation and operating costs of that system. This procedure, of course, is particularly important for programs that extend over a number of fiscal years, and is a necessary control on research and development projects that may commit heavy additional outlays in the future.

The second contribution is the utilization of cost data for assessing choices in achieving specified levels of deterrence capability — the systematic treatment of effectiveness. In this context operations research has become an integral part of military planning and programming (Quade, 1964; Enke, 1967, pp. 89–266). The third major contribution lies in the five-year projections. These have brought an articulation of planning and budgeting that has not hitherto been achieved in the defense establishment.

The program classification does not resolve all problems of either planning or management. It will not reveal whether more resources should be devoted to strategic retaliatory forces or to general purpose forces or to airlift and sealift forces. Moreover, the broad programs are not mutually exclusive and cannot be analyzed as if they were discrete (Wildavsky, 1966, pp. 306–7). A great many program elements serve more than one major program, or turn out to be useful for a second program although devoted initially to only one program. In these circumstances there are no rules for the determination of proper costing. The development and installation costs for the second program could reasonably be taken either at zero for this particular program element, or at average cost.

The program budget system of the Department of Defense cannot reveal whether the nation is better defended in one year than in another. Such a determination would require an assessment of military effectiveness against all potential adversaries and their probable response patterns. Neither, of course, can the program budget system reveal whether it is better to spend more on national defense and less on health and education. It can reveal military capability in relation to predetermined objectives and the estimated capability to be expected from additional military expenditures.

The program budget system is at its best in DOD when it assists in decisions about suboptimization — the evaluation of the most efficient means for attaining prespecified objectives (Hitch and McKean, 1960, pp. 158 – 64). The costs of attaining relative force levels can be ascertained. Alternative means of achieving a given force level can be explored systematically.

The general success of PPB in the Department of Defense is attributable to a number of factors, some of which were peculiar to the years after 1961 and some of which reside in the nature of military operations. There was readily available, as noted, a background of systems analysis research on the military, with personnel quite capable of continuing and extending this research. But undoubtedly the most important of the factors making for success was that military budgets were expanding rapidly in these years (Wildavsky, 1970, pp. 463 – 67). This meant that large sums were available for research, and that a new research staff could be created without disturbing existing organizational patterns or established interests. The availability of resources also meant that, "So long as dollar losses in one program were more than made up by gains in another, the pain of policy analysis was considerably eased" (Wildavsky, 1970, p. 466).

The technology of military operations also lends itself reasonably well to a PPB approach. Specific weapons systems are, in fact, very often alternatives, one to another, and can be analyzed in terms of least-cost combinations. It is possible to accept large margins of error in dealing with an intercontinental missile system. The potential effectiveness of a missile system can be estimated within a very broad range, as long as the Congress is willing to accept the generalized necessity for more destructive power.

It should be stressed that PPB, as developed in the Department of Defense, differs from older concepts of performance budgeting in two significant ways. First, the emphasis is on choices among programs, where such choices are grounded in systems analysis. Second, PPB is a centralizing decision process, not a technique for improving the effectiveness of program operation. Any benefits that accrue to the latter are of the nature of incidental spin-offs.

The experience of the Department of Defense does not define either the strengths or limitations of program budgeting as applied to nonmilitary government. In some nonmilitary areas program budgeting is much more difficult than for the military; in other areas it is somewhat easier. Unfortunately, there was no systematic appraisal of DOD experience with program budgeting prior to its introduction to nonmilitary departments and agencies. This has made it difficult to profit from experience.

The issues for civilian agencies can be grouped into (1) organizational patterns, (2) program definition, (3) costing, and (4) output criteria. An examination of these issues is followed by a general evaluation of program budgeting, including the experience of the Department of Defense.

Organizational Patterns

In the proposals of the first and second Hoover Commissions, performance budgeting, as it was then called, was viewed as a procedure that would encourage the decentralization of budgetary decisions. Performance measurements were to be developed at the bureau level. It was hoped that these would be useful as part of the materials for budget review, both within the Executive Office and the Congress. But performance budgeting was regarded primarily as a program management responsibility.

From the brief discussion of experience in the Department of Defense, it is evident that program budgeting is an instrumentality for the centralization of budgetary decisions, not for their decentralization. It is intended to be a technique of policy analysis, not a technique of management. There is an inevitable transfer of authority from the bureau level to the department level and from the department to the central budget office. Operational responsibility is not centralized, but budget planning is, provided, of course, that the centralizers encourage the development of the technique and utilize the findings. Recent developments in the PPB system as applied to federal civilian agencies suggest that this type of centralization will occur, even though highly diversified patterns have emerged in recent federal practice (Harper, Kramer, and Rouse, 1969, pp. 623–32). Indeed, recent experience suggests that program budgeting should be viewed as a device for strengthening central decision authority and for permitting departments and the Executive Office of the President to control and plan more effectively.[8] Procedures that have been established by the Office of Management and Budget, for example, call for additional staffing and the creation of analysis units at the top levels of management. These may be attached to existing budget offices or they may be attached to the office of the secretary within a department. Similarly, the role of Management and Budget in initiating PPB will strengthen its influence in resource allocation decisions and thus enhance the Executive Office of the President.

A different staffing pattern would produce different results. If those responsible for program budget analysis were attached to bureau chiefs, the bureau role in budget decision-making would be retained. It is conceivable that budget analysis staff could be distributed in accordance with the existing distribution

8. There have been expressions of concern that the centralization of resource allocation and management decisions has been carried too far even in the Department of Defense, with a consequent loss of efficiency and flexibility at lower echelons (Niskanen, 1967, pp. 17–20).

of administrative authority throughout a department or agency. But this has not and is not likely to occur; centralization and program budgeting are largely synonymous.

This means that program budgeting will encounter its most severe organizational difficulties in departments and agencies that have a long tradition of semiautonomous bureaus. This is the case with such federal departments as Treasury, Interior and Agriculture, for example, where bureaus have well-established patterns of congressional and interest-group support. In these circumstances program budgeting will encounter understandable opposition from the bureaus; unless bureau autonomy is reduced, program budgeting could become an informational and reporting classification, without visible impact on budget decisions and without the possibility for interprogram comparisons and evaluation.

The same considerations apply to state and local governments that may introduce program budget techniques. In fact, the instances of independent and relatively uncontrolled governmental units are much more widespread here. Every state government abounds with independent authorities that are organized outside the budgetary supervision of the governor. A great many mayors have budgetary authority over only a small fraction of the municipal activities within their boundaries. The adoption of program budget techniques by all such autonomous and semiautonomous agencies would provide an adequate information base for judgments about fragmented state and local government programs, but would not provide for centralized decision authority and the analysis of program externalities and alternatives.

The harmonization of program and organizational structure is a most difficult matter. It affects the measurement of cost, the selection of criteria for evaluating output, and the definition of programs and program elements.

The interesting case of estuaries in the programs of the Department of the Interior is illustrative. There are apparently nine bureaus in Interior that conduct programs in estuaries. These include such bureaus as the Geological Survey, the Fish and Wildlife Service, the National Park Service and the Bureau of Outdoor Recreation. This proliferation of bureaus in estuaries has been cited as an example of a department-wide problem that should be susceptible to a redefinition under PPB.[9] But it may well be that "estuaries" are not an appropriate program definition for Interior. The activities of the Bureau of Outdoor Recreation are national in scope, and estuaries are just one place where these activities are conducted. For those interested in how much resources Interior devotes to estuaries it would be useful to have an information

9. Statement of John Haldi, Joint Economic Committee, Subcommittee on Economy in Government, *The Planning-Programing-Budgeting System: Progress and Potentials,* September 1967, p. 193.

system that serves up the data. It does not follow that national programs should be subdivided into regional components and recombined "functionally." There is no more an a priori case for "estuaries" as a program definition than there is for "headwaters" as a program definition.

The relationship of program budgeting to legislative review will continue to be most uncertain. In the federal government, for example, Program Memoranda are developed for purposes of review by departments and the Office of Management and Budget. These are not made available to congressional committees. The legislative committees are, of course, interested in a review of programs and will examine program dimensions and program justifications, but they are also interested in a great many other things, including the control of administration and the modification of programs in the interests of their constituencies.[10] It is very likely that most legislative committees will continue to insist on budget justifications and budget classifications that will serve interests other than those of program review. This will require the continuation of traditional object classifications for legislative purposes as well as for management purposes in the control of inputs. In short, the need for multiple classifications will continue as long as the budget process serves multiple purposes.

The Definition of Program

A great many government budgets have traditionally been presented in terms of a functional classification that supplements a classification by organizational structure. The budget of the United States government, for example, has thirteen major functional categories under such headings as national defense, international affairs and finance, natural resources, commerce and transportation, interest, and general government. The functional classification of expenditures is intended to describe the broad purposes and programs of a government; it typically cuts across organizational lines and embraces the activities of a number of departments and agencies. Occasionally the classification reaches below the departmental level to place the activities of one bureau in a different grouping than the remainder of the department (Burkhead, 1956, pp. 113 – 25).

The planning-programming-budgeting system as it is now practiced by the federal government seeks to define programs within departments and agencies. The classification is broken down into three groups: program categories, program subcategories, and program elements. The program categories are

10. See the classic articles by Arthur W. MacMahon, "Congressional Oversight of Administration: The Power of the Purse," *Political Science Quarterly*, June 1943, pp. 161 – 90; ibid., September 1943, pp. 380 – 414. Also, Richard F. Fenno, Jr., *The Power of the Purse* (Boston: Little, Brown, 1966).

defined by each department or agency to embrace groupings that serve the same broad objective.

The Department of Health, Education and Welfare, for example, defines four program categories in addition to executive direction and management: education, health, social and rehabilitation services, and income security. Within "education" there are six subcategories:

Development of basic skills

Development of vocational and occupational skills

Development of academic and professional skills

Library and community development

General research (nonallocable research)

General support.

Within "Development of vocational and occupational skills" there are, for example, three program elements:

Improving the education of the general population

Improving the education of the economic and socially disadvantaged

Improving the education of the physically and mentally handicapped.

It is not intended that the program structure will necessarily reflect existing organizational structures. Where possible, it is hoped that research activities can be placed within a program format, but in some instances research and development activities may be of such generalized character that they are listed as a separate program subcategory or program element. For any one department, program categories would be expected to be fewer than ten. Subcategories might number from forty to fifty and program elements several hundred.

Each program is to be supported by a Program Memorandum (PM) to serve as budget justification, with an emphasis on the assumptions employed and the analysis of outcomes and alternatives. Special analytic studies (SAS) are undertaken to provide the underpinning for the Program Memorandum, but need not be phased directly with the budget cycle of an agency. All of these are linked together in the multiyear Program and Financial Plan (PFP) to show the relationship of budget to program.[11] "The basic purpose behind the PFP is to identify the extent to which future budget choices are already foreclosed so that remaining options are identified, and so that future consequences of present decisions are routinely identified and considered during the decision process" (Carlson, 1970, p. 373).

Program analysis documents prepared by the Department of Health, Education and Welfare for the 1968 budget suggest the kinds of studies that are intended for inclusion in the Program Memoranda for that department.[12] Nine

11. The terminology and general guidelines for the PPB system are contained in Bureau of the Budget, Bulletin No. 68–9, April 12, 1968.

12. Department of Health, Education and Welfare, *Selected Disease Control Program,* Pro-

programs, such as motor vehicle accident prevention, arthritis control, and lung cancer, are evaluated by estimates of benefits and costs and costs of deaths averted. The benefits are measured by discounted lifetime earnings.

A Program Memorandum for urban transportation, prepared by the Department of Transportation for FY 1970, identified highway program costs by four objectives: economic efficiency; safety; aesthetic environmental, and social values; and contribution to desirable urban development. The memorandum then analyzed selected issues such as: What steps should be taken to reduce peak-hour congestion, especially on high traffic-density radial corridors? Should a special program be established to provide convenient and inexpensive mass transportation for ghetto areas?[13] The memorandum discussed alternative approaches and costs for each of these issues, but did not incorporate benefit-cost or cost-effectiveness studies.

The Office of Management and Budget has used a procedure for "Issue Letters" to the departments and agencies as a technique for stimulating the analytical studies that are to be conducted. These studies are intended to define the Major Program Issues (MPIs) that will need special attention during the budget year. The issues to be subject to analysis are negotiated between OMB and the departments and agencies. For the FY 1970 budget there were 380 Issue Letters for seventeen departments and agencies. Apparently only about half of these were the subject of analysis; the system of Issue Letters is said to be in need of overhaul (Carlson, 1970, p. 375).

Program budgeting is intended to direct attention to the importance of trade-offs within programs and possibly among programs. If program objectives are defined, as in the above HEW case, by a reduction in deaths, then it is better to allocate resources toward program element A, where death reduction costs are lower, that to program element B, where they are higher. The definition of program thus becomes crucial in establishing the limits of the trade-offs that will be systematically explored (McKean, 1967, pp. 65 – 69). If programs are defined narrowly, that is, if there are a great many programs for a department or agency, the analytical task of measuring within a program is made easier, but the interdependencies among programs will be lost and the possibilities for exploring larger trade-offs submerged. In water resource management it might be desirable for some rivers to serve solely as sewage conduits, but that possibility will never be explored by those in charge of a "clean streams" program. The benefits from a two-year nursing education program cannot be compared with the benefits from a four-year nursing program if the two programs are in different departments.

---

gram Analysis 1966, (Washington, 1966) (mimeo).

13. See Joint Economic Committee, *The Analysis and Evaluation of Public Expenditures: The PPB System,* vol. 2 (Washington, 1969) pp. 676 – 97.

The reorientation toward an end-product approach inherent in the PPB system may be illustrated by a comparison of existing activity schedules for the Coast Guard with its proposed program structure.[14]

The present activity schedule consists of:

vessel operations
aviation operations
shore stations and aids operations
repair and supply facilities
training and recruiting facilities
administration and operational control
other military personnel expense supporting program
supporting programs.

The proposed program structure is:

search and rescue
aids to navigation
law enforcement
military readiness
merchant marine safety
oceanography and other operations supporting services
supporting services.

This program structure moves somewhat away from the input approach to budget classification, but continues to reflect activities more than outputs. The same is true of most of the program categories that have been developed in the federal government (Bureau of the Budget, 1970, pp. 269–95).

For state and local governments, a very different type of program structure is needed. A generalized example of this has been suggested by Hatry and Cotton and is reproduced in Table 6.1. In practice, the lettered "program subcategories" under each of the major programs would need to be further subdivided into program elements. It may be noted that this classification will not conform with organizational patterns. A mental health program for school children (II) may be administered by the board of education (III). Recreation activities (VI) may be conducted by the public housing authority (IV) or by the police department (I). Program budget categories, as noted above, must be defined and reviewed centrally. A crosswalk will be necessary if the categories are to be useful for budget management and control by program agencies.

One of the difficult classification problems in a program structure arises from government activities that serve more than one purpose and, hence, could be classified under more than one program. Examples are multitudinous. The educational activities of the armed services are both education and national defense. The federal program for school lunches contributes to education,

14. Bureau of the Budget, Bulletin 66–3, October 12, 1965, Exhibit 2.

Table 6.1. Illustrative PPBS Program Structure for State and Local Government

I. *Personal Safety*
   A. Law Enforcement
   B. Traffic Safety
   C. Fire Prevention and Control
   D. Safety from Animals
   E. Protection and Control of Disasters Natural and Man-made
   F. Prevention of Other Accidents

II. *Health*
   A. Physical Health
   B. Mental Health
   C. Drug and Alcohol Addiction, Prevention and Control

III. *Intellectual Development and Personal Enrichment*
   A. Preschool Education
   B. Primary Education
   C. Secondary Education
   D. Higher Education
   E. Adult Education

IV. *Satisfactory Home/Community Environment*
   A. Comprehensive Community Planning
   B. Homes for the Dependent
   C. Housing — other than that in A and B
   D. Water Supply
   E. Solid Waste Disposal
   F. Air Polution Control
   G. Pest Control
   H. Local Beautification
   I. Noise Abatement
   J. Intra-Community Relations
   K. Homemaking Aid/Information

V. *Economic Satisfaction and Satisfactory Work Opportunities for the Individual*
   A. Financial Assistance to the Needy
   B. Increased Job Opportunity
   C. Protection of an Individual as an Employee
   D. Aid to the Individual as a Businessman
   E. Protection of the Individual as a Consumer of Goods and Services
   F. Judicial Activities for Protection of Consumers and Businessmen, alike

VI. *Leisure Time Opportunities*
   A. Outdoor
   B. Indoor
   C. Recreational Activities for Senior Citizens
   D. Cultural Activities

VII. *Transportation — Communication — Location*
   A. Motor Vehicles
   B. Urban Transit Systems
   C. Pedestrian
   D. Water Transport
   E. Air Transport
   F. Location Programs
   G. Communications Substitutes for Transportation

VIII. *General Support*
   A. General Government Management
   B. Financial
   C. Purchasing and Property Management
   D. Personnel Services
   E. Unassignable EDP
   F. Legislative
   G. Legal
   H. Elections

Source: Harry P. Hatry and John F. Cotton, *Program Planning for State, County, City* (Washington: State-Local Finances Project, The George Washington University, 1967, pp. 17–18.)

health, and also to the level of farm income. Foreign economic or military aid may involve a substantial element of subsidy to specific domestic producers.

If it is determined that it is important to be able to add up programs to a nonduplicative total, it is necessary that arbitrary decisions be made as to whether a specific activity falls within one program or another. Moreover, there are political implications in such choices. A great many federal government education programs, for example, could be classified as health programs, welfare programs, or manpower programs. The volume of expenditures that may be affected by such decisions in the field of education may amount to as much as $1 billion (Hirsch, 1965, pp. 197–98). In other words, the federal government's education program may be made to look larger or smaller in comparison with other federal programs. There is no budget classification that is neutral in terms of the politics of policy.

If the emphasis is on a program classification that follows existing organizational lines, then the problem of assigning activities to specific programs is less serious. Where there is to be analysis and comparison of specific program subcategories, there is no reason why ad hoc classifications cannot be pursued. That is, for some purposes it may be desirable to regard the educational activities of the armed services as national defense, and for other purposes to regard these as manpower training. Again, the translation grid or crosswalk will be necessary to permit reclassification for specific purposes. The crosswalk is also necessary to link the Program and Financial Plan with the appropriation structure and the schedules showing new obligational authority.

In the Department of Defense, the introduction of program budgeting was not accompanied by administrative reorganization. The prevailing structure of each of the branches of the armed services was left intact, and program definitions that cut across service lines were developed centrally, in the Office of the Secretary of Defense. This approach avoids the disruption that inevitably accompanies an administrative reorganization, but it does not reinforce administrative responsibilities for the management of specific programs. To accomplish the latter it would be necessary to reorganize government activities in accordance with program definitions. Ideally this reorganization would start with major functional areas, such as health, education, transportation, and national defense; departments and agencies would be reorganized in these categories. Within each department and agency there would be further reorganization in accord with defined programs and program subcategories.

The multipurpose character of government activities will defeat efforts to achieve such a synchronization of program budget classification and organizational structure. It is not at all clear that such synchronization is possible or desirable. There is no way of ascertaining a priori that the urban transportation activities now under the jurisdiction of the Department of Housing and Urban Development properly belong there rather than in the Department of Transportation. Administrative traditions, the visibility of programs, the leadership and staff potential in one agency as compared with another — such considerations are as valid as the purely taxonomic in determining the organizational location of government programs. It is hoped, however, both in the federal and in state and local governments, that program budgeting can provide an informational base for examining programs that cut across departmental lines.

Management considerations will always influence program definitions and in many cases will be decisive, particularly for large and decentralized operations. Any federal or state department that operates field offices will necessarily conduct a number of its departmental responsibilities in a single regional office. This office, regardless of the number of programs in which it is involved, must be planned and budgeted as a unit. And, as long as legislators are elected from regions and are concerned with their constituents, there is high probability that a regional office will be subject to legislative review in terms of some vague measure of total effectiveness, and not in terms of its contribution to the designated national (or state) programs that constitute the budgetary units for the department of which it is a part.

In local governments a related problem arises when a number of programs must serve a specific clientele, as with welfare and family services. In some cities a family-centered approach to human resources is evolving with an administrative pattern that requires a high degree of coordination among traditional departments of health, welfare, education, housing, and sometimes police and recreation. The activities and programs of a great many departments may be involved in staffing a comprehensive neighborhood social services center. Such centers, in effect, become a new budget program compiled from the budgets of many existing departments and agencies. In these circumstances it is evident that a program budget format should not inhibit new organizational approaches. The program is more important than the budget format.

Finally, organizational problems are posed by the requirements for program projection. An essential element in program budgeting is its long-range aspect. This year's budget request must be related to a multiyear program and financial plan. Line administrators are usually in the best position to assess future program needs and requirements and to project the activities under their jurisdiction. A central planning or central programming unit may be too far removed from the scene. Realistic projections for the intermediate, if not for the longer, term require a sense of day-to-day operations. But projections must also be centralized if departmental and executive office objectives are to be related to long-term goals, and if there is to be appropriate attention to resource constraints.

Measurement of Costs

For the Department of Defense, one of the greatest strengths of program budgeting is its careful attention to cost. The interests of central management control over the defense establishment required that the future costs of initial expenditures on a weapons system be very carefully estimated so that a modest commitment in one year might not accelerate unreasonably in future years. The close attention to cost also requires careful examination of the relationship between installation costs and the resulting impact on current expenditure, and, of course, attention to the cost of alternatives, measured in terms of effectiveness.

In the nonmilitary sectors of government these kinds of costing problems, while always present to some degree, are not as acute. Apart from natural resource projects, initiation of a new program or program subcategory does not automatically commit a heavy volume of expenditure in future years. If capital costs are a relatively small part of the total, program levels can be expanded or contracted more easily than in the military. Nevertheless, the longer time period inherent in program budgeting should contribute to a more effective use of resources over that time period, whether the outlay be current or capital.

The end-product approach of program budgeting does not, in and of itself, require a distinction between current and capital outlay. Program cost must reflect both, as well as their interrelationships. But emphasis is necessarily centered on the program itself and its accomplishments rather than on the economic character of the outlay. In other words, decisions should be about program and program levels and not about composition of inputs. For state and local governments, however, there may be financial and planning considerations that require a distinction between current and capital outlay. In such cases there need be no conflict between program budgeting and capital budgeting. Indeed, they could be mutually reinforcing. But program budgeting does not require capital budgeting.

Program analysis requires the use of some of the traditional concepts of microeconomics. In existing programs to be extended, marginal cost, not average cost, must be related to marginal outputs. If possible, opportunity costs should be explored; the cost of one program may be appropriately viewed in terms of the benefits that are foregone from giving up resources for an alternative program. Where benefits can be stated in monetary terms, and accrue over time, they should be discounted back to present values (see Chapter 7).

An end-product approach to budgeting can assist in the analysis of the influences contributing to program cost changes. A budget program may require additional resources because output is increased, because there has been an increase in the cost of inputs, or because productivity has decreased. Input costs, in turn, may rise because factor prices of existing inputs have increased or because a higher quality of input is available, presumably accompanied by enhanced productivity. These components need to be separated if there is to be an understanding of the relationship of program costs to program outcomes. Where the end products of government programs can be reasonably well defined and changes in the quantity and quality of output distinguished, it should be possible to analyze the nature of program cost increases. But in many cases quality and quantity changes cannot be separated, and precision in measurement is lost (see Chapter 9).

Complications in the measurement of agency costs may emerge from the practice of interagency transfers. This practice is widespread in the federal government and not infrequent in state and local governments. An appropriation to one agency will be used to finance activities conducted by another. An appropriation to the Department of Agriculture for research purposes may be transferred to the National Bureau of Standards, where the research will be conducted. In a state government, an appropriation to the department of health for a nurses' training program may be transferred to the department of education, where the program is actually administered. The agency that conducts the program is engaged in the production of an intermediate product for the agency that finances the program.

The emphasis on the end-product approach would suggest that the activity be counted in the agency to which the original appropriation was made, not in the agency where the program was conducted. Once more, alternative classifications are required to show, for purposes of management control, all the activities conducted by any agency as well as the program to which the activities should be assigned.

In state and local governments a quite different problem is posed by the availability of grant funds for the conduct of some programs but not others. In assessing costs and undertaking interprogram comparisons, how should the grant funds be counted? The funds are certainly not costless to the federal government or to the state government that may make them available to a municipality. But they are costless to the municipality, whose resource requirements are measured by the amount of funds needed from its own revenue sources as controlled by the matching requirements (see Chapter 8).

An aggregate or national viewpoint, of course, would require that all the costs of the program, from whatever source, be arrayed against program outcomes. But from the vantage point of the recipient government, its own resource allocation decisions are not likely to take account of federal or state grants as a part of program costs. A more efficient use of local resources will be obtained by comparing local costs with total program outcomes, including those financed by state and federal grants.

Grants-in-aid pose a very different problem for the grantor, who may have no responsibility for the administration of the grant. Federal grantor departments, for example, may not be able to measure program outcomes that are under the supervision of state or municipal governments.

Output Criteria

The experiences with performance budgeting in the 1950s exhibited considerable variety; this is invariably the case with budgetary innovation. There are a great many parties at interest to be served by the budgetary process. Those who install a budget reform will necessarily be motivated by a desire to strengthen such aspects of budget decisions as are seen, from their vantage point, to be most in need of repair, or by such political or administrative objectives as are perceived by the innovators. The recent history of program budgeting exhibits the same characteristics; there are wide varieties of experience within the federal government and among state and local governments.

In New York City, for example, PPB efforts are characterized by detailed systems analysis of police, fire, and hospital departments, to identify work units and increase technological efficiency under conditions of severe budget constraints (Joint Economic Committee, 1967, pp. 89 – 99). In Vermont and Wisconsin emphasis has been placed on improved program definition and justification for purposes of legislative review (Joint Economic Committee, 1967, pp. 86 – 89, 99 – 108). In the U.S. Department of the Interior PPB has been directed to long-range planning of physical resource programs (Joint Economic Committee, 1967, pp. 52 – 70). In the Department of Health, Education and Welfare major emphasis has been placed on the development of Program Memoranda for internal decisions on resource allocation (Joint Economic Committee, 1967, pp. 3 – 46). In some areas PPB is deemed to be nonapplicable; the Department of State was exempt from PPB requirements in 1967. One of the major difficulties encountered here is that a great many federal departments and agencies conduct programs overseas; the State Department has only the most tenuous supervision over the entire range of foreign affiars.

Given the variety of emphases that emerge under the general rubric of PPB, it follows that careful attention to the specification of output is not always required. Where major attention is directed to planning and projection, existing organizational structures and their current and anticipated program definitions may be adequate. But where the emphasis is placed on defining governmental goals and objectives, and relating the activities of organizational units to such goals and objectives, attention to output criteria is necessary.

The fundamental difficulty is that much of government output, by its very nature, is ill-defined and diffuse. Where public goods are relatively "pure" and the exclusion principle does not apply, there are, by definition, no discrete outputs that are appropriable by individuals. There is, to be sure, a continuum of government output, ranging from goods and services that can be specified with accuracy to those that cannot be so specified. The tons of steel and barrels of cement that emerge from the production processes of the market do have their counterpart in government activities; resource development projects produce gallons of water and kilowatt-hours of electricity. But for the market sector these specified outputs are final product. For the public sector the specified outputs are intermediate product. The final outcome is the consequence of the expenditure for the well being of the citizenry, and the objective is to maximize that well-being. As a result, output criteria, for the great bulk of government goods and services, will consist of a group of indicators or proxies, although these indicators never constitute a single criterion that permits the measurement of attainment for a specific program.

Where government output appears to be measurable and discrete, as with miles of roads paved, tons of garbage collected, or acres of land reforested, closer examination will reveal that these units frequently are not, in fact, comparable. Some miles of road are more costly to pave than others; commercial garbage collected is a different unit than residential garbage; land may be reforested in many different ways. In any event, the outputs that appear to be capable of ready quantification are often simply indicators of broader program objectives such as "provision of transportation," "sanitation," or "preservation of natural resources," all of which are composite and multipurpose.

For example, in developing guidelines for PPB installations in state and local governments, Hatry has proposed that objectives be specified as carefully as possible and criteria developed in relation to the specifications (Hatry, 1967). For the local government program, "Personal Safety," the objective could be defined as: "to reduce the amount and effects of external harm to individuals and in general to maintain an atmosphere of personal security from external events." In the subcategory "Law Enforcement," the objective might be stated: "to reduce the amount and effects of crime and in general to maintain an atmosphere of personal security from criminal behavior."

In this subcategory the criteria for measuring attainment of the program objective would consist of such entries as (1) annual number of offenses for each major class of crime, (2) crime rates per 1,000 of inhabitants, (3) a weighted composite crime-rate index, (4) annual value of property lost, or (5) an index of overall community "feeling of security." Other measures are also possible.

In the subcategory "Fire Prevention and Fire Fighting," the objective might be stated as: "to reduce the number of fires and loss of life and property due to fires." The criteria to measure this subcategory could include such entries as (1) the annual number of fires of various magnitudes, (2) the annual loss of life, (3) annual dollar value of property loss (adjusted for price level changes), or (4) the average time required to extinguish fires — a proxy measure of effectiveness.

The criteria for these subcategories are capable of reasonable definition and quantification. But there is no objective way of determining that one criterion is more important than another, and there is no way of aggregating the criteria to a single measurement of output. The development of the criteria and their use in budget decision processes will surely increase the attention that is directed to performance and output. The criteria will not provide an unambiguous measure of attainment.

A very different approach to output criteria is reflected in the program documents of HEW. The 1966 analysis of maternal and child health-care is representative (Joint Economic Committee, 1967, pp. 10–46; Wholely, 1969, pp. 451–71).

In this document the general objective of maternal and child health-care programs is described as "Make needed maternal and child health services available and accessible to all, in particular, to all expectant mothers and children in health-depressed areas." It is pointed out that there is no universal index of good or bad health among children. Subordinate objectives can be defined, however, such as "Reduce numbers of chronic handicapping conditions . . . Reduce infant mortality, particularly in 'health-depressed' areas" (Joint Economic Committee, 1967, p. 14). The document continues with a definition of health-depressed areas and a listing of such areas in terms of the incidence of infant mortality. The measures of chronic health conditions and unmet dental needs are set forth. The economic analysis consists of estimates of costs, manpower requirements, and estimates of the effectiveness of programs designed to meet the specified subobjectives. These estimates are arrayed for a health-depressed community of 50,000, and additional estimates are provided for a national program for all mothers and children in poverty. The document concludes with the statement:

> The interrelationships among the effects of environment, education, and medical care make it extremely difficult either to predict the improvements in health which would result from improvements in the delivery of services or to predict the human or economic benefits that would result from improvements in health. Data are lacking, moreover, on the effectiveness of past programs in reducing mortality or in preventing disability. (Joint Economic Committee, 1967, p. 40)

This approach to program budgeting is comparable with the suboptimization that has been practiced in the Department of Defense. The program objective in terms of defense capability is assumed in advance to be worthy of attainment; the analysis consists of estimating the alternative costs of attaining prespecified objectives. For HEW no effort is made to justify one type of health care as against another. The costs of maternity care, child health-care, and dental care are set forth but no conclusion as to their relative merit is suggested. The costs of each, and alternative approaches, including manpower requirements, are clearly stated.

Program analysis of this type is most useful for current budget decisions, for planning an agency's program, and interrelating existing programs. Ironically, its usefulness may reside in the fact that its aims are so modest. There is no effort here to specify outputs that can be compared with each other. There is no effort to estimate externalities or to invite broad comparisons of health outcomes with other outcomes, such as housing, in their effect on human welfare. But in a great many governments and for many functional areas the modest objective of costing out alternatives in relation to the level of services performed is sufficient justification for the effort that may be devoted to program budgeting.

The Benefits and Costs of Program Budgeting

As noted at the outset, there are three somewhat separable objectives that may be served by program budgeting — the taxonomic, the analytical, and the projective. For any specific government a program approach may embrace any or all of these objectives.

The classification of government activities by broad purposes may permit a better view of program interrelations and facilitate the identification of the need for coordinating mechanisms. An overview of objectives and goals will help to avoid the rigidities of existing organizational structures. Moreover, an emphasis on the taxonomic approach to program budgeting permits cross-classifications that reveal the multiple objectives served by many government programs, and the relationship of one program to another.

The analytical objective is perhaps the most important, and the most difficult. The basic task — that of measurement and comparison of inputs and outputs of government activity and the exploration of trade-offs and externalities — requires ingenuity and skill. Most often, what is required is measurement at the margin — the incremental costs and incremental outcomes derived from changes in existing programs. Less frequently, it will be necessary to measure the costs and outputs of wholly new programs.

In the experiences with performance budgeting in the early 1950s, it was discovered that there are a number of government activities where an end-product approach is almost wholly elusive. Recent developments in the theory and practice of program budgeting have not resolved — cannot resolve — this basic difficulty. Service output in the market sector is difficult to measure and to compare over time because of changes in its quality. Measurement of the quality of government service output faces the same difficulty. There is the further difficulty that, in the absence of prices, it becomes necessary to estimate the welfare consequences of public goods and services by improved education, improved health, or an improved environment. It is the identification of the specific contribution of government services to these consequences that is virtually impossible. A related difficulty is that many government programs serve multiple purposes.

A further difficulty is encountered in relating activities to outputs in the matter of general staff services which cannot be specifically allocated. Revenue administration, research and development, and the work of personnel offices, accounting offices, and legal staffs fall in this category.

As a result of the foregoing considerations a program budget does not measure output as a true end product; it will typically measure activities at some point short of the end product. Within the scope of this objective, which is a more modest one than frequently claimed for program budgeting, the systems analysis and measurements inherent in the technique will provide useful budgetary insights. In fact, relatively simple evaluations may be more useful than complicated ones. There are ever-present dangers in the latter (Enthoven and Smith, 1970, pp. 498–501).

Paradoxically, the government programs that are most susceptible to analytical techniques and where relatively usable data are available, such as in agriculture, are those in which political constraints are most severe. In the human resources area, where political constraints are less binding and there is greater freedom for policy change, there is a severe shortage of data on outcomes and effects (Schultze, 1968, pp. 88–89).

It is the analytic component — the examination and ranking of alternatives — that is intended to distinguish program budgeting, as it is currently practiced, from earlier efforts at performance measurement. But the relationship of analysis to policy may be a tenuous one. Wildavsky has put the point most strongly:

> All the obstacles previously mentioned . . . may be summed up in a single statement: *no one knows how to do program budgeting.* Another way of putting it would be to say that many know what program budgeting should be like in general, but no one knows what it should be in any particular case. Program budgeting cannot be stated in operational terms. . . .The reason for the difficulty is that telling an agency to adopt program budgeting means telling it to find better policies and there is no formula for doing that. (Wildavsky, 1970, pp. 467–68)

Wildavsky does not deny the possibility for improved policy analysis, but would concentrate attention on areas that are tractable and would divorce policy analysis from the requirements of the annual budget cycle (Wildavsky, 1970, pp. 472–75). Certainly the experience in the federal government since 1965 illustrates that program budgeting might well have been introduced more cautiously and with less fanfare. But unless policy analysis is, at some point, linked to the annual preparation and submission of the budget, it will likely have little impact.

The third objective — to project government activities into the future — is a sine qua non of rational planning for the public sector. Projections do not, of course, have the precision of budget estimates for the forthcoming fiscal year. They should not be regarded as either targets or constraints, but as rough guidelines to the future. They should spell out the options that are available in the immediate years ahead and reflect built-in increases. However, even as rough guidelines, projections must be structured by a common set of assumptions with respect to the size of the budget and program emphases. In the absence of central planning in the federal government, there is no such set of assumptions, except for the immediate fiscal year ahead. In consequence, the experience to date with the Program and Financial Plans has not been successful (Carlson, 1970, p. 377). Agency projections have been predicated on vastly different assumptions with respect to political feasibility and resource constraints. There have been difficulties with the definition of the term "commitment" in determining the volume of resources that is supposed to have been "pledged" for future expansion.

Long-range planning continues to be viewed as a part of program budgeting in the federal government, at least as an ultimate goal. Recent experience in the states with the creation of new offices of state planning, however, points in a different direction. In New York and California, state planning offices are concerned with economic projections, with projections of state government programs, and with economic growth, but are not involved directly in budget preparation. In local governments, planning offices are traditionally separated, organizationally and procedurally, from budget offices. In general, recent state and local developments in program budgeting have been organizationally linked with the budget process, not with the planning process.

Program budgeting will undoubtedly make important contributions to an improvement in the quality of budgetary decisions in governments that introduce it and seek to develop it over a period of years. It will be particularly helpful to centralized management decision processes, in that it will facilitate judgments about the appropriate level of a given program. Thus, central budget offices and chief executives should be able to make more intelligent decisions about increases or reductions in program levels. This ability is as important during a period of retrenchment as it is in a period of expansion.

For the immediate future, program budgeting will be much less useful for comparisons among programs, particularly where they have diverse end products. Program budgeting does not facilitate a calculation of marginal social costs and marginal social benefits for such varied programs as explorations in space, foreign aid, or medical care for the aged. Whether program budgeting will improve the quality of legislative review decisions continues to be very much in doubt. Experience in Congress and in those state and local legislatures where a program format has been employed does not suggest that such improvement will be the case, although at least one U. S. senator has expressed enthusiasm in this regard (Proxmire, 1970, pp. 413 – 23).

The most ardent advocates of program budgeting often convey the impression that budget decisions are susceptible to solution by operations research, or that systems analysis, with accompanying quantifications, will yield an efficient decision in matters of resource allocation. This view overlooks the fact that budget-making is also conflict management and conflict resolution. There is no efficient solution to be revealed by careful economic analysis apart from the political realities defined by those who contend for shares of public resources. Program budgeting is not a neutral, nonpolitical tool. Ideally, what is consummated in program budgeting is a marriage of the analytical and the political:

> It may, indeed, be necessary to guard against the naiveté of the systems analyst who ignores *political* constraints and believes that efficiency alone produces virtue. But it is equally necessary to guard against the naiveté of the decision maker who ignores *resource* constraints and believes that virtue alone produces efficiency. (Schultze, 1968, p. 76)

Program budgeting techniques do become important as a part of budgetary strategy and may be significant in the tactics of conflict resolution. As Rowan has said, "power and influence flow not only from traditional sources but also from the ability to command data and analyses" (Rowen, 1970, p. 227). A similar point has been made with respect to "scientific objectivity" in budgeting for higher education: "In such a context the new science of management serves not so much to manage the university as to manage the impression that outsiders have about it" (Rourke and Brooks, 1966, p. 103). Program budgeting may acquire significance as a tactical maneuver in the struggle over relative shares of public resources. It may also be used as an instrumentality for creating a favorable citizen response to public programs. It has been so used by the Department of Defense (Wildavsky, 1964, pp. 135 – 42).

Program budgeting injects into the decision process a new set of actors — the analytic staff — or, as Schultze has termed them, "partisan efficiency advocates" (Schultze, 1968, pp. 95 – 97). The political scientists who view government budgeting as essentially a bargaining technique in the general setting of conflict resolution are appropriately concerned lest the systems approach substitute an apparent economic rationality for political rationality (Mosher, 1967, pp. 67 – 71; 1969, pp. 160 – 67). There is indeed a potentially serious loss in democratic values in an overquantified approach to budget decisions. Numbers can be misused and assume significance far beyond that justified by the margin of error attached to their compilation. Numbers are intended to discipline the political process, not substitute for it.

It is possible to be relatively complacent about the substitution of market oriented or systems oriented decision processes for political decision processes (Schick, 1969, pp. 137 – 51). In a technological world we are subject to the continued assaults of a computerized existence. But there are large segments of the population which are not complacent about the resulting dehumanization. Governmental organization and governmental decision structures are now, and in the foreseeable future will be, subject to two divergent and conflicting forces: the needs for centralization inherent in a technological society where externalities abound, and the needs for decentralization in the relations of public programs to the constituents they are intended to serve (see Chapter 8). Program budgeting strengthens the former set of needs; as currently practiced it runs counter to the latter set.

In examining the political character of program budgeting it is necessary to distinguish among three type of politics: policy, partisan, and system (Wildavsky, 1966, pp. 304 – 5). Policy politics is simply "Which policy will be adopted?" Partisan politics is "Which party will win office?" System politics is concerned with how decision structures will be set up. Program budgeting, Wildavsky argues, is very little concerned with partisan politics, considerably concerned with policy politics, but very much concerned with system politics. Program budgeting, if its objectives are to be realized, requires, either immediately or prospectively for any government agency, a change in existing decision structures and, in general, an increased centralization of decision authority.

The system politics inherent in program budgeting comes into direct conflict with the existing organizational patterns of most government agencies. Government is organized around ways of getting things done — around management concerns that typically require operations in terms of professional skills, as with an accounting unit, or in terms of work flow, as with a typing pool or a mail room. Government is not organized in terms of output, and therefore the units of an organization cannot easily be budgeted in terms of output. It cannot be anticipated that this condition will change. Management considerations will continue to dominate. The efficiency costs of governmental reorganization, measured in terms of management effectiveness, to achieve a complete output orientation would be exorbitant.

References

Bureau of the Budget. *Special Analyses, Budget of the United States, 1971.* Washington, 1970.

Burkhead, Jesse. *Government Budgeting.* New York: Wiley, 1956.

Burkhead, Jesse, Thomas G. Fox, and John W. Holland. *Input and Output in Large-City High Schools.* Syracuse: Syracuse University Press, 1967.

Carlson, Jack W. "The Status and Next Steps for Planning, Programing, and Budgeting," in Robert W. Haveman and Julius Margolis, eds., *Public Expenditures and Policy Analysis.* Chicago: Markham, 1970, pp. 367–412.

Commission on Organization of the Executive Branch of the Government. *Budgeting and Accounting.* Washington, 1949.

Enthoven, Alain C. "Economic Analysis in the Department of Defense." *American Economic Review,* May 1963, pp. 413–23.

Enke, Stephen, D. *Defense Management.* Englewood Cliffs: Prentice-Hall, 1967.

Enthoven, Alain C., and K. Wayne Smith. "The Planning, Programing, and Budgeting System in the Department of Defense: An Overview from Experience," in Haveman and Margolis, eds., *Public Expenditures and Policy Analysis,* pp. 485–501.

Fisher, Gene H. "The Role of Cost-Utility Analysis in Program Budgeting," in David Novick, ed., *Program Budgeting.* Cambridge: Harvard University Press, 1965, pp. 61–78.

Gross, Bertram M. "The New Systems Budgeting." *Public Administration Review,* March-April 1969, pp. 113–37.

Grosse, Robert N. "Problems of Resource Allocation in Health," in Haveman and Margolis, eds., *Public Expenditures and Policy Analysis,* pp. 518–48.

Hammond, Paul Y. "A Functional Analysis of Defense Department Decision-Making in the McNamara Administration." *American Political Science Review,* March 1968, pp. 57–69.

Harper, Edwin L., Fred A. Kramer, and Andrew M. Rouse. "Implementation and Use of PPB in Sixteen Federal Agencies." *Public Administration Review,* November-December 1969, pp. 623–32.

Hatry, Harry P. *Criteria for Evaluation in Planning State and Local Programs.* Washington: State-Local Finances Project, The George Washington University, 1967.

Hitch, Charles J., and Roland N. McKean. *The Economics of Defense in the Nuclear Age.* Cambridge: Harvard University Press, 1960.

Hitch, Charles J., *Decision-Making for Defense.* Berkeley: University of California Press, 1965.

Hirsch, Werner Z. "Education in the Program Budget," in Novick, ed., *Program Budgeting.* Cambridge: Harvard University Press, 1963, pp. 178–207.

Joint Economic Committee, Subcommittee on Economy in Government. *The Planning-Programing-Budgeting System: Progress and Potentials,* September 1967.

McKean, Roland N. "Remaining Difficulties in Program Budgeting," in Stephen Enke, ed., *Defense Management.* Englewood Cliffs: Prentice-Hall, 1967, pp. 60–73.

McNamara, Robert S., "The Formulation of Political Objectives and Their Impact on the Budget," in Samuel A. Tucker, ed., *A Modern Design for Defense Decision.* Washington: Industrial College of the Armed Forces, 1966, pp. 27–29.

Mosher, Frederick C. *Program Budgeting.* Chicago: Public Administration Service, 1954.

———. "Communication on PPBS." *Public Administration Review,* March 1967, pp. 67–71.

———. "Limitations and Problems of PPBS in the States." *Public Administration Review,* March-April 1969, pp. 160–67.

Mushkin, Selma J. "PPB in Cities." *Public Administration Review,* March-April 1969, pp. 167–78.

Niskanen, William A. "The Defense Resource Allocation Problem" in Enke, ed., *Defense Management,* pp. 3–22.

Novick, David. "The Department of Defense," in Novick, ed., *Program Budgeting,* pp. 81–119.

Proxmire, William. "PPB, the Agencies and the Congress," in Haveman and Margolis, eds., *Public Expenditures and Policy Analysis,* pp. 413–23.

Quade, E. S., ed. *Analysis for Military Decisions.* Chicago: Rand McNally, 1964.

Rourke, Francis M., and Glen E. Brooks. *The Managerial Revolution in Higher Education.* Baltimore: The Johns Hopkins Press, 1966.

Rowen, Henry S. "Assessing the Role of Systematic Decision Making in the Public Sector," in Julius Margolis, ed., *The Analysis of Public Output.* New York: Columbia University Press, 1970, pp. 219–27.

Schick, Allen. "Some Problems of Multipurpose Budget Systems." Washington: U. S. Bureau of the Budget, 1966 (mimeo).

———. "The Road to PPB: The Stages of Budget Reform." *Public Administration Review,* December 1966a, pp. 243–58.

———. *"Systems Politics and Systems Budgeting."* *Public Administration Review,* March–April 1969, pp. 137–51.

Schultze, Charles L. *The Politics and Economics of Public Spending.* Washington: The Brookings Institution, 1968.

Wholey, Joseph S. "The Absence of Program Evaluation as an Obstacle to Effective Public Expenditure Policy: A Case Study of Child Health Care Programs," in Joint Economic Committee, *The Analysis and Evaluation of Public Expenditures: The PPB System,* vol. 1, Washington, 1969, pp. 451–71.

Wildavsky, Aaron. *The Politics of the Budgetary Process.* Boston: Little, Brown, 1964.

———. "The Political Economy of Efficiency: Cost-Benefit Analysis, Systems Analysis, and Program Budgeting." *Public Administration Review,* December 1966, pp. 292–310.

———. "Rescuing Policy Analysis from PPBS," in Haveman and Margolis, eds., *Public Expenditures and Policy Analysis,* pp. 461–81.

Yoingco, Angel Q., and Antonio O. Casem. "Performance Budgeting in the Philippines." *Philippine Economic Journal,* no. 16, 1969, pp. 166–84.

SEVEN

Benefit-Cost Analysis

Benefit-cost analysis is a technique for assessing the economic utility of a public investment project. The technique can be used to indicate whether a specific expenditure should be undertaken. It can also be used to determine the appropriate scale of investment and thus the optimum size of a specific investment project, as well as the product-mix, capital intensity, and other aspects of project design. A benefit-cost approach can also be employed as the framework for a general theory of government investment. In this chapter emphasis will be placed on benefit-cost as a decision technique, although some attention is also directed to benefit-cost as investment theory.

Although benefit-cost has been most often used in analyzing the justification for investment in physical resources, in recent years it has been extended to the analysis of investment in human resources. As a decision technique the results of benefit-cost are, at best, a helpful guide. The outcome of the analysis alone does not constitute the decision.

Benefit-cost is simple in concept, reflecting a most elementary decision rule: No rational person could be expected to undertake actions where anticipated costs exceeded anticipated benefits. But the practical applications become more complicated.

Benefit-cost analysis is a part of established budgetary procedures in the field of water resources. The term is also used to describe a general method of analysis of any public expenditure, whether that expenditure represents investment in physical or human capital. As such, it may be distinguished from cost-effectiveness or cost-utility analysis, although existing terminology is by no means standardized (G. A. Steiner, 1965, p. 311; Goldman, 1967).

The term "cost effectiveness" emerged from the analysis of military programs where objectives were prespecified and the purpose of the analysis was to explore the relative merits of alternative means of accomplishing the specified objective. For example, if the objective is to attain a given level of deterrent strength to counter assumed levels of enemy capability, the task of the analyst is to ascertain the costs of alternatives for attaining this specified level. In these circumstances no careful quantification of benefits is required; emphasis is placed on exploring the relative costs of the technological alternatives that are available. Costs are to be minimized for a given output. The implicit question to be answered is, "Given that a specified objective is to be attained, what is the least-cost alternative way of attaining the objective?"

Cost effectiveness in this sense can be applied in other contexts, such as the analysis of pollution abatement in a water resource program for a river basin. Successive levels of pollution abatement could be specified and the costs of attaining each level by the available alternatives could be estimated. The evaluation of benefits that might accompany each level need not be worked out in detail. This approach does not require an exploration of the trade-offs among different pollution abatement objectives but it does require an exploration and cost analysis of the various means by which abatement levels could be attained.

On the other hand, benefit-cost analysis, as traditionally employed, does not prespecify a program level or assume in advance that a benefit is worth achieving. In fact, the analysis is specifically intended to compare costs and benefits of various projects, and the justification of specific programs and program levels within projects. The results of the comparisons indicate the activities and activity levels that are most justifiable. The optimum level of output is to be ascertained. The implicit question to be answered is, "Given that there are various projects to be undertaken, which, if any, are worth doing?"

The recent extension of the analytics of expenditure analysis, particularly as a part of program budgeting, has blurred the original distinction between benefit-cost and cost effectiveness. The latter is now employed as the generic term to embrace all manner of techniques for the analysis of inputs, technological alternatives, and outputs. Benefit-cost analysis, in this context, is simply the most prominent of cost effectiveness methods.

The estimation of both benefits and costs can be undertaken only in relation to an objective function. When economic welfare is viewed as a one-dimensional quantity, the objective function is usually taken to be an increase in national income or in aggregate consumption. In contemporary discussion priority is usually given to consumption, including government-provided goods, as against national income, on the ground that the ultimate purpose of investment, whether public or private, is to increase future consumption.

Other purely economic arguments of objective functions could also be specified, such as the supply of foreign exchange, or contribution to full employment, or even a desired state of income distribution. In practice there are usually many economic and sometimes noneconomic objectives to be served by public expenditure programs. The task of the analyst is to specify these objectives without attempting to weight or make comparisons among them (Eckstein, 1961, pp. 439 – 49) — this last is presumed to be the task of the policy-maker.

Once the objective function is specified, benefits consist of the present value of the time stream of the contribution to the objective function that will emerge from the project. Likewise, costs are estimated as the present value of the resources that are employed, valued at their opportunity cost, as a consequence of implementing the project. Benefits measure the contribution to the objective function; costs measure the reduction in the objective function.

A simplified formula for present value is

$$PV = \sum_{t=1}^{\infty} \frac{B_t - C_t}{(1 + r)_t}$$

where B is the benefit (e.g., addition to aggregate consumption), r is the rate at which future benefits are discounted over t years of project life, and C is the cost. In this simplified formula C includes both operating costs and the capital costs of amortization.

In terms of this formula a positive present value means that the project is a justifiable use of resources. Present values may also be expressed in terms of a ratio in which the numerator consists of discounted benefits and the denominator consists of discounted operating and capital costs. If the B/C ratio is greater than 1.0 the project is a justifiable use of resources. It should be stressed that both benefits and costs must be measured over time. The technique permits a broad view of project impacts; the economic consequences of the project may be traced through a series of effects on factor and product prices, repercussion effects on investment, and multiplier effects on income.

Benefit-cost analysis is grounded in formal welfare economics (Eckstein, 1958, pp. 19 – 46). This grounding derives from an analogy with private competitive markets. In such markets, assuming neither external effects nor decreasing costs, the interaction between consumers who maximize their utilities and producers who maximize their profits will attain the highest total utility for any given income distribution. The specific conditions for such an optimum can be set out in greater or lesser detail, but the essential requisites are that (1) consumers equate their valuation of the marginal unit of each commodity taken to the valuation of alternative consumption foregone and that (2) producers organize their inputs so that each commodity is produced by the method that sacrifices the least highly-valued of foregone alternatives.

Benefit-cost analysis accepts as a starting point the principles of market-based measures of the valuation of both benefits and costs. Since consumption is the essential argument in the implicit objective function of the traditional approach to benefit-cost, benefits are measured by the market price of the outputs from the public investment or by the price that consumers of the outputs would be willing to pay if they could be charged. Such prices are taken as indicators of the relative value that the economy places on the objective benefits of the investment. Costs are measured by the monetary outlays necessary to undertake the investment. Such outlays represent a measure of the worth of the least highly-valued (consumption) alternatives that would have to be given up to construct and operate the project in question.

To the extent that the assumed competitive characteristics of the economy do not obtain, benefit-cost analysis must be modified in application to any specific project. Externalities, for example, are not reflected in market pricing and may need to be incorporated in the benefits or costs of a public project. Market valuations may not reflect the whole of consumer valuations, as where esthetic considerations are involved. For any specific project it may be necessary to reject the prevailing income distribution and undertake investments that seek to alter that distribution.

It has been pointed out that benefit-cost is most effective in dealing with cases of intermediate social goods (Musgrave, 1969, pp. 797 – 806). This effectiveness depends crucially upon the availability of measures of benefits and costs. For those goods that are final products and for which exclusion is not practiced (see Chapters 2 – 3), consumer valuations are as difficult to ascertain in a benefit-cost framework as in any other. But where public goods are intermediate product, opportunity cost measures of benefits are more easily obtained by imputation to the intermediate good of its contribution to the market-produced final good.

Historical Development

Benefit-cost analysis originated, not in the writings of economists, but in the practices of federal administrative agencies in the United States and, in particular, in the practices of water resource agencies. In these agencies the analysis is operational in the sense that the technique is used for the evaluation of the feasibility of specific projects, for the selection of preferred projects from among a range of possible projects, and for the justification of the projects in the budgetary process. Benefit-cost analysis is an established part of the procedure by which water resource projects move through the proposal stage to legislative authorization and eventual construction. Although in recent years benefit-cost analysis has come to be employed in other areas of expenditure analysis, it continues to be most closely integrated with budget procedures in the area of water resources. Moreover, most of the conceptual problems of benefit-cost are well illustrated by experience in water resources.

The federal government has engaged in water resource development programs since 1802. In the early years of the nineteenth century these were primarily projects for the development of navigable waters. In the latter part of the nineteenth century programs for irrigation and flood control were added, and later, water resource development for hydroelectric power, water supply, recreation, and pollution abatement.

Water resource development provides a classic illustration of the complexities of a public good. For some water programs, the exclusion principle is clearly inapplicable. The protection of the flood plain cannot be extended to some residents without extending it to all residents of that plain. Water resource projects abound in externalities. The downstream dam may add to the value of the upstream reservoir; the reservoir may destroy or enhance a scenic view; fish and wildlife may be protected or annihilated by a project designed for another purpose. Furthermore, water resource projects are developmental in character. They often provide the social overheads in transportation or water supply that encourage private investment and economic growth. Water resource projects are often tied to distributional objectives, particularly on a regional basis. Specific groups within a region may have their interests promoted by the use of public funds. Political and social objectives may be advanced by water resource projects, as in the long-standing requirement in federal irrigation law that landowners with 160 acres or less shall be given preference in water supply.

The multiple and sometimes conflicting objectives that are served by water resource projects invite an intensification of the "purely" political aspects of public decision-making. Vote-trading to secure increased appropriations, described in such phrases as "log-rolling" and "pork barrel" has long characterized the legislative process in this area. Unless there are no budget constraints, that is, unless the Congress is prepared to appropriate funds for all water resource development projects that could be proposed, criteria must necessarily be established for limiting the range of choice. It seems likely that benefit-cost techniques were developed in order to provide economic criteria as a discipline to the political process.

In any event, as far back as 1902, the Rivers and Harbors Act required that engineering reports for projects proposed by the Army Corps of Engineers include a discussion of benefits and costs. This approach was pursued over the next several decades and was encouraged by the National Resources Council, the agency predecessor to the National Resources Planning Board, in the early 1930s. Benefit-cost analysis was first formalized in the Flood Control Act of 1936 with this declaration of intent: "that the Federal government should improve or participate in the improvement of navigable waters or their tributaries, including watersheds thereof, if the benefits to whomsoever they may accrue are in excess of estimated costs." Although federal water resource agencies other than the Corps of Engineers are not similarly bound by statutory prescription, conventional practice dictates adherence to benefit-cost analysis for all water resource project justification.

Operating Procedure

The practices that are followed by the Corps of Engineers, although more highly formalized than those of most federal agencies, will illustrate the procedures that are involved (Eckstein, 1958, pp. 2 – 8).

The initial demand for a water resource project may originate either with interested citizens in an area or with the federal water resource agency that is responsible for specific programs. For example, flood damage along a stream may give rise to demands by affected homeowners, business firms, and farmers for the provision of additional flood protection. Such persons may approach the district office of the Corps of Engineers to seek advice and assistance. The congressman for the affected district will also be consulted. If it seems desirable to undertake a survey, the congressman will attempt to secure authorization for it in the annual flood control legislation enacted by the Congress. This will authorize the Corps of Engineers to undertake a preliminary investigation. If the project appears to be feasible, a thorough exploration of project justification will be authorized by the Congress.

The Water Resource Development and Planning Act of 1965 established a federal Water Resources Council with responsibility for establishing river basin commissions, for coordinating planning among them, and for allocating planning funds. Specific projects may be subject to preliminary review by the Council, if they come within a major watershed.

Once planning funds are approved by the Congress, the district engineer will survey all engineering and economic aspects of the project and propose a feasible water use program. Hearings will be held at which affected parties at interest will testify. As a part of the survey, the district office will estimate the costs and benefits that are expected to result from the project and include these estimates in the project report.

This project report is reviewed by the Board of Engineers for Rivers and Harbors in Washington. The Chief of the Corps of Engineers will then add his recommendations to that of the Board, and the complete report will be sent to other interested federal agencies as well as to the Office of Management and Budget. The recommendations of the OMB are added to the project documents and these are transmitted to the Committee on Public Works of the House of Representatives.

This Committee will typically hold hearings on the proposed project; its staff will examine the project justification material. If the Committee's findings are favorable, it may then include the project for authorization in the annual flood control legislation. This legislation, if adopted, will authorize the project, but it will not provide funds. These must be provided separately by appropriation measures. In consequence, far more projects are authorized than are actually constructed. There is, however, no requirement that the projects once authorized need be rejustified subsequently, even after the lapse of several years' time.

At the successive stages of review and decision, the underlying benefit-cost analysis is of considerable, but not exclusive, importance in decisions concerning the project. In some cases, projects will be approved even though measurable costs exceed measurable benefits, particularly where intangible values, such as the saving of human lives, are thought to be present. In other cases, projects with favorable benefit-cost ratios will not be approved, or, if approved, will not be funded by the appropriations committees. There is nothing in federal legislation or practice that requires the benefit-cost ratio to control the decision.

It may also be noted that once authorized projects are constructed, there is no provision for a post facto review of the underlying benefit-cost analysis. Benefit-cost is used for project justification, not for the appraisal of outcomes.

The General Concept

In the most general sense the method of benefit-cost analysis encompasses all techniques for program or project evaluation that involve systematic comparison of benefits and costs in the context of an implicit or explicit objective function. Viewed this broadly, benefit-cost has relevance to private as well as public economic decision-making. The analysis of alternative investment programs engaged in by both government and business is an application of this generalized technique. It is conventional to refer to the investment decision-making procedures of private enterprises as capital budgeting and to those of the public sector as benefit-cost, but the two share a common foundation in the theory of capital.

The controversial issues with regard to investment criteria in general are as relevant to benefit-cost analysis in the public sector as they are to private investment. The parallelism of these general considerations, however, does not obliterate fundamental differences between public and private criteria for project selection. The major differences lie in the objective function, the nature of the constraints which set limits to the magnitude of the investment or expenditure, and the degree of interdependence and indivisibility among projects.

All programs and projects, whether public or private, are subject to some budget constraint. Much of the contemporary theory of capital budgeting is concerned with the specification of the appropriate constraints and the opportunity cost of funds for investment purposes by individual private enterprises. For public expenditure decisions, the legally-established budget for the governmental jurisdiction in question and its allocation among agencies and bureaus is the primary manifestation of the financial constraint. Both total budget expenditures and expenditures under large functional categories will be limited by such factors as an executive decision that total expenditure shall not exceed a specified amount, or that taxpayer resistance will not permit revenues to rise above a certain figure, or that the requirements of economic stabilization are such as to limit the total outlay. It is then necessary to establish a priority ranking of projects which is grounded in the relevant budget and other constraints.

Benefit-cost analysis is usually undertaken under the assumption that the economy is operating at generally full employment conditions, and that resources are scarce and must be valued at their opportunity cost. Where resources are unemployed, opportunity costs may be negligible. When this condition obtains it is possible to revise costs downward. A careful study of the 1957 – 64 experience with water resource projects in this country demonstrated that such downward revisions would range from 5 to 30 percent, depending on the type of project and the location of the construction site. (Haveman and Krutilla, 1968, pp. 65 – 86). An alternative approach, supported by Prest and Turvey, is to continue to use the market prices of employed resources, even where there is existing unemployment, in order to facilitate comparisons of the allocative consequences of public projects under alternative means for economic stabilization, such as tax reduction or increases in transfer payments.[1]

Criteria for Project Analysis

The framework for project analysis involves four elements: selection of the choice set; specification of constraints; measurement of benefits and costs; and determination of a choice model (Steiner, 1969, pp. 73 – 91).

THE CHOICE SET

The notion of a choice set reflects the need to limit the range of possible projects for comparison within a particular benefit-cost analysis. Without such limitation the context for any public sector benefit-cost study logically encompasses the entire budget and hence calls for comparisons among projects of all departments and agencies. There is a certain appeal to such a comprehensive conception in which the total budget, its departmental and agency breakdown, and the selection of individual projects are mutually and simultaneously determined. The practice of public budgeting, however, does not proceed in this manner. The usual situation is that the budget for particular agencies is taken as given. In this situation, the ranking of projects by benefit-cost considerations

---

1. A. R. Prest and R. Turvey, "Cost-Benefit Analysis: A Survey," *Economic Journal,* December 1965, p. 694. This article is the best available examination of the conceptual issues in this area. The authors of this volume have relied on this source in a number of ways not fully revealed by specific citations.

proceeds within the choice set of an agency or bureau at the subdepartmental level.

Steiner argues that the scope of the choice set is a crucial element in benefit-cost analysis of public projects. Unlike private investment decisions where individual projects do not substantially interact with one another, public investments are characterized by interdependencies, incompatibilities, rather rigid budget constraints, and a variety of nonbudget constraints. As a result, a specific project in the public sector cannot be evaluated solely in terms of its "absolute merit" but requires consideration in the context of that choice set comprising those projects that have a common budget constraint, or common interdependencies or incompatibilities.

Thus the scope of the choice set may be complicated. All water resource projects may be subject to the same budget constraint but be located in different regions with no interdependence or incompatibility. But a specific water project may be highly incompatible with other government programs in its region, as where a reforestation program and a reservoir are intended to occupy the same site.

CONSTRAINTS

The nonbudgetary constraints that must be taken into account in the ranking of projects encompass such limitations as are imposed by physical, financial, distributional, political, or legal considerations. These constraints may be expressed in absolute terms, as where a project's budget is fixed or where its geographic location is specified. They may also be expressed in relative terms and analyzed by estimating trade-offs. It may be possible, for example, to cost out the distributional value of flood protection for poor farmers as against flood protection for wealthy farmers, where the differences are measured in terms of the opportunity cost of water for one purpose as against the other.

Formally, constraints may be treated either as "side-considerations" or as elements in the objective function. The significant question with regard to the treatment of constraints is whether they can be removed. Certain physical constraints derive from the state of nature while other constraints arise from limitations of knowledge and technique, and these cannot be modified in the immediate future. On the other hand, laws, regulations, and administrative procedures can be modified. Those constraining elements which could be, but are not, removed constitute, in effect, values implicitly included in the objective function. The acceptance of constraints which are not immutable reflects, essentially, decisions about objectives rather than the incorporation of technical limitations into the project design.

MEASUREMENT

The issues which arise in the definition and measurement of benefits and costs constitute the subject matter of much of the remainder of this chapter. The purpose of this section is to outline in the most general sense the way in which the conceptualization of benefits and costs influences the ranking of projects. The essence of the definition of benefits and costs is that they are intended to measure the net contribution to a given objective function of a particular project. Benefits measure the direct and indirect contributions to the function by the project, while costs indicate the direct and indirect contributions to the function which foregone alternatives could have made. Thus, satisfactory measurements of benefits or costs require specification of the significant elements within the objective function, including relative weights where the function has multiple arguments, and of knowledge of how various project activities influence the elements in the objective function. Failure to satisfy either of these conditions results in faulty estimates of the relation of benefits and costs and unsatisfactory ranking of projects.

Market prices provide considerable information regarding benefits and costs, but often they are inaccurate measures of consumers' evaluation of activities and in no case do they measure such vital aspects of social welfare as freedom, equity, and justice. The literature of benefit-cost abounds with ingenious attempts to measure relevant yet elusive project outcomes. Nonetheless, as Steiner concludes, "Much work remains to be done" (Steiner, 1969, p. 86).

THE CHOICE MODEL

The final element in project analysis is the selection of the model or criterion for relating the estimated costs and benefits of diverse projects. Establishment of the constraints and of the objective function, along with the assumption that the measurements of costs and benefits are consonant with these considerations, in effect resolves the important issues which might otherwise be determined implicitly as a consequence of the selection of a choice criterion. It is precisely because the alternative criteria implicitly treat such elements as constraints, objective functions, interdependencies, and indivisibilities differently that they yield, at times, inconsistent results (Steiner, 1969, pp. 86–90). To the extent such elements have already been resolved and are reflected in the estimates of costs and benefits then there remain no substantive differences among the criteria but only certain formal relationships.

In selecting criteria for public investment it is useful to distinguish two major concerns. One centers around issues in the determination of the proper investment criterion under the assumption that projects are perfectly divisible, independent, have no externalities, are faced with the single constraint of a capital cost expressed in terms of a rate of interest, and certain other simplifying assumptions. Here the questions are much the same as those in the theory of investment for a business firm: What are the differences among the criteria, under what circumstances do they yield conflicting results, and which is the appropriate one to use under the given assumptions? The second concern is more specific to the problem of public investment and deals with the appropriateness of the various choice criteria for the particular circumstances and conditions of investment for which indivisibilities and dependencies abound and multiple constraints and complex objective functions are characteristic. While most of this chapter deals with efforts to establish measures of costs, benefits, constraints, and other relevant elements under these difficult conditions, this section is devoted to the question of how various choice models lend themselves to the incorporation of such measures.

Alternative Choice Models. Using the analogy of benefit-cost analysis and private investment decision-making, the selection of projects is essentially similar to the ranking of alternative private investment programs. If profits (revenues minus costs) are taken to be the sole element in the objective function and benefits and costs are measured only in terms of net revenues, then the enterprise can choose among several criteria for ranking investment alternatives. These criteria include the discounted present value of profits (benefit minus cost), the ratio of present value of profits to costs (benefit/cost), the internal rate of return or marginal efficiency of investment (the rate of discount which equates the present value of the stream of net returns with the original investment cost), and the payout period (the number of years it takes for net revenues to equal the original investment cost).

Obviously, the payout period is a crude, unsatisfactory standard for project ranking. It ignores the size of the stream of net benefits which occurs after the project has earned enough to cover its original costs. It is usually employed only where there is high uncertainty about the future.

To rank projects by the internal rate of return or the marginal efficiency of investment requires calculation of that rate of discount which equates the present value of the stream of net benefits with the original cost of the investment. This approach may be potentially difficult because the equation for its solution is of a degree equal to the number of years for which benefits are expected to accrue. There may be multiple solutions, with the need for further criteria in order to choose among these solutions.

Such a situation is illustrated in Figure 7.1, in which discounted present value is shown on the Y axis and the discounting interest rate on the X axis. Here the nature of the time stream of net benefits is not "well-behaved" since as the discounting interest rate increases, present value rises, reaches a peak, and then declines, becoming negative at rates above a certain level. Calculation of the internal rate of return for such a pattern of net benefits yields two interest rates which equate present value to zero.[2]

2. A time stream of net benefits with results of this type is: − 100, 90, 110, − 60, − 60.

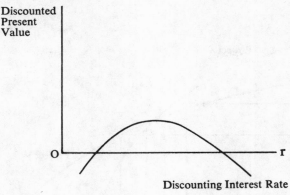

Figure 7.1. The Time Stream of Benefits

If for a given project the stream of net benefits is such that its present value declines monotonically as the discounting interest rate increases, a single internal rate of return will emerge. What then of the ranking of projects by this rate in comparison with benefits minus costs or with the ratio of benefits to costs?

In selection among a set of specified projects, these criteria may, on occasion, conflict. This possibility can arise with respect to the present value and the internal rate of return if, for example, there are two or more mutually exclusive projects identified in terms of given time streams of benefits and costs. The benefit minus cost (present value) standard establishes project priority in accordance with the amount of the present discounted value of net benefits. The internal rate of return criterion, on the other hand, ranks projects by the magnitudes of the rate of return at which present value is equal to zero. The possibility of conflicting criteria is illustrated in Figure 7.2 where two alternative projects W and V are shown. The internal rate of return, OS, for project V, exceeds that of W (OR) and so V would have a preferred position in the selection of projects by that standard. With regard to the benefit minus cost or discounted present value criterion, project V still outranks project W at discount rates in excess of OC, but at rates below OC the order is reversed, and W becomes the preferred project.

The simplest situation in which present value curves will cross occurs when one project has smaller net benefits which accrue relatively early while the other has larger net benefits concentrated in more distant time periods. At low discount rates the long-run future returns of the latter will provide it with a higher present value, but as the discount rate increases, the contribution of future returns weighs less and less heavily in present value until at some rate the present value of the first project becomes greater.

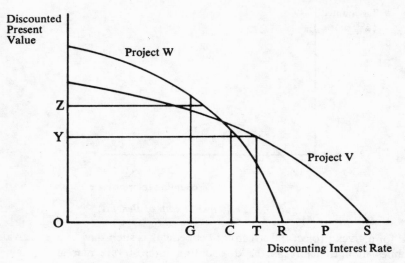

Figure 7.2. Criteria for Project Selection

Discussion of this inconsistency in the context of the investment decision of the private firm leads, in the usual treatment, to the conclusion that if the interest rate used to obtain the relative present value accurately measures the cost of capital to the firm, then this criterion rather than the internal rate of return will select the project which optimizes the firm's objective function of profit maximization. Investment choices, however, whether public or private, do not always involve mutually exclusive projects, or involve projects which have a single possible scale measured in terms of capital costs. As a result there is need for a standard of minimum qualification, in terms of the choice criterion to determine which mutually compatible projects shall or shall not be undertaken.

Project Ranking. Rankings of projects are not always necessary for investment choices. When projects are mutually exclusive, a conflict of the sort described above may occur so that a criterion is necessary to select the one which contributes most to the objective function. In such a situation, however, all that is required is to select the best project, not to rank the projects. Even if the context in which project selection takes place is such that potential projects are not mutually exclusive, so that several can be chosen, it still is not necessary to rank them. What is required is to establish either a minimum or cutoff internal rate of return or a particular discount rate for calculation of whether the discounted present value exceeds a minimum acceptable value.

In the situation depicted in Figure 7.2 if the projects were mutually compatible and did not involve any interdependencies, one, both, or neither could be chosen regardless of relative ranking. Selection would depend upon the minimum qualifying rate of return or on discounted present value with an assumed discount rate. According to the rate of return criterion, at a cutoff interest rate of *OC* both *W* and *V* qualify, while at a rate of *OP* only *V* is acceptable. From the perspective of the discounted present value approach, both projects would qualify at an interest rate of *OG* and a cutoff present value of *OY,* while only project *W* would qualify at that rate if the minimum present value were raised to *OZ.* If, however, the discounting interest rate were raised to *OT* only project *V* would be acceptable at the cutoff present value standard of *OY.*

The relevant issue appears to be not that of ranking but of acceptance or rejection of projects. In this regard, the rate of return criterion, by utilizing a present value of zero as its standard, is able to provide an invariant evaluation of projects which can be compared with an interest rate (so long as the stream of net returns is "well behaved"). The discounted present value criterion, on the other hand, yields judgments which will differ among themselves and with regard to the rate of return evaluations depending upon the discounting interest rate used (unless all projects are such that, in terms of Figure 7.2, none of the discounted present value curves intersect). Unfortunately, as has been pointed out, the unique evaluation yielded by the internal rate of return is not always consistent with maximization of the relevant objective function.

Leaving aside for the moment the substantive considerations in the choice among these conflicting criteria for public investment decisions, there remains the question of whether rankings of projects ever become necessary. So long as the minimum standards for approval of projects are accurate reflections of relevant constraints, there is no need for rankings as such. However, if budgetary or other constraints are not fully reflected in project acceptance standards, ranking provides a way to determine which of those projects nominally qualified shall in fact be undertaken. Again, in terms of Figure 7.2, let *W* and *V* now be two compatible yet competitive projects, each of only one possible size. On the one hand, if the nominal cutoff interest rate is *OC,* but funds sufficient to finance only one project are available, *V* is preferable by virtue of its higher internal rate of return. On the other hand, given a discount rate of *OG* and a requirement of positive present value, both *W* and *V* qualify, but, if funds are lacking, *W* is preferred on the grounds of its higher present value at the given discount rate. Thus, project selection can be based on rankings, and the two criteria under consideration may provide dissimilar rankings.

B/C and B − C. Selection among a group of mutually compatible projects raises still further difficulties. The discounted present value criterion, although it gives the correct answer to the simplified problem of choice among mutually inconsistent projects, has an inherent bias in favor of large projects which could lead to a less than optimal mix of investment opportunities. Suppose the constraint on investment to be not that of a given cost for capital funds, but of an absolute limit to the amount of funds available for investment. For example, let the discounted amount of capital funds available be 50. Referring to Table 7.1, Project 1, as the project yielding the highest present value, would be accorded top priority and would absorb all the funds. Yet, if there were available ten small projects of the character of Project 2 in Table 7.1, allocation of the 50 of funds to this group of projects would provide 60 of net benefits rather than the 50 associated with Project 1.

Table 7.1. Relationships among Criteria

Project No.	Discounted Benefits	Discounted Costs	Net Benefit (B – C)	Benefit-Cost Ratio (B/C)
1	100	50	50	2.00
2	11	5	6	2.20
3	20	15	5	1.33
4	104	100	4	1.04
5	20	16	4	1.25
6	12	8	4	1.50
7	13	10	3	1.33
8	10	7	3	1.47
9	2	1	1	2.00

In these circumstances the rate of discount as the implicit constraint to reflect the cost of capital is not the effective constraint. The effective constraint is the supply of capital funds. The criterion of acceptance of all projects with a positive present value cannot be implemented at the given discount rate because funds are insufficient to meet costs. One way to avoid this difficulty is to employ as the basis for ranking projects not the difference between benefits and costs but their ratios. The benefit-cost ratio does not bias selection in favor of large over small projects, but its rankings and the actual ratio for various projects still depend upon the discount rate. As a consequence, if the discount rate justified more projects with present values in excess of zero than the budget constraint allows, then there also will be more projects with benefit-cost ratios in excess of one than the same budget constraint will permit.

In these circumstances, it is possible to recalculate the discounted benefits and costs by successively higher interest rates until the number of projects which pass the test is consistent with the available budget. As rates increase, the present value of some projects will fall below zero and they will be eliminated as the benefit-cost ratio for certain projects now drops below one. The nature of the relation between the benefit-cost ratios and the difference between benefits and costs is such that the projects eliminated as the interest rate rises may not be the same ones. Inconsistent results can obtain even if this procedure is followed, but it does eliminate the need for project rankings and reestablishes a rate of discount as the relevant constraint, although such a contrived rate lacks the economic rationale of a rate selected as representative of social time-preference or the return to private investment (see below, this chapter).

The discussion, so far, has mainly concerned the relation of benefits minus costs to the rate of return. Clearly, comparison of the difference between benefits and costs and the ratio between them can be made only after some discounting interest rate has been selected to permit measurement of the present values of benefits and costs. Assuming that benefits and costs are estimated by the application of an arbitrary interest rate, what is the relation of present value to the ratio of benefits to costs? The relation between a ratio and the difference between the numerator and denominator conforms to no simple rule other than the obvious one that when the ratio is one the difference is zero. Beranek (1967, pp. 21 – 23), who has discussed the issue, is able to reach only the generalization that with respect to two projects, if the one which has a lower present value involves larger discounted costs, it will also have a lower benefit-cost ratio.

Tables 7.1 and 7.2 illustrate the relationship among benefits minus costs, the benefit-cost ratio, and the relative magnitude of discounted costs. Table 7.1 clearly shows that the ranking of a series of projects by net discounted present value does not conform to the ranking of the same projects by the ratio of benefits to costs. In Table 7.2 the generalization that consistent rankings result when the costs of the lower-ranking project are above those of the higher-ranking one is illustrated. In Comparison I, the project with the larger net benefits (Project 2) has lower costs; this project also has a higher benefit-cost ratio. Comparison II shows the converse of this case, since the project (6) with the larger net benefit has higher costs and a lower benefit-cost ratio. On the other hand, Comparison III indicates that a higher cost for a project with larger net benefits does not necessarily give it a lower benefit-cost ratio. Comparison IV summarizes these possibilities and serves to indicate the absence of a simple relationship.

These tables are also useful in revealing the importance of the netness of measures of costs and benefits in the determination of project rankings. If, for example, with respect to Project 1, 40 of its costs were now to be treated, instead, as deductions from benefits, the present value would remain at 50, but the benefit-cost ratio would rise to 6.0 (60/10). As will be seen in the discussion below, the allocation, in practice, of a particular element as a project cost or as a deduction from benefits is by no means a routine matter but involves basic questions with regard to constraints and the objective function.

Finally, there appears to be no systematic relation between ranking by the

Table 7.2. Differences in Project Ranking

		Projects Ranked By B-C (Net Benefits)	Relation Between and Among Costs (Discounted Costs)	Projects Ranked by B/C (B/C Ratios)
Project with larger net benefits has smaller costs	I	2>3 (6>5)	$C_2 < C_3$ (5<15)	2>3 (2.20>1.33)
Project with >B has higher costs	II	6>9 (4>1)	$C_6 > C_9$ (8>1)	6<9 (1.50<2.00)
Project with >B has higher costs	III	6>8 (4>3)	$C_6 > C_8$ (8>7)	6>8 (1.50>1.47)
Summary	IV	3>4,5,6 (5>4,4,4)	$C_{4,5} > C_3 > C_6$ 100, 16>15>8	6>3>4,5 1.50>1.33>1.04,1.25

internal rate of return and by the benefit-cost ratio. As was shown above, the present value of project costs and benefits varies with the discounting interest rate. Any comparison of internal rates of return with benefit-cost ratios involves the already discussed potential discrepancies of intersecting present value curves plus the differences in ranking occasioned by relating benefits to costs by means of their ratios rather than their differences. It is no wonder that no consistent relation emerges.

PROJECT SELECTION IN THE PUBLIC SECTOR

The significance of nominal differences among criteria becomes evident as one or another is applied in project selection in the public sector. The focus changes from the formal differences under conditions of certainty, independence, divisibility, and clearly specified constraints to the real world of public investment decision-making. Here, as Steiner argues, the issue is which among the alternative criteria can best provide a framework to encompass the considerable interdependence, indivisibility, and uncertainty, along with the rather strict budget constraints, which characterize public investment decision (Steiner, 1969, p. 89).

Analysis of project selection in the public sector involves the selection of a choice model compatible with the actual situation. The three main models for choosing among investment projects under the most simplified assumptions have just been described. None of them is consistent with the actual choice situation in the public sector, and, therefore, compromise is necessary. Most of the controversy over choice models for the evaluation of public projects is the result of different views on the relevance of such alternative models to the underlying situation of the public sector. Essentially, two distinct perspectives emerge. One treats the public sector as being able to obtain funds at a given cost. As a consequence, it is proposed to use that choice model which accepts projects whose present value, discounted at the given cost, exceeds zero. If, in fact, budgetary funds are so constrained that they cannot be augmented at the assumed cost, despite the continued existence of additional projects with positive present values, then this model is seriously inconsistent with reality. Under these circumstances, project ranking by the relative size of discounted present values will not optimize the returns from the constrained budget because the discount rate used (the given cost) is not a true measure of the opportunity cost of displaced alternative projects.

The other main perspective views the budget as strictly limited and incapable of increase at any price. The relevant choice model is one which derives implicitly that interest rate which, when used to discount returns, establishes a set of projects whose total costs just exhaust the budget limitation. Those projects are then selected whose internal rate of return exceeds the implicit interest rate. No rankings are necessary because this implicit rate establishes a cutoff perfectly consistent with available funds. In fact, some projects may not have unique internal rates of return, or the budget limitation may not be so severe, and additional funds may be obtainable at specified cost. In the latter situation, the implicit interest rate is not an accurate measure of alternatives forgone by the public project and inefficient project selection will ensue if this measure is employed.

These remarks deal only with one dimension of reality in public sector project selection. Granted that the nature of the budget constraint is the most significant aspect of the choice model, treatment of interdependencies, arguments in the objective function, indivisibilities, uncertainty, and other elements that depart from the simple assumptions of the pure choice models raise further difficulties in the attempt to select the approach that is most congruent with the purposes of the analysis.

Viewed in this context the preference for the present value criterion, which virtually all practitioners of benefit-cost analysis share, lies in its superior capacity to make explicit budgetary and other constraints, as well as project indivisibilities and interdependencies and to separate these from the determination of the proper rate of discount. Put another way, it permits specification in the formulation of the present value of a project of these elements rather than relegating them to behind-the-scenes adjustments of costs and benefits. This latter practice is necessary in the rate of return approach, to compensate for its inherent erroneous assumption that current outlay is the resource whose return is to be maximized.

A General Approach. One approach to the explicit incorporation of relevant aspects of public sector investment decisions is to rank projects by their present values estimated by a method in which the discounted present values of projects, calculated in accordance with the usual formula,

$$V = \sum_{t=1}^{\alpha} \frac{B_t - C_t}{(1 + r)^t}$$

are modified by factors which reflect the project's absorption of constrained elements or contribution to other national goals. For example, weights can be assigned to the dollar values of each of a number of financial constraints and projects ranked by their net benefits. There is reason to suppose that these weights may vary from project to project and from time to time. Steiner, expanding this notion, presents a "genuinely eclectic model" as:

$$V = \sum_{t=1}^{\alpha} \frac{B_t - C_t}{(1 + r)^t} - \sum_{j=1}^{n} p_j K_j$$

In this formula, each K_j represents the number of units of a constrained resource and p_j the shadow price of the binding constraint (for example, budget appropriation, foreign exchange, private investment opportunity foregone) (Steiner, 1969, pp. 87 – 88). It is possible to break down a constraint such as the budget into specification of sources of the constrained funds, such as taxation, borrowing, and curtailment of other public projects. The *ps* refer to the weights to be given to each of the corresponding constraints and may be positive or negative, although usually the latter. The weights thus represent quantitative estimates of the opportunity costs engendered by the use of each unit of the constrained factors. The advantage of this model is the highly general way in which constraints, opportunity costs, and indivisibilities can be incorporated. Steiner's conclusion on choice models seems especially apt:

> If there is a serious charge against the progress that the academic invasion of this area has achieved, it is that the mathematical structure of choice situations has been labored beyond the point of sensible return, and the confrontation of real problems with real data largely neglected. If the state of the art before 1950 was long on measurement and short on theory, the balance has been redressed and it is time to return to implementation. (Steiner, 1969, pp. 90 – 91)

The Estimation of Benefits

Unless there are very good reasons to the contrary, both costs and benefits are estimated in terms of constant prices over time. Cost estimates for physical capital projects, such as water resource development, are usually straightforward engineering calculations, with appropriate attention to external costs.[3] These might include the costs of relocating households or business firms, erosion losses during construction, or other third-party effects. The estimation of benefits presents more serious complications. And if benefit streams are not uniform over time, the calculations are most intricate.

One of the major strengths of benefit-cost analysis is that a very broad view may be taken of project effects in order to comprehend the full range of externalities. But this strength brings corresponding pitfalls. In consequence, a major difficulty confronting the practical application of benefit-cost is ascertaining when to stop counting and what not to count. A second problem is how to count; that is, how can benefits be aggregated in terms of a numeraire that will comprehend both market and nonmarket values?

The benefits that may be counted are also subject to political constraint. The legislature may approve only such projects as are to be constructed in a given region or for a specified purpose. A water resource project, for example, might yield substantial recreation benefits if the legislature were to authorize the development of lands adjacent to reservoir sites, but this may not be politically feasible. In some circumstances political constraints may be so severe that economic choice is kept within very narrow limits. The analyst has the responsibility to assess the constraints and their cost, in addition to examining the possibilities of maximizing an objective economic function (Marglin, 1967, pp. 19 – 39).

CLASSES OF BENEFITS

Water resource agencies in the U.S. government have traditionally approached the measurement of benefits by a classification that distinguishes among primary, secondary, and intangible benefits. Primary and secondary benefits are sometimes labelled direct and indirect.[4]

The primary benefits of a project consist of the value of the goods or services that "result from conditions with the project as compared with conditions without the project." The primary benefit of an irrigation project is the value of the additional crops produced on the newly irrigated land. The primary benefit from a flood control project is the estimated annual savings in flood damages. The primary benefit of a hydroelectric project is estimated in terms

3. The apportionment of joint costs in multiple-purpose water projects is an important exception to this generalization. In human resources analysis cost calculations are more difficult, both conceptually and empirically. In the analysis of military programs, costing also presents intricate problems (G. H. Fisher, "Cost Functions and Budgets," *The Analysis of Public Output* [New York: Columbia University Press, 1970], pp. 231 – 63).

4. See the President's Water Resources Council, *Policies, Standards, and Procedures in the Formulation, Evaluation, and Review of Plans for Use and Development of Water and Related Land Resources,* Senate Doc. 97, 87th Cong., 1st sess., 1962.

of opportunity cost — as the difference in the cost of electric energy produced as compared with the cost of the most economical alternative source of supply, usually thermal power, that might be produced at the same site. In the case of the irrigation and hydroelectric projects (this will also be true of many other water programs), there are, however, associated costs. For irrigated land, these are the costs of seed, farmers' labor, and materials and supplies necessary to produce the crop. For the hydroelectric project, the associated costs include the generators and penstocks required to produce the power. Where associated costs are private costs, they lie outside the budget constraint and must be subtracted from gross direct or primary benefits to yield a measurement called "primary benefits attributable to the project" (Federal Reserve Bank of Kansas City, 1958, pp. 9 – 16).

Secondary benefits are multiplier effects and investment effects that may be localized within a region or project area. Whether they may be appropriately counted in the numerator of the benefit-cost ratio has been a matter for considerable controversy (Marglin, 1967, pp. 79 – 82). Most of this controversy has centered on the practices of the U.S. Bureau of Reclamation. (McKean, 1958, pp. 154 – 63.)

The Bureau has traditionally distinguished two classes of secondary benefits. The first is described as "stemming from" the industries that supply the project area with goods and services. The second class is "induced by" the economic activities from processing, distributing, or consuming the output of the project itself. Secondary or indirect benefits will have secondary or indirect costs associated with them. These must be deducted in order to arrive at a net measurement of secondary benefits, which is termed "attributable secondary benefits."[5]

The objection to a general inclusion of all secondary benefits, from the standpoint of the national economy, is that multiplier effects and induced investment are not unique to government investment. All increments of expenditure, public or private, stimulate additional increments of economic activity that could be described as "stemming from" or "induced by" the original increment. The question of including secondary benefits ultimately involves consideration of the opportunity cost of the public project. Under the standard assumption of full employment such secondary benefits must be presumed to exist both with and without the project. But to the extent that a regional distribution of benefits is an element in the objective function, local multiplier and investment effects are of importance since they bring a redistribution of national income to favor the region (Haveman and Krutilla, 1968, pp. 37 – 64).

5. See Subcommittee on Evaluation Standards, Inter-agency Committee on Water Resources, *Proposed Practices for Economic Analysis of River Basin Projects* (Washington, 1958), pp. 8 – 10. Also, *Report of Panel of Consultants on Secondary or Indirect Benefits of Water-Use Projects* (Washington: Bureau of Reclamation, Department of the Interior, 1952).

A new irrigation project may serve as the basis for a major expansion in regional population and economic activity. A hydroelectric installation may attract new industry and bring important agglomeration effects. The Bureau of Reclamation, long sensitive to the regional development concerns of western states, has promoted the inclusion of secondary benefits as a device for justifying a larger volume of water resource development projects, to achieve a regional redistribution of income (Fox, 1957, pp. 504 – 5). The Bureau estimates secondary benefits as a part of its project reports, but does not formally include these in the numerator of the ratio.

In accordance with federal practice since 1962, there are a number of specialized secondary benefits which may be properly included in the numerator. These may include benefits from reducing a region's chronic unemployment or benefits that are derived from moving a local industry closer to capacity operations. More effective utilization of existing grain storage elevators as a result of increased grain production from an irrigation project, for example, would qualify as this kind of specialized secondary benefit. But, in general, secondary benefits of the multiplier or induced investment type may not be counted under existing federal practice.

A third general class of benefits is called intangibles and, by definition, monetary values may not be attached to them. For a water resource project, intangibles may include the improvement (or destruction) of the esthetic qualities of the landscape. Flood control projects may save human lives, and such estimated savings will at least be described in the general project justification, although the water resource agencies have abandoned, in recent years, any attempt to attach monetary values to the savings. The treatment of intangibles is particularly crucial in the application of benefit-cost analysis to human resources (see below).

There are also borderline areas where benefits are a mixture of elements that are tangible and measurable and intangible and unmeasurable. Recreation benefits that are associated with park areas established around reservoirs yield some particularly troublesome problems. Recreation enthusiasts will argue that there are evident intangible benefits to be derived from a day's boating or picnicking. How may these be priced out? Some federal water resource agencies have employed a standard benefit of $1.60 per visitor day at established recreation areas. This presumably represents a kind of average opportunity cost, that is, the amount that persons are willing to pay for the use of the facilities at the recreation area. Other more sophisticated techniques have been discussed in the literature, but have not yet found their way into operating procedures.[6]

---

6. See Marion Clawson and Jack L. Knetsch, *Economics of Outdoor Recreation* (Baltimore: The John Hopkins Press, 1966), esp. pp. 43 – 141.

Very often, in benefit-cost analysis, it is possible to establish trade-off values against intangibles, or to estimate the cost of honoring a specific constraint. The cost of maintaining esthetic considerations can be priced out in terms of the tangible values that would be sacrificed in the value of water supply, power, or flood damage prevention. Recreation can be evaluated indirectly by comparing the visitor days gained from one project design with the monetary losses to other water programs from that project design. The analysis of intangibles by way of trade-offs against tangibles may be more orderly, particularly at the margin, than efforts to construct hypothetical values for inclusion in the numerator.

THE DISCOUNT RATE

The most controversial aspect of benefit-cost analysis is the choice of the appropriate rate at which to discount future benefits and costs. A high discount rate reduces the present value of benefits, and thus the numerator in the benefit-cost ratio, so that a smaller number of public investment projects will be justified. Conversely, a low discount rate increases the present value of benefits, justifying a larger number of projects for investment.

The controversy has inevitably taken on ideological overtones. Those who favor an expansion of the public sector will rationalize arguments for a low discount rate. Those who would restrict public sector investment activities will seek to justify a high discount rate. Moreover, the difference between a low rate and a high rate is crucial, particularly for long-lived investments. It has been estimated, for example, that for federal water resource projects authorized in 1962, when a 2-5/8 percent rate was used, an increase in the discount rate to 6 percent would have brought 64 percent of the projects below the ratio of 1.0.[7]

There are a number of reasons for discounting. The most important is a productivity consideration: given a positive rate of return on investment in general, the resources used in a particular project could be invested elsewhere to yield resources in the future larger than the amount invested. This reason can be expressed alternatively as a time preference consideration: most people would prefer to receive an identical consumption benefit (income) now rather than in the future. Yet another reason, only partially separable from those mentioned, is that the future is uncertain; the expected future benefits from the project may not in fact accrue, or they may turn out to be less valuable than is currently expected — and expected future costs may turn out to be less burdensome than is currently anticipated.

7. Irving K. Fox and Orris C. Herfindahl, "Attainment of Efficiency in Satisfying Demands for Water Resources," *American Economic Review,* May 1964, pp. 198 – 206.

An alternative to the use of a preselected discount rate to establish present values is the calculation of the internal rate of return. As noted above, if the time stream of net returns is well behaved, the internal rate provides a single set of consistent rankings, unlike the present value criterion which can favor different projects at different discount rates. Two problems, nevertheless, arise in the application of this approach. First, an opportunity cost-rate must be chosen in order to decide where to stop as a cut-off. As the discussion below indicates, it is by no means clear, conceptually or practically, what constitutes the proper rate to serve as the required manifestation of opportunity cost. Second, the ranking of projects by their internal rate may not yield an ordering consistent with the relevant constraints, since ranking by internal rate of return assumes current outlay to be the sole constrained factor.

Consequently, there remains an ambiguity, despite the stable ranking. A "true" opportunity cost-rate must still be found if projects are to be carried to the margin.

Although the internal rate of return has been used rather widely in the analysis of human resources projects, it has been conventional to preselect a discount rate for physical resource development, particularly water resources. There are four possible approaches to the selection of the discount rate: private time preference and social time preference, and private productivity and social productivity. Private time preference is a simple expression of the uncertainty of the future — the view, possibly myopic, that present goods are to be preferred to future goods. Social time preference expresses a concern for future generations; the welfare of our grandchildren will be increased if investments are made now. Private productivity is the opportunity cost of private investment — the returns that can be secured from current investment in the private sector. Social productivity would measure these returns plus or minus the external effects of the private investment. Estimates of social productivity would be most difficult since the generalized externalities of private investment cannot be quantified accurately; no such estimates have ever been attempted.

The literature of controversy on this subject has centered on two of these concepts — social time preference and private opportunity cost (Prest and Turvey, 1965, pp. 697–98). Those who favor the time preference rate argue that the choice among projects whose costs and benefits lie in the future is meaningless unless based on relative preferences between the present and future. The debate has ranged widely and it is useful at the start to set out the broad framework within which it has taken place.

In a "perfect" private capital market, the rate of return to investment would be equal to the rate of time preference. As Hirshleifer, among others, has shown, in the Fisherian analysis of capital savers and investors equate at the margin time preference with the productivity of investment (Hirshleifer, 1958, pp. 330–33). Under these circumstances the utility sacrificed by saving is

exactly equal to the utility gained by the increment of future income obtained
from the investment of that marginal dollar. There is no divergence between
time preference and rate of return just as, in competitive equilibrium, there is
no divergence between supply price and demand price.

As imperfections in the capital market are introduced, various sources of
divergence emerge. First, following Baumol's discussion, taxation and risk
drive a wedge between private yields and the gross returns to investment
(Baumol, 1968, pp. 789 – 96). Corporate taxation, or for that matter any tax
which lowers appropriable returns to investment, reduces the interest payment
which borrowers are willing to pay, and therefore lowers the equilibrium time
preference. This can be shown in Figure 7.3. Let II be the gross marginal
efficiency of investment schedule, which, when related to SS, the private savings function, yields the perfect market interest rate r and investment of I. To
the extent that taxes and risk reduce the net private yield to investors, a new
schedule I′I′, lying below II, is appropriate and its intersection with SS at
interest rate r′provides a time preference rate equal to the net private, but not
to the gross, yield of investment and a new level of investment of I′.

Here, as Baumol points out, lies the fundamental source of discrepant

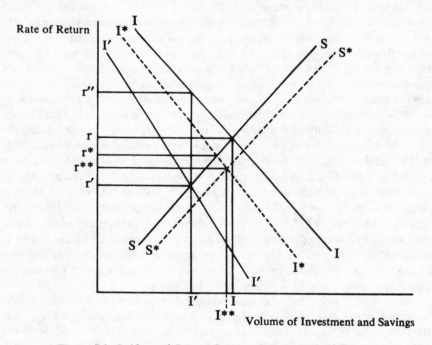

Figure 7.3. Public and Private Savings, Investment and Returns

discount rates for public projects. The time preference rate, r′, lies below the gross private rate of return, r″ at the equilibrium level of investment, I′. Furthermore, in terms of the social optimum, investment is not carried out to I, the point where private costs and benefits are equal. One remedy is to abolish taxation which reduces profitability and to provide a government subsidy to offset risk, raising I′I′ back to II. Such a policy, however, ignores not only the distribution and stabilization functions of business taxation, but also any elements of benefit taxation embodied in such levies. If it is agreed that business taxation is not motivated by efforts to compensate for external costs, neither the gross nor the net private marginal efficiency of investment curves reflect these external costs (and benefits), and they should be adjusted to encompass such considerations. If I′I′ measures the net private returns to investment (after taxes and risk) and II gross private returns, there is need for still another curve which shows "gross" social returns after taking account of the external economies or diseconomies of private investment, but which ignores taxation and individual risk. Presuming that diseconomies predominate, this curve can be shown as I*I*.

The intersection of I*I* and SS provides a rate of time preference and return, r*, that encompasses external as well as private costs and returns and therefore is a more appropriate measure of opportunity cost than the purely private rate, r. There remains, however, a further relevant consideration. Not only must the social costs of investment be considered, but it has been argued that the aggregate of private time preferences of individuals does not reflect true social time preference. One view is that any preference for present benefits over certain equivalent future benefits is inherently irrational and that the behavioral manifestations of such preference display a myopia with regard to the future which should not influence present investment decisions. If we grant that myopia is the result of the individual's realistic appreciation of the genuine personal risk of death, then this element, like risk to individual investors, does not reflect any true social risk that the future benefit will not in fact be forthcoming, and so should be ignored. A second argument for the adjustment of the private savings function is that the present generation's concern for the future is of the nature of a public good and that individuals do not express their preferences for such goods through market behavior. That is, the private lending behavior of individuals overstates their valuation of present consumption.

To the extent that these arguments are accepted, the SS curve shifts to the right to S*S* and its intersection with I*I* provides the socially correct discount rate, r**; this is an appropriate rate for both public and private investment. Yet, what can be observed or estimated are the before tax and risk rate of return (r″) and the equality of the returns inclusive of tax and risk to the time preference rate (r') at the indicated level of private investment I'. What policies are available to obtain the optimum investment level of I^{**}?

One possibility is to undertake public projects so as to raise the investment from I' to I^{**} by selecting projects with a return in excess of r^{**}. This is a superior alternative to using r' as the appropriate rate for public investment, but it is still open to the charge that at the margin private investment, shown at I', has a social return of r'' which is in excess of r^{**} and thus has a greater social return than acceptable public projects. The alternative is to attempt to devise a set of taxes and transfers to private investors and savers such that their private decisions would produce a level of investment at II^{**}. Such a system would in principle obviate the need for public investment, but the very essence of the rationale for the public sector is that because of decreasing costs, nonexclusion, and the nature of externalities, a system of taxes and transfers of this sort is impossible. The government itself must provide and distribute certain goods and services.

The conclusion, here, as with virtually the entire field of public policy, is that a choice must be made among second-best solutions. With this general conceptual framework it is possible to appraise the contending points of view and to examine some institutional considerations.

Those who urge that the appropriate discount rate is the marginal productivity of capital in the private sector contend that the source of funds for government investment is the private sector or that government investment will displace private investment that would otherwise be made. Obviously, it is uneconomic to invest for returns in the public sector at 4 percent when returns in the private sector are 15 percent and all externalities have been counted. Future national income increments will be greater, in these circumstances, if public investment is undertaken only when it is at least as profitable as private investment. Stated in these terms, the case is undoubted. The general welfare will be reduced if the public investment is permitted to displace private investment with a higher yield.

The advocates of private opportunity cost seek to strengthen their cause by a further appeal to the inclusion of consumption as well as investment in the linkage between private opportunity cost and private time preference. This concern with the value of foregone consumption probably emerged in response to the fact that many governments finance investment outlays from current taxes that have a restrictive effect on consumer expenditures. Mishan, for example, urges that if an individual can secure a certain yield p on private investment to perpetuity on everything he saves, his rate of time preference will also be equated to p. In perfect capital markets the appropriate rate of social discount must reflect marginal consumer valuations of savings and consumption. That is, individuals will value the sacrifice of consumption as equivalent to the certain returns from private investment. The relevant return to consumption, therefore, is the return that could be obtained on private investment (Mishan, 1967, pp. 139 – 46).

> Thus, whatever the social rate of discount adopted, no part of any dollar should be withdrawn from the private sector to finance public investment unless it can earn in the public-investment project at least as much as the certain yield p in the private sector. (Mishan, 1967, p. 143)

When the discount rate is linked to private opportunity costs, taxes must also be taken into account (Baumol, 1969, pp. 493 – 96). Where returns on private capital are taxed at 50 percent, as in the corporate sector, the appropriate private opportunity cost must be measured before taxes, not after taxes. The correct discount rate is an average grossed up in accordance with tax burdens in the sectors of the economy from which the resources are drawn.

The implication of Mishan's and Baumol's points is reflected in Figure 7.3 by the difference between r' and r''. At r', time preference and the after-tax rate of return on investment are equated at a level of investment of I'. Yet at this level of investment the before-tax private rate of return is equal to r''. Mishan and Baumol argue that r'' reflects social returns to private investment and any lower discount rate applied to public sector projects would displace private investments of higher social yield.

This approach would be quite satisfactory if, in fact, private capital markets were as competitive as the model assumes. But when returns on private investment incorporate monopoly elements or when private costs have been socialized, private sector profit rates will exceed the social rate, as was assumed in Figure 7.3 by the shift in the before-tax investment returns curve from II to I^*I^*. In consequence, consumer valuations of future consumption as against present consumption will be inflated at the margin.

There are abundant cases where private rates of return do not reflect the full range of social costs that are associated with private investment. Rates of return to automobile manufacturers, for example, do not incorporate the social costs of the automobile, embracing such externalities as air pollution, noise, increased delinquency and crime, the cost of automobile accidents, and the like. These imperfections cannot be offset or complemented by public actions to attain optimality. There is no way to incorporate into public sector decisions monopoly elements that are found in the private sector, and no easy way to shift the social costs back to the producing firm.

There are other difficulties in the application of private opportunity cost. There may, of course, be social benefits from private investment, as where a business firm trains its unskilled employees; or, on the other side, there may be external costs from government investment, as where a public hospital has a polluting smokestack (Baumol, 1969, p. 499). Estimates of the net of social costs and benefits from private investment are nonexistent, but casual observation of the existing state of environmental pollution, particularly in urban areas, would suggest that the social costs of private investment run high.[8] Indeed, in a market economy an important device for increasing the profitability of private investment is to externalize internal costs by shifting them to nonpurchasers of a firm's output. In some cases these costs, as with air pollution, may be for some time undetected. In other cases tax supported public programs may be introduced to offset the privately generated social costs. In any event, there is no reason to believe that the rate of private investment, at any one time, is optimal with respect to other objectives, such as growth and stabilization, or the maximization of consumption over time (Marglin, 1967, pp. 47 – 53). Both for reason of externalities and because of the importance of other macroeconomic objectives that are related to investment, there is no reason to believe that private profitability rates are appropriate for judging social profitability. In this, as in so many other instances, private market signals are not irrelevant, but the signals must be adjusted and interpreted.

Those who favor a social time-preference discount rate point not only to the limitations of the concept of private opportunity cost but also argue that there is a difference between individual time preference valuations and social time preference (Marglin, 1963, pp. 95 – 111). The latter is not a simple aggregate of the former, because it is possible to make all individuals better off by undertaking more investment collectively than each would find it desirable to undertake privately. Interdependence effects are prominent in individual choices between the welfare of this generation and of future generations. A social rate of time preference that is lower than present opportunity costs of private capital will justify a larger volume of public investment. This will favor future generations as against the present generation and sacrifice present consumption benefits in favor of future consumption benefits.

In a market economy there is no reason to believe that the savings and investment preferences of households and business firms will establish an optimum choice pattern between the consumption of this generation and the consumption of future generations. It follows from this approach that the choice between present and future generations must reflect a social rate of time preference, and this cannot be measured by private opportunity cost.

The generational issue is a complex one because the concern for future generations involves a valuation as between present and future consumption, and this valuation rests on an implicit prediction about the welfare of future generations. On the one hand, it has been suggested that even with modest growth rates we can confidently expect future generations to be much better off than present generations (Baumol, 1967, pp. 152 – 59; 1969, pp. 499 – 501).

8. For an impassioned discussion, see Ezra J. Mishan, *The Costs of Economic Growth* (New York: Frederick A. Praeger, 1967), esp. pp. 109 – 21, 148 – 54.

It would follow that it is appropriate to discount future welfare heavily as against present consumption. But, on the other hand, those who are concerned about environmental pollution are by no means confident that future genera-tions will be better off than the present generation. Market-guided resource allocation may well leave developed nations with a socially unproductive complex of air and water pollution and congested and noisy cities — this may be the heritage of the next generation. If this is the case, there should be a reordering of priorities between the present and the future and additional public investment in this generation to provide for an adequate legacy of clean air and water and efficient urban transportation systems.

The argument that a concern for future generations should be implemented by the use of a social time-preference rate is persuasive, but the difficulty is that there is no mechanism, in the absence of central planning, for arriving at a reasonable consensus on the value to be attached to the welfare of future generations. One study committee, recognizing the complexity of the problem, argued that for the federal government the appropriate discount rate should reflect the "administration's social rate of time discount." This would be established by the President after consultation with his staff agencies, such as the Council of Economic Advisers.[9]

In the absence of a consensus on the criteria for the selection of a discount rate it is not surprising that, in practice, arbitrary desicisions have been made. In the federal government the rate of discount has been determined, not by the productivity of investment in the private sector, or by an estimate of social time preference, but by the cost of federal funds. Since 1962, for water resource projects, this cost has been based on the interest rate payable by the Treasury on interest-bearing marketable securities that have a maturity of fifteen years or more on original issue. A 1967 survey by the General Accounting Office of ten federal agencies that used discounting for one or another budgetary pur-pose disclosed that the rates employed ranged from 3 to 12 percent.[10] This state of affairs is more indicative of confusion than of differences in budgetary constraints among agencies.

A compromise between public and private interest rates would suggest that the long-term interest rate on high-grade corporation bonds might be an appropriate discount rate. A variant of this proposal has been suggested by Krutilla and Eckstein, who urge that the appropriate rate is the opportunity cost of private tax funds under a balanced budget. In a set of ingenious calculations for the late 1950s these tax costs were estimated separately for the

9. Report of Panel of Consultants, Bureau of the Budget, *Standards and Criteria for For-mulating and Evaluating Federal Water Resources Development* (Washington, 1961), p. 67.

10. Subcommittee on Economy in Government, Joint Economic Committee, *Interest Rate Guidelines for Federal Decision-making*, 90th Cong., 2nd sess., 1968.

business sector and the household sector in accordance with the tax burdens falling on each. The tax cost of business funds was put at the average interest rate paid on borrowings by business firms, and the tax cost of household funds was put at the average interest rate paid on loans for household consumer durables. Krutilla and Eckstein concluded that the appropriate discount rate for that period was between 5 and 6 percent; at that time, average yields on federal long-term bonds were between 3 and 4 percent (Krutilla and Eckstein, 1958, pp. 78 – 130).

Other compromises or mixed approaches are evidently possible. Marglin, for example, has suggested a measurement that he labels "social-rate-cum-opportunity-cost" (Marglin, 1967, pp. 47 – 71). This would combine the long-term interest rate on government bonds with an allowance for the private investment, but not the private consumption, that is displaced by the government investment.

It is evident that the controversy over the discount rate is heavily value-laden. There are no "rules" to which one may repair for unequivocal solutions. Baumol puts the point most strongly: "At stake in the choice of an acceptable discount rate is no less than the allocation of resources between the private and the public sectors of the economy" (Baumol, 1969, pp. 489 – 90). The choice between public and private resource use can be approached directly, in a benefit-cost framework, by imputing additional values to public investment in behalf of future generations. The choice between public and private resource allocation would thus be made explicit.

But in the realm of public policy the choice of the appropriate rate of discount makes the decision an implicit one. The use of a social rate of time preference rests most strongly on the argument that a market interest rate cannot reflect citizen preferences toward future generations — the choice between consumption now and consumption in the future. Only a public policy to determine which persons shall assume the burden of sacrificing for future generations can reflect this choice (Marglin, 1962, pp. 194 – 205). Therefore, social time preference, politically determined, needs to be used for discounting in order that future generations shall be protected against the profitability of private investment in this generation. Otherwise, the apparent profitability of private investment may appear to be excessively attractive as compared with the true social profitability of public investment.

EXTERNALITIES AND DISCONTINUITIES

In the literature of welfare economics it is conventional to distinguish between technological and pecuniary externalities. These distinctions have been carried over into benefit-cost analysis (Krutilla and Eckstein, 1958, pp. 56 – 60). Technological externalities arise when the project affects the physical input-output relationships of other producing units, public or private. A simple example is where a downstream reservoir adds to the capability of an existing upstream reservoir. In this case the resulting benefits have a value that should be counted in the numerator of the benefit-cost ratio. Technological externalities may lead to costs as well as benefits, and these, since they do use constrained resources, should be subtracted from the value of the numerator rather than added to the denominator. This is not an insignificant decision, as was shown in the discussion of Table 7.1.

Pecuniary externalities may be defined as project influences on the factor and product prices of other producing units. A major public recreation facility may have adverse effects on the demand for, and, hence, price of, private recreation facilities in the project area. A major water resource project may raise wage rates, not only during the construction period, but during its operational phase. Such wage-rate increases may have all manner of side effects. Some marginal private firms might be put out of existence; some retailers might enjoy additional profits from higher levels of consumer demand.

Tracing out all the technological and pecuniary externalities that may arise from a project amounts to little less than a general equilibrium analysis for the whole economy of a region. Since this is more than can typically be undertaken, the benefit-cost analyst must be content with measuring only those important externalities that can be easily quantified. These are not likely to include such matters as wage-rate influences but could well include such pecuniary effects as reductions in the price of privately supplied electric energy.

The measurement of externalities becomes particularly treacherous when projects are large in relation to the economy of an area or when the project, regardless of size, passes a regional threshold of development. The provision of a major increment of industrial water supply, for example, may permit business firms not only to move toward capacity but to expand their scale of operation. A hydroelectric project that attracts an electrochemical complex may also attract additional processing and supplying activities. To dismiss these consequences under the general rule for excluding secondary benefits may considerably understate project benefits. On the other hand, inclusion of secondary benefits in their totality is inappropriate since the resource inputs for these activities would probably have found employment elsewhere. Some types of projects in some areas are a greater stimulus to economic growth than other projects. There is no reason to exclude all possible induced investment effects, even though secondary benefits may generally be excluded.

Discontinuities present a different kind of problem. Ideally, once it is determined that a project is justified and is to be undertaken, the project should be built to a scale such that the net marginal benefits from the last increment of expenditure are zero. However, the technology of project construction may prevent attainment of this ideal; engineering considerations may dictate that a project be built to a single size. Flexibility in project construction can eliminate some of the inherent problems of discontinuities, but is likely to raise costs. This problem is more serious, of course, for a single project than for a long-range investment program with multiple projects.

DISTRIBUTION AND COMPENSATION

Although benefit-cost analysis, in its formal aspects, purports to be concerned solely with efficiency criteria, as with so many other areas of public expenditure decisions, distributional considerations necessarily intrude. These enter via the political scene as regional interests press for development projects. Distributional considerations also enter in a far more complex way in the relative emphasis to be accorded specific programs in a multipurpose project.

A large river-valley development project may embrace many water programs. These might include (1) irrigation, (2) hydroelectric power, (3) industrial and municipal water supplies, (4) recreation, (5) pollution abatement, (6) flood control, and (7) navigation. Some of these project purposes will be at least partially substitutable, one for another, but others will not. Reservoir storage capacity can be used alternatively to provide for releases in the summer months to lower pollution levels downstream or to maintain reservoirs for recreational purposes. Some choices will have to be made to award the benefits of the project, at least at the margin, to either upstream recreationists or downstream users of industrial and municipal water. The upstream recreationists will be different people, with different incomes, than the downstream water-users. The difficulties of choice are compounded when some of the classes of benefits are more elusive than others. In these circumstances the best efficiency calculus will still leave a wide margin for political decision. Harsh choices are posed when a Grand Canyon project will reduce the esthetic value of a national park in order to supply additional water and hydroelectric power. As suggested above, trade-off analysis, useful for marginal decisions, is inadequate for such major controversies.

In some cases what appears to be a distributional issue in the choice of the groups to be favored could also be described as a difference between immediate and long-run efficiency criteria. Instances of this type arise with respect to hydroelectric power. An immediate efficiency judgment, for example, might suggest that storage capacity available for electric power generation be used only for peaking purposes, since peaking power can be sold at a higher price than firm power. In most areas, this means that hydroelectric output must necessarily be marketed to privately owned electric power companies which are in a position to pay for and utilize additional peaking capacity. However, there may be another class of electric power distributor — the municipally-owned systems and the cooperatives. Their demands are typically for firm power at a lower price. An immediate efficiency solution will thus favor privately owned companies. But there may be long-run efficiency considerations in a mixed public and private system of ownership and marketing of electric power. This system will require that public distributors be maintained in a status competitive with private distributors and that the former be permitted to purchase power at a lower price. Difficult and controversial choices of this kind can neither be avoided nor resolved by the techniques of benefit-cost analysis.

RISK AND UNCERTAINTY

The average anticipated net gains from a project may deviate from the actual gains. Costs may be greater or less and benefits greater or less than anticipated. The differences may be described under the general heading of risk and uncertainty.

The traditional distinction between risk and uncertainty is that the former can be described by a probability function based on experience with comparable activities; uncertainties, by definition, are not subject to probability determinations. In the literature of benefit-cost analysis the terms are often used interchangebly, or used to describe the same phenomenon (Eckstein, 1958, pp. 81 – 90; McKean, 1958, pp. 64 – 71). Very often, attitudes toward the inclusion of specific allowances for risk and uncertainty would appear to be a matter of value judgment. Those who are generally conservative in their approach to government investment criteria will favor such an allowance (Hirshleifer and Shapiro, 1969, pp. 505 – 30); those who are generally liberal will oppose the allowance (Marglin, 1967, pp. 71 – 74).

Where government agencies have had considerable experience in certain standardized kinds of projects, as with irrigation, a careful study of experiential outcomes should provide the basis for a probability distribution of risk. This distribution could be used to judge the outcomes of a proposed project, such as the probability that a reservoir will silt-up within a specified time period. Unfortunately, systematic studies of the outcomes of projects that have been constructed and operated are seldom undertaken. On the other hand, one of the advantages of public investment is that risks are pooled; this advantage should not be lost by applying financial, as distinct from engineering, risk calculations that are pertinent only for the private sector.

In a conservative approach to the benefit-cost criterion, it is possible to incorporate allowances for risk and uncertainty in a number of ways. One possibility is to establish a higher permissible ratio than 1.0, for example, 1.2 or 1.3. Another possibility is to use a somewhat higher rate of discount which will have the effect of reducing the number of projects that are economically justifiable. A third possibility is to establish an arbitrary cutoff point on the duration of benefits. A reservoir may have a physical life of fifty years, but the "project life" will be arbitrarily set at forty years. Where there is some knowledge about the kinds of risks and uncertainties to be anticipated, there may be reasonable grounds for choosing among the possible types of allowances or a basis for attaching probability weights to some classes of benefits. If the risks of technical obsolescence are anticipated to increase over time but not to terminate at a point in time, it may be desirable to introduce an adjustment in the discount rate, rather than an arbitrary cutoff point.

PRIVATE OPPORTUNITY COSTS

Benefit-cost analysis requires the extensive use of market measurements where they are available and their synthetic construction where they are not. Since the private conduct of economic activity differs in important ways, such as in tax status and the cost of financing, from its public conduct, there are often dangers in transferring market cost analogies into the public sector. These dangers are ever-present in applications of benefit-cost techniques.

For example, in estimating the benefits from a hydroelectric installation as part of a water resource project, it is customary to use as a point of reference the costs of providing power under private ownership at the project site for the most feasible available alternative, which is usually steam power-genera-tion. The difference between providing the power publicly and providing it privately becomes the net benefit assignable to the numerator of the ratio. Private costs, however, would include federal, state, and local taxes payable out of operating revenue, taxes that would not be paid if the project were public. Their inclusion in the estimate of private costs will widen the difference between the alternative costs of public and of private power, and increase the net benefits attributable to the project.[11] As against this, it should be noted that private taxes are not real resource costs, but are generally transfer payments and should not be included as part of alternative private cost.

A related problem arises in the case of private capital costs for power investment. If the estimates of private power costs include capital costs at market rates, the resulting cost measures will be higher than if a government capital cost rate were imputed to the private power alternative. In conse-quence, the calculated net benefits from public power investment will be correspondingly higher, the benefit-cost ratio will be more favorable, and a larger volume of public investment will be undertaken.

The use of private costs as a basis for measuring public power benefits will increase estimated benefits and yield a more favorable ratio for the public project. This introduces a "bias" in favor of public power as against private power, even as the use of a social time-preference rate for discounting benefits

11. Suppose that public power costs are one mill per kwh, and alternative private power costs are two mills per kwh if taxes are excluded and three mills if taxes are included. Since the net public power benefits are the difference between private and public costs, the inclusion of taxes in alternative private costs will raise public power benefits per kwh from one mill to two mills.

introduces a general "bias" for public as against private investment. But the use of a private cost for the evaluation of power benefits and a social time-preference rate for discounting are not necessarily inconsistent. The power program is concerned with the present value of benefits that could be either publicly or privately produced. This is a narrow question of foregone alternatives. The use of a social time-preference discount rate rests on considerations of intergeneration equity and hence on basic choices between present and future benefits.

COST ALLOCATION

Benefit-cost analysis is used primarily for justifying and ranking projects. The estimates of benefits, however, may also be used as a basis for allocating project costs, particularly where public policy requires or seeks to secure project revenue from specified classes of beneficiaries.

In federal water resources policy many of the problems of cost allocation are taken care of by traditional practice. Certain classes of beneficiaries are not charged for benefits they receive. Even though it might be possible to identify the beneficiaries and even though there might be some willingness to pay on the part of such beneficiaries, the federal government has not traditionally sought to recover costs from its programs for navigation or flood control; these have been financed from general revenue. On the other hand, the beneficiaries from programs for irrigation, hydroelectric power, and industrial and municipal water are expected to assume the full cost of such programs. Recreation occupies a middle ground; the beneficiaries are expected to pay a part, but not all, of program costs.

There is no doubt that an assessment of user charges against project beneficiaries will, in many instances, bring a reduction in the quantity demanded.[12] The demand for industrial and municipal water, for example, is sufficiently elastic with respect to price that the imposition of user charges will bring a substantial downward movement along the demand curve. User charges will lower the total required investment in water supplies at any one point in time and reduce the danger of overbuilding.

In consequence, cost allocation and accompanying user charges are not independent of the measures of benefits. A prior decision to impose charges is equivalent to a decision to restrict use, and this reduces anticipated benefits. In some cases, as in recreation, there may be very little knowledge of the responsiveness of demand to user charges or of the marginal costs of additional use. A period of experimentation may be necessary to provide information with which to estimate the demand for the facility.

12. This point of view is forcefully presented in J. Hirshleifer, James C. DeHaven, and Jerome W. Milliman, *Water Supply: Economics, Technology, and Policy* (Chicago: University of Chicago Press, 1960).

If user charges can be avoided, the traditional rules for the utilization of fixed investments should be employed. A facility should be built to a scale such that the user charges could be imposed to cover total cost. Once the facility is built, only the marginal costs of operating the facility should in fact be imposed, unless there is a need to ration the use of the facility. For such costs effective utilization is secured only when marginal cost pricing is employed.

Benefit-Cost Extensions

The year 1958 marked a turning point in both the conceptual treatment of benefit-cost and in the possibilities for its extension to other areas. In that year, three major volumes were published on the subject: those of Eckstein, Krutilla and Eckstein, and McKean. These volumes reflected the operating experiences of water resource agencies in the United States, but, more particularly, they provided the theoretical underpinnings for the analysis and explicitly described the strengths and weaknesses of the approach. That which had been the property of technicians in government agencies now became the property of professional economists.

In the years since 1958 benefit-cost techniques have been applied to many areas of government expenditure. The studies that have emerged are in many ways more sophisticated than those from the traditional water resources litera-ture. But there is an important difference. The extensions of benefit-cost analy-sis have remained largely academic in the sense that they are not yet incorporated into the required operating procedures of government agencies. Although a number of significant studies have been made of the benefits and costs of specific education programs, for example, there is no requirement that the U.S. Office of Education justify its budget requests in terms of benefit ratios, nor have these studies been used as the basis for appropriations by the Congress of the United States. However, it is anticipated that with the develop-ment of program budgeting in the U.S. government, benefit-cost techniques will be increasingly utilized as a part of the budgetary process.

PHYSICAL RESOURCE DEVELOPMENT

The extensions of benefit-cost have come in the areas of both physical resource development and human resource development. Investments in highways have been subjected to benefit-cost treatment, at the academic level and in some metropolitan area transportation studies.[13] There have also been studies of civil

13. Herbert Mohring and Mitchell Harwitz, *Highway Benefits: An Analytical Framework* (Evanston: Northwestern University Press, 1962).

aviation expenditures and government outlays for research and development.[14] Urban renewal has been subjected to a thorough analytic treatment.[15] Although it might be expected that benefit-cost for renewal would quickly find its way into practitioner hands in the central cities, operational progress in this area has been very modest.

The analysis of urban renewal has brought an important methodological extension of benefit-cost for application to the analysis of complex problems that combine investment in physical and in human resources. This approach, developed by Lichfield, consists of the preparation of a comprehensive balance sheet of the different consequences of alternative projects in the same area (Lichfield, 1965, pp. 207 – 50). The methodology is most useful for comparing two plans of development for a specific area (Lichfield, 1966, pp. 129 – 53). In the balance sheet the columns show the producers or operators of the renewal program, that is, the city council and current landowners. Current landowners, in turn, are subdivided into those that might be displaced and those that would remain. These may be further subdivided into classes of landowners, that is, commercial or residential. The numbers of landowners involved in each category are also noted. Benefits and costs for each group are then subdivided into current and capital outlays. Monetary values are inserted where possible, but in some cases other units of measurement are employed, as with timesaving for shoppers. Nonmeasurable or intangible benefits or costs are specifically designated as such.

There are parallel sets of entries for the consumers of the urban renewal projects. These consumers are divided into groups such as new occupiers, subdivided between public and private; vehicle users; car-park users; university faculty and students; and the shopping public. The instrumental objectives intended to be accomplished by the renewal program are entered for each class of user. Again, benefits and costs are measured in monetary terms if possible.

The basic accounts are then summarized for each of the producer-operator groups and for the consumer groups. The summaries are both quantitative and nonquantitative. Supporting schedules can be used to aggregate the capital costs and current costs in relation to the specified instrumental objectives. If it were deemed useful, it would be possible to expand the classification to designate the classes of producer-operators or consumers within specific areas of the city.

14. See Gary Fromm, "Civil Aviation Expenditures," in Robert Dorfman, ed., *Measuring Benefits of Government Investments* (Washington: The Brookings Institution, 1965), pp. 172–222; Frederic M. Scherer, "Government Research and Development Programs," ibid., pp. 12–57.

15. Jerome Rothenberg, "Urban Renewal Programs," in Dorfman, ibid., pp. 292–341, and Rothenberg, *Economic Evaluation of Urban Renewal* (Washington: The Brookings Institution, 1967).

The great strength of this balance sheet approach to a complex problem is that no single ratio emerges. The analysis is structured by classes of beneficiaries and the costs associated therewith, and by the spatial dimensions of the project. Those who are charged with making final decisions are not in a position to depend solely on numbers whose specificity is misleading. Rather, the way in which the information is presented emphasizes the very complexity of the project and its multiple objectives and does not permit the quantified values to overpower the nonquantified values.

The other strength of the analysis is that it permits an assessment of gains and losses for affected groups. This information will point to the potential sources of resistance as well as to the potential beneficiaries. The political authorities may wish to consider taxes and user charges against some of the prominent beneficiaries or compensation to some of the losers, in the interest of equity and in the interests of securing wider agreement for the support of the project.

Lichfield has demonstrated the usefulness of the balance-sheet approach in the complicated case of urban renewal. It is incomplete in that not all externalities can be identified, but it is nevertheless an approach to a general equilibrium analysis. There are other areas of both physical and human resource development where a similar approach could be utilized. It would appear, for example, that the analysis of urban transportation projects would lend itself to this technique, as would comprehensive programs for changes in urban educational systems.

HUMAN RESOURCE DEVELOPMENT

The most important extensions of benefit-cost techniques have been directed to the study of human resource investment, and in particular to education. Much of the underlying stimulus to this development has come not from those primarily interested in benefit-cost techniques, but from the general attention that has been directed toward the economics of human resources. These developments are most commonly associated with the work of Schultz and Becker.[16]

The conceptual breakthrough that has made these developments possible is the measurement of the economic value of education by its effect on lifetime earnings. In its first applications this measurement permitted the estimation of rates of return on investment in education at both the high school and college levels. The approach is to compare, on a cross-section basis, lifetime earnings of those who have attained various educational levels. Allowances are incorporated, where possible, for other factors that might influence differences

16. See Theodore W. Schultz, *The Economic Value of Education* (New York: Columbia University Press, 1963); Gary S. Becker, *Human Capital,* (New York: Columbia University Press, 1964).

in lifetime earnings, such as race, ability, age, and sex. The results may be expressed by internal rates of return, or an applied predetermined discount rate. Further, earnings do not always reflect contributions to national income.

Using the lifetime earnings approach, studies have been made of the returns to high school dropout programs and on-the-job training programs.[17] Educational expenditures for combatting poverty have been thoroughly examined.[18] In addition to education, the other area of human resources that has received considerable benefit-cost attention is health.[19] Specific diseases, such as heart disease, cancer, and strokes have been subjected to economic analysis, and there has been some effort to measure the costs and gains from medical research. The economic value of a human life has also been examined.[20] Benefit-cost studies have also been incorporated in the program budget analysis of the Department of Health, Education and Welfare. Education programs have been examined for their effects on discounted lifetime earnings, and health programs for the costs of averting deaths from various causes.

Benefit-cost applied to human resources expenditures brings to the surface a number of problems which are present but which may not be as prominent in applications to physical resources. The difficulties that are encountered with intangibles, complex and interrelated outcomes, and distributional values become far more serious. And in some areas, such as education, there is as yet no way to conceptualize a production function or even to trace rough relationships between inputs and outputs.

For example, the emphasis on discounted lifetime earnings in the measurement of the benefits of education programs has severe conceptual limitations. An increase in the earning capacity of students is surely only one of the benefits of an educational program. Other benefits will include such noncommensurable outcomes as increased skill in communication, an enhanced enjoyment of literature and esthetics, and a sensitivity to group and interpersonal relationships. The volume of intangibles in education is very large in relation to the volume of tangible benefits.

17. Burton A. Weisbrod, "Preventing High School Dropouts," in Dorfman, op. cit., pp. 117–49; Jacob Miner, "On-the-Job Training: Costs, Returns, and Some Implications," *Journal of Political Economy*, October 1962, pt. 2, pp. 50–79; Michael E. Borus, "A Benefit-Cost Analysis of the Economic Effectiveness of Retraining the Unemployed," *Yale Economic Essays*, Fall 1964, pp. 371–429.

18. Thomas I. Ribich, *Education and Poverty* (Washington: The Brookings Institution, 1968).

19. See, for example, Herbert E. Klarman, "Syphillis Control Programs," in Dorfman, op. cit., pp. 367–410; Klarman, "Present Status of Benefit-Cost Analysis in the Health Field," paper presented at the 94th annual meeting, American Public Health Association, 1966.

20. T. C. Schelling, "The Life You Save May Be Your Own," in Samuel B. Chase, Jr., ed., *Problems in Public Expenditure Analysis* (Washington: The Brookings Institution, 1968), pp. 127–62.

The discounting technique, since it is narrowly economic, also produces some distortions that may be offensive to ethical values. Thus, studies show that educational programs that bring benefits at the elementary school level are less "valuable" than programs that bring benefits to children in secondary schools, because the gains in earnings are more distant in the first case. Similarly, there are fewer benefits to be derived from improving the lifetime earnings of older workers than of younger workers, and fewer benefits from improving the educational attainment of women, because they will devote less time to gainful employment.

On the distributional side, educational gains from a given amount of additional resources are likely to be more evident in suburban schools than in slum schools, and there is no easy way to aggregate small educational gains plus reductions in distributional inequality in comparison with large educational gains and increases in distributional inequality.

Choices among health programs, on the basis of benefit-cost analysis, raise another set of ethical problems. Measuring discounted lifetime earnings does not reveal the value of alleviating pain and suffering; some diseases have a high death rate, others are debilitating, others are merely uncomfortable. And there are distributional values here as well. A tuberculosis control program will save the lives of lower-income nonwhites with limited earning capacity, but a cancer control program will save the lives of higher-income whites. A program for the control of alcoholism will bring greater benefits to Protestants and Catholics than to Jews, among whom there is a lower incidence of that disease. In general, choices among health and education programs that are predicated on discounted lifetime earnings will structure the choice against those who have low earnings, those whose earnings will materialize only at some future point in time, or those whose participation in the labor force is limited: nonwhites, the very young, the aged, and women.

It may be an appropriate economic policy to concentrate expenditures in areas that maximize the future level of national income. But the maximization of social welfare may dictate attention to considerations, such as equality of opportunity, that transcend the limitations of values defined in such narrow terms.

A General Appraisal

Major attention has been directed here to benefit-cost analysis for water resource projects because it is in this area that the technique developed and because here it has had a high operational content. The procedural routines under which water resources projects are evaluated, justified, proposed, and adopted are based on benefit-cost analysis. This operational experience, extending over several decades, has provided, at two points, an important disciplinary ingredient in public investment decisions. First, it has established a framework for reasonably consistent and uniform project evaluation at the staff level. It has encouraged attention to measurement techniques and has stimulated engineers and hydrologists, for example, to think systematically about the economic aspects of projects. Second, benefit-cost has disciplined the political process. It has tended to inhibit congressional approval of those projects that are without economic justification. It has tended to substitute measurable findings for rhetoric and opinion. The interest of congressmen in larger appropriations to improve the economic welfare of their constituents is certainly legitimate, but it is only one of the objectives to be served by projects. It may be anticipated that similar disciplining will obtain as benefit-cost analysis moves increasingly from the academic to the operational in other areas of physical and human resource development.

Experience with water resource development projects suggests that benefit-cost has its greatest strength where the choice set is narrow — where it is used to compare projects that are roughly similar in purpose and that may be expected to have about the same volume of externalities. Although one project is never, of course, exactly like another, certain classes of projects are far more amenable to analysis and comparison within the class than are projects that serve very different purposes. For example, benefit-cost is well adapted to the analysis of alternative investments in harbor facilities along the St. Lawrence Seaway. It is much less well-adapted to comparisons among major river-development projects of a multipurpose variety and even less well-adapted to comparisons among major governmental functions. Even more equivocal is comparison of the benefit-cost ratio for a water resource project with the ratio for an educational project.

Where there are major complementarities between the public and private sector and among programs within the public sector, benefit-cost loses its precision. Threshold effects in water resource development are of this type, as noted above. In the human resources area a program for preschool education may need to be combined with income maintenance and improved public health facilities. Only then may the outcomes from the preschool program be measurable and favorable.

The greatest dangers in application come when the volume of intangibles is large. As Dorfman said in summarizing a conference on benefit measurement:

> The practioners were very skeptical and inclined to doubt whether the most important social effects of government investment could ever be appraised quantitatively by cost-benefit analysis or any other formalized method. One of them likened the problem to appraising the quality of a horse-and-rabbit stew, the rabbit being cast as the consequences that can be measured and evaluated numerically and the horse as the amalgam of external effects, social, emotional, and psychological impacts, and historical and aesthetic considerations that can be adjudged only roughly and subjec-

tively. Since the horse is bound to dominate the flavor of the stew, meticulous evaluation of the rabbit would hardly seem worthwhile.[21]

When the intangibles are distribution values, the task of measuring appropriate trade-offs is particularly crucial. Benefit-cost is primarily concerned with establishing a criterion for judging economic efficiency in terms of national income gains. The measurement of benefits "to whomsoever they may accrue" is distributionally neutral. But, in the world of public investment decisions, nothing is distributionally neutral. Every government investment decision, in physical or human resources, favors some groups or persons more than others. Those favored, or relatively disfavored, may be classified by their income position, by their ethnic status, by their occupational status, or by their geographic location. And distributional considerations are quite as legitimate as efficiency considerations in public investment decisions. There is no basis for presuming that the distribution of national income is any less important than the size of the national income in the determination of aggregate welfare.[22]

Although the importance of distributional judgements has come to be increasingly recognized in recent years, there is not now nor can there be an adequate calculus for combining efficiency and distributional considerations. Maass has proposed that administrative agencies in government concentrate on measuring benefit-cost ratios in efficiency terms, and that the executive then propose explicit trade-offs with distributional objectives (Maass, 1966, pp. 208 – 26). Congress would then be in a position, if the alternatives are reasonably well defined, to arrive at a decision that must and will be broadly political.

Weisbrod has proposed a public policy objective of "grand efficiency," to combine economic efficiency and distributional considerations (Weisbrod, 1968, pp. 177 – 209; 1969, pp. 177 – 97). Project justification would include a display of distributional effects, measured in such terms as income class, ethnic status, and area. This, at least, would make distributional considerations explicit. Alternatively, weights might be attached to different classes of benefits, based on previous legislative action with respect to income distribution as reflected in personal income tax schedules. Income benefits received by low-income groups for a given type of project would thus be weighted more (or less) than benefits received by higher-income groups. Calculating the weights on the basis of previous legislative actions would not, of course, be determinative of what the weights ought to be or will be for future decisions.

The determination of a "proper" distribution of income will always be a

21. Dorfman, op. cit., p. 2.

22. For an excellent study of the relationship between efficiency and distribution in Corps of Engineers projects in southern states see Robert H. Haveman, *Water Resource Investment and the Public Interest* (Nashville: Vanderbilt University Press, 1965).

matter for the broadest kind of political decision-making. In a well-ordered public finance system it might be desirable to effectuate distributional policy solely by taxes and transfers from the national government. But since allocational decisions always have distributional consequences the world of policy will reflect the reality of this mixture. The best that economists can do in this situation is to improve their measurements of the distributional effects of specific projects in the hope that political decision-makers will understand better the consequences of their actions. This effort should include estimates of trade-offs to show the distributional consequences of the sacrifice of specified classes or increments of benefits. Alternative distributional consequences are as worthy of study as alternative techniques for cost minimization.

If benefit-cost techniques are to have operational usefulness, they must, of course, be related to administrative organization and to the responsibilities of existing governmental units. It may be an interesting academic excercise to analyze in benefit-cost terms major incremental additions to an urban transportation system. However, unless there is a competent area-wide transportation agency, the application of the technique becomes an almost meaningless exercise. In these circumstances, central authority must have general planning responsibility and general control over sources of funds and project revenues if rational investment decisions are to be made. In the absence of these responsibilities, benefit-cost techniques can make little operational contribution.

Perhaps the most disturbing tendency, almost inherent in benefit-cost analysis, is the encouragement that it gives to attach monetary values to intangibles, and the corresponding encouragement to emphasize those costs and benefits that can be measured rather than those that cannot. Esthetic considerations in urban renewal may be as important as measurable effects on neighborhood land values. It may be more important for the social fabric to introduce programs to strengthen the education of the underprivileged than to strengthen those who are already privileged. In its built-in emphasis on measurable outcomes, to the neglect of the nonmeasurable, and in the absence of attention to distributional concerns, benefit-cost may be positively misleading.

If, as was asserted in the first chapter of this volume, the value content of contemporary public-sector decisions is increasing, a technique that consciously avoids social and political values must be used with the greatest of caution.

References

Baumol, William J. "On the Appropriate Discount Rate for Evaluation of Public Projects." Joint Economic Committee, *The Planning-Programing-Budgeting System: Progress and Potentials,* 90th Cong., 1st sess., 1967, pp. 152–59.

————. "On the Discount Rate for Public Projects." Joint Economic Committee, *The Analysis and Evaluation of Public Expenditures: The PPB System,* 91st Cong., 1st sess., Vol. 1, 1969, pp. 489 – 503.

————. "On the Social Rate of Discount." *American Economic Review,* September 1968, pp. 788 – 802

Beranek, William, "A Note on the Equivalence of Certain Capital Budgeting Criteria," in Richard E. Ball and Z. Lew Melnyk, eds., *Theory of Managerial Finance: Selected Readings.* Allyn and Bacon, Boston: 1967, pp. 21-24.

Eckstein, Otto. *Water-Resource Development.* Cambridge: Harvard University Press, 1958.

————. "A Survey of the Theory of Public Expenditure Criteria," in National Bureau of Economic Research, *Public Finances: Needs, Sources, and Utilization.* Princeton: Princeton University Press, 1961, pp. 439 – 494.

Federal Reserve Bank of Kansas City. *Monthly Review,* October 1958, pp. 9 – 16.

Fox, Irving K. "National Water Resources Policy Issues." *Law and Contemporary Problems,* Summer 1957, pp. 472 – 509.

Goldman, Thomas A., ed. *Cost-Effectiveness Analysis.* New York: Frederick A. Praeger, 1967.

Haveman, Robert H., and John V. Krutilla, *Unemployment, Idle Capacity, and the Evaluation of Public Expenditures.* Baltimore: Johns Hopkins Press, 1968.

Hirshleifer, Jack. "On the Theory of Optimal Investment Decision." *Journal of Political Economy,* August 1958, pp. 329 – 52.

Hirshleifer, Jack, and David L. Shapiro. "The Treatment of Risk and Uncertainty." Joint Economic Committee, *The Analysis and Evaluation of Public Expenditures: The PPB System,* 91st Cong., 1st sess., 1969, pp. 505 – 30.

Krutilla, John V., and Otto Eckstein. *Multiple Purpose River Development.* Baltimore: The Johns Hopkins Press, 1958.

Lichfield, Nathaniel, "Spatial Externalities in Urban Public Expenditures: A Case Study," in Julius Margolis, ed., *The Public Economy of Urban Communities.* Washington: Resources for the Future, 1965, pp. 207 – 47.

————. "Cost-Benefit Analysis in Urban Development — A Case Study: Swanley." *Regional Science Association Papers,* Vol. 16, 1966, pp. 129 – 53.

Maass, Arthur. "Benefit-Cost Analysis: Its Relevance to Public Investment Decisions." *Quarterly Journal of Economics,* May 1966, pp. 208 – 26.

Marglin, Stephen A. "Economic Factors Affecting System Design," in Arthur Maass, Maynard M. Hufschmidt, Robert Dorfman, H. A. Thomas, S. A. Marglin, and G. M. Fair, *Design of Water-Resource-Systems.* Cambridge: Harvard University Press, 1962, pp. 159 – 226.

————. "The Social Rate of Discount and the Optimal Rate of Investment." *Quarterly Journal of Economics,* February 1963, pp. 95 – 111.

————. *Public Investment Criteria.* Cambridge: The M.I.T. Press, 1967.

McKean, Roland N. *Efficiency in Government Through Systems Analysis.* New York: Wiley, New York, 1958.

Mishan, E. J. "Criteria for Public Investment: Some Simplifying Suggestions." *Journal of Political Economy,* April, 1967, pp. 139 – 46.

Musgrave, Richard A. "Cost-Benefit Analysis and the Theory of Public Finance." *Journal of Economic Literature,* September 1969, pp. 797 – 806.

Prest, A. R., and R. Turvey. "Cost-Benefit Analysis: A Survey." *Economic Journal,* December 1965, pp. 683 – 735.

Steiner, George A. "Problems in Implementing Program Budgeting," in David Novick, ed., *Program Budgeting.* Cambridge: Harvard University Press, 1965, pp. 308 – 52.

Steiner, Peter O. *Public Expenditure Budgeting.* Washington: Brookings Institution, 1969.

Weisbrod, Burton A. "Income Redistribution Effects and Benefit-Cost Analysis," in Samuel B. Chase, Jr., ed., *Problems in Public Expenditure Analysis.* Washington: Brookings Institution, 1968, pp. 177 – 209.

———. "Collective Action and the Distribution of Income: A Conceptual Approach." Joint Economic Committee, *The Analysis and Evaluation of Public Expenditures: The PPB System,* 91st Cong., 1st sess., 1969, pp. 177 – 97.

EIGHT

Fiscal Federalism

In a federal system of government there is more than one level of authority. Each level has responsibility for making some independent decisions. The levels are therefore, and necessarily, coordinate.

In complicated federalism, as in the United States, there is no single system, but multitudinous systems. The national government may have statutes that are intended to be reasonably uniform in application among the states, but, in fact, differences in the fiscal positions of states, or in the application of administrative discretion, may establish markedly different patterns in the distribution of responsibility between the several states and the national government.

Each state will also establish a different internal pattern of governmental and fiscal responsibility and sometimes these patterns will vary among the cities or counties of a state. For some purposes each state system may be viewed as "federal" in character. And subordinate units of government, likewise, may exhibit, within any state, substantial variation in relationships with systems, school districts, or special districts. These systems within systems are not confined to the United States. In Canada, for example, the Toronto municipal government pattern is a federation within the Province of Ontario, which in turn stands in a federal relationship to the Dominion of Canada. Although it might be more appropriate to describe all of these systems under the general rubric of "multilevel finance," the more traditional term "federalism" will be retained here. The legal, political, and fiscal relationships that accompany a federal system are most intricate. Although an effort will be made here to concentrate on the fiscal issues, it is not possible to isolate the fiscal dimension from others.

In any economy there are changes in technology, in the relative prosperity of regions, and in the degree of factor mobility among the regions.[1] In the public sector there are resulting changes in the productivity of revenue sources and expenditure requirements. In addition, new public policy concerns emerge, matched or unmatched, by the emergence of administrative competence. All of these factors of change impinge on a federal system, requiring continuous readjustment in the distribution of governmental authority and fiscal capacity. These readjustments are a source of friction; the costs of agreement are high in a system of federalism.

It may be that the fundamental conflict in any organization is between centralization and decentralization. Whether the organization is a household, business firm, or government, there will be conflict between the center and its constituent members, and such conflict appears to be endemic. National economies that are organized along socialist lines are as much subject to this conflict as those organized along capitalist lines.

Existing federations, such as Canada, India, and Nigeria, have faced serious civil strife from demands for regional autonomy. Czechoslovakia and Yugoslavia have recently moved toward more regional autonomy in both political and economic policy. Even unitary states, such as France and Great Britain, must acknowledge the existence of new forces for regional "nationalism," forces which in some cases have appeared to be dormant for centuries.

It may not stretch the parallel too far to observe that contemporary demands for community control of education, welfare, and the police function in the United States are comparable to these regional demands in national states. In many instances it would appear that the contemporary demand for regional autonomy or community control reflects more of a concern over the decision process than over the outcomes of the process. This is a distinction that is not harmonious with the traditions of economic analysis, where means and ends are conventionally, and sharply, separated. Economists do not typically regard the process of decision as an end in itself and have been concerned with decision processes either as technical exercises in the aggregation of preferences or in terms of agreement and information costs. What appears to have happened in recent years is that the practical difficulty of securing agreement on the objectives of public policy and the theoretical difficulties of a "logical" aggregation of social values has led to concern for the process by which public decisions are reached; this concern is a substitute for the evaluation of the outcome. In a federal system this means that there is a continued search for both the techniques with which economic objectives can be attained and for a viable pattern of centralized and decentralized decision structures.[2] Issues

1. Throughout this chapter the term "region" will be used as a synonym for state or province to connote generally a spatially-defined political jurisdiction — a component of the national government or national economy.

2. The philosophic dimensions of the controversy over centralized and decentralized authority lie outside the scope of this volume. It may be noted, however, that the recent demands

related to centralization and decentralization are not identical with those related to federalism, but the two sets of issues become very much intermingled.

A federal system seems to encompass all the stresses and strains that are possible in the attempt to attain social objectives by means of governmental organization. It is not surprising that federalism should be the subject of extravagant praise and extravagant condemnation. The U. S. federal system, for example, has been described as "perhaps the greatest mark of American political genius" (McConnell, 1966, p. 357). It has also been described as a system which favors capitalists, landlords and racists. "Thus, if in the United States one disapproves of racism, one should disapprove of federalism" (Riker, 1964, p. 155).

In general, the theory of federalism has been characterized by rationalization, and the practice of federalism has been characterized by expediency. There are few "principles," political, economic, or administrative, available to guide the student of the subject. If there is any area of public finance that is characterized by multiple and conflicting objectives, it is intergovernmental relations.

This chapter will first examine the political arrangements that characterize a federal system and then the fiscal objectives that should be attained under the system, in terms of stabilization and growth, allocations and distribution. The third section of the chapter will be devoted to the devices for fiscal accommodation, with particular reference to grants-in-aid.

Political Organization

CHARACTERISTICS OF FEDERALISM

In a unitary government, such as that of Great Britain, authority is centralized, and local governments possess only such jurisdictional power as is granted by the Crown. The powers of local government can be modified by act of Parliament, although at any one time local authorities have substantial discretion. In a federal system the national government is not the source of all legal authority. The federal principle, according to the standard legal definition, is "the method of dividing powers so that the general and regional governments are each, within a sphere, co-ordinate and independent" (Wheare, 1964, p. 10). A federal system must be established by a written constitution.

---

for regional autonomy, student autonomy, and community control are typically regarded as an attempt to countervail the impersonality and bureaucracy of large organizations. The basic conflict can be described as one between the gains in operational efficiency from centralized techniques and the gains from decentralized administration responsive to humanistic considerations. The economic aspects of this conflict are examined briefly above in Chapter 1 and the relevant decision processes in Chapter 5.

Since the establishment of a federal system is in the nature of a bargain between the central government and its regional constituencies, and since the terms of this bargain are continuously subject to modification, it follows that there must be a judicial system with responsibility for interpreting the constitution and developing a legal framework for the resolution of conflict. A federal system must possess a supreme court with constitutionally established authority to participate in the processes of change and adaptation. Similarly, the states or provinces must be party to the amendment of the constitution.

Federal states usually emerge out of confederation rather than from the decentralization of unitary states. Historically, there would seem to be little doubt that military considerations are of primary importance in the initial creation of a federal system. The center is always endowed with authority for the maintenance of a military establishment, either to protect the constituent states or to engage in aggressive warfare against other states. This was surely the case with the U. S. federal system in 1787. Military considerations also seem to have been important in the creation of the large number of federations among the newly independent nations of Asia and Africa in the years since World War II. As Riker points out, however, the conditions for the continuation of a federal system may differ in important ways from the conditions that called it into existence.

EVOLUTION OF A FEDERAL SYSTEM

It is characteristic of almost all federal systems that they evolve in the direction of fiscal and administrative centralization. Peripheralized federalism tends to be replaced by centralized federalism. The center undertakes new public programs; its revenue and expenditure increase more rapidly than the revenue and expenditure of the constituent units; the number of central government employees increase more rapidly than the employees of the states or provinces. The reasons for this development do not appear to be either simple or obvious. Wars or depressions will encourage the growth of the center. The growth of military expenditures and the prominence of nationalism are, of course, of great importance. National economic and social planning must be centralized. The increased specialization and interdependence of national economies, and improvements in the technology of transportation and communication, are also important. In developed countries the increased mobility of labor undoubtedly contributes to the dominance of national influences. The national government also has traditionally acquired more elastic sources of revenue than the constituent units have, so that the national fisc is typically stronger than regional fiscs. Where political parties are national in scope there is a resulting centralizing thrust. There are undoubtedly other factors that have contributed to centralizing tendencies, but it should be stressed that centralizing trends do not operate uniformly. States or provinces may, from time to time, retrogress as well as progress, as will their constituent jurisdictions.

The observable centralizing trends in fiscal affairs appear, however, to generate a reaction. In every federal system strong movements for regional autonomy emerge, based on considerations of ethnicity, language, religion, and economic development. The center must engage in continuous bargaining with the states, and the fiscal bargain is only one of those that must be struck.

Political organization for a workable federalism may be viewed simply as the outcome of a bargain, as the consequence of an interplay or political power-struggle between the center and the provinces, or between those who favor centralization and those who favor decentralization, or between those whose political interests are favored by centralization or decentralization. Such elements of political bargaining are obviously present in any federal system and very often appear to dominate the whole relationship.

If there is any economic rationality in a federal system, this rationality must rest on grounds of economic efficiency in resource allocation. The critical assumptions are that, first, a group of individuals who reside in a "community" or "region" possess preference patterns that are homogeneous and that differ from the preferences of individuals who live in other communities or regions; the preference variability within regions is less than among regions. Second, individuals within a region have a better knowledge of the costs and benefits of public services for their region. In addition, of course, there must be a mechanism for revealing and aggregating preferences within a region. Therefore, if decisions concerning the allocation of public resources, the level and composition of such resources, and the ways in which private resources are to be devoted to a public purpose are to be left to the authority of the region, there is a greater opportunity for preferences for public expenditures to be optimized, with given costs and technology. Regional sovereignty is roughly analogous to consumer sovereignty, or is a spatial arrangement that approaches consumer sovereignty in the public sector.

The existence of regional differences in tastes and preferences implies that the polity is composed of many publics, not just one, and that "publics" must be defined regionally or spatially, not just in terms of interest groups or other functional representation. As an administrative matter the center cannot be expected to respond to any but the most gross of regional differences; Gargantua, by definition, is insensitive. Moreover, the cost of delivering certain kinds of public services may be lower if they are disjoined regionally. Therefore, a polycentric system is necessary if regional consumer sovereignty is to be implemented and if public service costs are to be minimized.[3]

It would be difficult to take exception to this kind of generalized rationale for a pattern of regionalized decisions. But against the undoubted existence of regional differences in tastes and preferences runs another hard fact of exis-

3. An elucidation of this view is contained in Vincent Ostrom, Charles M. Tiebout, and

tence: there is no common agreement as to what may be appropriately recognized as a "legitimate" or "essential" regional difference. Almost every public program that is of interest to one region is also of interest to another region and hence assumes a "national" dimension. The citizens of Region A may have a low preference for public education, but the citizens of Regions B . . . Z may have an interest in the education of the children of Region A as long as there is interregional commerce and some labor mobility among the regions. There are externalities for every program in Region A. Sometimes these are significant and sometimes they are trivial.

Moreover, the boundaries are different for each program area. Two or three politically bounded regions may be concerned with water resource development in a given river basin, but four or five regions may be concerned with a common program for the abatement of air pollution. A region may be safely awarded considerable autonomy in the education of elementary school children, but somewhat less autonomy in the education of high school students and even less in education at the college level. Political boundaries, no matter how drawn, cannot appropriately coincide with the full range of relevant program areas. Political participation is also significant in this context. The larger the unit the less is direct participation possible in governmental decisions, although the decisions by the large units may be ones of most influence on the lives of citizens. Smaller units provide for greater participation, but that participation may be in trivial matters (Dahl, 1967, pp. 953 – 70).

The basic economics of a federal system imply that it is desirable, in the interests of maximizing the welfare of the total society, to recognize that some welfare-yielding public activities are regional in impact and that variations in preferences, costs, and benefits for such activities differ systematically from area to area. Furthermore, it is implied that such recognition and its implementation will not involve externalities of such scope and dimension as to reduce the welfare of other regions. To put the matter another way, a federal system implies regional autonomy; this autonomy implies a regional veto. One region can stand against all other regions in the exercise of its decisions concerning some public programs, or at least within specified limits of some public programs, without finding these decisions overruled by other regions acting in concert against it.

WORKABLE THEORY

The foregoing generalized language suggests the difficulties that are encountered in efforts to devise workable arrangements in the real world. Such terms

Robert Warren, "The Organization of Government in Metropolitan Areas: A Theoretical Inquiry," *American Political Science Review,* December 1961, pp. 831 – 42.

as "regional sovereignty," "regional welfare," and "regional externalities" are not precise, nor are their "national" counterparts. In consequence, students of federalism, both political scientists and economists, have had the greatest difficulty in moving from general constructs to the world of public programs. There are serious difficulties in measuring differences in tastes, costs, and benefits and in demarcating the spatial boundaries of these differences. The variations that are observed may reflect differing income distributions or imperfections in political mechanisms rather than the regional variations in preferences and cost conditions.

Moreover, there is simply no way to measure whether the welfare of regions B . . . Z is affected with sufficient adversity by the actions of Region A as to justify intervention in the affairs of Region A with a presumed loss to its welfare.

The phraseology that has been used to describe federal systems, as in the United States, is uncomfortably vague and usually is restricted to an examination of federal-state relationships rather than to an examination of federal-state-local relationships. Even the interpretation of the history of federal-state relations in the United States is subject to considerable controversy. For example, the traditional view of these relations is that, until the Supreme Court decisions beginning in 1937, dual federalism prevailed. The national government and the states each had generally exclusive areas of authority and jurisdiction, with very few concurrent powers. This was changed, it is usually argued, as the New Deal legislation and its eventual affirmation by the Supreme Court extended the scope of national programs into areas that had been hitherto reserved to the states. Since the 1930s we have had not dual federalism, but cooperative federalism. A steadily increasing number of powers have been exercised concurrently by the national government and the states.

This view has been challenged by Grodzins and Elazar. Their thesis is that the history of federal-state relations in the United States has always been one of cooperation, not of the separation of functions by levels of government (Grodzins, 1965, pp. 165 – 84; Elazar, 1962; Elazar, 1966). The proper analogy is with a marble cake, not a layer cake. Nothing unusual occurred in the 1930s; the New Deal was an extension of traditions that dated back to the experiences of the nineteenth century.

The Grodzins-Elazar thesis has in turn come under attack by Scheiber, who argues, from a careful examination of the history of specific federal-state programs, that there have been significant changes in the distribution of federal and state authority and that these changes have not occurred in a smooth, evolutionary fashion (Scheiber, 1966). He finds, for example, that the New Deal brought very sharp changes in the pattern of federal-state-local relations in the United States.

Finally, in recent years a new term, "creative federalism," has come to be employed to describe some of the dimensions of federal programs initiated or reemphasized since 1965. Creative federalism seems to embrace such characteristics of intergovernmental relations as federal-city grant programs, which increasingly bypass the states, an increased emphasis on economic growth, new "partnerships" with private business firms, and possibly new budgetary techniques such as those of the Planning-Programming-Budgeting System (Scheiber, 1966, pp. 14–16). Creative federalism has been described in glowing terms as a new way of organizing federal programs, one in which "Simultaneously, the power of states and local governments will increase; the power of private organizations, including businesses, will increase; and the power of individuals will increase" (Ways, 1966, p. 122). This is a definition so broad as to be meaningless.

The fiscal and administrative patterns that accompany a federal system are subject to as much difficulty of analysis and appraisal as the nature of the system itself, whether dual, cooperative, or creative. The traditional view of fiscal and administrative patterns is that the continued increase in the power of the center and the growth of its administrative establishment maintains and revitalizes the center. At the same time the fiscal support of state or provincial programs by grants-in-aid maintains and revitalizes the states or provinces. Fiscal support is not only the lubricant of the continuously changing relations between the center and the regions, it is the lifeblood of a federal system.

This "administrative theory" of federalism has likewise come under attack. Riker, examining specific functions that are exercised by the national government and the states, finds no consistent pattern of administrative sharing, and concludes that the maintenance of the vitality of federalism in the United States has come about more from the influence of organized political parties than from fiscal support and administrative sharing (Riker, 1964, p. 50).[4]

The foregoing welter of conflicting historical interpretations and the use of ill-defined phrases does not make for clarity in isolating the leading characteristics of a federal system, in this or any other nation. One conclusion, however, seems to be inescapable. A federal system is a politically conservative system. The sharing of responsibility and authority for governmental programs is inherently ponderous. The veto power retained by the provinces or local governments can at least retard and frequently prevent the introduction of measures of social legislation, or delay their implementation once national legislation has been adopted. The doctrine of states' rights, as it has emerged

4. For other discussions of the relationship of political parties to federalism see David B. Truman, "Federalism and the Party System," in Aaron Wildavsky, ed., *American Federalism in Perspective* (Boston: Little, Brown, 1967), pp. 81–109; Morton Grodzins, "American Political Parties and the American System," ibid., pp. 109–43.

in the American context, is a doctrine of conservatism and resistance to the introduction of measures of social welfare.

James Madison, after the experience of Shay's Rebellion, apparently understood this point very well. He wrote:

> The influence of factious leaders may kindle a flame within their particular States, but will be unable to spread a general conflagration through the other States. . . . A rage for paper money, for an abolition of debts, for an equal division of property, or for any other improper or wicked project, will be less apt to pervade the whole body of the Union than a particular member of it; in the same proportion as such a malady is more likely to taint a particular county or district, than an entire State. (Madison, pp. 61 – 2)

A federal system is a device for the economic and political recognition of pluralism. It is not the only such device that is available, and its costs may be very high. These costs include the inherent resistance to change and adaptation that are endemic in a system of coordinate and concurrent powers. Alexis de Toqueville may have made the most profound remark on this subject when he spoke of "the good sense and practical judgment of the Americans . . . in the ingenious devices by which they elude the numberless difficulties resulting from their federal constitution" (quoted by Martin, 1965, p. v).

Fiscal Objectives

The contributions of economists to the theory and practice of fiscal federalism have been meager. In this area, at least, economists are less critical than political scientists. The latter explore the discrepancies that emerge between national policy and regional policy and examine the political consequences of regional autonomy. Political scientists investigate the role of interest groups in the federal system and assess the relative administrative competence and responsiveness of federal, state, and local agencies. Among economists there has been very little effort to analyze the macro aspects of federalism, in the sense of comparing economic objectives and outcomes of federal and unitary states.[5] Economists will typically accept the existence of a federal system, or indeed extol its virtues as "democracy by decentralization," and then proceed to explore how traditional economic objectives, such as efficiency or stabilization, can be accomplished within the federal framework.

This is not to say that the economic model should come first, to be followed by the specification of the political model. In a political world economic rationality, particularly when it is narrowly defined, does not have priority.

5. One prominent exception is Anthony Scott, "The Economic Goals of Federal Finance," *Public Finance*, 1964, pp. 241 – 88.

There must always be a compromise between political and economic objectives. But neither is it necessary for the economist to adapt his models to a federal system that he uncritically accepts.

Perhaps this observed tendency to avoid the significant issues is attributable to a harsh reality: some of the problems in the economics of federalism are virtually intractable, the operational state of existing analytical techniques being what it is. For example, the optimum size of local governmental units is a matter of considerable economic importance, given the present worldwide rates of urbanization and growth. In the few efforts that economists have made to address themselves to this problem it is possible to discern some "principles" in terms of economies of scale, and spillovers of benefits and costs. Unfortunately, in the real world both scale effects and spillovers are sufficiently elusive of measurement and aggregation that the economic analysis here has had to confine itself to rather empty if/then propositions.

Whatever the difficulties are with the existing state of analysis of the economics of federalism, they will be accepted here in an examination of the conventional approaches that have been attempted. These approaches may be subsumed under traditional neo-Keynesian objectives: stabilization and growth, distribution and allocation. A fourth objective that is commonly associated with federalism and may be considered an aspect of allocation — the provision of minimum service levels — will also be examined.

STABILIZATION AND GROWTH

Provincial or state governments have very little responsibility for the achievement of economic stabilization. Their economies are open, it may be assumed, with a substantial volume of interstate trade, with the demand for a state's exports determined nationally, and with substantial mobility of capital and labor. Any effort to employ fiscal techniques for the stimulation of levels of income and employment within their boundaries, as by expenditure on physical capital facilities in time of deflation, will have modest outcomes. Local employment may be increased, but effects on the resident population may be offset by the in-migration of the unemployed from other states. Local expenditure will increase but multiplier effects within the region will be small, since a substantial portion of the increases in state spending will spill over to other states. State fiscal policies intended to counter an inflationary situation will face comparable obstacles. Increases in state taxes, without corresponding expenditure benefits, will place the state's economy at a competitive disadvantage. Expenditure reduction, with tax rates unchanged, will have similar consequences. In neither case is it likely that the reduction in regional aggregate demand will be sufficient to affect local price levels where there are integrated national markets for goods and factors.

Also, it may be assumed, states will not possess the customary tools of national monetary policy. In contemporary federal systems, states and provinces do not have authority to create money. States must also be concerned about their external debt, much of which is likely to be held by persons and institutions in other states. As a consequence, the requirement for a balanced budget, often enforced constitutionally, will conform with the economic, as well as the political reality of an open system where policy parameters are largely exogenous.

From time to time, in this country, there have been proposals that the national government attempt to coordinate the fifty states in an intergovernmental fiscal policy. The "coercive" techniques for such coordination would not be difficult to devise. Grants-in-aid, for example, could be made conditional on adoption by the states of specified stabilization policies. But nothing has ever come of such proposals nor is such coordination likely to occur since the required degree of coercion would interfere with the states' prerogatives in fiscal affairs. Therefore, stabilization, in this and other federal systems, is a national objective, to be implemented by national policies. States and local governments are in the position of adapting their fiscal positions to policies that are determined exogenously, in very much the same way that business firms and households must adapt their budgetary decisions to the fiscal and monetary actions of the national government.[6] States and local governments can be expected to respond to central government policies in ways that appear most desirable from the state and local government vantage point, but these governments cannot be induced to coordinate action without basic changes in the structure of federalism which would have the effect of eliminating essential federal characteristics.

In the interests of regional growth, state or local government officials may pursue policies that are intended to attract economic activity to their jurisdictions, by offering tax inducements or capital facilities whose costs are borne by the general taxpayer. If the total volume of economic activity is, as a practical matter, exogenously or nationally determined at full employment levels, state or local subsidization to attract economic activity has unfortunate allocational consequences; the gains of Region A are the losses of Region B. The distributional consequences of such inducements to business location may also be unfortunate. The subsidies to the incoming business firm are often paid at the expense of nonbenefiting taxpayers within the jurisdiction. If subsidies must be paid they could be better paid to induce business firms to remain in areas where there is an adequate supply of labor and an existing infrastructure.

6. For a somewhat different view of local stabilization policies, see James M. Buchanan, *Public Finance in Democratic Process,* (Chapel Hill: University of North Carolina Press, 1967), pp. 270–75.

DISTRIBUTION

There are three partially separable economic issues associated with distributional policy in a federal system. The first is that of the overall distribution of income — the range of issues that are examined as a part of the distribution branch of the total public household. The second is that of horizontal equity among individual taxpayers — the search for a decision rule that will assure the equal treatment of equals in a system of multilevel finance. The third issue is equalization of the fiscal position of the states or local units within a federal system. This last requires the selection of criteria to measure, and means to assure, equality with regard to governmental services or taxable capacity, or perhaps levels of real expenditure. These three issues are, however, only partially separable, and in some instances are entangled with allocational considerations.

Aggregate Income Distribution. In the overall distribution of income in a federal system it must be determined whether the national government or the state governments have final authority. It would be a coincidence if state policy and national policy were in agreement on appropriate distributional policy, and therefore whichever level is the last to redistribute will control the policy. It is usually argued that if the states have ultimate control over income distribution there would be unfortunate barriers to the optimal location of population and economic activity. Upper-income individuals and some business firms would migrate from high tax (redistribution) states to avoid tax burdens. It is usually contended that the states should modify the distribution of income in the first instance, and the national government should then determine the final distribution (Musgrave, 1959, p. 181).

This general precept is reasonable enough when the distribution branch, as is typical in fiscal theory, is conceived as being subject to implementation solely by taxes and transfers. But distributional concerns are only partially implemented by taxes and transfers in state-local finance. Implementation also comes by way of resource allocation — by decisions to spend more or less on programs that benefit specific income groups. Expenditures for education will have different distributional consequences than expenditures for police and fire protection. Although these considerations are also relevant for national finance, distributional and allocational concerns are substantially more intermingled at the state and local levels.

Equity Among Individuals. The second distributional concern is for the provision of horizontal fiscal equity among individuals. This problem does not arise in a unitary state where the central fisc presumably treats all individuals alike with respect to their taxes and benefits, regardless of where they live. It does arise in a federal system, and there are two ways of dealing with it. One approach is that first introduced by Buchanan (1950, pp. 583 – 99), who urged that in establishing criteria for horizontal equity it is necessary to compare the fiscal positions of individuals across regional lines. A second approach is concerned with the region as an entity and not with the individuals who comprise it. Here it is assumed that the region is sufficiently homogeneous with respect to tastes, costs, and incomes so that horizontal equity criteria can be established for regions in relation to each other.

Buchanan's criterion is that all citizens should receive equal treatment with respect to taxes and benefits from governmental services, regardless of the state in which they live. Unless this is done, the citizens of low-income states will be subject to excessive fiscal pressure as such states attempt to tax more heavily in order to provide adequate levels of governmental services. Resource allocation will be distorted, as citizens move to higher-income states where governmental services can be provided at lower tax burdens with respect to income.

The remedy is to equalize the fiscal residuals of individuals — the net difference between tax burdens and expenditure benefits. Buchanan assumes that within a region the benefits of government goods and services are uniformly distributed among the populace; that is, individual preferences and other characteristics are such that within a region all persons value equally the service provided by the level of state and local expenditures.

The fiscal positions of individuals are identical with an average fiscal position of the region as a whole. The fiscal residuals can be equalized, if they can be measured approximately, by varying the national government rate of personal income tax among the several states. Alternatively, the central government could require redistributive payments among the states to equalize fiscal capacity. These payments would approximate an equalization of the residuals and would be more feasible than tax rate discrimination.

Buchanan's proposal is conceptually interesting, but of no practical importance. Aside from its constitutional infirmity, as Buchanan himself noted, it is by no means clear that the provision of spatial horizontal fiscal equity among individuals is of such importance as to countervail other fiscal objectives. Central government tax rates that discriminated geographically would destroy any authority the states possessed over their vertical money income distributions. And the equalization of fiscal residuals would not guarantee that all individuals would end up at an optimum on their indifference curves between public and private goods. As Scott has pointed out, the true test of fiscal equity among individuals is the achievement of geographical indifference with respect to tax-benefit combinations (Scott, 1964, pp. 253 – 55). This condition is not assured by the equalization of the residuals, since some individuals will prefer to live in a high-tax, high-benefit jurisdiction.[7]

7. Further discussion of the Buchanan concept is contained in Musgrave (1961, pp. 116–22); comments by Buchanan, ibid., pp. 122–29; A. T. Eapen, "Federalism and Fiscal Equity Reconsidered." *National Tax Journal,* September 1966, pp. 325–29; A. D. Scott, "The Evaluation of Federal Grants," *Economica,* November 1952, pp. 377–94; Buchanan, "Federal Grants

Equity Among States. The alternative approach is to emphasize, not the position of individuals with respect to the combined central-state fisc, but the position of states in relation to each other and to the central fisc. Here the constituent units within the states are implicitly extinguished, and it is assumed that states are reasonably homogeneous, internally, with respect to tastes and preferences. Equalization must be defined in relation to established statewide political jurisdictions. The individual's position in the state has no significance.

In this approach there is a substantial range of choice among equalization objectives, as Musgrave has pointed out (Musgrave, 1961, pp. 97 – 116). The possibilities include (1) the equalization of actual outlays or performance by the states, (2) the equalization of differentials in need and capacity, and (3) the equalization of state fiscal potentials. To highlight the issues, Musgrave assumes no spillovers of benefits or tax burdens and no fiscal retaliation; in addition, equalization grants are limited to transfers among states so that the central government budget is in balance. What any one state gains in subsidies others lose in transfers.

Equalization of outlays or performance levels requires transfers from above average revenue-need states to below average revenue-need states, until all states achieve equivalence. Any expansion of revenues by a particular state either reduces the subsidy received or increases its required transfer payments, so that only a portion of the increase remains with the taxing jurisdiction. Such an arrangement would be seriously disincentive in terms of a state's own tax revenues, with the possibility that the states might move toward a zero level of taxation.

Equalization of differentials in need and tax capacity removes this disincentive by the elimination of a state's own tax rate in the formula for subsidization, but introduces the inequities that follow from the receipt of subsidies by states without regard to the extent of efforts on their own behalf.

The equalization of fiscal potentials is more attractive. In one variant of this approach subsidies are based on the state's own tax effort and tax base in relation to the average tax base and rate. The outcome of such a scheme is complex, but in general it provides the greatest subsidy to states whose tax base is lower than average and whose tax rate is above average. Another variant to equalize fiscal potential would provide a subsidy to achieve average performance per dollar of self-financed outlay. Finally, capacity and need may be

---

and Resource Allocation," *Journal of Political Economy,* June 1952, pp. 208 – 17; A. D. Scott, "Federal Grants and Resource Allocation," *Journal of Political Economy,* December 1952, pp. 534 – 36; with Buchanan's reply, pp. 536 – 38. An extension of the Buchanan concept to urge that fiscal residuals be adjusted by interstate grants to slow down the migration of the indigent from the south is contained in James M. Buchanan and Richard E. Wagner, "An Efficiency Basis for Federal Fiscal Equalization," *The Analysis of Public Output,* (New York: Columbia University Press, 1970), pp. 139 – 58.

combined in such fashion that subsidies adjust revenues so that any state can provide average performance levels per dollar of self-financed outlay at average tax rates on its own tax base.

The strength of the fiscal potential approaches is that they reduce the free ride inherent in capacity equalization. At the same time, since the subsidies depend on a state's own tax rate, the equalization of fiscal potentials reintroduces substitution effects. Both incentives and disincentives accompany schemes to equalize fiscal potentials and vary in accord with the base, rate, and need of individual states in relation to the average of all states. Effects do not all tend in one direction, but do promote the equalization of effort and performance which, after all, is the objective sought.

Specific formulas for the accomplishment of equalization objectives can be developed, as Musgrave has shown (Musgrave, 1961, pp. 98 – 116). But even if agreement can be reached on the equalization objective, implementation is another matter. The assumptions that simplified the description of alternative concepts of equalization no longer can be accepted. For example, when the region is treated as an entity, attention must be directed to benefit and cost spillovers.

Expenditures in one state may give rise to substantial out-of-state benefits, as where those educated in State A migrate to State B. On the cost side State A may be in a position to shift a portion of its tax burdens to the residents of other states, where property and income taxes are imposed on business firms that export goods across state lines. This increases A's fiscal capacity at the expense of B's.

It might be possible to secure some rough estimates of benefit spillovers that would be sufficiently accurate for implementation of an equalization scheme. Rough estimates of exported taxes are also possible. But the practical difficulties are overwhelming for any equalization scheme that requires a computation of the taxable capacity of states.

Traditionally, the measurement of taxable capacity has attempted to index the relative position of the states by some readily available indication of economic activity, such as personal income (ACIR, 1967, pp. 79 – 87). Tax effort, then, is simply the ratio of state and local tax collections to state personal income, and the states are ranked by this index. An alternative is to formulate a representative or model state-local tax system, based on average practices of the states or some set of standard provisions for tax bases and rates.[8] This model is then applied state-by-state to estimate the resulting yields, which are then converted to an index designating the taxable capacity of the

---

8. See Advisory Commission on Intergovernmental Relations, *Measures of State and Local Fiscal Capacity and Tax Effort,* (Washington, 1962.)

state. Tax effort, again, is the ratio of actual state-local tax collections to the estimated yield from the model tax system.

Neither the ratio of tax collections to state personal income nor model tax-system yields is in any way a satisfactory measure of taxable capacity. The level of personal income would need to be modified by the distribution of that income within a state and perhaps by its composition with respect to labor and property income. The measures used extinguish important differences among the municipalities in a state. Measures of personal income and model tax-system yield both overlook the circumstances that affect taxable capacity within a given state. Some states have additional taxable capacity because their citizens have, on the average, a propensity to gamble at race tracks, or to buy lottery tickets. Other states have additional taxable capacity because some kinds of economic activities have been traditionally subject to heavy state-local tax burdens, such as the extractive industries. And it is by no means clear that taxable capacity can be isolated from the preferences of the community with respect to public versus private goods.

In addition, political circumstances are relevant. At any one time, in any one state, taxable capacity is influenced by constitutional restrictions, by the political program of the governor and his willingness to seek higher tax rates, by the attitudes of legislators and their constituents, by the political parties, and by the attitudes toward taxpaying assumed by local governments. In short, equalization schemes that depend on operational measures of taxable capacity among states are subject to severe limitations. Such measures at the intrastate level would probably be somewhat more meaningful.

ALLOCATION

The foregoing discussion emphasizes that a federal system complicates the achievement of the traditional goals of the public sector. The utilization of fiscal and monetary policy for purposes of stabilization is weakened in a federal system, in contrast with a unitary system. Distributional objectives are even more difficult to attain in a system of multilevel finance. Comprehensive horizontal equity among individual taxpayers is unattainable because of the different net fiscal benefits available to taxpayers in different governmental units. Even when states are treated as homogeneous units there are great complications in any attempt to equalize service levels or fiscal capacity among them.

The economic rationale for a federal system must reside in the allocations branch. As noted above, the case rests on the belief that preferences and costs for public goods will differ less among citizens in specified geographic areas than among the population as a whole. Therefore, a federal system will be more efficient in optimizing preference patterns than will a unitary system, where geographic differences in attitudes between public and private goods would presumably be obliterated. However, it may be noted that in an "ideal" unitary system it would still be possible to recognize differences among regions. For example, in two regions that had uniform costs and incomes but differing preferences for regional public goods, centrally-collected taxes for government goods and services could be lower in one region than in another.

The general rule for allocations of public goods is that for Pareto optimality to obtain, taxes must be collected on a benefit basis, in accord with individual marginal valuations of public goods, and that quantity must be determined at the point where the sum of the marginal valuations is equal to marginal cost. In a federal system with semiautonomous regions the benefit principle cannot be linked to specific individual valuations but must be linked with regional benefits. This may afford an approximation to individual Pareto optimality if, again, costs, benefits, preferences, and incomes are reasonably homogeneous. In fact, the homogeneity assumption is necessary to the very concepts of regional cost and benefit.

It would appear to be an unwarranted extension of the benefit basis to assert that regional taxes must be collected by the region, as has been argued (Buchanan, 1957, p. 176). There is no economic virtue attached to the proposition that each government must collect the revenue that it spends, and to justify this proposition on political grounds would require the invocation of some mystical virtue attached to self-reliance. It is quite possible for the central government to collect taxes in the region and establish a pattern of subventions, with the regional government responsible for determination of the expenditure level and mix.

Before examining efficiency conditions, it may be noted that very little is known about the economic cost of federation. Scott argues that there is an "opportunity cost of federating" (Scott, 1964, p. 242). GNP must be smaller, to some extent, in a federal system than in a unitary system, although larger than in a balkanized system, since any degree of regional authority over economic or fiscal policy is likely to interpose some barriers to factor and product mobility. These barriers will reduce, to some degree, the volume of total economic activity. In addition, it appears likely that a federal system will, in many instances, fail to achieve appropriate economies of scale. The boundaries of major governmental subdivisions, in every federal system, may not be immutable but they do change slowly. With technological improvements in transportation and communication it would seem reasonable that, over time, the scale for the provision of many state and local area services could be increased with consequent reductions in average unit cost.[9] The observable

9. This is a reasonable a priori assertion, but empirical documentation is most difficult. Accurate measures of governmental service output are unattainable for many programs. Therefore costs per unit of output cannot be accurately measured either for a cross section of local government activity or over time for individual units.

failure to reorganize governmental boundaries precludes securing whatever economies of scale may emerge.

The size of the local government unit required to secure consensus is likely to be smaller than the size of the government unit required for economies of scale (Rothenberg, 1970). Moreover, as Rothenberg has pointed out, there are two other dimensions involved in the selection of appropriate size: the minimization of political externalities, such as the need for bargaining across jurisdictional lines, and the maximization of social redistributive goals. Both of these dimensions indicate larger units than those required to secure the maximization of a home-rule type of consensus.

These considerations on the production side point toward a lower GNP in a federal than a unitary system, but there may be some offsets. Centralized administration, it is often argued, produces serious diseconomies of scale. A federal system may also provide more opportunity for technological innovation, as in the Brandeis concept of the states as "laboratories of experiment." Some states may develop "model" programs in specific areas that can be emulated by other states with a saving in installation cost. There may be production-side efficiencies to offset some of the production-side inefficiencies that characterize a federal system. And there may be consumer efficiencies, if there is an appropriate clustering of individuals with common tastes and preferences, provided that there is sufficient mobility to permit the clustering. It is possible, of course, that measured GNP would be smaller under a federal than a unitary system, but that regional decisions, reflecting a commonality of tastes and preferences, would attain a higher level of real income. It is also possible that a federal system may have an easier task in equalizing incomes among regions than a unitary system (Shoup, 1969, pp. 631 – 34)). Unfortunately, there have been no studies of the relative costs and gains of federal and unitary systems, and such studies would be most difficult to undertake. Moreover, the issues are usually formulated in terms of a static model; it is not at all clear whether a federal or unitary system is more responsive to changes in tastes and technology.

If it is accepted that the GNP is likely to be lower under a federal system, that is, where the cost of federation has already been paid, then allocational efficiency must be attained within the limits of this lowered GNP. This efficiency can be approached, as with distributional concerns, by seeking to (Pareto) optimize the position of individuals and their preferences, or by seeking allocational efficiency for the local governmental unit in its collective rationality.

The Tiebout Effect. Since it is impossible to determine individual tax burdens at the equilibrium level of government services through the revelation of citizen preferences, the most straightforward individualistic solution argues that optimization is attained as households move from one locality to another in order to secure that bundle of government goods and services and tax payments which satisfies the preference pattern of the household. This kind of optimizing is known as the Tiebout effect (Tiebout, 1956, 1961).

The Tiebout effect is equivalent to a market mechanism in local finance, with the results intended to be Pareto optimal in individualistic terms. The mobility and competitiveness of households is presumed to bring an equilibrium, after allowance for the cost of movement, between public goods benefits and costs at the margin. Mobility will result from either tastes or income. Those who value public goods highly will tend to live in the same community with others who value public goods highly, and this will be equitable for that community if incomes or other proxy measures of tax liabilities are also comparable. If tastes are similar but incomes differ, those with low incomes and a high preference for public goods will seek to enter the high-income community. At this point exclusion will be practiced to produce an income-segregated community.

A closer approximation to a consumer optimum is achieved at the expense of a production distortion (Scott, 1964, p. 267). Employees may locate at a distance from their place of employment such that the costs of the journey-to-work are substantially increased. This may be an acceptable cost for individuals, but there may be substantial social costs arising from the additional transportation facilities, such as congestion and air pollution. Also, once household moving costs are introduced it is evident that the Tiebout option is available to some but not to others. It is, in fact, available to those who by nature of their occupation are required to move frequently, or those who by virtue of their wealth or income have the means to transfer their residence. Thus, "some will remain behind" (Scott, 1964, p. 268). And those who remain behind have available only the possibility of influencing their neighbors to modify the existing bundle of local public benefits and costs through instrumentalities of political persuasion. This equilibrating mechanism may or may not be as effective as a shift in residence.

As an explanation of the clustering of tastes and incomes for bundles of local government goods the Tiebout analysis is most realistic. This is, in fact, what evidently occurs in income-segregated communities in this country, where zoning and subdivision regulations are imposed to exclude low-income families. The metropolitan-wide social costs of income segregation are, however, neglected in this model. The concentration of low-income families in the central city, so characteristic of metropolitan social patterns, raises the demand for public services, contributes to the erosion of the central city tax base, and permits the high-income communities to avoid at least a part of the cost imposed on local government by the area as a whole.

The Tiebout effect is a kind of simulated market solution. Decentralized decisions with regard to residence, based on individual preference functions, promote Pareto optimality with respect to bundles of local public goods and services. At best the Tiebout effect ignores the social costs of communities segregated on the basis of taxpaying capacity and even fails to allow full individual adjustment, since the selection of a residence area implies acceptance of a specific package of service levels and tax burdens, all aspects of which are not likely to conform to individual taxpayer preferences. The nature of local public goods, however, introduces a further dimension that must be examined.

Breton has pointed out that the polar condition of pure public goods — availability in equal amounts to all — is not characteristic of local public goods (Breton, 1965, pp. 175 – 87). He would prefer the term "nonprivate good" to describe a wide range of local government services that are available in unequal amounts, although the amount available to one does not reduce the amount available to others. The incomplete publicness attributed to local public goods is, of course, also characteristic of all public services, whether local, state, or national. But for local goods, availability depends particularly on accessibility, or the distance between the household and the point of production. This will be the case with hospital services, parks, and playgrounds, and police and fire protection that may not be distributed uniformly throughout the local government jurisdiction. In other cases, as with vaccinations, objective benefits are an increasing function of the number of persons in the jurisdiction who are vaccinated. A part of education benefits may also share this characteristic; average benefits rise with an increase in the number educated. Breton feels that local public goods could be classified by an ascending order of publicness in accordance with availability.

The existence of nonprivate goods does not nullify the possibility of attaining Pareto optimality, provided that tastes are identical among individuals for local goods and that all taxes are imposed on the basis of objective benefits to the recipient. If tastes were not identical, benefit taxation would necessarily differ among individuals.[10] The basic problem is one of mapping, and perfect mapping would be one "in which all the objective benefits of local goods are exhausted within the boundaries of the local jurisdiction, the benefits of provincial goods within the provincial jurisdiction, the benefits of national goods within the national jurisdiction, and so on" (Breton, 1965, p. 180). Local goods would be supplied by the local jurisdiction, and provincial, national, and international goods by their jurisdictions. With identical tastes for local goods in each locality and taxes on objective benefits, a system of grants could be devised that would be Pareto optimal. Complications would arise if benefits

10. For an interesting exchange on the nonprivate goods concept, see J. C. Weldon, "Public Goods (and Federalism)," *Canadian Journal of Economics and Political Science,* May 1966, pp. 230 – 38, with a reply by Breton, pp. 238 – 42.

were not exhausted within the boundaries of each jurisdiction, that is, if there were spillovers. Matching grants would be necessary to correct for these; it would be a higher-level government responsibility to estimate the spillovers. Further complications would arise where there were specific government services whose benefit area did not coincide with any existing jurisdiction.

The crucial assumptions in Breton's rarified case are equal tastes for local goods within each jurisdiction, although unequal among jurisdictions, and taxes levied on the basis of objective benefits. To the extent that these assumptions are unrealistic, or that tastes and objective benefits are incapable of measurement in the absence of preference revelation, the model is irrelevant. Perhaps the most important concept that Breton has introduced is that of nonprivate goods. This may not be the most felicitous terminology, but at least it does stress that a great many local goods and services are not "pure." Their provision tapers from the point of production; accessibility is spatially determined; they are consumed (and provide benefits) in unequal quantities.

Collective Decisions. The second approach to allocational efficiency looks not to individual Pareto optimality but to the conditions of collective rationality for the local government unit as a whole. In this approach it is conventional to assume that (1) tastes are uniform among all individuals in the local jurisdiction, or, less strenuously, that (2) tastes are sufficiently uniform that differences may be safely neglected. In any event, the local jurisdiction is examined as a collectivity in its relations with the outside world, in benefit-cost terms. The question is whether the political domain of benefits coincides with the political domain of costs. If the political-decision unit coincides with the area of benefits and costs, an optimal production level for the collective can be attained. If it does not coincide, programs for compensation among jurisdictions must be worked out.

The issue, then, is spatial spillovers. If the benefits of local government goods spill out into other jurisdictions, local goods will be under-produced within the jurisdiction.[11] If the costs of local government goods can be made to spill out into other jurisdictions, by exporting tax burdens, local government goods will be overproduced.[12] Any specific local government may be favored as the recipient of spill-ins of benefits from other local governments, or disadvantaged from spill-ins of other local government costs.

Since externalities of this type may be assumed to be substantial, there is no

11. One of the first to point this out, and to conclude that local expenditures for education were particularly liable to this suboptimization was Burton A. Weisbrod, *External Benefits of Public Education* (Princeton: Industrial Relations Section, Princeton University, 1964).

12. For an exploration of the complexities, see Alan Williams, "The Optimal Provision of Public Goods in a System of Local Government," *Journal of Political Economy,* February 1966, pp. 18 – 33.

reason to expect any local government to achieve a collective production optimum, except by accident, for any single service, to say nothing of a bundle of goods and services.[13] Central intervention would be required, such as a National Social Diseconomies Board, to estimate the externalities and arrange a pattern of compensating taxes and transfers. Such boards, of course, do not exist.[14] Functional grants-in-aid are a rough way of accounting for such diseconomies.

The operational difficulties in attaining efficient allocation in a federal system by way of collective rationality are formidable. Nevertheless, this approach is more appropriate than individualistic solutions. A federal system accepts the existence of subordinate governmental units of greater or lesser autonomy. The economic position of individuals must therefore be examined in relation to "citizenship" in such units, as well as to "citizenship" in the national economy. To abstract individuals from their relationship to the subordinate units would nullify the basic characteristic of the federal system, since it would eliminate the political autonomy possessed by such units. The appropriate conceptual framework is the examination of the conditions for and the procedures necessary to assure a maximum of collective rationality.

MINIMUM SERVICE LEVELS

A final fiscal objective of a federal system may be noted briefly — the provision of minimum service levels. This objective combines distributional and allocational concerns. Here the central fisc determines that the national interest requires specified public services to be provided at a level consonant with some roughly defined national standard. National standards may reflect considerations of spillovers, as in education, where population mobility may be such as to require a national minimum level of skills. Or minimum levels of service may reflect a national judgment that specified social services, such as maternal and child care, should be available to all citizens. In effect, a category of merit wants is established and implemented by intergovernmental devices.

At the state-local level one device for establishing a minimum service level is the mandate. School districts, for example, may be required to spend a minimum amount per pupil, and state aid will partially assist in meeting this minimum.

13. The best empirical study is Werner Z. Hirsch, Elbert W. Siegelhorst, and Morton J. Marcus, *Spillover of Public Education Costs and Benefits* (Los Angeles: Institute of Government and Public Affairs, University of California, 1964).

14. It has been demonstrated that a decision rule in terms of maximizing average net benefits per household will permit the delineation of service boundaries by central authority in certain simplified cases. See Eugene Smolensky, Richard Burton, and Nicholas Tideman, "An Operational Approach to an Efficient Federal System," (Chicago: Center for Urban Studies, University of Chicago, 1968) (mimeo).

Fiscal Arrangements

The political issues examined in the first section of this chapter — the distribution of governmental authority between the center and the states, the reconciliation of regional sovereignty and national sovereignty, and the concessions to minority interests that are essential in a federal system — are bound up with fiscal issues. The devices for accommodating the complex of national interests and the complex of provincial or state interests are largely fiscal measures. The distribution of fiscal authority must, in a general way, be consonant with the distribution of governmental authority. At the same time, in the arena of public-policy conflict, the fiscal issues take on a significance of their own.

In the Federalist papers Hamilton wrote:

> Money is, with propriety, considered the vital principle of the body politic; as that which has sustained its life and motion, and enables it to perform its most essential functions. A complete power, therefore, to procure a regular and adequate supply of it, as far as the resources of the community will permit, may be regarded as an indispensable ingredient in every constitution . . . . the federal government must of necessity be vested with an unqualified power of taxation in the ordinary modes . . . . the individual States should possess an independent and uncontrollable authority to raise their own revenues for the supply of their own wants. (Hamilton, pp. 182 – 3, 190, 193)

This is an appealingly simple prescription, but Hamilton must have known that fiscal arrangements are not this precise. Sources of revenue are never "independent" in any federal system, since they are dependent on the income and wealth of an identical body of taxpayers. The whole is, indeed, the sum of its parts. A federal system is not static; as revenue sources change over time in their responsiveness, and as new expenditure requirements emerge, there must be new agreements between the center and the states, and agreement costs in this area are relatively high. The necessarily continuous reassessment of national-state-local fiscal relations required in a federal system poses the most controversial of political problems.

FINANCIAL PRINCIPLES

If there were a "pure" system of dual sovereignty then there could be "pure" financial principles. These would include financial independence defined to exclude any exchange of revenues between the center and the states. The center would not provide subventions for the states; the states would not support the center. A second principle would be financial responsibility. Expenditures, by the center and by the states, would be financed from taxes collected from revenue sources available to the center or to the states. A third principle would be autonomy. There would be no direct or indirect pressure on either level to alter revenue or expenditure (Dehem and Wolfe, 1955, pp. 64 – 72). However, as was pointed out above, the objectives of the economics of federalism are not harmonious with those of the politics of federalism. Neither are they harmonious with "pure" finance. Pursuit of financial independence and responsibility, for example, will produce tax rate differentials among states which may lead to misallocation of labor or capital. Income differentials may persist among the states and indeed may be accentuated if financial independence and responsibility are pursued. If there are rational distributional objectives these will be thwarted.

Because of conflicting objectives the "pure" principles are always modified by central authority. Autonomy is violated by conditional grants from the national government that encourage (coerce) the states to redirect their resource allocation patterns. The national government expresses some concern about regional income differentials and modifies grant patterns in the interests of regional income redistribution. The national government formulates stabilization policy quite independently of the states' interests in budgetary policy, and the states are forced to adapt their fiscal policies to those of the national government.

There is no consistent integration of macro-policy objectives in any federal system or systematic review of trade-offs among such objectives. There is little attempt to pursue consistent programs to equalize fiscal capacity or service levels and no attempt to affect the inherent allocational inefficiency of a federal system. Instead, there are a number of traditional techniques for fiscal accommodation (Blough, 1962, pp. 384 – 405).

FISCAL ACCOMMODATION

The first of these is simply centralization — the transfer of program and administrative responsibility from the states to the national government, to conform with the observable and historic increase in the fiscal power of the center as against the states. In practice, however, the outright transfer of programs or functional responsibility has not been historically significant. In this country, for example, welfare financing and administration has tended to move from the local governments to the state, and the federal government has assumed increased financial responsibility. But the states do not surrender their responsibilities. Rather, the national government adds its fiscal and perhaps its administrative support to programs that the states traditionally have performed. At the same time there is centralization of programs and administrative as well as financial responsibility, in that the national government undertakes more and different programs. The states do not abandon the programs they have administered; these are expanded absolutely, and the relative position of the state-local system tends to decline.

A second traditional technique for fiscal accommodation in a federal system is the separation of revenue sources. The national government, either under the constitution or by agreement with the states, restricts its revenue structure to specified sources; other specified sources remain with the states, and over-lapping taxation of the same general revenue source will be eliminated. The Dominion government in Canada, from 1942 to 1947, and with some varia-tions thereafter until 1962, made block grants to the provinces, which in turn relinquished income and estate taxes. In this country the separation of revenue sources has been traditionally practiced for only one levy — the property tax, which has been, with the exception of a brief period during the Civil War, the sole province of the state and local governments. There has been a plethora of proposals for extending the separation of revenue sources, but this appears to be an area in which coordinated action is impossible to achieve.

A third technique for revenue coordination is the tax supplement, under which the national government collects a levy at a specified rate and the states are encouraged to impose an additional levy on the same tax base, which levy will also be collected by the national government, and the supplement rebated to the state or local jurisdiction. This device is used for the personal income tax in Sweden, where municipalities may add a specific levy to the national tax (Groves, 1952, pp. 234 – 38). It is also used for local government supplements to the statewide sales tax in a number of states in this country.[15]

State supplements to national levies or local supplements to state or county levies have the advantage of administrative simplicity. The constituent units in the system will exercise their fiscal sovereignty within a framework of regional benefit taxation. Higher preferences for public goods within a region can be matched by increased willingness to pay. Presumably the supplemental local rates chosen are those which roughly equate tax receipts to aggregate benefits from additional governmental expenditures. The sovereignty accorded to the underlying jurisdiction by tax supplements is a restricted one. The higher jurisdiction retains authority to prescribe the tax base and exemptions, and the supplementing jurisdiction may choose only the rate at which the supplement is to be added, usually limited by a ceiling.

Revenue sharing is generically akin to tax supplements. Under this proce-dure the central government administers the levy and simply rebates a portion to the constituent jurisdiction, usually on the basis of collections. The local government has no option with respect to the rate or base of the tax; it is collected uniformly throughout the jurisdiction of the central government. Revenue sharing is widely practiced by states in this country for such levies as the sales tax, gasoline tax, and miscellaneous imposts such as liquor license fees. It is not now employed by the federal government, but recent proposals

15. This arrangement is sometimes dubbed the "piggy-back." A further variant is the adop-tion, by a few states in this country, of definitions of taxable income and exemptions that are identical with those of the federal government. The state income tax is then collected at a specified fraction of the taxpayer's federal income tax liability. West Virginia and Alaska use this system.

in this area are of sufficient importance to warrant special examination (see below).

A fourth technique available for smoothing relations between the center and the regions is described under the general head of "cooperation." This technique may extend to the exchange of information among departments of revenue or to joint audits of taxpayer returns. The objectives are the minimization of administrative costs and a reduction in costs of taxpayer compliance and litigation.

A fifth device, deductibility, is most widely applied in this country under the federal personal and corporate income tax. This permits the taxpayer to deduct, as an expense in computing his federal income tax liability, payments made to state and local governments such as personal income tax, sales taxes, and property taxes. Deductibility means that the superior government partially immunizes the state-local taxpayer from the burden of state-local levies. Thus, deductibility is a technique by which the national government strengthens state-local government taxable capabity (Break, 1967, pp. 28 – 61). The strengthening of local taxable capacity, however, is not uniformly spread among the citizenry. Those in upper-income brackets benefit more than those in lower brackets.[16] It is not at all clear that the benefits of deductibility enter the tax consciousness of state-local political decision-makers or of any taxpayers except those in the highest brackets. In studies and analysis of regional disparities in tax effort, state-local tax burdens are not typically measured net of deductibility. The revenue loss to the national government is probably greater than the realized addition to state-local fiscal potential.[17]

The techniques of fiscal accommodation that have been examined thus far — centralization, separation of sources, supplements and deductibility — are concerned with vertical adjustments in a federal system. Generally, these are arrangements for augmenting the tax bases or strengthening the administration of state and local levies. Tax credits are a sixth technique which may serve comparable purposes, but which may also be used for horizontal accommodation, to assure a uniform pattern of taxation among the provinces or states.

Tax credits permit the taxpayer, under conditions specified by the superior government, to deduct, from his liabilities to the superior government, the tax payments that he has made to a state or provincial government. In this country tax crediting is used for the federal death duty, to achieve a modest measure

16. For an empirical study for the U. S., see Benjamin Bridges, Jr., "Deductibility of State and Local Nonbusiness Taxes Under the Federal Individual Income Tax," *National Tax Journal,* March 1966, pp. 1 – 17.

17. An additional technique for strengthening state-local fiscal capacity in this country is the exclusion of interest on state and local government bond issues from income reported for federal tax purposes. Again, the revenue loss to the federal government probably exceeds the gains (through lower interest rates) that accrue to state-local units.

of uniformity in state death duties and to assure that the states do not destroy this source of state revenue by engaging in competition through tax concessions to the wealthy aged. Crediting is also used to assure uniformity in state tax levies for unemployment compensation.

Tax credits permit a considerable degree of "coercion" and "dictation" from the superior government. The national government may and will prescribe the conditions under which credits are to be extended, and states must conform with the prescriptions if their residents are to enjoy the tax advantage that is extended. Crediting could thus be used to enforce a high degree of uniformity among the states in their tax structures and choice of rates, bases, and exemptions. Concomitantly, the price of the uniformity is the loss of state autonomy in the selection of the objects and the distribution of tax burdens. Crediting could be used to eliminate overlapping and conflicting state tax laws and to achieve horizontal coordination among the units in a federal system. It could also be used to require the states to increase their tax burdens in specified ways. The national government could adopt a nationwide sales tax, and provide that liabilities paid under any conforming state sales tax statute could be used to satisfy the federal liability. States that conformed could retain the revenues in their own coffers; states that did not conform would find that their residents paid the national levy to the national government. Like deductibility, crediting is not distributionally neutral. Wealthy taxpayers will gain a relative fiscal advantage as compared with taxpayers who are less wealthy. Neither does it contribute to allocational efficiency, since the tax will appear to be costless to the subordinate unit (Shoup, 1969, pp. 616 – 17).

The foregoing devices for fiscal accommodation in a federal system are designed, or may be designed, to achieve horizontal and vertical coordination of revenue without reference to expenditure coordination. Centralization is the exception; this will affect both revenue and expenditure by the transfer of responsibility. The major device for fiscal accommodation on the expenditure side is the grant-in-aid; although directed at expenditure coordination, the grand-in-aid may also have a great many effects, intended and unintended, on the revenue structures of provinces or local governments.

The Grant-in-Aid

In the first section of this chapter it was noted that a prominent rationale for the successful continued implementation of a federal system is the concept of shared power. As new program responsibilities emerge, the national government may marshall resources for their support, but the administrative responsibilities for the new programs are shared with underlying governments as a means of contributing to their continued vitality and for adapting details of application to local circumstances. The grant-in-aid is the major device for such patterns of shared responsibility; the grant-in-aid thus becomes the major instrumentality for the continued viability of a federal system.

In the second section of this chapter it was noted that the application of a spatial conception of the benefit theory of taxation requires that the geographical area of benefit be circumscribed and that the residents of this area support those public expenditures that benefit the area. Therefore, a grant-in-aid from the national to the regional government will contribute to an efficient allocation of resources only if the grant is to finance national benefits derived from the program which extend to the entire nation and only if there are no important side effects on other programs and other revenues. In principle such grants-in-aid should be extended to the point where the last dollar of expenditure brings an equivalent national marginal social benefit. It is necessary to finance the state-benefited portion of the program from state resources and the national-benefited portion of the program from national resources.

But in the world of fiscal federalism it is not at all clear that grant programs are formulated, adopted, or implemented with such efficiency objectives in view. Neither is it clear that they are introduced to maintain the continued viability of state or provincial governments. Grant-in-aid programs are adopted for a number of reasons, most of which can be grouped under two general headings — program concerns and fiscal concerns, with a substantial overlap between the two.

PROGRAM AND FISCAL OBJECTIVES

The generalized influences that give rise to increases in public expenditures were examined in Chapter 1. An increase in income, given some positive elasticity in the demand for public goods, is reflected in larger outlays for health, education, space exploration, and recreation. The externalities associated with urbanization increase, with additional requirements for public sector activity, particularly in metropolitan areas. The growth in general affluence leaves some families, regions, and ethnic groups lagging behind, and there are demands for redistributional public expenditures. As these issues emerge, political leaders respond or formulate programs that will induce a favorable response. Interest group support is organized for increases in public sector activities. Where states or local governments are already administering the program or a related program, and with politically determined constraints on state-local revenues, expansion appears possible only by way of a grant-in-aid from the federal government. Where the program is relatively new or untried it may be centralized at the outset. In some cases the national government initiates a new program by means of a grant-in-aid. Historical experience in this country does not suggest that there are uniform precedents for choices between federal administration of a program and federal support of a program by way of a grant-in-aid.

But the emergence of new program concerns or enhanced citizen interest in existing programs would not give rise to grants-in-aid were it not for the fiscal disparities that exist between the federal government and state and local governments. As noted, the revenue sources utilized by the national government in this country are more elastic than those utilized by state and local governments — a condition that generally obtains in all federal systems. The federal government thus acquires, under full employment and reasonably steady growth, control over an increasing share of the gross national product. States and local governments can typically obtain increased shares only by increases in tax rates. The property tax base, so important to local governments, lags behind the growth in income as capital-output ratios decline for the economy as a whole. Very simply, then, if the states are not to suffer a serious deterioration in their responsiveness to demands for public programs, with resulting political malaise, tax rates must be increased or their fiscal capacity must be supplemented from the federal government. Grants-in-aid thus offer a means of sharing central revenue sources. These conditions obtain in other federal systems — India, Canada, Australia — as well as in the United States.[18]

The reasons for the discrepancies between state-local fiscal capacity and federal government fiscal capacity are wholly institutional, that is, political and structural and not "purely" economic. At some level of abstraction the fiscal capacity of any national government must be the aggregate of the fiscal capacity of its constituent units, provided only that there are effective means of taxing economic activity that crosses state lines. But this is not the reality of fiscal federalism in the United States. State and local legislatures have not availed themselves of the same kinds of tax bases, at the same rates, as has the federal government.

It is commonly asserted that the reasons for this situation lie in such matters as the veto power that is often exercised at the state level by well-established interest groups opposed to an increase in public budgets. This veto power, it is asserted, can be more effective at the state and local levels than at the national level, where a different and more "liberal" confluence of political forces is at work. Certainly, such veto groups have been successful, in many states, in limiting by constitutional restriction the taxing and borrowing powers of states and local governments, and then compounding the restrictions by making amendment to the constitution a most tortuous affair. Fear of loss of

18. In the United States in the years 1956 – 66 state-local taxes increased as a proportion of GNP from 7.5 to 9.4 percent while federal taxes in relation to GNP declined slightly, as a result of the federal revenue reduction of 1964, from 15.9 to 14.6 percent. Nevertheless, federal expenditures for nonwar purposes from own resources increased by 162 percent in these years, while state-local expenditures from own resources increased only 107 percent (ACIR [1967], pp. 47 – 52).

economic activity also limits states and local governments in their willingness to be first to impose additional taxes; business firms threaten an exodus from the state in the face of higher tax rates. In some cases states may find their fiscal capacity limited by administrative ineptitude — which in turn reflects an unwillingness to secure administrative ability for purposes of revenue collection. It is also evident that states and local governments are limited in their general fiscal capacity by lack of access to a central bank. Because of this concern for borrowing, states and local governments conduct their affairs more nearly like business firms, with attention to credit ratings and the esteem in which they are held by investment bankers. And finally, it is typically argued that the federal government has "pre-empted" the best sources of revenue — the individual and corporation income tax — leaving inferior sources of revenue to states and local governments.

In this pattern of conventional rationalization of the disparities between national and state-local fiscal capacity it would appear that the most important causal factor is "unwillingness." States and local governments are the captives of a set of political and economic forces that have reduced their fiscal capacity. Larger public budgets, financed from state-local taxable resources, might well provide additional social overheads and increased economic activity over time. But in state-local fiscal affairs attention is focused more frequently on short-run tax burdens.

In a federal system without clearly designated areas of expenditure responsibility, program concerns and fiscal disparities are the generalized forces that account for the establishment and expansion of grants-in-aid. In varying degrees these forces will also influence policies for other devices for fiscal accommodation, and in some cases will dictate that new national programs be undertaken. Specific grants-in-aid reflect the continued interplay among program and fiscal objectives as does the establishment or extension of a national program. Program objectives will be defined by the interaction of interest groups, administrators, legislators, and chief executives. In this mutual adjustment the professional administrator has a very large role not only in the formulation of the program but in the policies for implementation. It is he who defines the standards for the grant program and interprets the standards as he administers the aid. The federal administrator is in a position to influence the quality of administration of the recipient government; the grant-in-aid provides a high degree of leverage. In consequence, a pattern of bureaucratic federalism has developed, with the application of standards that differ from state to state or city to city. And since there are major differences in federal-state-local relationships among program areas, there is a resulting system of federalism by function as well as federalism by bureaucracy.[19]

---

19. For significant case studies in a functional area, see Robert H. Connery, et al., *The Politics*

Fiscal objectives are somewhat independent of program objectives. A grant-in-aid may be partially equalizing among recipient states; that is, a larger proportion of total program expenditures may be grant-aided in poor states than in rich states. The matching requirements will thus be inverse to some measure of "richness," usually per capita income (Davie and White, 1967, pp. 193 – 203). The grant may be designed for demonstration purposes; that is, to exhibit the worth of a new program in the hope that support may be found for its continuation from state and local resources. Such grants tend to become more or less permanent as beneficiary groups and state-local administrators become accustomed to federal assistance and are able to maintain sufficient political support to assure continuation.

A grant-in-aid program may have the fiscal objective of stimulus. The matching requirements may be modest, and this and other conditions of the grant may encourage the recipient government to "overspend"; that is, to allocate from its own resources a larger expenditure to the aided program than it would in the absence of the grant program.

A grant-in-aid program may also be of the nature of "general support," where its principal purpose is to add to the taxable resources of the recipient units, leaving such units with broad discretion in the expenditure of the grant. State aid to education is often, in effect, a general support program. There may be matching requirements and equalization features, but general support is the dominant characteristic (Benson, 1964, pp. 205 – 35).

FISCAL RESPONSES

Even as there may be differing fiscal objectives in a pattern of grants-in-aid, so may there be differing response patterns from recipient governments, and these responses may not always be anticipated. Response patterns may be classified as neutral, substitutive, or stimulative. In a neutral response pattern the additional program expenditure is equivalent to the amount of the grant. In a stimulative program the recipient government "overspends" — that is, secures additional resources from its own taxpayers to increase program outlays by more than the grant. In a substitutive response the recipient government reduces expenditure from its own resources with a corresponding reduction in taxes or increase in expenditure for other nongrant purposes.

Alan Williams has shown how the graphic technique to analyze consumer response to varying price offers can be applied to the responses of the recipient government (Williams, 1963, pp. 171 – 80). Figure 8.1 illustrates the difference

---

of Mental Health (New York: Columbia University Press, 1968), esp. pp. 87 – 466.

in response between a lump-sum grant and a categorical grant. The line AB shows the possibilities for the division of local expenditure. Assuming that it is possible to conceptualize a community indifference curve, the resulting equilibrium position would be at point I. If the grant is for a specific service, the new possibility line is shown as AC, and the community can now move to a new equilibrium at point II, which is superior to point I. It may be noted that the categorical grant provides more of both the grant-aided service and the nongrant-aided service, since there are both income and substitution effects. The income effect occurs as the reduced price of the aided program lowers the average price level. The substitution effect occurs as a larger portion of the aided program is purchased. A lump-sum grant equal to the categorical grant received at point II would permit the recipient government to move to an even better position. In these circumstances the possibility line is shown as DE and the new equilibrium point at III, superior to either I or II.

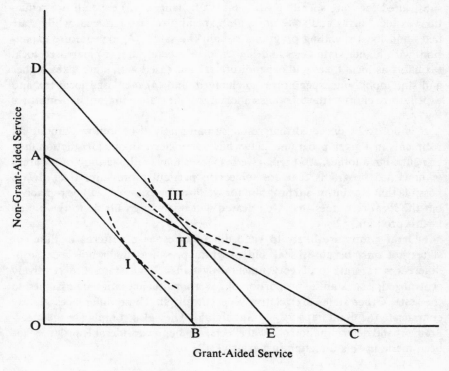

Figure 8.1. Responses to Grant Patterns

Other response patterns, including the stimulation of additional expenditure from local tax resources and the establishment of minimum service levels can also be analyzed graphically (Williams, 1963, pp. 176 – 80). It is also possible to ascertain, again given a community indifference curve, the responses that would occur from variations in matching provisions and open-end versus closed-end grants (Mushkin, Cotton, and Lupo, 1968, pp. 32 – 39). Unfortunately, there is no way to decide whether the response patterns that are optimal from the standpoint of the local government are also optimal from the standpoint of the central government.

Break points out that when one looks at both the grantor and grantee, and when expenditure effects are combined with tax changes and with effects on nongrant expenditures, a state-local aid program may produce six basic response patterns (Break, 1967, p. 100). These may be described as: (1) tax substitution, where state taxes have been substituted for local taxes with no change in spending; (2) expenditure substitution, where local spending is substituted for state spending, with taxes unchanged; (3) expenditure reduction, as local taxes and state nongrant expenditures are reduced, while state taxes and local spending programs remain the same; (4) expenditure expansion, with higher state taxes and higher local expenditure; (5) increased local tax effort as local taxes and expenditure are increased with state taxes higher and state nongrant expenditures unchanged; and (6) increased local tax and expenditure effort with state taxes unchanged but state nongrant expenditures lower.

It is not to be expected that response patterns will be uniform among all recipients in a given program. That which is replacive in one jurisdiction may be neutral in another. And replacive responses may spill over into other areas of nonaided programs that are subject to particular pressure. It is always possible that a grant-in-aid program for welfare, for example, will be replacive, but the local resources that are released will be made available to the public health program.

Federal grants are likely to yield different response patterns in different states not only because fiscal and program pressures differ but because of differences in state-local governmental systems. Some states are relatively centralized; a substantial proportion of governmental activities are assigned to the state. Other states are relatively decentralized. These differences greatly complicate the fiscal impacts of grants-in-aid. They also complicate the measurement and determination of fiscal effects, although considerable progress has been made in this direction in recent years.[20]

20. See, for example, Seymour Sacks and Robert Harris, "The Determinants of State and Local Government Expenditures and Intergovernmental Flows of Funds," *National Tax Journal,* March 1964, pp. 75 – 85. Alan K. Campbell and Seymour Sacks, *Metropolitan America* (New York: The Free Press, 1967), Chapters 3 – 5. See also discussion in Chapter 9.

The foregoing confluence of program and fiscal considerations, and their complex interactions, suggest that it is difficult to alter grant-in-aid patterns once they are introduced — a suggestion that is most evidently supported by U.S. experience. There has been some success, in state aid programs for education, in consolidating, from time to time, specific (categorical) grant programs into general grants to extend a larger measure of discretion in resource allocation to the school districts. But this has not been the case with federal grants to states or cities. Here the grant program tends to find its political support in a defined clientele and administrative group which will oppose a transfer of decision authority over grant funds to a broader or higher-level administrative authority. At the same time, fiscal responses are built into state or local government budgets, and changes in grant programs would bring new "distortions" in resource allocation.

These considerations suggest that a taxonomy of grant programs is not straightforward; classification is complicated by the multiple and frequently conflicting purposes of specific intergovernmental fiscal arrangements. However, the following outline may be useful:

A. Use of proceeds
  1) general
  2) categorical
B. Level of grantor and recipient government
  1) federal to state
  2) federal to state to local
  3) federal to local[21]
  4) state to local
C. Distributional intent
  1) equalizing
  2) nonequalizing
D. Conditions attached
  1) matching or nonmatching
  2) open-end — closed-end
  3) other statutory or administrative requirements

In the context of practice in this country it may be noted that almost all federal grants are categorical in nature.[22] Where specific categorical grants are lumped together in a program area, the term "functional grants" is sometimes used (ACIR, 1967, p. 7). But, all federal grants are directed toward specific

21. In recent years this pattern has been complicated by grants to local, nongovernmental community organizations under the federal poverty program.

22. The magnitudes involved are set forth in Break (1967), pp. 4 – 6, 97 – 99, 127.

programs; there are no general-purpose or block grants. At the state level education grants may properly be classified as general in nature; one state — New York — uses a general purpose per capita grant payable to counties and municipalities. Revenue sharing, which is similar to block grants is, however, widely practiced in state-local relationships.

The role of the states in the administration of grant programs has been a most controversial aspect of intergovernmental policy in the United States. The major federal grants, for highways and welfare, are now paid to states. The highway programs are administered at the state level in cooperation with the U.S. Department of Transportation. Welfare funds, however, are frequently re-granted to local units of government.

The alternative pattern is subvention directly from the national government to local units, avoiding the intermediation of state administration and state policy. In recent years both the numbers of such programs and the amounts granted under them have been slowly increasing as a proportion of total grants. The most important of these are the aid programs for airports, urban renewal, public housing, and the Model Cities and poverty programs (Martin, 1965, pp. 115 – 35). It is reasonable to anticipate that federal-urban grant programs will increase in importance with the continued fiscal and program difficulties of the cities. It is also reasonable to expect that from time to time the governors of the states will assert their interests in the control of federal funds that enter their states and will attempt to defeat the "circumvention" that is developing.

Grants may also be classified according to their spatial equalizing or non-equalizing nature, as noted in the second section of this chapter. Grants that are paid on a per capita basis are mildly equalizing with respect to fiscal capacity since people are more uniformly distributed than income. In general, there are relatively few federal grants with important equalization effects. Some categorical programs are aimed at providing transfers to disadvantaged groups, and it may be anticipated that this type of equalization will increase.

In addition to grants whose amounts vary inversely to fiscal capacity, equalization can be implemented by variations in matching requirements. Poor states may be required to match at a lower ratio than richer states. Again, federal practice employs this device sparingly. Matching, however, can serve objectives other than equalization. Where one of the objectives of the grant program is stimulation, matching may provide the appropriate "coercion" of the recipient unit to furnish additional program resources from its own tax base.

Ancillary conditions may also be attached to the grant to again "coerce" the recipient governmental units to adopt practices that are judged by the grantor government to be desirable. These may extend to regularizing civil service practices in the recipient government, the establishment of procedures for accounting and auditing, or the elimination of conditions, such as ethnic discrimination, that violate national laws or directives.

Finally, grants may be distinguished as open-end or closed-end. The recipient government may be encouraged to apply for a grant whose limit has not been determined in advance, or may be determined in accordance with a general standard of need, specified only within broad limits by the legislature. A closed-end grant limits by legislation or administrative regulation the amount to which the recipient government is entitled.

The most common popular criticisms directed against matching or categorical grants-in-aid are that they distort the resource allocation patterns of the recipient government and that they impose an excessive degree of administrative control on the recipient government. Contemporary journalism on this topic is burdened with polemic and invective, which is perhaps understandable in view of the uncertain nature of the basic concepts of federalism.

Some of the elements in the controversy over resource distortion can at least be untangled. For example, suppose that the federal government establishes a grant program for public health clinics to provide that neighborhood centers serving a population of no less than 50,000 would be supported by capital funds and operating funds, provided that 25 percent of such funds were made available from local tax resources. This could be justified on distributional grounds as a means of increasing the volume of medical services at the neighborhood level. Viewed in allocational terms, such a program means, in effect, that a national policy has been declared with respect to local public health clinics, and implies that the national benefits from such clinics are judged to be equal to 75 percent of their costs. Local communities are thus induced or coerced to reallocate public resources under their control in the direction of public health clinics. The local community is, in effect, given a new cost function that requires a recalculation of its optimum local expenditure pattern. Public health clinics may have previously appeared to be inferior, in terms of benefits and costs, as compared with such other programs as recreation or streets and roads. Now the local costs are reduced by three-fourths. A national judgment has been substituted for a local judgment. National benefits have been redefined; there is no resource distortion from a national viewpoint. It has simply been decided that public health clinics provide national benefits. This may imply that the previous local allocational pattern was nonoptimal from a national viewpoint, although optimal from a local viewpoint. From the vantage point of local government, resource distortion will occur only if the required local matching funds reduce the resources available for other programs. The administrators of benefited groups whose programs for recreation or for streets and roads may now be reduced may well feel that distortion has occurred.

Since optimum resource allocation will necessarily differ as between the national government and local governments, that which is optimum from one vantage point will necessarily be distortion from the other.

The perennial controversy over "federal controls" by way of grants-in-aid is a reflection of the conflict discussed above between program considerations and fiscal considerations. The Congress and federal administrators, as noted, are typically interested in program support, not in generalized fiscal support of subordinate governments. Therefore, program objectives will be defined in the legislation and in its administrative regulations. The attainment of these program objectives requires some "controls," which may indeed be cumbersome and expensive to comply with. To the extent that fiscal considerations or "general support" is the more prominent objective of the aid, to that extent can "controls" be reduced. But even in general-support grants there must be control by way of audit. All constitutions require that monies shall be expended for the purposes for which they were appropriated, and an audit of the accounts of the recipient government is necessary to assure that this is, in fact, the case. To the extent that broader program grants can be substituted for categorical grants, or that categorical grants can over time be consolidated, to that extent controls can be minimized. In every federal system the grantor government is, for these purposes, the "superior" government and will necessarily impose conditions on the grantee.[23]

REVENUE SHARING

The legal, political, and fiscal complexities of intergovernmental fiscal relations in the United States are well illustrated by the controversy that has recently been directed to proposals for revenue sharing. The proposals, and the discussion associated therewith, illustrate the basic institutional difficulties that are associated with a federal system — the veto power that the constituent units possess, and their consequent ability to redefine national policy in terms of state and local policy; the continued conflict between program objectives and fiscal objectives; and the difficulty of predicting response patterns in any grant-in-aid system.

Proposals for revenue sharing emerged prominently in this country after 1964, at a time when neo-Keynesian economics was at the peak of political and popular acceptance. The Revenue Act of 1964 was successful in bringing an

23. In the complexities of federal grants to urban areas in this country, the grantor government also faces problems of efficient allocation, usually described as the need for "coordination" of grant programs. The Demonstration Cities and Metropolitan Development Act of 1966 and the Intergovernmental Cooperation Act of 1968 require, in effect, that regional planning agencies be established with authority to review grant programs for the region, and that the federal government coordinate its grant programs with the regional plans. This expands the role of the grantor from that of program aid to a positive role in the encouragement and support of regional planning, and "intervention" in the structure of local government. It has been proposed that the national government be given an even stronger role at the community level by the appointment of federal coordinators with responsibility across program lines. (See James L. Sundquist and David W. Davis, *Making Federalism Work* [Washington: The Brookings Institution, 1969]).

increase in economic activity by way of tax reduction. With a more rapid growth rate in the U. S. economy, it could be forecast, with reasonable accuracy, that the federal budget would continue to generate a full employment surplus in future years. This surplus would be available for additional federal expenditure, for additional tax reduction, or for grants to the states.

The initial proposal for block grants to the states as shares of federal revenue is described as the Heller-Pechman plan.[24] The plan was remarkably uncomplicated (Heller, 1966, pp. 117 – 72; 1968, pp. 3 – 38). The federal government would collect 2 percent of the federal individual income tax base on behalf of the states, that is, two percentage points in each bracket of net taxable income. The use of the tax base rather than tax collections for revenue sharing would stabilize the states' shares, while leaving the federal government free to vary tax rates in accordance with requirements for economic stabilization.

The amounts so collected would be placed in a trust fund and paid to the states on a per capita basis, thus accomplishing a modest redistribution from rich to poor states. If additional redistribution were desirable, a portion of the revenue could be paid to states with low per capita income. The trust fund device would insulate the payments from the annual uncertainties of congressional appropriation. The plan might start at a lower level of sharing — perhaps one half of 1 percent — and build up to the 2 percent level over a period of years. In full operation the plan would afford the states access to an elastic source of revenue, since it may be anticipated that taxable income will continue to increase as a fraction of the national income. This will occur with increased incomes and mild inflation as long as personal income tax exemptions and rates are held constant.

The plan was viewed by its authors as a means of strengthening fiscal federalism by restoring state revenue sources. The plan would permit the states, many of whom have lagged behind in their tax effort, to increase state-local expenditures and thus reduce the administrative responsibility of the federal government. State and local governments would be efficient partners in federalism. "There are also more positive reasons why the states and their subdivisions should have a stronger role. Creative federalism requires diversity and dissent and innovation. Yet these cannot simply come down from on high. They have to well up from below. The danger if they do not is that the central government will grow stronger in authority and weaker in ideas"

24. In the fall of 1964 President Johnson appointed a task force on intergovernmental fiscal relations, whose chairman was Joseph A. Pechman. Walter W. Heller, then chairman of the Council of Economic Advisers, worked with this group, and the resulting proposal for revenue sharing came to be known as the Heller-Pechman plan. In addition, numerous legislative versions of revenue sharing were introduced in the Congress in 1965 and 1966 (ACIR [1967], pp. 67 – 70, 312 – 22). Extensive hearings on these proposals were held by the Subcommittee on Fiscal Policy of the Joint Economic Committee in the summer and fall of 1967.

(Heller, 1966, p. 124). Revenue sharing was not viewed as the sole means of disposing of the fiscal dividend. Over a period of years tax reduction and increases in direct federal expenditure, as well as categorical grants-in-aid, could be accommodated.

The major criticisms of the Heller-Pechman plan and other proposals for revenue sharing have centered on whether the states are appropriate administrative units for the control of block grants and the closely related question of whether it is possible to devise a "pass-through" that would assure that the block grants would in fact be channeled to metropolitan areas where fiscal pressures are generally most severe.[25]

Unfortunately, the examination of issues of this type must necessarily turn on value judgments as to whether states, and their governors and legislatures, can be "trusted" to behave in accordance with whatever national "priorities" are implied in the desire to provide states and localities with substantial block grants. It is certain that response patterns would be very mixed. Some states would undoubtedly reduce the rate at which state tax burdens are increasing, thus providing, in effect, for tax reduction from the shared revenue. Other states would undoubtedly channel the revenues toward the most pressing fiscal problems at the state level — such as higher education or state subvention of elementary and secondary education. Other states would surely respond to the demands of metropolitan areas and "pass-through" the funds to hard-pressed cities. Only one thing is certain. Revenue sharing with the states would increase the political power of governors and state legislatures at a time when the urban fiscal crisis is severe.

To meet the criticisms of those who were concerned about the pass-through to the cities Heller and Pechman have suggested that it would be possible to deal with this in a number of ways.[26] Governors could be required to prepare plans for the use of funds in accordance with general guidelines laid down by Congress. Consultation with local officials and interest groups could be required. The development of such state plans would bring a reexamination of state-local fiscal relations in all states.

A second possibility is to provide a minimum pass-through to local governments in all states — perhaps 40 to 50 percent of all shared revenue. A third possibility would provide for a minimum pass-through to all local governments plus a per capita allocation to cities above a specified size.

None of these possibilities is wholly satisfactory. There is no reason why a requirement to develop a state-local expenditure plan would instill in gover-

25. See papers by Richard Ruggles, Lyle C. Fitch, Carl Shoup, and Harvey E. Brazer in Harvey S. Perloff and Richard P. Nathan, eds., *Revenue Sharing and the City* (Baltimore: Johns Hopkins Press, 1968), pp. 39–106.

26. Joint Economic Committee, Subcommittee on Fiscal Policy, *Revenue Sharing and its Alternatives: What Future for Fiscal Federalism?* (Washington, 1967), pp. 115–16.

nors a sense of responsibility for the fiscal problems of urban areas. The minimum pass-through to local governments would undoubtedly tend to become the maximum pass-through. Moreover, any specified minimum overlooks the great differences that now exist among state-local expenditure systems. The division of expenditure assignment varies greatly among the states, with some systems highly centralized, others decentralized to the county level, others to the municipal level. The degree to which welfare and education are state-supported functions is typically crucial in determining the extent of centralization within a state. Local expenditures as a proportion of total state-local expenditures in 1962 varied among the states from 39 percent to 78 percent (Campbell and Sacks, 1967, p. 44). No general formula can be written that will have uniform applicability. A per capita allocation to cities encounters difficulties in specifying the appropriate city size and again overlooks the differences in the assignment of local expenditure responsibility as between counties and cities.

It would be possible to incorporate the pass-through complications, state by state, in specific legislation for each state. This would require a broad grant of discretionary authority to a federal agency charged with responsibility for examining state-local fiscal systems, and the relative needs and resources within each system. On the basis of such examination specific legislation could be drafted for each state. This would not be an insuperable task, although no national government now administers grants of this magnitude and complexity.[27]

The administration of President Nixon decided, late in 1969, to incorporate revenue sharing in its fiscal program and introduced legislation to that end. It was proposed, as with Heller-Pechman, that the amounts shared were to be based on a specified proportion of the individual income tax base, rising from one-sixth of 1 percent in the last half of fiscal year 1971 to 1 percent by 1976.[28] Each state's share would be determined by its population and revenue effect. The latter would be defined as the ratio of general revenue collected from its own sources as a fraction of the state's personal income. This would have the effect of giving a state with tax effort (so defined) at 10 percent above the national average a 10 percent bonus above its basic per capita share.

Under the administration's proposal the pass-through to local governments would be restricted to general governments, such as municipalities, counties,

27. Some federal systems incorporate elements of discretion in grants. The Australian Commonwealth Grants Commission has continuing authority for discretionary grants to the three states with the weakest fiscal position; the Finance Commissions in India have broad power to recommend tax shares that differ among the states; the Planning Commission in India has considerable discretion in the allotment of development grants among the states.

28. See *Budget of the United States for the Fiscal Year 1971, Special Analysis* (Washington, 1970), pp. 223–24.

and towns, but school districts and other special districts would be excluded. The amount of the pass-through would be measured by the ratio of local general revenue to the total of state and local general revenue and each local government would receive a payment that corresponded to its share of the total of all locally-raised general revenue within the state.

Although the base for revenue sharing might be expanded in the future, it should be noted that the amounts involved in the administration's proposal are miniscule — in 1976 the sharing would amount to about 4 percent of the probable volume of state-local general revenue collections. Further, the bonuses are paid to states on the basis of effort, not of need. This will not improve the relative position of urban areas. As in all aspects of fiscal federalism, the administration's proposal is a compromise among conflicting objectives.

The institutional reality is that over time, all federal systems, by the very nature of the power devolution that is constitutionally prescribed, develop wide variations in their patterns of state-local expenditure and revenue. These institutional differences in fiscal systems are superimposed on the regional economic systems that differ in their resource endowments, growth rates, and extent of urbanization. Thus, disparities develop among states and within states, and relatively straightforward schemes such as revenue sharing cannot eliminate the disparities and, indeed, may accentuate some of them.

Of the many confusions and contradictions that beset a federal system one of the critical ones is whether fiscal arrangements are intended to preserve and strengthen that system or whether fiscal arrangements, irrespective of the federal structure, are intended to achieve specified economic objectives, such as minimum program levels, equalization, or allocative efficiency. This is the confusion that has been reflected in the proposals for revenue sharing. If the objective is simply to strengthen the federal system by strengthening the revenue position of the states, of governors, and of state legislatures, the plan is well devised. If the objective is to increase the quantity and quality of programs for education, welfare, health, and housing in the cities, or to reduce fiscal disparities within states, then revenue sharing is relatively inefficient. Federal categorical grants to the states or local governments can accomplish these objectives with greater flexibility and program efficiency, where the latter is measured in terms of program output in relation to federal resource input.

The implicit theme of this chapter is that a federal system is expensive. Its costs must be measured in both political and economic terms. Its benefits are not self-evident. If it were possible to choose between a federal system and a unitary system, on broad grounds of political responsiveness and economic efficiency, the federal system would have few votes. However, the choice is never made on these terms.

References

Advisory Commission on Intergovernmental Relations. *Fiscal Balance in the American Federal System,* Vol. 1, Washington, 1967.

Benson, Charles S. "State Aid Patterns," in Jesse Burkhead, *Public School Finance: Economics and Politics.* Syracuse: Syracuse University Press, 1964, pp. 205 – 35.

Blough, Roy. "Fiscal Aspects of Federalism," in Arthur W. MacMahon, ed., *Federalism Mature and Emergent.* New York: Russell and Russell, 1962, pp. 384 – 405.

Break, George F. *Intergovermental Fiscal Relations in the United States.* Washington: The Brookings Institution, 1967.

Breton, Albert. "A Theory of Government Grants." *Canadian Journal of Economics and Political Science,* May 1965, pp. 175 – 87.

Buchanan, James M. "Federalism and Fiscal Equity." *American Economic Review,* September 1950, pp. 583 – 99. Reprinted in Buchanan. *Fiscal Theory and Political Economy.* Chapel Hill: University of North Carolina Press, 1960, pp. 170 – 89.

————. "Federal Expenditure and State Functions." *Federal Expenditure Policy for Economic Growth and Stability.* Washington: Joint Economic Committee, 1957, pp. 174 – 79.

Campbell, Alan K., and Seymour Sacks. *Metropolitan America.* New York: The Free Press, 1967.

Dahl, Robert A. "The City in the Future of Democracy." *American Political Science Review,* December 1967, pp. 953 – 70.

Davie, Bruce F., and Joseph T. White, "Equalization Alternatives in Grant-in-aid Programs: Allotment Formulas and Measures of Fiscal Capacity." *National Tax Journal,* June 1967, pp. 193 – 203.

Davis, Ruffus. "The 'Federal Principle' Reconsidered," in Aaron Wildavsky, ed., *American Federalism in Perspective.* Boston: Little, Brown, 1967, pp. 3 – 33.

Dehem, R., and J. N. Wolfe. "The Principles of Federal Finance and the Canadian Case." *Canadian Journal of Economics and Political Science,* February 1955, pp. 64 – 72.

Elazar, Daniel J. *The American Partnership.* Chicago: University of Chicago Press, 1962.

————. *American Federalism: A View from the States.* New York: Crowell, 1966.

Grodzins, Morton. "The Federal System," in *Goals for Americans, Report of the President's Commission on National Goals.* Englewood Cliffs: Prentice-Hall, 1965, pp. 265 – 84.

Groves, Harold M. "New Sources of Light on Intergovernmental Fiscal Relations." *National Tax Journal,* September 1952, pp. 234 – 38.

Heller, Walter W. *New Dimensions of Political Economy.* Cambridge: Harvard University Press, 1966, pp. 117 – 72; idem. "A Sympathic Reappraisal of Revenue Sharing," in Harvey S. Perloff and Richard P. Nathan, eds., *Revenue Sharing and the City.* Baltimore: John Hopkins Press, 1968, pp. 3 – 38.

Madison, James, Alexander Hamilton, John Jay. *The Federalist.* New York: The Modern Library, 1937.

Martin, Roscoe C. *The Cities and the Federal System.* New York: Aldine · Atherton, 1965.

McConnell, Grant. *Private Power and American Democracy.* New York: Knopf, 1966.

Musgrave, Richard A. *The Theory of Public Finance.* New York: McGraw Hill, 1959.

————. "Approaches to a Fiscal Theory of Political Federalism," in *Public Finances:*

Needs, Sources and Utilization. Princeton: National Bureau of Economic Research, Princeton University Press, 1961, pp. 97–122.

Mushkin, Selma J., John F. Cotton, and Gabrielle C. Lupo. *Functional Federalism.* Washington: State-Local Finances Project of the George Washington University, 1968.

Oates, Wallace E. "The Theory of Public Finance in a Federal System," *Canadian Journal of Economics,* February 1968, pp. 37–54.

Riker, William H. *Federalism.* Boston: Little, Brown, 1964.

Rothenberg, Jerome. "Local Decentralization and the Theory of Optimal Government," in *The Analysis of Public Output.* New York: Columbia University Press, 1970, pp. 31–64.

Scheiber, Harry N. *The Condition of American Federalism: An Historian's View.* Subcommittee on Intergovernmental Relations, Committee on Government Operations, U. S. Senate, 89th Cong., 2d sess., 1966.

Scott, Anthony. "The Economic Goals of Federal Finance." *Public Finance,* no. 3, 1964, pp. 241–88.

Shoup, Carl S. *Public Finance.* Chicago: Aldine · Atherton, 1969.

Tiebout, Charles M. "A Pure Theory of Local Expenditures." *Journal of Political Economy,* October 1956, pp. 416–24.

———. "An Economic Theory of Fiscal Decentralization," in *Public Finances: Needs, Sources, and Utilization.* Princeton: National Bureau of Economic Research, Princeton University Press, 1961, pp. 79–96.

Ways, Max. " 'Creative Federalism' and the Great Society." *Fortune,* January 1966, pp. 121–23, ff.

Wheare, K. C. *Federal Government.* 4th ed. New York: Oxford University Press, 1964.

Williams, Alan. *Public Finance and Budgetary Policy.* London: Allen and Unwin, 1963.

NINE

Determinants and Consequences
of Public Expenditures

The positive theory of the public sector, as with other subdivisions of economics, has as its concern the formulation and testing of behavioral hypotheses. Economists' interests in the positive aspects of government behavior naturally lie in those hypotheses that concern real or financial resources. The main hypotheses relevant to the positive theory of public economics encompass those that deal with the determination of levels of public expenditures and revenues along with those that explain the consequences of such outlays and revenue collections upon the economic status of society. Because this book is concerned with public expenditures, positive theories of taxation and tax incidence and the empirical studies of these matters are excluded from discussion here, except insofar as revenue considerations are relevant to expenditure determination. Furthermore, as the introductory chapter explains, stabilization aspects of expenditures are not systematically examined in this study, and, therefore, there is no development here of those aspects of positive theory that deal with the effects of budget policy on aggregate demand.

An Overview of Positive Aspects

A CLASSIFICATION

Within these limits the positive aspects of public expenditures analysis may be classified to encompass: (1) specification and measurement of inputs and outputs of the public sector; (2) analysis of supply and demand for public sector outputs; (3) investigation of the distribution of public outputs among individuals and firms (that is, the incidence of expenditures); (4) study of the consequences of such outputs for the "state of society;" (5) examination of governmental budgetary procedure from the standpoint of organizational behavior. This taxonomy seems to encompass the major empirical public expenditure traditions.

The primary focus of this chapter is on the economic issues of measurement of public sector outputs and the supply and demand for government expenditures. It does not cover in equivalent detail the full range of positive aspects of public expenditures. Each of the five aspects of positive public expenditure analysis are described in brief outline in this section and the nature of their empirical study is illustrated by a few representative examples. The various specific areas of positive analysis are developed in greater detail in subsequent sections of the chapter.

Measurement of inputs and outputs is one of the economist's stocks in trade. Nonetheless, the conceptualization and estimation of service outputs, whether public or private, has proved virtually intractable. Inability to measure units of service outputs is a serious if not fatal barrier to the estimation of production functions, cost and supply curves, and productivity changes. In addition, it imposes extreme difficulties in determination of identified demand relationships. Furthermore, lack of clear-cut measures for governmental outputs greatly hampers the practice of program budgeting, the major technique for rational public sector allocational decision-making. The lynchpin of empirical studies of economic behavior, relatively unambiguous measures of output, is lacking for the public sector. Still, available data on public expenditures subdivided by function and, for federal systems, by levels of government provide a basis for both crosssectional and intertemporal analysis, As a consequence, there exist empirical analyses of historical trends in public outlays as well as comparative studies of levels of expenditure at a given date.

The provision of services by governments, even if not generally capable of measurement in unambigous units, has an effect on the character of society. Just as an increase in the production and distribution of agricultural products is likely to reduce the incidence of malnutrition in a society, so also does the provision of education, highways, police and fire protection, hospitals, military capability, and other services by the public sector affect the quality of life. Yet, measures such as reduced crime, mortality, and morbidity rates and higher achievement test scores represent not quantity or quality of public services provided but the effects of such services along with other determining factors. While it is true that private final goods also influence the quality of life, the motives for their production and consumption are reflected in individual and not collective behavior. Today there is emerging a tradition of analysis of the consequences of private economic behavior that can be illustrated by studies of the effects of smoking or of the the release of the waste products of production and consumption into the atmosphere, water, or land. In the public sector, however, systematic examination of the consequences of policies is an integral rather than subsidiary element in decisionmaking because public activities represent a collective attempt to influence the state of society. Political scientists, economists, and sociologists have studied such associations as those between public hospital outlays and morbidity, or educational outlays and pupil performance as a means of establishing relations between public sector activities and their consequences for social conditions.

The study of the statutory impact of taxes and of household and business response to taxation has produced an enormous literature on shifting and incidence and heated controversy over the relevance and usefulness of the conventional analysis. Although, as has been indicated above, taxation is not a major concern of the present work, the distribution of public expenditures are examined here. The issues involve first, attempts to assign public expenditures or the services provided by the public sector to particular groups in the economy, usually categorized by income class. A second concern is to examine reactions with regard to production, consumption, and the provision of services by decision-making individuals and firms to the availability, free of direct charge, of various public services. One rather conspicuous illustration here is the question of whether measures such as increases in welfare payments or the establishment of a guaranteed annual income reduce or increase work incentives. Less obvious is the response of businesses to increased public expenditures on police and fire protection or of households to greater public adult education. Another important facet of this same issue might be termed "expenditure capitalization" as an analogue to tax capitalization. This arises mainly when spatial considerations cause an increase or decrease in the value of real estate or real business property as a result of a public action such as the building of a park, an incinerator, an airport, or highway.

These efforts at empirical analysis of the consequences of expenditure, along with similar attempts for taxation are, at best, extremely limited in scope. They do not in any way go beyond examination of impact or first round shifting toward the ultimate general equilibrium effect of taxes and expenditures. Such objectives are far beyond the capacity of present analytic and empirical techniques and appear destined to remain so.

Finally, positive studies have been made of the budgetary process and the underlying political structure as a means of explaining the emergent pattern of agency requests and legislative authorizations and appropriations. Here the major research has been performed by political scientists who have examined the budgetary process at the state and federal level with regard to systematic relations between the size of the budget appropriation and individual agency requests and a variety of factors such as agency "acquisitiveness," executive tenure, and the numbers of years a party has been in office.

The content of this chapter thus concerns those aspects of the positive theory that focus on the explanation of variations in the levels of public expenditures and determination of the quantity and quality of goods and services provided by such public outlays. In a sense, benefit-cost studies are applications of that aspect of positive public expenditure theory that investigates the consequences of public sector outputs and goes on to place an economic valuation on these consequences relative to their costs. Benefit-cost has, however, received separate treatment in Chapter 7, partly because of its importance, but mainly because its focus on the valuation of benefits and costs of individual projects requires the use of techniques quite distinct from those relevant to the establishment of statistical regularities. The subject matter of this chapter deals mainly with the problems, methods, and results of attempts to derive statistical regularities which underlie public expenditure decisions and the consequences which ensue from them. So much for our overview of the aspects of positive analysis of public expenditures. The remainder of this chaper is concerned with the details.

Quantity and Quality of Public Services

Empirical study of the public sector is beset by many difficulties. Until the U. S. Census of Governments of 1941, systematic and comparable expenditure data for other than central governments scarcely existed. Even today comparisons among countries and among governmental units in the same country present serious data problems. In addition, there has not yet emerged a widely accepted objective function for governmental units. As a result, no single conceptual model can be set forth analogous to models of consumer or business behavior for which relevant variables can be deduced from theoretical considerations. Instead of empirical studies functioning essentially to provide unbiased estimates of parameters for theoretically specified variables, as they do for consumer and business demand and supply, empirical studies of the public sector attempt to identify variables that appear to be statistically related to expenditures. Further, any attempt to apply one or another model based on preference maximization to the behavior of governmental units must contend with the powerful possibility theorem of Kenneth Arrow (1963) which denies the existence of any consistent procedure for the aggregation of individual preferences. These and other difficulties of empirical analysis of public bodies will be discussed below. Yet the basic problem underlying almost all of the others remains the inability to develop an unambiguous definition and measure of the quantity and quality of public services. This difficulty has proved to be an enormous barrier to clear-cut empirical conclusions in the economic analysis of the public sector.

STATISTICAL PROBLEMS

There is little need to emphasize the importance of being able to specify the quantity provided of a particular public service. From the standpoint of demand it is essential to relate variations in a set of independent variables such as income, price of the service, and population to variations in quantity demanded. But if operational measures of quantity cannot be defined for public sector outputs, it is impossible to describe what is demanded in varying quantities by different government units with differing characteristics.

Likewise, with regard to supply it is necessary to be able to measure units of output to estimate the contribution of various quantities and types of inputs and of alternative organizational structures. If there do not exist unambiguous measures of output or product there is no way to express the production relationships which underlie cost and supply functions. In this regard Margolis writes:

> Over the past decade there have been many statistical studies of the variation of urban public expenditures. All of them are incomplete because the data are inadequate to test interesting hypotheses. The major data shortcoming is the absence of measures of product. A larger expenditure figure is always an ambiguous number. Does a higher police expenditure per capita mean a greater preference for law and order via police services; or does it mean that the crime problem is greater and, therefore, the higher expenditures are needed to reach the same service level; or are the greater expenditures necessary because different urban forms make certain services more costly; or is there a shift in the composition of public and private provision of services? (1968, pp. 530–31)

Clearly, the absence of an unambiguous scale for measuring units of public service outputs does not preclude all empirical analysis of expenditures by governments. Absence of a measure of quantity, for example, in no way inhibits study of the association of observed public expenditures with various characteristics found within the spending jurisdiction. Nor does the lack of measures of quantity preclude analysis of social conditions such as levels of or changes in measures of mortality and morbidity or of pupil achievement in relation to public expenditures on public health facilities or education. However, if it is not possible to relate community characteristics to the quantity of particular government services taken or inputs purchased to quantities produced, then it becomes impossible to separate demand from supply elements in the determination of spending and, as a result, also impossible to identify the effects of particular independent variables upon expenditures or the consequences of expenditures. This circumstance explains why most empirical analyses of public sector economic behavior, whether or not their authors recognize it, are studies of factors associated with public spending rather than studies of the demand for or supply of publicly provided goods or services.

CONCEPTUALIZATION OF PUBLIC SECTOR OUTPUTS

Despite the absence of sufficiently well-defined measures of public outputs to permit empirical supply and demand analysis, it is important to try to conceptualize the nature of the products of various governmental activities. Hirsch describes public sector outputs as

> Those amounts, basically expressed in physical units, that result from, or exist from the production process, which can be described as follows: Various input factors enter a pipeline in which production converts them into outputs. Since the process takes time, it is usually advisable to assign a time dimension to the production process. Output is measured in terms of the number of basic output units of specified quality characteristics per unit of time. There is another aspect in which time plays a role: Output can be produced at either a steady or a varying rate, which can affect the cost of production as well as the value of the output. (1968, p. 479)

Application of this clear-cut conception to operational measurement of public outputs has proved virtually impossible. Shoup (1969, p. 78) reminds us, however, that "no physical-unit concept of output has been devised for a large portion of the private sector, particularly trade and the professions. Quality differences in products as they leave the factory pose the same question. Housing is another illustration." The problem of quantification is not limited to the public sector.

The difficulty in measuring service outputs obviously derives from the very notion of a service. Unlike a commodity, a service is not a tangible physical entity and, therefore, cannot be counted in the same way as such entities. Activities can be counted, and so it is possible to measure the number of concerts given, operations performed, teeth extracted, tons of refuse removed, classes taught, and so on. These enumerations are not deemed satisfactory indications of service-outputs for two interrelated reasons: they do not discriminate sufficiently for differences in quality, and they may not reflect the service output actually desired or intended. An aggregation of classes taught does not allow for variation in the nature of the teaching or physical circumstances. One might better add apples and oranges than classes taught in graduate physics and in kindergarten. Efforts to remedy this difficulty by creation of fine divisions of types of activities or performances introduces the second problem. The objective of a service is a particular outcome such as increased knowledge or curing an illness, not an activity such as teaching a class or performing a surgical operation.

Operational measures of service outputs are estimated by techniques that parallel the two problems just mentioned. One approach accepts performances or activities as the fundamental measure of units of service output and attempts to control for quality variation. This procedure is always subject to the criticism that the performances tabulated are not appropriate indications of the service-outputs provided. The other approach tries to measure the quantity of service by the effect on the putative objective. Here medical service outputs are measured in terms of rates of mortality and morbidity and not operations performed or patients diagnosed. Both views have merit, but economic analysis has stubbornly eschewed measurement of quantities of goods in terms of their consequences because of the considerable advantages in maintenance of the distinction between output and valuation. For services, no less than goods, this distinction appears to have great usefulness.

Although the general problems of service measurement are difficult, the presence of market prices for services in the private sector greatly facilitates quantification. This follows because the market price for private services presumably equates, at the margin, the value of the service to the consumer with its costs to the producer. As a consequence, for any marketed service total expenditures are, in effect, a measure of price times quantity, although in practice the quantity dimension cannot be isolated. If, in empirical analysis, elements associated with variation in the costs of production of such services (input prices and internal efficiency) can be specified and their effects taken into account in the analysis it becomes possible to isolate the determinants of increases in quantity and to identify the usual demand-determining variables such as price, income, and family composition in the context of either family budget or aggregate time series study.

Even for a marketed commodity, however, the derivation of supply relationships presents unusual features. Lacking an overall measure of units of output, the discrete performances that make up the service can be examined and their costs analyzed in relation to the quantities provided over different time periods. If performance quality can be taken into account and producers of services are presumed to maximize profits as assiduously as those who produce the usual kinds of goods, supply curves for performances sold on the market can be estimated.

It is possible, then, to derive identifiable demand and supply relationships for marketable services, but it is by no means easy to develop quantifiable measures of units of output for such services. For publicly provided services, where market prices do not exist to permit separation of demand from supply considerations, measures of units of output are essential if such identification is to be achieved. Yet measurement of units of public service outputs has proved extremely elusive. The essence of the problem is that for services the distinction between the product and the effects or consequences of the product is blurred on the demand side, while the distinction between the product and the production process is likewise blurred on the supply side. For example, the services of the police are demanded to provide protection, and it is difficult to separate the activities performed (patrol, investigation, and others) from the consequences of these services as manifested in the reduction of crime. Yet with regard to commodities, it is steak, for example, for which demand is estimated and not the consequences of consuming the commodity. If consequences such as protection, deterrence, and fire prevention are to be taken as that which is demanded of services, it would appear that the analogous demand for commodities should be described and measured in terms of status, warmth, energy, and similar dimensions of the consequences of consuming goods.

Clearly, this is obviously not an operationally useful approach. The alternative appears to be consideration of the service activities themselves as units of output. This approach requires an implicitly accepted connection by the demander between the service performed (street patrol, services of a TV repair man) and that which he "truly" demands (protection, a repaired TV set). Still, this implicit link between commodity and "source of utility" is also present in the demand for goods. Kelvin Lancaster (1966) has convincingly argued that consumer demand is at base the demand for qualities that yield utility and not for goods in themselves. Consumers may, in fact, purchase goods that do not maximize the utility-yielding qualities potentially attainable at a given outlay. With services, the consumer may find that the qualities he wished to obtain may not, in fact, be present to the extent expected. Yet one would not say that fewer goods were produced because the consumer had not obtained so much of the qualities he desired from the bundle of goods actually taken as he might have with a different mix of goods. So also with services it does not appear reasonable to conclude that fewer services are provided if they do not lead to the desired effect. In the case of both goods and services we need invariant measures of quantities produced and demanded — measures independent of the consequences of the use of the commodities. At the same time, it is also valuable to inquire in a systematic way about these consequences, some of which are of great concern to economics and others of which are more properly the concern of other social sciences.

The perspective developed above parallels the viewpoint developed by Bradford, Malt, and Oates (1969). They distinguish "the services directly produced ('D output') and the thing or things of primary interest to the citizen consumer ('C output')" (p. 186). The individual's utility function contains C but not D. On the other hand, for each individual, the level of C is functionally dependent upon D and any other government service which contributes to C output and a number of environmental factors. With regard to police services, D is represented by a vector that includes "the number of city blocks provided with a specified degree of surveillance,. . . the number of blocks provided with readily available police-officer reserves, the number of intersections provided with traffic control, and so on" (p. 186). C output however, is measured in terms of the probabilities that a citizen will be subjected to certain kinds of accidents or criminal acts. Cost analysis of both C and D output is conceptually possible. D output is a function of a vector of inputs and is amenable to conventional cost estimation techniques. Costing of C output, however, involves estimation of the effects of a wide range of environmental factors and their interaction with public sector outputs. Bradford, Malt, and Oates' conceptualization of health and hospital services clearly illustrates their approach:

> The components of the I-vector [I = Inputs] would now consist of medical personnel, beds, medicines, surgical equipment, etc. A given I would then map into a vector D, whose components would indicate the number of (potential) treatments for various maladies (e.g., a certain number of flu shots, appendectomy operations, and so on). The consumer, however, is less concerned with the treatment itself than with his cure from the disease; a flu-shot, for instance, is not equivalent to avoiding a case of influenza. The C-vector is thus best associated with the dimensions of the individual's state of health and as such is jointly determined by available health treatment (D) and by a number of exogenous variables reflected in the vector E (e.g., the age of the residents, past accidents, and the presence or absence of epidemics). Like the degree of safety from criminal acts, the state of health of the members of a community depends on several environmental variables as well as on the quantity and scope of available health treatment. (p. 193)

As a subsequent section of this chapter shows, explanation of "social states" and their dynamics, is, so far, beyond the capacity of contemporary social science.

Useful as this framework is, it remains incomplete. The objectives of collective budgetary decision-making transcend the concepts of both C and D outputs. As emphasized in Chapter 5, achievement of objectives such as participation by citizens in public sector activities and the engendering of feelings of community and cohesiveness in the society also are elements in public outputs. A full analysis of the outputs of government budgetary actions would extend beyond the enumeration of services or effects on probabilities of illness or criminal activities. These kinds of outputs of organizational behavior are not limited to the public sector, but they tend to exert far more influence on public policy than on private decisions where, if recognized at all, they are peripheral considerations.

In summary, the position developed above is based on the recognition that all final demand derives from the demanders' concern with the characteristics and effects of the good or service demanded. Yet, it is only a good or a service performance for which an operational demand in terms of an offer of a price can be made. A consumer, for example, is willing to buy at various prices so many pounds of steak per week, and it is in terms of pounds of steaks and not calories, texture, cholesterol content, or other effects that this demand is expressed. So also is a consumer ready to purchase at various prices different

numbers of seats at concerts given by various artists or different numbers of
visits to physicians for a variety of treatments. Here again, demand is measured
in terms of what it is that can be bought; that is, seats purchased or physician
visits are not aesthetic satisfaction or cures attained. Indeed, a service has been
demanded (and supplied) even if the patient dies or the tenor fails to reach the
high note. There is little rationale for treating government services any differently. The ultimate desire by the public may be for protection, increased
knowledge, deterrence, or whatever. But governments cannot buy these things.
Unlike most consumers, however, they generally do not purchase from private
producers the services that they expect to yield these consequences, but instead
purchase labor and intermediate products and produce the services themselves. Nonetheless, the quantity of services performed by governments (streets
patrolled, classes conducted) are analogous to the quantities of services performed by private producers (concerts given, hospital days provided). Measures of the effects of the provision of these services are important, and indeed
determine their valuation, but are not themselves measures of quantity. Protection services provided by Brinks, Pinkerton, and other private agencies are not
sold on the basis of the number of robberies, burglaries, and other crimes that
occur in the organization that employs them. Instead, at higher prices, more
men, patrols, and supporting equipment and services can be purchased. Why
should the quantity of preventive services provided by governments be conceived of in terms of reduction in incidence of unwanted activities when private
services are not marketed in accordance with such measures? Tempting as it
is to go from expenditure to consequence, economics has profited greatly from
the intermediate step of specification of units of output and their cost.

The Determinants of Public Expenditures

Despite the confusion surrounding the measurement of public sector outputs,
the growing abundance of data on observed public expenditures has been
accompanied by an enormous outpouring of studies of determinants of such
expenditures. These studies range from international time-series and cross-
sectional comparisons to analyses of particular levels of government (for example, counties) within a given political jurisdiction (for example, state). Among
the more general and less strictly statistical approaches are a few efforts to
develop an explanation of how public expenditures evolve as an economy
develops. Discussion of these concerns, along with some other broad generalizations that have been offered to explain public expenditures will be followed
in this section by a summary review of the statistical studies of determinants
of public expenditures.

EXPENDITURE DEVELOPMENT

The seminal view on the behavior of public expenditures over time is Adolph Wagner's notion that the share of the public sector in the economy will rise as economic growth proceeds. Musgrave (1969) points out, however, that Wagner's prediction was based on anticipation of a major expansion of public enterprise as growth occurred; not only has this failed to materialize but it is not the kind of activity which one wishes to explain within the context of public expenditure development. The relevant expenditures are those for which no saleable product results — that is, either transfer payments or expenditures for services provided without direct charge. The question at issue concerns the influence of economic considerations on the level of such expenditures as an economy develops from low to high per capita income. As far as possible in this analysis social, political, and other "conditioning" factors are held constant to concentrate on economic considerations.

While many authors have examined expenditure development in this context, Musgrave's recent treatment seems most complete (Musgrave, 1969, pp. 69 – 90; see also Gupta, 1969, pp. 35 – 40). At the outset Musgrave rejects the notion that the development of public expenditures as a whole can be explained by a common set of generalizations. Instead, he divides expenditures into public capital formation, public consumption, and transfer payments. He does acknowledge, however, that if the preferences of the people indicate a fundamental dislike for high taxes, they appear to view public expenditures in general as substitutes for private expenditures and the aggregate of public expenditures is itself a proper unit for analysis.

Public capital formation is not an unambiguous concept because by definition all capital formation in socialist economies is public. To avoid confounding public capital formation with the historical extensiveness of collectivism, Musgrave conceives of public capital as investments that cannot be provided privately because of widespread externalities, decreasing costs, or deficient capital markets. Within this framework, early stages of development appear to call for a high ratio of public investment to GNP to provide the infrastructure required to increase productivity. Transportation, irrigation, and training are among vital social overheads that permit the specialization and expansion of markets essential to growth. In addition, in early stages of growth the absence of developed markets for private capital coupled with relatively limited taxable capacity often necessitates public investment in nonexternality yielding capital formation. As development proceeds, both of these conditions wane and a reduction in the share of public capital formation can be expected until, with the advent of significantly higher per capita incomes, new forces emerge to raise this share once again. Primary among these forces is public capital formation to complement, protect, or service private investment and consumption, as with highways, defense, and sanitation. Also of crucial importance is the need for increased human capital, provided primarily in public schools, to operate the extremely complex technologies of advanced stages of economic growth. In virtually all of these cases, expansion of private capital formation also is required so that there is no necessity for the share of public in total capital formation to rise.

The behavior of public consumption raises the question of distinguishing final from intermediate public goods and services. Final public consumption will increase with development if the demand for such goods and services is income-elastic. Expenditures for intermediate public goods will depend on the relative income elasticities for those final private goods involving a high component of public intermediate goods. The distinction between final and intermediate public goods, while clear enough for items such as public police and fire protection provided to private enterprises, is far from clear for traffic patrols, weather reporting, and garbage collection. Musgrave recognizes the need for increased public outlays to offset the external costs of private activities such as congestion and air and water pollution, but he notes that private expenditures also may be undertaken to compensate for these external costs, as when an individual builds a swimming pool to avoid the traffic to and from the beach. It is not clear that on balance public consumption expenditures will rise as a share of total outlays.

Price as well as income elasticity is relevant to the demand for both public capital and consumption. Musgrave ignores such considerations on the ground that there is no reason to expect the relative prices of public and private goods to vary systematically as growth occurs. William J. Baumol (1968) pointed out that the relative prices of those commodities, for which technology does not permit rapid increases in productivity, will rise as the real costs of production elsewhere decline. It appears that in many public sector activities, both consumption and investment, productivity rises very slowly. As a result, overall productivity rises less rapidly in the public sector than in the private sector as per capita income growth proceeds. A price elasticity of less than one in the face of relatively higher prices for public goods as income grows would lead to not only higher public expenditures for goods and services but also to a rising share (Gupta, 1969, pp. 37 – 38).

Public redistribution in relation to GNP may be expected to fall with rising per capita income if the aims of redistributive policy are to provide a minimum absolute standard of consumption, while this ratio will tend to remain constant if the aim is to provide a certain relative degree of equality of income. In either case any systematic effect of growth in reducing inequality will reduce transfer payments, and vice versa. To the extent that growth increases personal risks with respect to income by more frequent obsolescence of skills or lessened family cohesiveness, increased transfers are necessary. Further, higher per capita income reduces the need for capital expansion and, therefore, may lessen

concern for the disincentives to saving and supply of effort that some economists contend results from redistributive transfers. Logic does not provide a
clear answer here, although Musgrave leans toward anticipation of a declining
share for redistribution.

The effects of other developmental factors such as demographic trends,
social and political changes, and intermittent international warfare should be
added to the systematic influence of rising per capita incomes on public expenditures. With income per capita constant, rising population implies a
greater need for certain spatially determined functions as well as public measures to combat congestion. Yet there are economies which arise out of increased density. These matters and the influence of specific demographic
trends are discussed below in the section on cost relationships. Social and
political developments involve changing preferences and the process by which
collective decisions are made. Some discussion of these matters appears later
in this chapter and also in Chapter 5 above.

The long-run effects of the public expenditure increases necessary to support
wartime levels of government outlays have been analyzed by Peacock and
Wiseman (1961). They conclude that the increased outlays during wartime
break through a threshold limitation on taxation, thereby permitting perma-
nently higher postwar civilian expenditures. This thesis is not widely held,
however, since there is evidence that after deferred civilian public spending has
taken place following the war, public outlays return to the pre-war trend level.
Pryor's analysis of data for Britain (1968, p. 443 – 446) indicates only a one-
year displacement of civilian public expenditures after World War II.

COMPARATIVE EXPENDITURES

It is interesting not only to analyze the effects of economic growth on public
expenditures but to compare public expenditures in alternative economic systems. Collectivist economies, by the essential nature of their economic organization, channel a greater share of national income through budgetary
mechanisms. Still, regardless of the extent of government employment of
factors of production, it is possible to distinguish the quantity of expenditures
for certain common functions performed by governments in virtually all
economies. Such functions include education, social welfare, domestic protection, national defense, and health and hospitals. Pryor (1968) has examined
public expenditures in communist and capitalist countries during the past
decade. He considers as broad determinants of expenditures the economic
system, the level of economic development, and other influences that include
what Musgrave calls "conditioning factors." In effect, Pryor adds the economic system as an independent variable but, in view of a lack of institutional
or theoretical evidence, he pursues an inductive approach instead of testing
certain a priori hypotheses.

EMPIRICAL DETERMINANTS: INTERNATIONAL COMPARISONS

Both Musgrave and Pryor pursue their interests in expenditures by recourse
to data. For one analysis Musgrave employs date from time-series studies of
national public expenditures for the United States, the United Kingdom, and
Germany, from 1890 to approximately 1960. All these countries reveal a trend
towards a higher ratio of government expenditures to GNP for both military
and civilian purposes. Among civilian purposes the three countries show social
services (education, welfare, housing) as increasing the most. The increases
comprise both transfer payments and government purchases in roughly equivalent proportions. Simple income elasticities and marginal propensities to spend
show government expenditures in the United Kingdom and Germany responding more to increased GNP in the earlier part of the century, while responsiveness in the United States becomes greater in the more recent period. Musgrave
reports that time-series data for the U.S. and U.K. indicate a constant ratio
of public capital to consumption outlays of about 20 to 30 percent. Finally,
Musgrave interprets the findings as a contradiction to the Peacock-Wiseman
displacement thesis, since it appears that after some postwar adjustments
civilian public expenditures return to the prewar trend determined by the
underlying developmental situation (Musgrave, 1969, pp. 92 – 110).

Pryor (1968) has collected, made comparable, and analyzed an enormous
amount of data on public expenditures in market and centralized economies.
His manipulations of these data center around the influence of the character
of the economic system, the level of development, and other factors in relation
to total public consumption expenditures and its functional components. The
fundamental method used involves comparison of seven market economies
with seven centralized economies roughly paired for per capita GNP in about
1960. As dependent variables Pryor makes use mostly of the ratio of expenditures to GNP. These ratios are compared cross-sectionally and ratio-income
elasticities are estimated for cross-sections and time-series data.[1] In addition,
there are countless special regressions and other comparisons.

For the level of economic development Pryor's time-series analysis of the
fourteen countries from 1950 to 1962 shows eleven with statistically significant
ratio-income elasticities for total public consumption expenditures, excluding
the military. Close examination of his findings leads him to conclude that the
connection between per capita incomes and the share of public expenditures
is primarily manifest as an economy passes through the transition from
agricultural-rural to industrial-urban and per capita incomes rise from around
$200 to $600. Once this transition is attained, Pryor holds that the relation of
expenditures and incomes "appears more random."

Another test for the hypotheses on public expenditure development is com-

---

1. A ratio-income elasticity is the percentage change in the ratio of the measure of public
consumption expenditures to the GNP that occurs when per capita income changes by 1 percent.

parison of cross-sectional data for countries at different stages of development. Here, noneconomic conditioning factors tend to confound hypothetical relationships and expenditure data, even for current outlays, generally are far from comparable. In addition, any international cross-section regression analysis that includes per capita income as an independent variable is liable to be distorted. As a consequence of the great differences in income among developed and underdeveloped countries, this variable has attributed to it a major portion of the variance of virtually any dependent variable in regression analysis. When Musgrave regresses total current expenditures against per capita income for some forty-five countries, the result is a coefficient of multiple determination of .57. His results are virtually identical to those of Gupta (1969) who finds an R^2 of .59 for a similar cross-section analysis of 53 noncommunist countries using data from 1958 to 1962. While Gupta discusses cogently the major obstacles to interpretation of the results of such cross-section studies, he fails even to group countries by per capita incomes or to separate expenditures by broad purpose. Musgrave, however, does separate countries into high- and low-income groups and finds the R^2's drop to .049 and .015 respectively (Musgrave, 1969, pp. 112-113).

The previous discussion suggests that the total of public expenditures may not bear any systematic relation to per capita income, but rather particular components would show such relationship. Musgrave finds conflicting evidence. For countries whose per capita income is less than $600, civilian (nonmilitary) expenditures correlate positively with income and more highly (R^2=.715) than do total expenditures (R^2=.271). For countries with incomes in excess of $600 per capita, however, the relation of civilian expenditures to income is negative as is the case for total expenditures. Social security expenditures, also analyzed by Musgrave, yield coefficients of determination of .62 and .42 respectively for country groups below and above $600 per capita. Here again the correlation coefficients are higher than for total expenditures. Other national cross-sectional studies of expenditures (Martin and Lewis, 1956) have shown that administrative and economic expenditures of low-income countries are relatively well explained by income levels, but education and health prove to be more variable. Pryor's results are consistent here; he finds in cross-sectional analysis only internal security, foreign aid, and research and development associated with variations in per capita incomes (p. 287).

Musgrave concludes that the absence of a clear indication of a rising share of public expenditure in the cross-sectional findings may be a revelation of the underlying indeterminateness of the effects of economic factors or of the failure in the statistical analysis to control adequately for noneconomic influences on expenditures. He interprets the positive relationships observed from time-series studies as an indication of rising outlays for social services that reflect social and cultural tendencies toward equality, which have accompanied growth in incomes in almost all nations.

For the influence of the economic system, Pryor finds that public spending is relatively higher in centrally planned economies for education, research and development, and non-military security, excluding traffic control. The economic system is not significant for defense, welfare, and health; nor does the elasticity of the ratio of expenditures to incomes for any type of expenditure vary systematically with the economic system between 1950 and 1962. In fact, in a great many cases, the variation among countries within the same economic system exceeds that between the two systems. Pryor concludes that (1) "The policy dilemmas facing decision makers of public consumption expenditures are quite similar in all nations regardless of system" (p. 285); and (2) "public finance institutions which appear different may actually act in very similar ways." "For questions concerning the determinants of public consumption expenditures — in contrast to problems dealing with the politics surrounding their administration — Anglo-American economists seem considerably more justified in their neglect of the differences in budgetary institutions in the two systems than some continental economists and their fetishness with institutional details" (p. 287).

NATIONAL STUDIES

Time-series data can be used to test for the effects of a few fundamental economic determinants of public expenditures, but paucity of observations inevitably leads to use of cross-sectional analysis when concern is for specification of a wide range of economic and other factors. Because of lack of comparability of data, differences of political and institutional arrangements, and the already mentioned statistical problem occasioned by inordinate variations in incomes, international cross-sectional study cannot provide a satisfactory framework for the search for statistical regularities in public sector expenditures. The focus turns, then, to those countries whose federal character provides a multitude of governmental jurisdictions which possess independent or quasi-independent expenditure authority thereby permitting systematic examination of the fiscal behavior of such jurisdictions. Indeed, under such circumstances expenditures or jurisdictions with common functional responsibilities which lie within certain boundaries can be aggregated and compared with other aggregates, thus providing an enormous number of combinations for exploration and explanation. Despite these advantages, fiscal analysis of cross-sectional data from governmental units within a given country or from various different countries presents many problems.

CONCEPTUAL PROBLEMS IN IDENTIFICATION OF
DETERMINANTS OF PUBLIC EXPENDITURES

Specification of the determinants of public expenditures faces two distinct methodological difficulties. One, the statistical difficulty of identification, arises because in the analysis of public spending those variables systematically associated with the demand for activities and services provided by the public sector are also associated with variations in the supply of such services and in the determination of public revenues. For example, personal income is a determinant both of the demand for public services such as education, protection, and streets and roads and of the supply of these same services insofar as income affects either tax receipts or factor costs. That is, areas where incomes are higher tend to be those where wages and salaries also are higher and where the revenues available to finance expenditures are greater. As is well known from econometric theory, when no important variables that influence demand can be specified that do not also affect supply, a supply equation cannot be identified. So also, a demand equation cannot be specified if there are no supply determinants that do not also affect demands (Baumol, 1965, pp. 221–28). A major shortcoming of empirical studies of the public sector stems from this inability to identify demand and supply relationships and, therefore, to estimate price and income elasticities with confidence.

The second methodological problem in the specification of determinants of public spending derives from the collective nature of public sector decisions. Economic models for estimation of behavioral relationships hinge on assumptions with regard to the underlying objectives of the decision-making unit. For consumer behavior it is presumed that the decision unit (the individual or the family) acts to maximize its utility. Therefore, observed behavior in the light of prevailing prices and in incomes reveals the nature of the underlying preferences. For business behavior, the situation differs in that it is hypothesized rather than presumed that businesses act to maximize one or another operational objective function (for example, profits) so that their observed behavior can be used to test the various hypotheses presented. The collective nature of public bodies, however, makes it impossible to apply either of these models. Even if two governmental decision-making bodies were confronted by identical objective circumstances (prices, technological possibilities, incomes) and the pattern of preferences of the citizen members of the two body politics were identical, there is no assurance that they would undertake the same pattern of public expenditures.

Explanations for potentially different fiscal behavior even where "objective circumstances" are identical all hinge on the collective nature of public decisions. The Arrow possibility theorem shows that there is no logically consistent mechanism for the aggregation of individual preferences to provide the basis for a collective choice. Thus, no set of impersonal rules can be devised to resolve the problem of collective choice. Observed behavior of any governmental unit will reflect the character of its organizational arrangements and its decision makers. Different decision-making bodies, for example, may be attempting to maximize rather different objective functions such as economic welfare, social welfare, prospects of reelection, exportation of fiscal burdens, or the welfare of some special group. Regularities will not emerge from the correlation of public expenditures with objective characteristics of communities or nations if expenditures are intended to attain highly different objectives. If objectives sought through collective decisions are presumed to be similar or identical, variations in the efficiency with which the intended objective is achieved will also diminish the probability of the emergence of statistical regularities between outlays and characteristics. Furthermore, for reasons already discussed, citizens may be loath to reveal their preferences for fear that their tax burdens will be increased as a result. Consequently, given similar preference patterns among citizens, different bodies politic will vary in their ability to perceive these preferences, and, again, will react differently in their spending policies.

Variations in the objective function, administrative efficiency, and knowledge of preferences of citizens may distort behavioral regularities in public expenditures. The presence of these factors greatly weakens the deductive approach to the specification of independent variables for an explanation of public spending. A deductive approach necessitates a detailed model of behavior that under given conditions or constraints spells out those factors that influence the objective function. Statistical fitting of the data either assigns magnitudes to the underlying behavioral relations (elasticities of demand in consumer behavior) or tests the hypothesized objective function (are profits maximized by business behavior?). If, however, the behavior of different units represents attempts to attain a variety of objectives, by a range of more-or-less efficient methods, with more-or-less complete information about the wishes of its members, construction of useful deductive models is hardly likely. In addition, there is a growing body of evidence that whatever collective decision makers try to do, it is not to maximize any objective function. Lindblom (1961, pp. 308 – 09) argues, for example, that the objective function is defined by the set of decisions itself ex post and has no operational meaning to decision-makers ex ante.

One may conclude from this methodological morass that, while empirical regularities may be observed in public expenditures, they should not be interpreted as indications of rationality or necessarily as evidence that a particular hypothesis has been confirmed. Because deductive models are so difficult to apply, validation of alternative explanations for public expenditures has come to be based on the relative magnitudes of variance explained by one or another set of regressors without regard for the logic of the underlying model. Recourse to the size of multiple correlation coefficients as a primary criterion leads to acceptance of results that are not stable. Addition of further variables or replication of the analysis in a different locale or time period may produce substantially different coefficients than those found in the original analysis.

Such behavior suggests bias in the estimated parameters. Difficult as the task is, reliable statistical estimates of determinants of government expenditures requires testing logical hypotheses derived from conceptual approaches to the behavior of the public sector which permits identification of relationships. Margolis raises similar concerns. He concludes,

> Certainly it is reasonable to attempt to apply private market analogies to public processes. If successful, we would have a rich body of theory to extend to the huge but neglected public sector; possibly the normative theorems might be transformable into administrative rules. Unfortunately, it is more difficult in the public sector to use predictive tests to judge the usefulness of abstract models and, therefore, discussions about the reasonableness of models will be more common. (1968, p. 536)

Further Issues in Empirical Studies of Public Expenditures. A survey of the rapidly proliferating empirical studies of public expenditures is beyond the scope of this chapter. A most useful review is by Roy Bahl (1968). Presented here is only a discussion of the major approaches taken to the search for empirical correlates of public expenditures in the United States and some highlights of the results.

The Unit of Analysis. Except for a few time-series studies, the great preponderance of empirical analysis of public expenditures in the United States has been of the cross-sectional variety. The choice of a unit of analysis has varied between an attempt to employ a building-block approach in which decision-making governmental units are treated as observations, and a more aggregative conception of units that consolidates governments within a region, such as a state or a standard metropolitan statistical area, and considers the total region as an observation.

There are serious problems with both approaches. The former has the apparent advantage of focusing on the behavior of a decision-making unit. Recognition, however, that in the United States a local government, such as a city or school district, receives intergovernmental aid as determined by other governmental units and may vary in its functional responsibilities from state to state and even within a state, substantially weakens the notion that a local government is an autonomous decision-making unit whose behavior can be compared directly with other similar bodies. However, attempts to circumvent these difficulties by aggregations of governmental units, such as all those in a state, into a single observation for comparison with other state aggregates, introduces the biases associated with estimates of statistical parameters from aggregated data. The underlying behavioral relations of individual governments within a state may be quite different from those revealed by analysis of statewide or other aggregates.

Attempts to resolve these problems have ranged from the use of "assignment" variables to reflect differences in the functional responsibilities of similar types of local governments (Campbell and Sacks, 1967) to efforts to include as independent variables interstate variations in such factors as political organization and allocation of taxation powers.

The Statistical Models. Given the unit of analysis, empirical studies of public expenditure can be characterized by the nature of the dependent variable and the kinds of independent variables chosen to account for its variation. The objectives sought by statistical analysis of public expenditure data are extremely varied. A major, yet seldom attained objective, is the specification of elasticities of demand and supply for public expenditures in general or for some particular level of government, functional category, or some combination.

Whether due to recognition of the aforementioned problem of lack of identification or because other concerns were involved, a great many models with objectives other than estimation of elasticities have been tested empirically. It is possible to distinguish studies concerned simply with explaining the variance of some measure of public expenditure (Burkhead, 1961) from studies that pursue more specific objectives as, for example, estimates of the effects on expenditures of intergovernmental grants, political and legal arrangements, level and sources of tax revenues, and size of the governmental unit. Specific dependent variables studied have included total expenditures; expenditures per capita, per pupil and per square mile; expenditures as a share of income and of property valuation; and the ratio of the expenditures of one level of government to the total. Each of these measures of expenditures can be calculated for the nation as a whole; for each of the fifty states, for local governments, for SMSA's, and for arbitrarily defined geographic regions. Furthermore, expenditures may be broken down by functional category, broad purpose (for example, civilian-military), whether resource-using or not, and by other criteria. The range of potential statistical questions regarding public expenditures is enormous, encompassing, in effect, combinations of alternative measures of expenditures with various degrees of aggregation and categorization.

In addition, dependent and independent variables may be expressed in terms of observations at one point in time for different units, at various points in time for the same unit, or as rates of change or first-differences over a period of time. This last category represents efforts to test models whose results more properly permit inferences to be drawn about the effects of temporal changes in the independent variables. Still, analysis of first-differences or rates of change from cross-sectional data is not equivalent to time-series and cannot be interpreted as depicting statistical regularities of the historical past.

The choice of independent variables must be related to the objectives sought and to the specific dependent variable selected to reflect the purpose of the statistical inquiry. For cross-sectional analysis encompassing entire states as units of observation it has been traditional since the early work of Fabricant (1952) to ignore intergovernmental financial transactions and to concentrate on a few basic variables such as income, density, and urbanization, which are regressed on per capita total expenditures and on per capita expenditures for each of a number of functional areas (for example, education, health and hospitals, police and fire protection). These three variables are generally found to be positively related to almost all categories of public expenditures, although the portion of variance that they explain has declined with the passage of time. Later modifications of this model include nonlinear treatment of the independent variables (Kurnow, 1963) and the addition of a number of demographic and political factors (Fisher, 1964).

A major innovation in studies of expenditures has been the explicit inclusion of amounts of state and federal aid as independent variables. Inclusion of these variables that usually have a positive influence on spending has led to higher portions of variance explained and to testing of hypotheses on the extent to which aid stimulates expenditures by recipient governments or substitutes for expenditures permitting lower taxes or greater outlays for nonaided functions (Sacks and Harris, 1964). Considerable controversy has raged about whether inclusion of grants-in-aid in estimating equations of this sort is a legitimate statistical procedure. The primary objection is that the inclusion of such aid introduces an element of circularity into the analysis in that a component of the dependent variable is used to account for its variance. In addition, the amount of aid, where grants are determined on a matching basis, is not a determinant of total expenditures but is, in a sense, a consequence of such expenditures. It should be pointed out, however, that to the extent grants-in-aid are based on allocation formulas rather than matching arrangements, the concern that amounts of aid are determined by expenditures is unwarranted. The problem of statistical circularity can be handled by subtraction of aid from the dependent variables so that the analysis correlates amounts of aid with expenditures by the recipient governmental unit or of its own revenues. Osman (1968) shows that federal aid continues to exert a significant positive influence over state expenditures when such adjustment is made.

In any event, quite apart from this statistical problem the full impacts of grants-in-aid are not revealed by their estimated effects on expenditures for the nominally aided function. A grant-in-aid for one purpose may affect expenditures for a variety of other functions. These effects may extend to governments other than the one which receives the aid.

Empirical studies of relationships among categories of expenditures within and between government jurisdictions are just beginning to emerge. For example, a recent study (Russett, 1969) examines the displacement of various civilian private and public expenditures associated with defense outlays. The extent of displacement is determined by the simple time-series correlation between categories of nondefense spending and defense outlays. A measure of proportionate reduction for each category is also obtained by dividing its estimated regression coefficient by the mean expenditure for the category during the period studied, 1939 to 1969. The results for the United States show that military outlays primarily displace personal consumption of durables and services and private fixed investment. On the whole, civilian government spending is inversely related to defense expenditures, but to a lesser degree than consumption and investment. Among categories of public spending, federal aid to education, welfare, and health and hospitals suffered the sharpest relative declines in the years in which military spending rose. Comparison with Canada, France, and the United Kingdom reveals varied patterns. In France the major impact of defense has been on civilian consumption expenditures by government with private consumption and fixed investment also affected adversely. In the U.K. the burden fell mainly on private investment and civilian government with virtually no reduction in private consumption. In contrast, Canadian experience reveals heavy displacement of private consumption, some reduction in private investment, but little effect on government civilian outlays.

Whatever the particular set of independent variables chosen, studies of statewide expenditures have, for the most part, employed the same set of variables to analyze total current expenditures and a variety of functional components of the total. Clearly, those variables pertinent to educational outlays need not be identical to those relevant for exploration of expenditures for highways or welfare. While there is value in comparison of estimates of regression coefficients for the same set of independent variables from successive cross-sections, the desire to test models particulary germane to specific functional areas has led to a number of studies within states of expenditures limited to a single function. At the same time, recognition that statewide aggregation might obscure regularities of behavior by local governments is manifest by studies that take as their unit of analysis diverse elements such as standard metropolitan statistical areas, school systems, villages, town, cities, and countries, and special districts. The major conceptual difficulty of such studies is the inconsistent pattern of the assignment of responsibilities for specific functions to particular governmental units. Some cities, for example, may have responsibility for welfare expenditures, while others may not because welfare is a county responsibility. To the extent that functional responsibilities are essentially consistent within a state, separate state-by-state analysis of local governments resolves this problem at the expense of fewer observations and the possibility that results depend upon the special organizational or legal characteristics of the particular state under study. An alternative approach is to include one or more independent variables to reflect variation in the assignment of governmental responsibilities. Then similar units of government can be analyzed together even if their functional responsibilities do not fully coincide (Campbell and Sacks, 1967).

The statistical models described so far are primarily those of the economists whose concern is to estimate the effects of factors believed to be associated with the demand for public expenditures and also to assess the influence of intergovernmental grants-in-aid. Multiple regression has been used almost exclusively because of its apparent suitability to the objectives sought. Those in the field of political science are, naturally, more interested in the implications of the relations of political factors to public expenditures, and their studies reflect this concern. Thomas Dye (1966) in a study of policy outcomes among states accepts this multiple regression model as appropriate and considers economic factors as prior to political in such determinations. His summary analysis treats statewide income, density, urbanization, and educational level as measures of economic development, all presumably positively associated with expenditures. These variables are taken into account before examination of the incremental contribution of the political system as measured by partisanship, party competition, voter participation, and malapportionment. These two sets of variables are related to a variety of policy outcomes including public expenditures for education, welfare, and highways. The net partial correlation coefficient for the four political system variables taken together does not exceed .12 for any of the three expenditures when the effects of the economic development variables are taken into account. Reversing the procedure, however, and considering the economic development variables after taking account of the political system ones yields correlations of over .40 for two of the three categories of expenditures.

A fatal shortcoming here, well known to econometricians, is that the absence of an explanatory model for the noneconomic variables permits inclusion in a single estimating equation of the most diverse and intercorrelated set of regressors. Dye's effort to provide a model and design for his analysis (1966, pp. 1 – 45) fails to deal adequately with this problem.

Other studies of expenditures by political scientists concerned with whether certain political characteristics are associated with larger or smaller expenditures use statistical methods, such as analysis of variance, that simply test for differences rather than attempt to measure the magnitude of relationships as in correlation analysis. Lineberry and Fowler (1967), for example, found evidence of higher spending in cities governed by mayor-council arrangements than in those possessing city managers.

Supply of Public Services

The studies discussed above are primarily demand oriented. They attempt to explain expenditures in terms of factors largely associated with demand. In fact, expenditures are jointly determined by demand and supply, and the determinants of the supply or costs of public sector services have received relatively little attention.

No doubt the already mentioned difficulties of definition and measurement of public outputs constitute the major reason for the paucity of studies of production functions and cost relations. In principle, standard approaches to the estimation of industrial or sectoral production or cost functions apply to the public sector. Conventional supply curves, however, based as they are on assumptions of profit maximizing market behavior have little place in the public sector. If public sector outputs were quantifiable it would be possible to relate, ex post, observed measures of quantities of similar outputs by different governmental units to observed measures of inputs used and, thereby, to estimate production coefficients. Given these coefficients and prices of inputs, cost curves could be derived. As an alternative, cost curves could be estimated directly by cross-section or time-series analysis of variations in expenditures in relation to variations in quantity of output, taking into account output quality and other determinants of cost such as differential factor prices. A rather different approach involves the use of technical engineering data to construct cost relationships. This method, which has been used to estimate industrial production functions, generally fails to deal satisfactorily with returns to scale since underlying technical relationships cannot specify the limitations of management and administration that often arise in practice to offset apparent scale efficiencies.

EMPIRICAL STUDIES OF PRODUCTION AND COST FUNCTIONS

The problem of measurement of outputs has been treated in several ways in empirical studies of the supply of public services. Certain kinds of publicly provided services are rather amenable to quantification in physical units. Water for residential and commercial use and refuse collection are perhaps the clearest illustrations. For such services relating the quantity of output to quantities of inputs and thereby obtaining coefficients of production is feasible. Even when measurable physical units of output can be identified, it is necessary to introduce variables to reflect what Hirsch (1968) calls, "service conditions affecting input requirements," and a factor to reflect differential technologies in the conversion of inputs into outputs. For refuse collection, service conditions might encompass population density or distance to dump or incinerator. In general, an equation to reflect the underlying production function for a service would be:

$O = (I, S, T),$
Where:
O = number of basic service units of given quality per period
I = input factors

S = service conditions affecting input requirements
T = state of technology

Conversion to a cost function for direct statistical estimation requires, in addition, a measure of quality of service since observed performances will vary in quality. Also, if factor prices vary, this must be taken into account in relating expenditures to the quantity of services obtained. Thus, a cost function for a service would be:

C = (O_1, Q, S, F, T)
Where:
C = total cost (total expenditures) on service
O_1 = output is physical terms independent of quality
Q = measures of quality of service
F = factor prices for inputs

Hirsch (1968, pp. 495 – 98) has estimated such functions for several public services performed in cities in St. Louis County. Throughout these analyses Hirsch assumes that there is no variation in factor prices and that the level of technology is the same in all cities. The latter assumption, which implies that there are no differences in efficiency from one governmental unit to another, permits attribution of observed differences in expenditure to quantity and quality of service provided and service conditions but not to greater or lesser facility in the transformation of inputs into services. In the equation for refuse collection, quality is measured specifically by collection frequency and pickup location and quantity by number of pickup units. The equations for police and fire protection use indices of scope and quality of service, while measures of area and population serve as indicators of quantity.

A problem arises if quality is measured by an index that includes average salaries paid or some other variable that is, in effect, a component of expenditures. Other things equal, quality is greater if more frequent pickups occur, but if more costly personnel are employed it does not necessarily follow that the quality of service is higher. Cost studies of services must avoid the tautology of identifying use of higher-priced inputs with greater quality and then interpreting a significant regression coefficient for such an index as evidence regarding cost relationships.[2]

Where satisfactory measures of units of physical output that reflect the service provided are unattainable, indicators of output performance are often used instead. In education, for example, the conceptually appropriate output

2. For a discussion of this issue and an attempt to resolve it in the area of educational expenditures, see Jerry Miner, *Social and Economic Factors in Spending for Public Education* (Syracuse: Syracuse University Press, 1963), pp. 81 – 84.

of a local public school is some measure of the provision of units of educational services adjusted for quality. Failing to obtain these kinds of measures, indicators of output such as performance or achievement test scores, school continuation rates and number of degrees awarded have been employed. The deficiency of these indicators is that, due to the presence of counter-productive "service conditions," large inputs may yield low outputs according to the indicator, while, in fact, commensurately large service outputs are being produced. Put differently, the production function relevant to public sector outputs is one for the conversion of inputs into public sector services (educational instruction) and not one for the conversion of inputs into test score achievements or retention rates of schools. Estimation of such functions can be extremely useful, but they require identification of significant service conditions and their effects must be successfully partialled out. This has proved inordinately difficult when service conditions vary systematically with those inputs, whose independent effects the analysis attempts to estimate. The controversy over the Coleman Report (Coleman, et. al, 1968), hinges on this inability to separate variations in race, social class, income, and native intelligence from those of teacher characteristics, school physical facilities, and current expenditures for materials, supplies, and other supporting inputs.

Kiesling (1967) has estimated a production function for achievement test scores in New York State school systems in which expenditure per pupil and intelligence scores have positive effects and the number of pupils a negative influence. The results of this study, which takes entire school districts as the unit of analysis, clearly involve aggregation bias, since there is no way of relating specific conditions in a particular school or classroom to the intelligence and achievement of particular pupils. Katzman (1968) studies test scores in individual schools in Boston as did Burkhead, Fox, and Holland (1968) in Atlanta and Chicago. Neither was able to identify any systematic relation of achievement with per pupil expenditures, but both found achievement positively related to socioeconomic status and to teacher characteristics.

The most comprehensive review of educational production and cost relations is in Guthrie, Kleindorfer, Levin, and Stout (1969). This study focuses on the distribution of educational resources among socioeconomic groups and the consequences of observed patterns of inequality. The authors' conclusion, based on their original research and the work of others, is that pupil performance is influenced by "items such as quality of physical facilities, ability of instructional staff, and adequacy of instructional materials. The achievement of high quality on each of these service dimensions costs money. Thus, quite understandably, the dollar amount spent per pupil also appears frequently as a significant predictor of pupil performance" (p. 144).

Still neither these investigators nor any others are able to estimate systematic functional relationships between inputs and outputs or between expenditures and outputs. It appears that as long as public service outputs are measured in terms of indicators of performance and not direct physical units the underlying production functions will remain elusive.

Almost all analyses of cost or production functions for public services raise the question of returns to scale and the optimum size of a government service-providing unit. The main obstacle to clear conclusions here as elsewhere in public sector supply is specification of output units of constant quality. Frequently population size of the government unit is treated as a measure of output quantity. Evidence of returns to scale is adduced if beyond a certain point expenditures per capita vary inversely with population in a multivariate analysis. Such interpretation is subject to considerable qualification insofar as population is seldom an appropriate measure of the scale of service outputs and may be positively associated with demand and with the quality or scope of the service.

A DEDUCTIVE APPROACH TO PUBLIC SECTOR COSTS

Empirical supply and cost analysis of public services has not and is not likely to yield firm conclusions with regard to the average and marginal costs of various services. Shoup (1969) presents an interesting and useful effort to derive such cost functions deductively in a manner similar to that of conventional price theory. The approach consists of deducing the behavior of total, average, and marginal costs of provision of various levels of services for specific governmental functions. Concern is directed toward variations in these costs as changes occur in number of persons served, in area served, and in number of service units supplied to each member of the group (pp. 79 – 86).

Shoup's approach applies to group consumption goods, that is, to goods that are not easily subject to exclusion by markets. He distinguishes among such group consumption goods those that are collectively consumed — for example, national defense where the marginal cost of another consumer is zero — from other group consumption goods that are noncollective — for example, traffic control. His method is first to hold constant area served and derive cost relations as the number of service units and numbers of persons served vary. Then, he holds service levels constant and varies area and population and develops costs under these conditions.

For example, assume that area served is held constant, and measure on the X axis of Figure 9.1 units supplied to each member of the group. If the service is a pure public good, in the sense that one person's consumption does not reduce the amount available for others (Shoup's collective-consumption good), the marginal cost of supplying one person with a given unit is also the marginal cost of supplying all persons with that unit. The marginal cost of the service unit itself can have the usual features of being relatively constant over a range and then rising. However, as shown in Figure 9.2, if the service in question

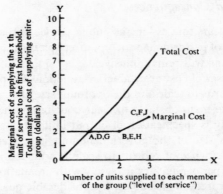

Figure 9.1. *Marginal and Total Cost of Group-Consumption, Collective-Consumption Good, for Level of Service and Number in Group*

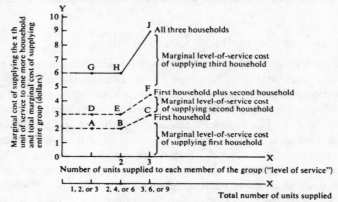

Figure 9.2. *Marginal Cost of Group-Consumption Good for Level of Service and Number in Group (Noncollective-Consumption Group)*

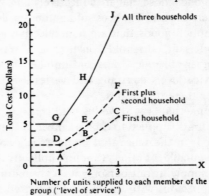

Figure 9.3. *Total Cost of Group-Consumption Good, for Level of Service and Number in Group (Noncollective-Consumption Good)*

cannot easily be subject to exclusion, but one person's consumption does reduce that of another (Shoup's group consumption but noncollective consumption good) marginal cost will increase with both number of units and number of persons supplied. In the case of collective consumption goods, average cost per capita always declines as numbers served increases. When complete joint consumption does not prevail, total costs of provision of a given quantity of service units rise as numbers of persons served increase. Here, the behavior of average per capita costs depends on the rate of increase in total costs; this behavior is illustrated in Figure 9.3. If the increment to total cost of additional numbers served starts at a low level and rises gradually, average per capita costs may fall over a substantial range. Eventually, as the group's size increases the incremental costs become so large that average per capita costs begin to rise.

When area served is allowed to vary, the behavior of costs of provision of a specified service level to a given population depends on a number of considerations. For many governmental functions minimum costs must be incurred that do not increase until a threshold size of the area served is reached. Here increase in population and concomitant rise in density lowers per capita costs of given service levels. An increase in density achieved by reduction in area with constant population would not be associated with such lower costs. Other functions such as police control may exhibit reduced cost with lower density, but whether per capita costs are lower for large areas with proportionately large populations or smaller areas with lower populations depends on the characteristics of the service and technology. Shoup points out that for a particular service the lowest cost technology for a small area of high density may be quite different than that for a large area of low density.

These logical deductions about costs are carried further by Shoup in detailed discusssions of specific functions such as defense, highways and streets, education, crime prevention, and health. Their major implication for empirical studies of public expenditures is that many of the traditional variables used as independent variables such as density, measures of area covered or served, and population operate on costs in different ways for different functions and vary even for the same function under differing technologies. Great care should be employed in their use and interpretation.

SOURCES OF EXPENDITURE INCREASE

The studies of cost and production relationships discussed above focus on efforts to derive timeless relations between inputs and outputs. They are applications of the static analysis of cost to public sector outputs. A related but distinct empirical concern is to explain the historical record of public expenditures for specific functions in terms of variations in the quantity of services, their quality, and their unit costs. Regardless of the forces that may explain the demand for public services, the existence of rising outlays for purchase of inputs implies either (1) more service outputs, (2) better quality services, (3) higher unit costs or, (4) some combination thereof. A number of studies attempt to distinguish among these elements in the explanation of historical trends in expenditures.

One illustration of such an effort is the study of Bradford, Malt, and Oates (1969) concerning the costs of local public services. The authors observe that rates of growth in expenditures for education, health and hospitals, and police and fire protection from 1947 to 1967 rose by approximately five times more than the wholesale price index. In all cases they try to separate measures of expenditures that reflect units of common services from those including expenditures for improved quality or quantity. For education, they measure current costs per pupil-day and, for health and hospitals, cost per patient-day deflated by an index of hospital personnel per patient to reflect quality improvements. For police and fire protection, they take urbanization as an indication of the need for improved quantity and quality and hold this constant by separate estimates of growth in expenditures in four major cities whose density did not increase during the period under consideration. These comparisons all indicate that measures designed to represent unit costs rose more rapidly for these public services than did the costs of conventional private goods. The authors conclude that their evidence supports Baumol's hypothesis of "a relatively static technology in the production of local public services."

Incidence of Public Expenditure

Analogously to taxation, incidence and shifting of public expenditure may be defined as the final resting place of the benefits of expenditures and the process by which benefits to the recipient are transferred to the bearer of the ultimate incidence. Further, the notion of impact also has relevance to expenditures in that there are those who by virtue of legal regulations or geographic location are entitled to receive transfer payments or government services. Impact applied to expenditures concerns identification of those who legally are entitled to receive expenditures or services financed by them just as taxation impact means identification of those legally obligated to pay taxes. Finally, there are economic effects of expenditures that transcend the question of specification of those who obtain the ultimate benefits and extend instead to overall consequences on employment, regional economic prosperity, supply of effort and savings, and similar considerations.

There are many reasons why the application of such concepts to expenditures is even less productive than their application to taxation. Most significant is that despite its unsatisfactory aspects the notion of the burden of a tax has a clear quantitative component in the dollar amount of tax payments. Difficulties arise when attempts are made to estimate aspects of tax burden that are not simply reflections of dollars paid in tax liabilities. For expenditures other than transfers, the relevant notion of benefits essentially concerns the attribution to households and business firms of the quantity of services provided. Furthermore, unlike taxation, which is levied in pecuniary terms upon well-defined bases (income, sales, wealth, production) and is therefore susceptible to analysis in terms of the reactions of decision units, the impact of expenditures is far more diverse.

In the most general sense, incidence and effects refer to analysis of the consequences of taxation and expenditures. Just as a tax may reduce or expand work effort or savings or decrease wages and increase prices or influence the value of capital assets, so may public expenditure, for example, increase or decrease work effort. Indeed, there is a recent outpouring of empirical studies that concern the response of work effort to various arrangements for public assistance payments. The relatively direct consequences of public expenditure, however, go far beyond effects on prices, work efforts, and assets into such diverse influences as those on rates of crime, delinquency, morbidity and mortality, likelihood of nuclear conflict, academic achievement of students, and speed and convenience of communication and transportation. If the incidence and effects of expenditures are thought to be efforts to specify their consequences, a vast array of concerns are introduced that have no counterpart in the study of the incidence of taxation. These concerns do not arise for taxation because, while taxes influence economic and even noneconomic behavior and may influence overall growth and regional economic well-being, they do not in themselves influence the provision of specific services. In effect, the appropriate parallel for incidence appears to be between taxation and unrestricted transfer payments, with goods and services expenditures by government and restricted transfer payments, such as those for physicians' services, falling outside the conventional framework.

In any event, economists have avoided analyzing the wide-ranging consequences of public expenditures within the notions of incidence and effects, although they have at times tended to confuse these consequences with measures of service outputs. Furthermore, disenchantment with the traditional concepts of tax incidence as being relevant only under the most limiting partial framework has led away from the classical theory to more operational notions. For example, Musgrave's conception of differential tax incidence posits a comparison of the distributions of income that would emerge under alternative taxes of equal yield while holding public expenditures constant in real terms. Analogously, differential expenditure incidence can be defined as the effect of alternative types of expenditures of equivalent magnitude on income distribution while holding taxes constant (Musgrave, 1959, pp. 211–17). Unfortunately, no empirical basis exists for isolation of these effects, and empirical studies of tax incidence concentrate on allocation of actual tax payments by income class.

This approach also serves as the basis for empirical studies of the distribution of public expenditure benefits. Rather than pursuing the will-o'-the-wisp of measurement and allocation of quantities of public services received or their valuation students of public expenditures have instead attempted to allocate amounts spent according to income class. That is, they endeavor to determine the pro-rata share of public outlays for the provision of services and transfers received by each income group. Despite the strong similarity of such endeavors to empirical analysis of tax incidence, an important difference remains. Allocation of taxation by income class proceeds from certain crude assumptions about tax shifting and incidence. For example, indirect taxes are almost always assumed to be shifted forward and direct taxes not shifted at all, except for the corporation income tax whose inconsistent treatment reflects the confusion in contemporary incidence analysis. Allocation of public expenditures, however, does not follow crude assumptions about shifting but rather what might be termed crude assumptions about impact. That is, expenditures are distributed among income classes in accordance with estimates of the outlays incurred to provide the services received by the income group. While this appears to be the only operationally feasible approach it is possible for expenditure shifting to occur that might deprive certain groups of benefits and transfer them to other groups. Shoup (1969, pp. 88–93) points out several possibilities where nominal beneficiaries of public services are forced to relinquish their benefits by subsequent developments. As an illustration, he cites higher rents charged in a residential area because a public park has been constructed in the neighborhood. Another illustration, resembling shifting of commodity taxation, is the increase in physicians' fees which has accompanied medicaid so that allocation of all receipts of transfer payments for this purpose to those on social insurance misstates the incidence of the benefits.

In studies that have attempted to allocate public expenditures among income groups (Adler, 1951; Gillespie, 1965, Tax Foundation, 1967), the standard pattern involves division of expenditures into general outlays and the specification of certain major outlays. The former category includes all government functions whose benefits are such that "there is no clear basis for allocation to subgroups within the economy" (Gillespie, 1965, p. 160). General expenditures, which include items such as national defense, general government, civilian safety, police, and prisons, are rather close to being pure public goods in the sense of being available in equal amounts to all consumers, although some of them clearly are intermediate rather than final services. It is conventional to allocate them to income classes either by population or by income. Clearly, the latter category provides for an allocation of more of the expenditure "incidence" to the higher income classes. Gillespie's study treats about 85 percent of federal and 15 percent of state and local outlays as falling within the general category.

Incidence of remaining major expenditures, such as education, social security, highways, and public health, is estimated separately by procedures adapted to the function. Social security and other transfer payments based on "objective" characteristics of families or individuals can be allocated on the basis of surveys of the incidence of such characteristics by income group. Unexceptionally, such transfers, whose receipt usually is contingent upon low-income status, are observed to be distributed highly inverse to income. Allocation of other specific expenditures focuses on methods for distribution of services by income class, and procedures are far from uniform.

The final goal of many empirical studies of tax and expenditure incidence is a net relation by income class of the balance between tax burdens and expenditure benefits. The significance of this fiscal incidence or residual is, of course, no better than the assumptions that underlie it. Table 9.1 summarizes a number of such estimates with net incidence indicated as the difference in percentage points between the allocated share of expenditures and taxes for each income class. Despite variations in magnitudes, the procedures used in all of the studies assign high positive net fiscal benefits to low-income groups, moderate net burdens to the highest group, and rough equality of benefit and burden to middle range income groups. Also, they show that state and local fiscal systems have less redistributive impact than the federal system, although because of the importance of defense outlays this tendency is considerably weakened if federal expenditures are assigned in accordance with population rather than income.

Public Expenditure and Social States

The economist's interest in government expenditure deals essentially with its role as a dependent variable. In addition to economists, students of public expenditures, especially political scientists and sociologists, are concerned with these expenditures as independent variables in the explanation of such diverse phenomena as reelection of public officials, educational performance of pupils, highway safety and construction, crime rates, rates of mortality and morbidity, and even the state of international tensions.

There is a tendency on the part of some to identify desired or intended consequences of public expenditures as indicators of public outputs. Although social states are dependent upon such expenditures and outputs, they are distinct from them. Thus, it is possible and desirable to distinguish (a) a production function for police patrol services that relates a variety of inputs (vehicles, officers, communications equipment, foot patrolmen) to a measure of area patrolled at given frequency and quality from (b) a quasi-production function for crime that relates rates of criminal activity to a variety of factors including an index of patrol services along with density, property values, characteristics of the local population, and other potential influences.

In a sense the problem here resembles that of estimating factor productivity.

Table 9.1. Distribution of Net Fiscal Incidence of Taxation and Government Expenditures as Estimated in Various Studies[1]

	Under $1000	$1000–1999	$2000–2999	$3000–3999	$4000–4999	$5000–7499	$7500 & over
All Governments							
1938/39	34.8	6.1	.6	.7	2.6	6.4	–15.3
1946/47	60.9	17.4	7.3	3.3	–4.5	–9.6	–23.4

Source: John H. Adler, "The Fiscal System, The Distribution of Income and Public Welfare," in Kenyon Poole, ed., *Fiscal Policies and the American Economy* (Englewood Cliffs: Prentice-Hall, 1951), pp. 359–409.

	Under $2000	$2000–2999	$3000–3999	$4000–4999	$5000–7499	$7500–9999	$10,000 & over
Federal	24.0	19.7	9.4	–2.7	–2.6	0.4	–13.3
State & Local	31.1	24.7	9.1	1.4	–0.3	1.3	0.1
All Governments	55.1	44.4	18.5	–1.3	–2.9	1.7	–13.2

Source: W. Irwin Gillespie, "Effects of Public Expenditures on the Distribution of Income," in Richard A. Musgrave, ed., *Essays in Fiscal Federalism* (Washington, D.C.: The Brookings Institution, 1965), pp. 122–86.

	Under $2000	$2000–2999	$3000–3999	$4000–4999	$5000–7499	$7500–9999	$10,000–14,000	$15,000 & over
1961								
Federal	65.9	22.9	15.8	4.9	–0.3	–4.3	–8.1	–23.8
State & Local	19.6	9.2	3.6	1.5	–0.4	–1.4	–1.8	–3.3
All Governments	85.4	42.1	19.5	6.4	–0.2	–5.6	–10.0	–27.0
1965								
Federal	63.3	32.0	14.5	3.9	–1.9	–4.6	–8.4	–33.9
State & Local	14.6	6.3	1.8	0.7	–0.6	–1.8	–2.3	3.9
All Governments	80.9	38.3	16.3	4.6	–1.5	–6.4	–10.6	–27.7

Source: Tax Foundation, *Tax Burdens and Benefits of Government Expenditures by Income Class, 1961 and 1965,* (New York: Tax Foundation, 1967).

1. The numbers in the table are determined as the difference between the estimated share (percent) of expenditures received by an income class and the estimated share of taxes borne by the same income class.

If only one input is required, total and partial factor productivity are identical, and measures of the quantity of the input and of the output suffice. To the extent that quality differences in the input or output are not susceptible of complete incorporation in their measurements, an ambiguity occurs in the attribution of output changes to productivity as against changes in the quantity of inputs. If production entails more than one input factor, so that an index serves to measure inputs, the additional problem of partial versus total factor productivity arises. Even when total factor productivity is considered it is possible that what appears to be productivity may reflect omitted inputs, failure to adjust adequately for quality improvements in inputs, or improper relative weighting of inputs in the index. In specification of the determinants of social states and their changes these problems of identification, weighting, and measurement of arguments in the function are extremely complex. In terms of an equation the situation can be depicted as:

S.S. $= (C, T, O_1 \ldots n \text{ [or E]})$
Where
S.S.   = measure of situation at point in time within an area with regard to specific social state (e.g., crime rate, mortality rate, accident rate)
C   = conditions related to social state (for example, nutrition, density, income, demographic factors)
$O_1...n$ = physical measures of different public sector outputs where possible or,
E_1 = measure of public expenditure where physical measures are unobtainable.

There is no explicit independent variable to reflect technology since this equation does not depict a proper production function.

The use of public expenditures as an independent variable can serve two essentially distinct purposes. From the standpoint of the explanation of public sector outputs, expenditures can serve as a composite index of inputs. Relations between quantities of public outputs and levels of expenditures indicate productivity or efficiency if differences in service conditions, factor costs, and output quantity are constant or can be taken into account. If, however, as is generally the case, these three intervening elements cannot be fully accounted for, empirical analysis will be unable to separate variations in the efficiency with which inputs are transformed into public service outputs from variation in service conditions, or output quality. As a result, an apparent observation of higher expenditures leading to lower or constant output may in fact reflect improper specification or measurement of service conditions negatively associated with output but positively related to expenditures.

From the viewpoint of social states and their differences over space or changes over time, public expenditures represent not a proxy for resource inputs but a measure of public service outputs which may or may not influence the social state in question. Here analogy with a production function is less appropriate because a social state (say health) can scarcely be viewed simply as a technical consequence of a number of "inputs," although the comparison is not entirely without relevance. Within any governmental jurisdiction there is seldom present a decision unit which is attempting to integrate a variety of diverse elements to affect some social condition. Perhaps national, regional, or sectoral planning embody elements of such decision making, but usually in western nations public sector outputs alone are controlled with a view toward affecting social outcomes, and the rest of the determinants are taken as outside the influence of the public sector.

The focus in this section is on the concern for the contribution, if any, that public expenditures as proxies for public service outputs make to comparative social states over time or space. Statistical analysis of such relationships requires measures of social states as the dependent variable and a sufficiently specified set of independent variables so that an unbiased estimate of the influence of expenditures emerges. Unfortunately, in the absence of adequate operational theories of social states, it is difficult to achieve satisfactory specification. Further, for a variety of reasons, expenditures for many functions tend to be concentrated in areas where service conditions are inimical to high public sector productivity in the simple sense of a ratio of public outputs to inputs. A consequence of the failure to specify adequately these service conditions leads to attribution of low outputs to high expenditures. For example, this phenomenon probably accounts for the findings in cross-sectional studies of low educational achievement in schools operating compensatory educational programs. In addition, systematic productive inefficiency (in the conventional sense of getting fewer outputs for given inputs) by governmental units spending larger amounts would also wash out positive associations between public outlays and social states. There is no avoiding the fact that statistical studies of the effects of expenditures are subject to considerable ambiguities of interpretation.

Empirical Studies of the Effects of Expenditure

OUTPUTS AND SOCIAL STATES

Sharkansky (1967, 1969) asks with regard to public outlays, "what do we get for our money?" To find the answer he regresses state public expenditures for 1962 on a number of statewide measures of what he terms public-service outputs. Some of these measures, such as welfare payments, number of hospital beds, or perhaps graduation rates from high school correspond to the concept of output developed here. Most, however, measure some aspect of what has here been termed social states. For example, Sharkansky also includes as public-service outputs the percentage passing the Selective Service mental examination, infant mortality rates, motor vehicle death rates, and a variety of crime rates. In addition he includes some measures of utilization of public facilities such as visits to state parks and rates of acquisition of hunting and fishing licenses. Altogether, in the 1967 study, sixty-eight variables representing public service outputs are included and broken down under the headings of: education, highways, public welfare, health and hospitals, natural resources, and public safety.

To represent expenditures for each function, Sharkansky uses three different measures: (1) combined state and local general expenditures per capita (for the particular function), (2) the same expenditures per $1000 of state personal income, and (3) the same expenditures as a percentage of total general expenditures. In multivariate analysis six common variables are used to reflect nonexpenditure influences regardless of function. These are: (1) federal aid, (2) state and local employees per 10,000 population, (3) average salary of state and local employees, (4) nonlocal share of state-local revenues, (5) per capita personal income, and (6) population. Sharkansky's 1969 study uses only the first of the above expenditure measures and a series of variables especially pertinent to each function as the nonexpenditure influences.

The results of simple correlations of the three measures of expenditures with the 68 measures of service output show a substantial number of significant relationships in all areas except public welfare and health and hospitals. For the most part, however, these significant correlations are negative except for education where they are split about half and half. Inclusion of the six common nonexpenditure influences permits estimation of partial correlations with the expenditure variables. For the categories of education and highways fewer partial than simple correlations are significant, but this actually is an improvement since the number and significance of negative correlations are reduced. Partial correlations give substantially better results for public welfare where for several of the measures significant positive correlations emerge. The few significant simple correlations for health and hospitals disappear with the inclusion of the nonexpenditure variables, and slightly fewer significant negative partial than simple coefficients characterize the measures for natural resources. Finally except for murder, taking into account nonexpenditure factors, substantially reduces the negative simple correlations of crime rates with expenditures.

One way of reducing the influence of nonexpenditure determinants of social states or of public sector outputs is to employ time series data. Relations between changes in output or social states and changes in expenditures within a given jurisdiction are very likely to be distorted by exclusion of "service conditions." Many such conditions tend, however, to remain relatively constant over time. Sharkansky (1967) uses percentage changes from 1957 to 1962 in the same variables as in his cross-sectional analysis for 1962 to examine patterns of temporal simple and partial correlations. By and large, there are fewer significant correlations in the analysis of changes, although a dramatic increase occurs in simple and partial correlations in health and hospital outputs when changes are taken as the measure of expenditures. Of great importance, however, is the very many fewer negative correlations that ensue from the analysis of changes. Only for measures of education do spending measures continue to exhibit a substantial number of inverse relationships with outputs or social states.

There is no doubt that Sharkansky's findings, which he interprets as general indications of relatively little connection between expenditures and public service outputs, are largely a function of his technique. Correlation of miles of highways and numbers of hospital beds with current spending rather than capital outlays of the recent past surely misses some rather vital links between expenditures and outputs. Inclusion among nonexpenditure variables of factors themselves highly correlated with expenditures tends to reduce partial correlations. The procedure of the 1967 study — using a common set of nonexpenditure indicators for all functions — seems unlikely to account for the particular service conditions associated with specific functions. Prices are not considered, and while the contemporary American economy may be characterized by rather small spatial variations in prices, omission of this factor from the time-series study seems quite inappropriate. The effects of changes in expenditures may emerge only with a lag. In addition, no measures whatsoever of quality of service are included so that higher expenditures associated with superior service have the effect here of reducing positive correlations. Finally, the analysis provides no way of allowing for the contribution of public expenditures to the output of intermediate services.

These criticisms are aspects of shortcomings that result primarily from the absence of an adequate theoretical framework. As the previous discussion has emphasized, the relations among service outputs and the linkages of service outputs to social states are manifold and complex. They cannot be dealt with by crude empiricism but require careful conceptual and analytic treatment, with each area of concern receiving separate consideration for its special nature and characteristics. Sharkansky's work nevertheless raises the proper questions and provides useful tests of some of the simplest and most obvious hypotheses. Clearly, there is much further work to be done.

Organizational Theory

By far the major portion of public expenditures is appropriated in annual or biennial budgets of governmental units. It is only to be expected that attention has been directed to the budgetary process as a source of explanation of expenditures. A number of excellent studies have recently appeared which describe, from the viewpoint of organizational theory, the procedure of public budget-making. These studies deal not only with the budget cycle and the responsibilities of various agencies and organizations within the government, but also attempt to interpret the role of interest groups, legislative coalitions, and potentialities for trade-offs among issues. Some of these subjects are examined in Chapters 5 and 8. Important as such descriptions and analyses are, for the most part they do not employ systematic testing of hypotheses and, therefore, do not rightly have a place in this discussion of empirical approaches to public expenditures. One portion of the tradition — the application of organizational theory to American budgetary institutions and the examination of the determinants of agency requests and subsequent appropriations — has been pursued on a statistical basis. It therefore is relevant to the concerns of this chapter.

Since agency requests are observed to be highly related to ultimate appropriations, explanation of their determination and of reasons for inordinate deviations of appropriations from requests goes to to heart of the question. Evidence for the close association of agency requests and appropriations comes from Richard Fenno, Jr. (1966), and Davis, Dempster, and Wildavsky (1966) for the federal government and from Sharkansky (1968) for the state governments. Fenno and Davis et al. have studied the relationship of federal government agency budgetary requests and congressional appropriations. They find strong evidence that, for the most part, legislators and executives mechanically follow incremental policies in budget determination. Fenno found that during the period 1947 to 1962, the House of Representatives failed to appropriate an amount within ten percent of the amount requested by the agency only 22 percent of the time. Fenno also discovered that agency appropriations were within 20 percent of the appropriations for the previous year 75 percent of the time.

Further evidence for the incremental rule emerges from the study of the budgets of twenty-six agencies of the federal government by Davis et al. Statistical techniques were employed to determine which among eight simple decision-rules best explained the observed budgetary data and to ascertain whether relationships between requests and appropriations remained stable over time. The rule which most often explained agency requests is the extremely simple one which ties the budget bureau's recommendation to a percentage of the congressional appropriations for that agency in the previous year. Congressional appropriations for a certain year are found to be best explained as a percentage of the agency request for that year. Combined, the implication of these rules is a determination of appropriations based on incremental rules of thumb, little related to the objective conditions so much emphasized in empirical studies of public expenditures. The study does find indications of shift points in relationships; the most important of such shifts occurred with the advent of the Eisenhower Administration.

Sharkansky (1969, pp. 67 – 74, 97 – 112) attempts to go beyond the generalized rules which account for the several budget requests and appropriations. He develops a series of hypotheses designed to explain both normal and deviant cases: (1) for the most part agencies follow an incremental policy in their requests; (2) certain "assertative" or acquisitive agencies request more than incremental increases; (3) requests by such agencies tend to be cut by a greater proportion than those of other agencies; (4) nonetheless, the growth rate of assertive agencies' appropriations exceeds that of other agencies; (5) the effectiveness of assertive or acquisitiveness by state government agencies varies directly with the number of elected executive state officials, the governor's potential for continuation in office, the degree of party competition and state personal income per capita and inversely with the strength of the governor's veto power over appropriations, and the current level of state expenditures and debt per capita.

While Sharkansky does identify those traits associated with agency assertiveness he does not go on to attempt to relate the extensiveness of these characteristics to the degree to which agency requests exceed normal or expected increments. He suggests that the presence of interest groups or sympathetic appropriations committee chairmen may be crucial factors.

If, in turn, the attitudes and behavior of committee chairmen, interest groups, and other correlates of agency behavior within government prove to be closely associated with characteristics and conditions found in the populations served by the governmental units under study, little gain in explanation of expenditures results from the investigation of budgetary procedures, conditions, and arrangements. In other words, if the outcomes of budgetary decisions are determined by external politics, study of internal politics is not likely to be productive. Reliable evidence on this question does not exist; but familiarity with the enormously diverse patterns of executive budget making and legislative budgetary enactment in the decentralized system in this country conveys the overwhelming impression that these internal differences do matter.

A positive theory of public expenditures, it would appear, ultimately must combine the objective circumstances and preferences of the relevant body politic with the organizational characteristics of the governing body. The theory of organization has much to tell the student of public expenditure determination. A systematic study of organizational theory and an empirical examination of behavioral hypotheses derived from such theory will, at minimum, be helpful to the analysis of the role of public expenditures in a mixed economy.

References

Adler, John H. "The Fiscal System, The Distribution of Income and Public Welfare," in Kenyon Poole, ed., *Fiscal Policies and The American Economy.* Englewood Cliffs: Prentice-Hall, 1951, pp. 359 – 409.

Arrow, Kenneth. *Social Choice and Individual Values.* 2d ed., New York: Wiley, 1963.

Bahl, Roy. "Studies on Determinants of Public Expenditures: A Review," in Mushkin, Selma J., and John F. Cotton, *Functional Federalism: Grants-in Aid and PPB Systems*. Washington: State-Local Finances Project of the George Washington University, 1968, pp. 184 – 207.

Baumol, William J. *Economic Theory and Operations Analysis.* 2nd ed. Englewood Cliffs: Prentice-Hall, 1965.

————. "Macroeconomics of Unbalanced Growth, The Anatomy of the Urban Crisis." *American Economic Review,* June 1967, pp. 415 – 26.

Bradford, M. A., R. A. Malt, and W. E. Oates, "The Rising Cost of Local Public Services." *National Tax Journal,* June 1969, pp. 185 – 202.

Burkhead, Jesse. "Uniformity in Governmental Expenditures and Resources in a Metropolitan Area: Cuyahoga County." *National Tax Journal,* December 1961, pp. 337 – 48.

Burkhead, Jesse, Thomas G. Fox, and John W. Holland. *Input and Output in Large City High Schools.* Syracuse: Syracuse University Press, 1968.

Campbell, Alan K., and Seymour Sacks. *Metropolitan America: Fiscal Patterns and Governmental Systems.* New York: The Free Press, 1967.

Coleman, James S., et al. *Equality of Educational Opportunity.* Washington: U. S. Government Printing Office, 1966.

Davis, Otto A., M. A. H. Dempster, and Aaron Wildavsky. "A Theory of the Budgetary Process." *American Political Science Review,* September 1966, pp. 529 – 47.

Dye, Thomas R. *Politics, Economics, and the Public: Policy Outcomes in the American States.* Chicago: Rand McNally, 1967.

Fabricant, Solomon. *The Trend of Government Activity in the United States Since 1900.* New York: National Bureau of Economic Research, 1951.

Fenno, Richard F., Jr. *The Power of the Purse.* Boston: Little, Brown, 1966.

Fisher, Glenn W. "Interstate Variation in State and Local Government Expenditures." *National Tax Journal,* March 1964, pp. 57 – 74.

Gillespie, W. Irwin. "Effect of Public Expenditures on the Distribution of Income," in Richard Musgrave, ed., *Essays in Fiscal Federalism.* Washington: The Brookings Institution, 1965.

Gupta, Shibshankar P. "Public Expenditure and Economic Development — A Cross Section Analysis." *Finanzarchiv,* October, 1968, pp. 26 – 41.

Guthrie, James W., George B. Kleindorfer, Henry M. Levin, and Robert T. Stout. *Schools and Inequality.* The Urban Coalition, 1969.

Hirsch, Werner. "The Supply of Urban Public Services," in Harvey S. Perloff and Lowdon Wingo, Jr., eds., *Issues in Urban Economics.* Baltimore: The Johns Hopkins Press, 1968, pp. 477 – 525.

Katzman, Martin T. "Distribution and Production in a Big City Elementary School System." _Yale Economic Essays,_ Spring 1968, pp. 201 – 56.

Kiesling, Herbert J. "Measuring a Local Government Service: A Study of School Districts in New York State." _Review of Economics and Statistics,_ August 1967, pp. 356 – 67.

Kurnow, Ernest. "Determinants of State and Local Expenditures Re-examined." _National Tax Journal,_ September 1963, pp. 252 – 55.

Lancaster, Kelvin. "Changes and Innovation in the Technology of Consumption." _American Economic Review,_ May 1966, pp. 14 – 23.

Lindblom, Charles. "Decision-Making in Taxation and Expenditures," in _Public Finances: Needs, Sources, and Utilization._ Princeton: Princeton University Press, 1961, pp. 295 – 329.

Lineberry, Robert L. and Edmund P. Fowler. "Reformism and Public Policies in American Cities." _American Political Science Review,_ September 1967, pp. 701 – 16.

Margolis, Julius. "The Demand for Urban Public Services," in Harvey S. Perloff and Lowdon Wingo, Jr., eds., _Issues in Urban Economics._ Baltimore: The Johns Hopkins Press, 1968, pp. 527 – 65.

Martin, Alison and W. Arthur Lewis. "Patterns of Public Revenue and Expenditure." _Manchester School,_ September 1956, pp. 203 – 44.

Musgrave, Richard A. _The Theory of Public Finance._ New York: McGraw-Hill, 1959.
_____. _Fiscal Systems._ New Haven: Yale University Press, 1969.

Osman, Jack. "On the Use of Intergovernmental Aid as an Expenditure Determinant." _National Tax Journal,_ December 1968, pp. 437 – 47.

Peacock, Alan and Jack Wiseman. _The Growth of Public Expenditures in the United Kingdom._ Princeton: Princeton University Press, 1961.

Pryor, Frederic L. _Public Expenditures in Communist and Capitalist Nations._ Homewood, Ill: Richard D. Irwin, 1968.

Russett, Bruce M. "Who Pays for Defense." _The American Political Science Review,_ June 1969, pp. 412 – 26.

Sacks, Seymour and Robert Harris. "The Determinants of State and Local Government Expenditures and Intergovernmental Flows of Funds." _National Tax Journal,_ March 1964, pp. 75 – 85.

Sharkansky, Ira. "Government Expenditures and Public Services in The American States." _American Political Science Review_, December 1967, pp. 1066 – 77.

_____. _The Politics of Taxing and Spending._ New York: Bobbs-Merrill, 1969.

Shoup, Carl. _Public Finance._ Chicago: Aldine · Atherton, 1969.

Tax Foundation. _Tax Burdens and Benefits of Government Expenditures By Income Class, 1961 and 1965._ New York: Tax Foundation, 1967.

Name Index

Subject Index

341